# International Criminal Justice

# International Criminal Justice

## Legitimacy and Coherence



*Edited by*

Gideon Boas

*Associate Professor, Faculty of Law, Monash University, Australia*

William A. Schabas

*Professor of International Law, Middlesex University, London, UK*

Michael P. Scharf

*Case Western Reserve University School of Law, USA*

**Edward Elgar**

Cheltenham, UK • Northampton, MA, USA

Published by
Edward Elgar Publishing Limited
The Lypiatts
15 Lansdown Road
Cheltenham
Glos GL50 2JA
UK

Edward Elgar Publishing, Inc.
William Pratt House
9 Dewey Court
Northampton
Massachusetts 01060
USA

A catalogue record for this book is available from the British Library

Library of Congress Control Number: 2012942066

MIX
Paper from responsible sources
FSC® C018575

ISBN 978 1 78100 559 0

Typeset by Columns Design XML Ltd, Reading
Printed and bound by MPG Books Group, UK

# Contents


*About the editors* vii
*List of contributors* ix
*Preface* xi

1 What is international criminal justice? 1
*Gideon Boas*

2 Order in the courtroom: the unique challenge of maintaining control of a war crimes trial 25
*Michael P. Scharf*

3 Making war crimes trials work – balancing fairness and expedition 44
*Iain Bonomy*

4 Applied rights in international criminal law: defence counsel and the right to disclosure 68
*Peter Morrissey*

5 Complexities in prosecuting international crimes: the ICC Libyan warrants 105
*Mark Ierace*

6 International criminal justice and the past 123
*Gerry Simpson*

7 International criminal justice in historical context: the post-Second World War trials and modern international criminal justice 145
*Robert Cryer*

8 Terrorism and international criminal law: questions of (in)coherence and (il)legitimacy 190
*Ben Saul*

9 The International Criminal Court and the complexities of international criminal justice 231
*James Potter*

10 Women and international criminal law: steps forward or dancing backwards 254
*Helen Durham*

11 Have recent changes designed to benefit victims of international crimes added to the legitimacy of international criminal justice? 269
*Sam Garkawe*

12 International criminal justice and military perspectives 304
*Geoffrey Skillen*

*Index* 319

# About the editors

**Gideon Boas** is an Associate Professor of the Monash Law Faculty and a Barrister. He was a Senior Legal Officer at the International Criminal Tribunal for the former Yugoslavia (ICTY), where he was the senior adviser to the Trial Chamber in the *Milošević* case. He has consulted for a range of governments, including the Australian federal government and Victorian government departments, as well as the United Kingdom Foreign and Commonwealth Office. He has also consulted for international organisations and NGOs, writing briefing papers and providing training. Gideon has been pro bono legal counsel for accused war criminal Radovan Karadžić, and has provided expert advice on extradition and other matters. He has published many books, book chapters and articles on international criminal law and justice.

**William A. Schabas** is Professor of International Law at Middlesex University in London. He is also Professor of International Criminal Law and Human Rights at Leiden University, Professor of Human Rights Law at the National University of Ireland Galway, chairman of the Irish Centre for Human Rights, and a visiting professor at the Paris School of International Affairs (Sciences-Po). He is the author of more than 20 books and 300 journal articles, on such subjects as the abolition of capital punishment, genocide and the international criminal tribunals. Professor Schabas was a member of the Sierra Leone Truth and Reconciliation Commission. He is a president of the Irish Branch of the International Law Association and chair of the Institute for International Criminal Investigation. He is an Officer of the Order of Canada and a member of the Royal Irish Academy, and holds several honorary doctorates.

**Michael P. Scharf** is the John Deaver Drinko-Baker & Hostetler Professor of Law and Director of the Frederick K. Cox International Law Center at Case Western Reserve University School of Law. In February 2005, Scharf and the Public International Law and Policy Group, a non-governmental organization he co-founded and directs, were nominated for the Nobel Peace Prize by six governments and the Prosecutor of an International Criminal Tribunal for the work they have done to help in the prosecution of major war criminals, such as Slobodan Milošević, Charles Taylor, and

Saddam Hussein. During the elder Bush and Clinton Administrations, Scharf served in the Office of the Legal Adviser of the US Department of State, where he held the positions of Attorney-Adviser for Law Enforcement and Intelligence, Attorney-Adviser for United Nations Affairs, and delegate to the United Nations Human Rights Commission. During a sabbatical in 2008, Scharf served as Special Assistant to the Prosecutor of the Cambodia Genocide Tribunal. He is the author of over 70 scholarly articles and 14 books. Since 2011, Scharf has been President of the Hague-based International Criminal Law Network.

# Contributors

**The Right Honourable Lord Iain Bonomy** is a judge of the Supreme Courts of Scotland and was from 2004 until 2009 a permanent judge of the International Criminal Tribunal for the former Yugoslavia.

**Robert Cryer** teaches at Birmingham Law School.

**Dr Helen Durham** is Strategic Adviser, International Law for the Australian Red Cross.

**Sam Garkawe** is Associate Professor, School of Law and Justice, Southern Cross University.

**Mark Ierace SC** is the NSW Senior Public Defender and a Senior Visiting Fellow at the University of New South Wales, where he teaches International Criminal Law. Between 2000 and 2004 he was a Senior Trial Attorney for the Office of the Prosecutor in the International Criminal Tribunal for the former Yugoslavia, where he led the trial team in *Prosecutor v Galić* (the siege of Sarajevo).

**Peter Morrissey SC** is a senior barrister with extensive experience in domestic and international criminal litigation. In Australian courts, he has appeared in many high profile criminal trials. He was also lead counsel for Sefer Halilović, acquitted before the Trial Chamber at the International Criminal Tribunal for the former Yugoslavia (ICTY), and for the appeal, which was dismissed in 2007. Peter has advised on several other cases at the ICTY. He teaches postgraduate subjects in international criminal procedure and has also published in this area.

**James Potter** is LLM (International Law) Australian National University, LLB Australian National University.

**Ben Saul** is Professor of International Law, Faculty of Law, the University of Sydney.

**Gerry Simpson** teaches international law at Melbourne Law School and the London School of Economics.

**Geoffrey Skillen** is former Director-General of Legal Services, Australian Defence Force and Principal Legal Officer, Office of International Law, Attorney-General's Department. He is the current Chair of the National Advisory Committee on International Humanitarian Law, Australian Red Cross.

# Preface

Books about international criminal law abound, whether technical manuals, textbooks, tomes on the yet-to-blossom International Criminal Court, or a growing plethora of monographs. There are also many works on associated areas such as transitional or restorative justice. International criminal justice as a discipline throws up numerous conceptual issues. While a predominantly legal response to mass atrocity satisfies traditional conceptions of justice, particularly in the milieu of international law, international criminal justice is so much more than this, engaging disciplinary areas such as politics, history, sociology and psychology to name but a few. The contribution that this book of edited essays seeks to make to this crowded field is to address some of these themes, from a mixture of traditional and more radical perspectives.

This book is one of the significant outcomes of a major project into the nature and content of international criminal justice. The purpose of the International Criminal Justice Project, funded by the Australian Research Council, is to explore the many facets of a sometimes strange and always complex discipline.

The contributions in this book critique some of the fundamental questions about international criminal justice. The first chapter, written by Gideon Boas, considers an essential yet often neglected topic: what is international criminal justice? Michael Scharf writes about the unique challenge of maintaining order in the courtroom where the most serious of international crimes are being tried. Lord Iain Bonomy of the Scottish Supreme Courts and a former Judge of the International Criminal Tribunal for the former Yugoslavia (ICTY) has written about the twin pillars of international criminal trials – fairness and expedition. Peter Morrissey SC and Mark Ierace SC, both former counsel before the ICTY, write about aspects of defending and prosecuting international crimes. Gerry Simpson tackles some critical questions relating to international criminal justice and the past, while Robert Cryer considers the historical context of the post-Second World War trials and their relevance to modern international criminal justice. Ben Saul discusses terrorism, counter-terrorism and the relationship of this borderline trans-international criminality in the context of international criminal justice. James Potter considers the role of the

International Criminal Court in the complex relationship of factors around international criminal justice. Helen Durham writes about the unique and often misunderstood relationship of women to international criminal justice. Sam Garkawe tackles the framework of international criminal justice as it concerns victims. Finally, Geoffrey Skillen examines international criminal justice in the context of Defence Force perspectives.

We hope that the contributions in this book stimulate some thought and debate around profound and underlying questions in the discipline of international criminal justice.

Gideon Boas
Melbourne 2012

William A. Schabas
Middlesex 2012

Michael P. Scharf
Cleveland 2012

# 1. What is international criminal justice?

**Gideon Boas***

## I. INTRODUCTION

What is understood by the phrase 'international criminal justice' is surprisingly difficult to articulate comprehensively. At a fundamental level, it describes the response of the international community – and other communities – to mass atrocity. This seems to be a broadly accepted definition. How we respond to war, to the rupture of society and to systematised murder and persecution, is at the heart of the issue. What forms of transitional justice are attempted and how their goals are achieved, or at least attempted, are all important responses.[1] But international criminal justice is about more than responses. How do we learn from history, or sometimes fail to do so? Can we use our understanding of human psychology to respond better to mass atrocity, or to prevent or address it sooner? What of the sociological elements that are infused in our response to heinous international crimes; how do these affect our understanding and practice of international criminal justice?

This chapter explores some different perspectives and disciplinary approaches to this complex area, including political, historical and sociological perspectives. This is important because, while as international lawyers we have raised important questions about legitimacy and coherence, we do not always open ourselves to a genuinely multidisciplinary approach to the debate about international criminal justice.

One might say that the obvious embodiment of international criminal justice comes in the form of international war crimes trials. All alternative

* The author is grateful to Mr Andrew Roe for his research assistance in the preparation of this chapter.

[1] See eg, Gary Jonathan Bass, *Stay the Hand of Vengeance: The Politics of War Crimes Tribunals* (Princeton University Press 2001).

responses, at least in the context of contemporary international relations, might be referred to as 'other'.

The trial of individuals for the commission of the core international crimes – genocide, crimes against humanity or war crimes (and possibly aggression, after 2017 before the International Criminal Court (ICC)) – is a powerful tool in the armoury of international criminal justice. The proliferation of international and internationalised war crimes tribunals which began in the 1990s[2] culminated in the creation of the ICC, a project that might be said to have been first seriously considered by Gustave Moynier in the 1860s.[3] As recent referrals to the ICC by the Security Council of the situations in Sudan and Libya confirm, the international community very much views war crimes trials as an important response to conflict and atrocity. This preference and its implications for international criminal justice form an important theme that must continue to be discussed.

There is of course a range of responses to atrocity. Truth and Reconciliation Commissions, of which there have been over 30 since the 1970s,[4] reflect a less retributive, more reconciliatory emphasis. Other community-based approaches reflect a more culturally specific response to the subject matter of international criminal justice. Examples of this include the *Gacaca* Courts in Rwanda,[5] the *Fambul Tok* in Sierra Leone[6] and the *Mato Oput* in Northern Uganda.

---

[2] International Criminal Tribunal for the former Yugoslavia, International Criminal Tribunal for Rwanda, Special Court for Sierra Leone, Special Panels for the Dili District Court, Extraordinary Chambers in the Courts of Cambodia and Special Tribunal for Lebanon.

[3] Jackson Maogoto, 'Early Efforts to Establish an International Criminal Court' in Jose Doria, Hans-Peter Gasser, and Mahmoud Cherif Bassiouni (eds), *The Legal Regime of the International Criminal Court: Essays in Honour of Professor Igor Blishchenko* (Martinus Nijhoff 2009) 3, 5. Maogoto notes that Moynier was not originally in favour of establishing an international criminal court, believing that, like many humanists of the time, descriptions of human suffering would shock the public into outrage and by extension pressure states to adhere to the humanitarian norms and rules, at 5.

[4] Paavani Reddy, 'Truth and Reconciliation Commissions: Instruments for Ending Impunity and Building Lasting Peace' (2004) 41(4) *UN Chronicle* 19, 19. See the discussion of 'Alternative Paradigms' in Mark Findlay and Clare McLean, 'Emerging International Criminal Justice' (2007) 18 *Current Issues in Criminal Justice* 457, 469.

[5] See Phillip Clark, *The Gacaca Courts, Post-Genocide Justice and Reconciliation in Rwanda: Justice Without Lawyers* (Cambridge Studies in Law and Society 2010).

[6] See Elisabeth Hoffman, 'Reconciliation in Sierra Leone: Local Processes Yield Global Lessons' (2008) 2 *The Fletcher Forum of World Affairs* 129; Tim

Another aspect of the international criminal justice patchwork is the extent to which it engages other disciplines. As already mentioned, this field has been traditionally viewed as a strictly (or predominantly) legal discipline, with images of the trial of the major war criminals at Nuremberg, and more recently the Slobodan Milošević or Charles Taylor trials, standing as masculine statements that impunity will not stand. However, an increasing sensibility has emerged in relation to other disciplines and views. Clearly, a discussion about what constitutes international criminal justice requires a broader analysis than that offered by international criminal law. Like international justice itself, different voices contribute to the content and meaning of this complex topic, and struggle to influence outcomes and processes.

Further fundamental questions about the coherence and legitimacy of international criminal justice itself are prompted by whether these voices are heard, and how they influence our understanding and responses. It is the purpose of this chapter then to examine some of these threads, to hear some of these voices, and to consider them under the broad question: what is international criminal justice?

## II. RETRIBUTIVE CONCEPTIONS OF INTERNATIONAL CRIMINAL JUSTICE – WAR CRIMES TRIALS

### A. Development of International War Crimes Trials

A reasonable place to start is the development of international war crimes trials. The first real example of such trials followed the Second World War. The Nuremberg, Tokyo and other post-war trials launched the new UN Charter world conception of international criminal justice. The goal of Nuremberg was to bring to justice the most senior German perpetrators of atrocities committed at the beginning of and during the war. American prosecutor, Robert Jackson, emphasised that while the trial was clearly one carried out by victorious nations over the vanquished, this did not mean that the court could surrender to an inevitable 'victor's justice'.[7] These Nazi war

Kelsall, 'Truth, Lies, Ritual: Preliminary Reflections on the Truth and Reconciliation Commission in Sierra Leone' (2005) 27(2) *Human Rights Quarterly* 361.

[7] Of course, all the post-Second World War tribunals were classic examples of victor's justice, even if the expression of it accorded with established principles of criminal justice. For a discussion of this aspect of the Nuremberg, Tokyo and other post-war trials, see eg, Antonio Cassese, *International Criminal Law* (Oxford

criminals were to be given a 'fair and dispassionate hearing',[8] a fair trial, and accorded the presumption of innocence. Moreover, he emphasised that the purpose of the trial was to incriminate the German leaders, not to act as an indictment upon the German people.[9] The individual was thus on trial, but not the State, nor the population. The extent to which these impressive and lofty goals were achieved has been heavily debated since that trial over 60 years ago,[10] and will no doubt continue to be assessed in light of the work of the modern war crimes tribunals.

## B. War Crimes Trials from the 1990s – The New Model

While some important domestic war crimes trials were held between the 1940s and the 1990s,[11] in reality, very little occurred on the international front until the creation of the International Criminal Tribunal for the former Yugoslavia (ICTY) in 1993 to try those accused of committing war crimes in the course of the Bosnian conflict. The aims and goals of this tribunal were not dissimilar to those in Nuremberg – to provide redress for the victims of atrocities, to express the moral outrage of the international

---

University Press 2003) 332–33; Cherif Bassiouni, *Crimes against Humanity in International Criminal Law* (Kluwer Law International 1999) 552–54; Timothy L H McCormack, 'Selective Reaction to Atrocity: War Crimes and the Development of International Criminal Law' (1997) 60 *Albany Law Review* 681, 717; Gerry J Simpson, 'Problems Confronting International Law and Policy on War Crimes and Crimes against Humanity' (1997) 60 *Albany Law Review* 801, 805–6; Timothy L H McCormack, 'From Sun Tzu to the Sixth Committee: The Evolution of an International Criminal Law Regime' in Timothy L H McCormack and Gerry J Simpson (eds), *The Law of War Crimes: National and International Approaches* (Martinus Nijhoff 1997) 31; Richard H Minear, *Victor's Justice: The Tokyo War Crimes Trial* (Princeton University Press 1973).

[8] Yale Law School – Lillian Goldman Law Library, 'Nazi Conspiracy and Aggression' (*The Avalon Project – Documents in Law, History and Diplomacy*, 2008) vol 1, ch V, 'Opening Address for the United States' <http://avalon.law.yale.edu/imt/chap_05.asp> accessed 23 February 2012.

[9] Ibid.

[10] For a small sample of some of this debate, see: Gerry Simpson, *Law, War and Crime* (Polity 2007); Bass, above note 1.

[11] Obvious examples include the trials of Adolf Eichmann in Israel, Klaus Barbie in France and Ivan Polyukhovich in Australia. Mark Findlay and Clare Mclean highlight that 'the intervention of the Cold War saw both the concept and practice of international criminal justice removed from the forefront of global politics and relations' (Findlay and McLean, above note 4, 458).

community, to provide a vehicle of retributive justice and, of course, to stand as a deterrent to those who would repeat such heinous crimes in the future.

There were, however, some noteworthy differences and interesting features to this new model. For a start, it (happily) lacked features of victor's justice that had marred the successes of the post-Second World War tribunals. Of course, the Serbs complained that they were the target of the tribunal and that this was a new version of victor's justice, wielded by the US, Germany and others through the UN system. Such accusations are understandable but quite wrong.[12] They also distract argument away from other far more legitimate challenges to the ICTY and other international tribunals, which relate to the politics of selecting which crimes to prosecute, in which regions of the world, and why.[13]

Another feature of the Yugoslav and Rwanda Tribunals was the fact that the Security Council created them as a measure under Chapter VII of the UN Charter, to restore and maintain international peace and security. Apart from an early challenge within the ICTY[14] and some initial scholarly disquiet,[15] this extraordinary development in the armoury of the Security Council has quickly been accepted as legitimate. Of course, this has now been replaced by the methodology of referring matters to the ICC by way of

---

[12] See Gideon Boas, *The Milošević Trial: Lessons for the Conduct of Complex International Criminal Proceedings* (Cambridge University Press 2007) 38; Michael P Scharf, 'The Legacy of the Milosevic Trial' (2003) 37(4) *New England Law Review* 915, 921–23; Enrique Carnero Rojo, 'The Role of Fair Trial Considerations in the Complementarity Regime of the International Criminal Court: From No Peace without Justice to No Peace with Victor's Justice' (2005) 18 *Leiden Journal of International Law* 829, 867–68.

[13] See Robert Cryer, *Prosecuting International Crimes: Selectivity and the International Criminal Law Regime* (Cambridge Studies in International and Comparative Law 2005) Part II; Gerry Simpson, 'War Crimes: A Critical Introduction' in Timothy L H McCormack and Gerry Simpson (eds) (above note 7, 1, 8–9); Alfred Rubin, 'International Crime and Punishment' (1993) 33 *The National Interest* 73; Ian Brownlie, *Principles of Public International Law* (6th edn, Oxford University Press 2003) 575.

[14] See *Prosecutor v Tadić* (*Decision on Defence Motion for Interlocutory Appeal on Jurisdiction*) (ICTY, Appeals Chamber, Case No IT-94–1-AR72, 2 October 1995).

[15] See eg, V Gowlland Debbas, 'Security Council Enforcement Action and Issues of State Responsibility' (1994) 43 *International Criminal Law Quarterly* 55; Gabriël H Oosthuizen, 'Playing Devil's Advocate: The United Nations Security Council is Unbound by Law' (1999) 12 *Leiden Journal of International Law* 549.

Security Council resolution (a technique ironically supported enthusiastically by the US, which is not a State Party of the Court and was, under George Bush's administration, the Court's arch enemy).

The fact that the ad hoc tribunals were set up under Chapter VII of the UN Charter made their relationship with the conflict in their respective regions necessarily deeper than a traditional criminal jurisdiction. Any criminal court established as a measure to re-establish peace and security must surely need to contribute to reconciliation and sustained post-conflict measures to stabilise the region. Additionally, to the tribunals' credit, they espoused broader goals of accountability and justice – in their judicial and political rhetoric[16] as well as in substantive areas of their core work. An important example of this goal-setting was reference to reconciliation as a mitigating factor in sentencing.[17]

Other interesting aspects of the new tribunal model were the development of a human rights regime, and the effect of the *jus cogens* norm of a right to a fair trial on the work of these courts.[18]

## C. The Special Place of the International Criminal Court

Like Nuremberg, the modern war crimes tribunals focus primarily on the senior participants in the conflicts addressed. The era of ad hoc and hybrid tribunals might be seen, in one sense, as preparatory work for the creation of the now functioning ICC. Determined somewhat optimistically in its statute to 'put an end to impunity', the ICC operates on a predominantly similar model to that of the ad hoc tribunals. Its struggle for existence through several International Law Commission drafts and the derelict Cold War years may have created an odd psychological facet to the Court, which on one level is played out in its substantive legal work. The Court is regarded,

---

[16] See eg, statements made by ICTY President Patrick Robinson in his addresses to the United Nations General Assembly and Security Council: ICTY, 'Statements and Speeches of the ICTY' (*UN ICTY*, 2011) <http://www.icty.org/sid/10259> accessed 5 October 2011.

[17] See eg, *Prosecutor v Plavšić* (*Sentencing Judgment*) (ICTY, Trial Chamber, Case No IT-00–39&40/1S, 27 February 2003) [94]. This case was followed in *Prosecutor v Jokić* (*Sentencing Judgment*) (ICTY, Trial Chamber, Case No IT-01–42/1-S, 18 March 2004), the Trial Chamber noting that 'the parties agree that Miodrag Jokić was instrumental in ensuring that a comprehensive ceasefire was agreed upon and implemented, at [90]; *Prosecutor v Blagojević and Jokić* (*Judgment*) (ICTY, Appeals Chamber, Case No IT-02–60-A, 9 May 2007), the Chamber stating that the conduct of an accused that promotes reconciliation in the former Yugoslavia has been considered as a mitigating circumstance, at [330].

[18] See generally Boas, above note 12, Chapter 1.

and regards itself, as the pre-eminent expression of global retributive justice. It is empowered to investigate crimes within its various jurisdictional limitations, and is used as an increasingly important aspect of the Security Council's (albeit selective) redress of atrocity. An important example is Security Council Resolution 1970, referring the Libya situation to the ICC.[19]

The Court is under pressure to investigate an enormous range of crimes and conflicts, develop technical assistance to states through a policy of positive complementarity, and develop an expeditious and efficient pre-trial, trial and appeal model – a task acknowledged by its own judges to be proving difficult.[20]

## D. Where Do War Crimes Trials Leave Us in Relation to Understanding International Criminal Justice?

As Bass put it, the various objectives for international war crimes tribunals include the following: 'to bring justice, establish peace, outlaw war altogether, erase bitterness, or to establish new international norms that will help lift us out of anarchy'.[21] Considering these lofty goals, can it be said that war crimes trials are a successful method of achieving international criminal justice? Do they at least contribute to ending impunity? Are they really a deterrent for murderous dictators and would-be *genocidaires*? Do they promote reconciliation in transitional communities? Or do they adversely impact on community rebuilding and on victims' need to establish the truth, to be heard and to take control of their own narrative?

Of course, it is not simply a question of spouting platitudes about impunity and justice. For war crimes trials to work, the accused must be tried fairly and expeditiously, account must be given of the role and rights of victims (individual and community) and the place of reconciliation must at least be considered in the process. These tribunals face a number of

---

[19] SC Res 1970, 6491st mtg, UN Doc S/RES/1970 (26 February 2011) ('SC Resolution 1970').

[20] Eric Ellis, 'Room for Everyone at the Hague' (*The Global Mail*, 8 February 2012) <http://www.theglobalmail.org/feature/room-for-everyone-at-the-hague/42/> accessed 23 February 2012.

[21] Objectives for international war crimes tribunals include 'to bring justice, establish peace, outlaw war altogether, erase bitterness, or to establish new international norms that will help lift us out of anarchy' – Bass, above note 1, 284; see also Colonel Murray C Bernay, 'Memorandum 15 September 1944' in Bradley F Smith (ed), *American Road to Nuremberg – The Documentary Record, 1944–1945* (Hoover Institution Press 1981) 36.

impediments, some external and others self-created, in achieving even the most basic aspect of these goals.

The most pressing external problem facing the international tribunals has been a varying preparedness on the part of states to support them. For example, states have at times demonstrated a reluctance to arrest accused perpetrators. This can be explained in part by the 'unwillingness of even liberal states to endanger their own soldiers either by arresting war criminals or in subsequent reprisals',[22] and in part by the way in which national interest 'shaped by political culture ... dictates whether or not states support the international criminal tribunals'.[23]

International criminal tribunals also face challenges partly of their own making, as their internal procedures have tended to frustrate the expedient running of the trial process. These impediments, such as a lack of prosecutorial restraint, a preparedness on the part of the courts to implement their powerful case management provisions and trial inefficiencies, have been rehearsed at length elsewhere,[24] but they continue to plague the work and viability of these important institutions.

At the same time, the international tribunals have enjoyed a number of successes in attempting to fulfil their mandate to try those accused of war crimes. Firstly, it is important not to take the existence of international criminal tribunals and international criminal law for granted. The existence and legitimacy of international criminal law as a body of law was questioned as recently as the 1980s,[25] although thankfully that debate can now be put firmly to one side. The creation of these tribunals as a juridical response to mass atrocity is itself an achievement, and the broader impact of these tribunals both in a punitive sense and as a deterrent should not be underestimated.[26]

---

[22] Bass, above note 1, 277.

[23] Ibid.

[24] See generally, Gideon Boas et al, *International Criminal Law Practitioner Library – Volume III– International Criminal Procedure* (Cambridge University Press 2011); Boas, above note 12.

[25] Georg Schwarzenberger, 'The Province of International Judicial Law' (1983) 21 *Notre Dame International Law Journal* 21, 25. Indeed, Schwarzenberger had maintained such a view since 1950. See generally Georg Schwarzenberger, 'The Problem of an International Criminal Law' (1950) 3 *Current Legal Problems* 263.

[26] However, Bass takes a more sceptical view as to whether war crimes trials are an effective deterrent, noting that it is 'far from clear that war crimes tribunals have much of a deterrent effect' – Bass, above note 1, 291, 294–95. On the other hand, Peter Galbraith states: 'I thought the whole war crimes issue was a very effective tool to stopping war crimes' – Bass, above note 1, 295. Wippman, quoted in Findlay

Secondly, despite the myriad complexities associated with war crimes trials, the fact that modern international criminal law has been crafted from next to nothing in under 20 years, is an extraordinary achievement. A significant number of trials have been held at the international criminal tribunals and, while far from perfect, they represent something of a credible system of criminal justice that responds to unspeakable crimes. The oft-referred-to 'road from Nuremberg to The Hague' was a difficult one, and many questions await reply from the ICC, but the international community continues to value such a juridical response.[27]

## E. National War Crimes Trials – A Lack of Action

Despite ratification of the Rome Statute of the ICC leading to the implementation of legislation in numerous countries, and despite the ICC clearly being set up by states as a court of last resort, there is little evidence that states are enthusiastically taking to the task of trying war criminals under their domestic criminal justice systems. While Belgium in the early part of the twenty-first century exploded into action as the State of universal jurisdiction, the *Arrest Warrant* case before the International Court of Justice (ICJ)[28] and some bullying from the then US President George W Bush and his Secretary of Defense, Donald Rumsfeld,[29] extinguished this brief excitement. The general disposition of states – particularly those of the common law persuasion – is well reflected in the experience of Australia, Canada and the United Kingdom, where few prosecutions have been

---

and McLean, above note 4, 474, notes '[t]hat for many "deterrence is the most important goal" of tribunals'.

27 Not only have the ad hoc and hybrid tribunals been created and supported, but the ICC has been the recipient of two Security Council referrals (despite three of the Council's permanent members not having ratified its Statute), including as recently as SC Resolution 1970 of February 26th 2011, referring the Libya situation.

28 *Arrest Warrant of 11 April 2000 (Democratic Republic of the Congo v Belgium) (Judgment)* [2002] ICJ Rep 3.

29 Following action sought by Iraqi victims against US President George H W Bush, Vice-President Dick Cheney and others for committing war crimes in the 1991 Gulf war, overt threats by US Secretaries of State Colin Powell and later Donald Rumsfeld (including the refusal to fund a new NATO headquarters in Belgium) led to a series of amendments brought by the Belgian Prime Minister that significantly emasculated the Belgian law, including the removal of the *partie civile* component and recognition of a wide range of immunities under international law. For a detailed account of these events, see Steven Ratner, 'Belgium's War Crimes Statute: A Postmortem' (2003) 97 *American Journal of International Law* 888.

launched, and fewer still have been successful.[30] Whether the unwillingness of able states to prosecute crimes of mass atrocity is a threat to the capacity of the retributive model is difficult to assess, but it seems likely to be one.

## F. The Threat to International Criminal Justice Posed by Guantanamo Bay and the 'War on Terror'

Another, slightly sinister, development in the response to mass atrocity has arisen following the 9/11 terrorist attacks on the World Trade Centre in the US in 2001. The 'war on terror' (a phrase coined by the Bush administration) has led to some genuine challenges to the legitimacy and coherence of international criminal justice.[31] The use of Guantanamo Bay as a holding station for state-sanctioned torture[32] and exclusion from state-based jurisdiction for the purpose of denying accused persons basic criminal process rights (including the *jus cogens* norm of a right to a fair trial),[33] poses a serious threat to international criminal justice and the rule of law. The war on terror also gave birth to the implementation of counter-terrorist measures that threatened some of the fundamental criminal process rights in countries that have a highly developed system of criminal justice.[34] Finally, and

---

[30] See generally, Gideon Boas, 'War Crimes Prosecutions in Australia and Other Commonwealth Countries: Some Observations' (2010) 21(2) *Criminal Law Forum* 313; Helen Durham and Michael Carrel, 'Lessons from the Past: Australia's Experience in War Crimes Prosecution and the Problem of the Applicable Legal Framework' (2006) 2 *Asia-Pacific Yearbook of International Humanitarian Law* 135; Aegis Trust, *Strengthening UK Law on Genocide, War Crimes and Crimes against Humanity – House of Lords Briefing Note on Planned Amendments to the Coroners and Justice Bill*, June 2009; Sharon A Williams, 'The Prosecution of War Criminals in Canada' in Timothy L H McCormack and Gerry J Simpson (eds), above note 7.

[31] See Marco Sassoli, 'The Status of Persons Held in Guantanamo under International Humanitarian Law' (2004) 2 *Journal of International Criminal Justice* 96; Knut Dörmann, 'The Legal Situation of "Unlawful/Unprivileged Combatants"' (2003) 849 *International Review of the Red Cross* 45; Daryl A Mundis, 'Military Commissions: The Use of Military Commissions to Prosecute Individuals Accused of Terrorist Acts' (2002) 96 *American Society of International Law* 320; Kenneth Anderson, 'The Military Tribunal Order: What to Do with Bin Laden and Al Qaeda Terrorists? A Qualified Defense of Military Commissions and United States Policy on Detainees at Guantanamo Bay Naval Base' (2002) 25 *Harvard Journal of Law & Public Policy* 591.

[32] Sassoli, above note 31.

[33] See *Hamdan v Rumsfeld*, 548 US 557 (2006).

[34] Much criticism has been made of such measures in a large number of jurisdictions. See generally Ben Saul, '"Why Do They Hate Us? … They Hate Our

significantly, responses to the Al-Qaeda attacks have led the US and its allies into full-blown international armed conflicts, some with lawful justification (Afghanistan) and some without (Iraq).

Some of these measures have an inevitable and unavoidable relationship with international criminal justice. The development and application of substantive and procedural criminal law in one jurisdiction affects that in another. The preparedness of one or more states to bypass fundamental principles and defensible interpretations of the law when trying certain kinds of defendants, or deciding whether to prosecute one conflict or party over another, has certain consequences. It creates a challenge to the legitimacy of a juridical response to atrocity and social rupture, because inconsistent and *sui generis* responses open international criminal justice up to allegations of partiality and prejudice – perhaps a modern, post-Nuremberg version of 'victor's justice'. Also, varying structures and practices across war crimes tribunals can lead to a sense of incoherence, which in turn raises questions of legitimacy.[35]

Another unavoidable development is the employment of permissive universal jurisdiction as a structural underpinning in international criminal justice. While international criminal tribunals can rely upon Security Council resolutions, engaging the UN Charter's Chapter VII powers, or, in the case of the ICC, multilateral treaty agreements or self-referral measures, the reality is that the entire system of international criminal justice is predicated on various expressions of universal jurisdiction.[36] Natural law conceptions of humanity and protection of communities are infused in the dialogue of what constitutes international criminal justice; these require a sense of an 'international community' acting 'collectively' against certain opprobrious behaviour. In this way, international criminal justice is an expression of global community – a dysfunctional one, to be sure. But, just as any

---

Freedoms": The Globalisation of Terrorism and Counter-Terrorism' in Swawkat Alam, Natalie Klein and Juliette Overland, *Globalisation and the Quest for Social and Environmental Justice: The Relevance of International Law in an Evolving World Order* (Routledge 2011) 205; Ben Saul, 'Defining Terrorism to Protect Human Rights' in Deborah Staines (ed), *Interrogating the War on Terror: Interdisciplinary Perspectives* (Cambridge Scholars Publishing 2007) 190–210.

35 See discussion in Boas et al, above note 24, Chapter 1.

36 See *The Princeton Principles on Universal Jurisdiction* (Program in Law and Public Affairs 2001) <http://lapa.princeton.edu/publications.php>. Principle 1(4) specifically considers due process requirements founded on the International Covenant on Civil and Political Rights (adopted 16 December 1966, entered into force 23 March 1976), 999 UNTS 171, arts 14, 15, at 29. All international criminal tribunals mirror this, therefore any system of international criminal justice should be taken to require this also.

community needs rules and a predictable application of those rules, so must international criminal justice reflect such principles.

All of this suggests that while war crimes trials remain the preferred model for addressing mass atrocity (at least at the UN level), serious questions about coherence and legitimacy remain. The risk is that a pluralistic and diverse expression of principle could unravel into a chaotic and fragmented system of justice. The US system of military tribunals post-9/11 certainly showed just how much of a threat this is. Worse perhaps is that a lack of commitment from states – political, strategical and financial – is always a danger.

## III. RESTORATIVE JUSTICE

For all the emphasis that has been placed on a retributive model, this is not the only way of defining international criminal justice. As Richard Goldstone has pointed out, prosecution is 'not the only form [of justice], nor necessarily the most appropriate form in every case'.[37] Restorative justice approaches mass atrocity and social rupture from a very different perspective. It focuses upon discovering the truth, reconstructing the narrative of a conflict or human rights-violated society, and re-empowering victims and victimised communities.

Different conceptions of the relationship between restorative and retributive justice have been advanced. One conception is that restorative justice operates on a fundamentally different level to international war crimes trials. While international criminal tribunals can be said to operate as a retributive/guilt-based justice model, restorative justice is designed to function on the level of establishing the truth and on reconciliation and healing.[38] Under this approach, the two are 'mutually exclusive, incapable of happy coexistence'.[39]

Another view is that the two can, with institutional transformation, coexist in a transitional context – that there is also scope for restorative themes to be incorporated into the procedural framework of international

---

[37] Richard Goldstone, 'Justice as a Tool for Peace-Making: Truth Commissions and International Criminal Tribunals' (1996) 28(3) *New York University Journal of International Law and Politics* 485, 491.

[38] Findlay and Mclean, above note 4, 469, referring to David Dyzenhaus, 'Judicial Independence, Transitional Justice and the Rule of Law' (2003) 10 *Otago Law Review* 345, 366.

[39] Ibid.

trials.[40] The problem with this attempt to marry the retributive with the restorative is that the forensic requirements of war crimes trials are in some respects manifestly incompatible with restorative approaches.

One such example of an attempt to integrate formal and informal approaches can be seen in Sierra Leone. Following that bloody conflict, which involved numerous rebel groups and the displacement of nearly half of the population of the country, a UN-backed peace agreement was finally reached in 2002. This was preceded by the *Lome Peace Accords* in 1999 which provided for the creation of a Truth and Reconciliation Commission. This had a legislative mandate to:

> create an impartial historical record of violations and abuses of human rights and international humanitarian law related to the armed conflict in Sierra Leone; … to address impunity, to respond to the needs of the victims, to promote healing and reconciliation and to prevent a repetition of the violations and abuses suffered.[41]

In 2002, at the request of the Sierra Leone President, a Special Court was created to try those responsible for crimes committed during the conflict, independently of the Commission. The Sierra Leone Commission concluded in 2004, releasing its final report. It has been criticised as being a 'deeply flawed and problematic process'[42] and as being in conflict with the Special Court.[43] This was for a variety of reasons, including the relationship between the Commission and the Court, internal organisational problems within the Commission and the cultural difficulty of encouraging public truth-telling.[44] Others, including one of the Commission members, William Schabas, believe the Sierra Leone model 'may help us to understand that post-conflict justice requires a sometimes *complex mix of therapies*, rather

40 Ibid.

41 Truth and Reconciliation Commission Act 2000, *Sierra Leone Gazette*, No 9, 10 February 2000, s 6(1).

42 Sierra Leone Working Group on Truth and Reconciliation, *Searching for Truth and Reconciliation in Sierra Leone – An Initial Study of the Performance and Impact of the Truth and Reconciliation Commission* (Pambazuka 2006) <http://www.pambazuka.org/en/category/comment/32255>.

43 Laurel E Fletcher et al, 'Context, Timing and the Dynamics of Transitional Justice: A Historical Perspective' (2008) 31(1) *Human Rights Quarterly* 163, 183. These views have been shared by others, including for example Rosalind Shaw, *Rethinking Truth and Justice in Sierra Leone – United States Institute of Peace Special Report SR-130* (United States Institute of Peace 2005).

44 Kelsall, above note 6.

than a unique choice of a single approach from a menu of alternatives'.[45] At any rate, while the Truth and Reconciliation model may well have benefits in a transitional environment, it seems that a cooperative or integrated approach with war crimes trials carries some difficulties.

An even less successful attempt to integrate formal and informal approaches to international criminal justice occurred in the former Yugoslavia, where a Truth and Reconciliation Commission was formed in 2001 to operate parallel to the ICTY. However, after facing considerable internal conflict, numerous withdrawals by key personnel, concerns over resources and the mandate of the Commission, and little substantive progress, it ceased to exist in 2003, without an official statement or decree.[46]

## A. Truth and Reconciliation Commissions

Of course, Truth and Reconciliation Commissions have for some time been used as an expression of international criminal justice – indeed, their use predates the modern system of international war crimes trials. The truth commission model, which is mostly utilised in a period of political or post-conflict transition,[47] is defined by Freeman as:

> an ad hoc, autonomous, and victim-centred commission of inquiry set up in and authorized by a state for the primary purposes of (1) investigating and reporting on the principal causes and consequences of broad and relatively recent patterns of severe violence or repression that occurred in the state during determinate periods of abusive rule or conflict, and (2) making recommendations for their redress and future prevention.[48]

---

[45] William Schabas, 'Conjoined Twins of Transitional Justice? The Sierra Leone Truth and Reconciliation Commission and the Special Court' (2004) 2(4) *Journal for International Criminal Justice* 1082, 1088 (emphasis added).

[46] See Nenad Dimitrijevic, 'Serbia after the Criminal Past: What Went Wrong and What Should Be Done' (2008) 2 *International Journal of Transitional Justice* 5; Tatjana Peric, 'Facing the Past: Religious Communities, Truth and Reconciliation in Post-Milošević Serbia' (6th Annual Kokkalis Graduate Student Workshop, Cambridge (USA), February 2004).

[47] Ibid. See also Mark Freeman, *Truth Commissions and Procedural Fairness* (Cambridge University Press 2006) 12–13; Steven R Ratner, Jason S Abrams and James L Bischoff, *Accountability for Human Rights Atrocities in International Law: Beyond the Nuremberg Legacy* (3rd edn, Oxford 2009) 228–29.

[48] Freeman, above note 47, 18.

The South African Truth and Reconciliation Commission[49] is often cited as the eminent example of a restorative response to social rupture. As Schabas points out, it is in that category of commissions established when social transition is already well underway (following the abolition of apartheid), and was therefore more likely to succeed.[50] Established in the mid-1990s, the Commission was tasked with the underlying goal of uniting the still heavily divided nation. Victims of gross human rights violations were encouraged to come forward and give statements about their experiences, some of which were shared with the broader community. The central involvement of victims in the process has been credited with having 'an unparalleled impact on the level of public awareness and engagement in a truth commission process'.[51] Perpetrators were also encouraged to give testimony, the Commission utilising a truth-for-amnesty procedure. Although questions have been raised about the frankness of disclosure by perpetrators and the satisfaction felt by victims, this Commission is broadly viewed as a successful use of restorative justice, and was credited with assisting South Africa in the transition to full democracy.[52]

The value of Truth and Reconciliation Commissions has also been expressed from the perspective of story-telling as a therapy. The use of narrative to expose truth and correct false and damaging stories, can have considerable value for individual victims and communities.[53]

Truth and Reconciliation Commissions are a global phenomenon and have been established in states including Argentina, Chile, El Salvador, Uganda, Germany, Zimbabwe, Guatemala and most recently Burundi and East Timor. They will no doubt continue to be relied upon as a mechanism of international criminal justice. Their effectiveness will probably much depend on the social context in which they are created and how they are designed to interact with juridical responses to crimes committed.

---

49 Ibid 26 – see generally regarding the South African Truth and Reconciliation Commission.

50 William Schabas and Shane Darcy, *Truth Commissions and Courts: the Tensions between Criminal Justice and the Search for Truth* (Kluwer Academic Publishers 2004) 15.

51 Freeman, above note 47, 26.

52 See Sam Garkawe, 'The South African Truth and Reconciliation Commission: A Suitable Model to Enhance the Role and Rights of the Victims of Gross Violations of Human Rights?' (2003) 27 *Melbourne University Law Review* 334.

53 See Teresa G Phelps, 'Narrative Capability: Telling Stories in the Search for Justice' in Severine Deneulin, Mathias Nebel and Nicholas Sagovsky (eds), *Transforming Unjust Structures: The Capability Approach* (Springer 2006) 1.

## B. Community-based Responses to Mass Atrocity

Moving perhaps further towards the perimeter of international criminal justice is a range of community-focused programmes for transitioning societies. Alternative forms of justice such as localised courts are approaches that can 'more accurately reflect sociolegal norms of the places most immediately afflicted by mass atrocity'.[54]

An interesting example of this approach is the *Gacaca* Courts used in post-genocide Rwanda. While the international response to the 1994 genocide came in the form of the International Criminal Tribunal for Rwanda (set up to try those most responsible for the genocide) and national courts (which prosecuted others), the Government also employed traditional justice methods in 2001. The decentralised nature of the *Gacaca* Courts allowed greater engagement at a community level for victims. The courts were not permitted to try serious offenders, but rather property and other more minor offences. From a practical perspective, the national courts could not hear cases for all the detainees who were incarcerated awaiting trial – as Drumbl pointed out, it would take over a century to hear that many trials. The *Gacaca* were to allow for mechanisms that were more akin to Rwandan social and legal cultures, the purpose being to give greater social ownership of the process, leading to a deeper reconciliatory effect.[55]

Another example is support for local peace alternatives in Northern Uganda (ceremonies such as *Mato Oput* – a ritual of the clan group that involves both the political and spiritual sphere).[56]

These alternatives are seen as important paths in the reconciliation process. They can provide a sense of ownership within a community and an alternative to perceived paternalistic responses from external forces. However, traditional justice methods are not without their critics. Tim Allen notes that crimes committed in Uganda have no parallel in traditional alternatives to justice, and that the ceremonies were never designed to be used for crimes of the gravity dealt with under international criminal law.[57] In Rwanda, reports varied considerably as to the success of this process.[58] Others note that community-based responses are a reworking of tradition; some view this as a positive while other organisations, such as Human

---

[54] Mark A Drumbl, *Atrocity, Punishment and International Law* (Cambridge University Press 2007) 70. See also Kelsall, above note 6.

[55] See Kelsall, above note 6.

[56] Ibid.

[57] Tim Allen, *Trial Justice: The International Criminal Court and the Lord's Resistance Army* (Zed Books 2006).

[58] See Kelsall, above note 6.

Rights Watch, do not disapprove of traditional justice but note that these methods do not meet international standards of justice.[59]

## C. Different Disciplinary Approaches and Concerns with International Criminal Justice

The expressions of international criminal justice discussed thus far can all be – and often are – considered from a legal perspective. War crimes trials are an inherently juridical response to atrocity. While reflecting a more restorative, truth-finding approach, Truth and Reconciliation Commissions must be partly understood from the perspective of the legal structure of, and constraints on, their work: how will testimony be taken? Are amnesties available and, if so, what test will be applied and by whom?

The international lawyer's reflex is to sublimate other threads, or voices, in the myriad conceptions of international criminal justice.[60] Part of this reflex is founded in the sense that international criminal *law* equates to international criminal *justice*. However, while war crimes trials are a species of any criminal trial, they are also much more than this. This is a space in which other disciplines can help us understand more broadly what is international criminal justice. Other disciplinary perspectives – historical, political, sociological and victimological – are all worthy contributors to the debate on defining international criminal justice.

## D. Politics

Consider for a moment the relationship between politics and international criminal justice. Politics has been, and in mainstream international criminal law still is, considered something inherently undesirable. This perspective, as Gerry Simpson puts it, views the trial ideally as 'a place liberated from politics and the contamination politics threatens'.[61] In fact, war crimes trials are infused with politics in a range of critical ways: in a practical sense, from their creation, implementation and ongoing support; in a conceptual sense, from the fact that all law is an expression of politics; and finally, in the sense that war crimes trials invariably mean different things to different people. Clearly, the creation of any of the ad hoc and hybrid criminal tribunals is a product of the political relationship between states. The

---

59 Ibid.

60 See eg, Boas, above note 12, 4 – arguing that international criminal trials are a forensic process and that extra-legal considerations are to be pushed aside (a position from which I now somewhat resile).

61 Simpson, above note 10.

creation of the ICC represents a major shift in international norms relating to the prosecution of international crimes.[62]

The same is true for Truth and Reconciliation Commissions and other ways of responding to mass atrocity. Indeed, one simply needs to take a step back and ask a simple question to see just how profound the role of politics is in international criminal justice. Why is there a court to try crimes in the former Yugoslavia, Rwanda and Sierra Leone but not in Somalia, Zimbabwe or Sri Lanka? Why is there a Security Council Resolution referring Sudan and Libya to the ICC but not Yemen or Gaza? Politics dictates expressions of international criminal justice, and in doing so shapes our consciousness about where, why and how it applies. Of course, what we do only serves to highlight what we do not but perhaps should do.

## E. Victimology

A critical sociological and psychological element of international criminal justice concerns the role and status of victims. This is an emergent area of research which raises difficult theoretical, methodological and conceptual questions. What constitutes victimhood, the role and significance of individual and collective victims, the experience of indirect victimisation, and access to justice and victim rights, must all be considered within the wider debates surrounding the normative evolution of international criminal justice.

Within this area, the line between victim and witness (and therefore between possible conflicting roles, participation and interests within proceedings) remains unclear.[63] The appropriate boundaries for victim participation and its implications for the relationship between different expressions of international criminal justice remains a contested area in which the legitimate interests of victims need to be considered in relation to the efficiency and fairness of the proceedings and the rights of the accused.[64]

While many expressions of international criminal justice promote a certain type of justice based on Anglo-Continental legal tradition, legal anthropology reveals a diversity in conceptions of justice, from the manner

---

[62] Nicole Deitelhoff, 'The Discursive Process of Legalization: Charting Islands of Persuasion in the ICC Case' (2009) 63(1) *International Organization* 33.

[63] See Pascale Chifflet, 'The Role and Status of the Victim' in Gideon Boas and William A Schabas (eds), *International Criminal Law Developments in the Case Law of the ICTY* (Martinus Nijhoff 2003) 75.

[64] See Sam Garkawe, 'Victims and the International Criminal Court: Three Major Issues' (2003) 3 *International Criminal Law Review* 347.

in which people, and more importantly victims, conceptualise rights, to their understanding of an individual's duties vis-à-vis ethnic or cultural groups and attitudes towards appropriate punishment.[65]

Where victims' ideas of justice do not align with international legal regimes, the result is their exclusion from a legal political system.[66] This requires a discussion of the diverging ideas of justice in the context of victimology.[67] One (traditional, forensic) view of international criminal justice is that it is designed to be the 'end of impunity', and not the 'end of suffering'.[68] On this view, it is a system that punishes people 'for the fact that they have breached the law, not for the fact that they have inflicted trauma as perceived subjectively [by victims]'.[69] Victims are not owed convictions but society at large has a right to pursue a conviction.[70]

On the other hand, the endless stories of victims re-traumatised by the process of testifying in international trials, the further marginalisation of victims from the trial process through the 'paperisation' of trials and dissatisfaction with sentences, are all legitimate concerns that call for a revision of traditional common law perspectives of the victim in criminal justice. The ICC may have addressed the lack of victim rights by granting participation and compensation rights, but this process is yet to pass the true test of time.[71]

Furthermore, complaints about the truth and reconciliation process and community-based models raise questions about how international criminal justice is responding to the critical needs and rights of victims, and being

---

[65] Kamari Maxine Clarke, 'Global Justice, Local Controversies: The International Criminal Court and the Sovereignty of Victims' in Marie-Bénédicte Dembour and Tobias Kelly (eds), *Paths to International Justice: Social and Legal Perspectives* (Cambridge University Press 2007) 138.

[66] Ibid 187.

[67] Marlies Glasius, 'What Is Global Justice and Who Decides? Civil Society and Victim Responses to the International Criminal Court's First Investigations' (2009) 31(2) *Human Rights Quarterly* 496, 516. Glasius goes further, noting: 'Both secondary sources in Uganda and the DRC and primary research for this article in the CAR suggest that victims have a distinct and sometimes passionate interest in the doings of the Court.'

[68] Uwe Ewald, 'Large-Scale Victimisation and the Jurisprudence of the ICTY: Victimological Research Issues' in Uwe Ewald and Ksenija Turković (eds), *Large-scale Victimisation as a Potential Source of Terrorist Activities: Importance of Regaining Security in Post-Conflict Societies* (IOS Press 2006) 171, 173.

[69] Mina Rauschenbach and Damien Scalia, 'Victims and International Criminal Justice: A Vexed Question?' (2008) *International Review of the Red Cross* 441, 550.

[70] Larry May, *Crimes against Humanity: A Normative Account* (Cambridge University Press 2005) 220.

[71] See Garkawe, above note 64.

shaped by them. The future for the relationship between international criminal justice and victimology rests on finding a middle ground between community-based responses and a purely legalistic characterisation of the purpose of internationalised justice.

## F. Psychology

Another, less obvious, lens through which to view international justice is the field of psychology. The application of psychological theory and research to this field provides a unique insight into the psychological processes both underpinning and resulting from crimes of atrocity. Psychology can offer explanations as to how and why perpetrators of heinous crimes, including genocide, come to engage in behaviour typically regarded as 'inhumane'. In the aftermath of such devastation, psychology can also aid in the understanding of the various behavioural and emotional reactions experienced by victims at both the individual and community levels.[72] It can also inform governmental and international bodies of the most efficient and effective ways of promoting the resilience and recovery of those affected by international crime.

### The psychology of genocide

An example of the place of psychology in international criminal justice can be seen in an examination of perpetrators of genocide.[73] One approach (dispositional) groups together explanations of genocide occurring as a result of the specific internal characteristics of perpetrators. It is an individual approach which states that people, especially leaders, commit acts of genocide due to some form of pathology or dysfunction within themselves; that is to say, perpetrators possess internal traits or profiles predisposing them to genocidal behaviour. While some authors use simple descriptors such as 'sadistic' or 'authoritarian' to describe perpetrators of genocide,[74] others have suggested more specifically that a series of traits play a role in genocide, including social conformity, xenophobia, submissiveness and a deep ideological commitment.[75] However, while it might be reasonable to accept that theories of pathological and personality dysfunction explain the

---

72 Thomas Blass, 'Psychological Perspectives on the Perpetrators of the Holocaust: The Role of Situational Pressures, Personal Dispositions, and Their Interactions' (1993) 7 *Holocaust Genocide Studies* 30.

73 Ibid.

74 John Steiner, cited in Blass, above note 72.

75 Steven K Baum, *The Psychology of Genocide: Perpetrators, Bystanders, and Rescuers* (Cambridge University Press 2008).

genocidal behaviour of some leaders, it has been argued that theories such as these cannot alone account for the millions of people who, having previously been considered to be mentally healthy members of society, come to partake in genocidal behaviour alongside these leaders.[76]

Situational approaches focus instead on the role of external social factors in the development of genocidal behaviour, including obedience to authority.[77] Others have suggested that the concept of identity is central to the act of genocide. Moshman, for example, argues that genocide occurs as a result of four overlapping phases of extreme identity formation: dichotomisation, dehumanisation, destruction and denial.[78] Dichotomisation refers to the way in which people classify themselves according to different dimensions (gender, religion, age, profession, etc), and how in some instances people may come to define themselves in one dimension instead of many different dimensions, creating a simple 'us and them' mentality.[79] The second phase, dehumanisation, involves ranking one side of this dichotomy above the other, such that those deemed to be without a certain dimension are considered to be inferior and even sub-human. The prime example of this phenomenon is the Holocaust in the Second World War, during which those of Jewish ancestry were deemed to be inhuman by those who prescribed to the Nazi ideology. Conceptualising the other as non-human allows for the cessation of any moral obligations towards that group, resulting in destructive behaviour toward those of 'inferior' status. Finally, in an attempt to align their moral identities, members of the 'superior' group partake in the process of denial, in which true acceptance of what has occurred is avoided. Each stage in Moshman's theory is thought to reinforce the other, such that dehumanisation increases the salience of dichotomisation, and involvement in destruction strengthens the ideas of dehumanisation. Thus, the extreme development of identity based on a singular dimension can create the perception of a dichotomous society in which one group dominates over the other, often leading to violent and genocidal behaviour.[80]

Examined from these different (non-legal) perspectives, psychology might be seen at once as a tool for 'treating' the consequences of mass

---

[76] Blass, above note 72.

[77] Ibid.

[78] David Moshman, 'Us and Them: Identity and Genocide' (2007) 7 *Identity: An International Journal of Theory and Research* 115.

[79] Gordon McCormick, 'Terrorist Decision Making' (2003) 6 *Annual Review of Political Science* 473.

[80] Moshman, above note 78.

atrocity, but also for understanding the 'why' and 'how', and thus becoming a means of preventing, predicting and responding better and more quickly to events.

## G. History

Another discipline of inevitable importance to international criminal justice is history. As vehicles for truth-telling and teaching history, war crimes trials have attracted a large body of literature. However, the potential for war crimes trials to explain events and set a historical record is limited. Constrained by the rules of evidence and the overarching forensic purpose of the criminal trial,[81] only fragments of the story can emerge. Reference to the didactic function of international war crimes trials in the judgments themselves demonstrates a view that these are vehicles for story-telling. In reality, however, their accounts are usually a collage of the reports and testimony of historical 'experts' led by the prosecution and defence, possibly with a random layering of accounts by victims and political leaders who testified.

Truth and Reconciliation Commissions offer a better vehicle for truth-telling – after all, that is their primary purpose. While they are themselves imperfect, they are probably better equipped to piece together the history of events and the stories of victims and victimised communities.[82] However, through whichever practical lens one views international criminal justice, the presence of history is palpable. Indeed, failure to remember similar events, obsessions with past wrongs and judicial or other preoccupations with the precedent-setting of international war crimes trials, are but a few examples of how history is perpetually infused into any dialogue about international criminal justice.

## H. Use of Force as a Means of Expressing International Criminal Justice

A final word on international criminal justice is required. Since the NATO bombing of Serbia in 1999, an interesting development is the growing prevalence of the use of force by the international community as a 'tool' of international criminal justice. International military action in Kosovo and Iraq were both justified in part by rhetoric of justice, and both led to the

---

81 See Boas, above note 12, 4.
82 See Phelps, above note 53.

arrest and trial of those countries' leaders for genocide and other crimes.[83] Neither were sanctioned by the Security Council. It is hard to imagine that one of the key aims of these military incursions was not the removal of these dictators.

Since these conflicts, a key development has been the creation of the ICC, adding another dimension to this international policing. The provision for Security Council referral under the Rome Statute has been exercised twice in relation to alleged crimes against humanity and genocide – in Sudan and Libya.[84] While neither has been particularly successful, it does suggest something of a shift in the international political landscape.

The situation in Libya in particular is fascinating. A mandate to set up a no-fly zone and protect civilians metamorphosed into something quite different. The substantial provision of strategic aid to rebel forces in order to assist them in setting up a strong and permanent opposition force, coupled with attempts to target and kill Colonel Gaddafi in air strikes, set up a very different international landscape. Considered in light of the much-lauded assassinations of Osama Bin Laden in Pakistan and Anwar al-Awlaki in Yemen, a very uncertain picture of international criminal justice begins to emerge.

## IV. CONCLUSION

Peter Goodrich suggests that 'justice is best understood as an imperfect and flawed practice of virtue … an always-failed attempt to actualize an ethical commitment and accounting of the past'.[85] Looked at through a purist lens, justice must always fail: how can it account for the evil of Milošević, Saddam Hussein, Omar Al Bashir or Klaus Barbie? In any case, one

---

83 See Corneliu Bjola, *Legitimising the Use of Force in International Politics: Kosovo, Iraq and the Ethics of Intervention* (Routledge 2009) 45; Richard Falk, 'Humanitarian Intervention after Kosovo' in Aleksandar Jokic (ed), *Lessons of Kosovo: The Dangers of Humanitarian Intervention* (Broadview Press 2003) 43. See also arguments by then UK Prime Minister Tony Blair for a reinvigorated doctrine of humanitarian intervention – Tony Blair, Speech Made Justifying Military Action in Iraq, Speech of 5 March 2004 at Sedgefield, UK, cited in Gerry Simpson, 'International Law in Diplomatic History' in James Crawford and Martti Koskenniemi (eds), *The Cambridge Companion to International Law* (Cambridge University Press 2011).

84 See SC Resolution 1970; SC Res 1593, 5158th mtg, UN Doc S/RES/1593 (31 March 2005).

85 Peter Goodrich, 'Justice and the Trauma of Law: A Response to George Pavlich' (1998) 18 *Studies in Law, Politics, and Society* 271, 275.

person's Barbie might be another's Bush. But justice is not pure and therefore neither can international criminal justice be. It is a work in progress, driven by a mixture of moral values and pragmatic responses.

There are many different ways to skin the international criminal justice cat, and a range of options is provided by restorative and retributive justice models. Examining these from different disciplinary perspectives can only serve to amplify our understanding and improve our capacity to respond to mass atrocity. This chapter has attempted to discover what is international criminal justice, but, truth be told, it means different things to different people at different times. The Mothers of Srebrenica will never be satisfied that justice has been done, even when Radovan Karadžić and Ratko Mladić are locked up for life. This is much like Arendt's account of the Eichmann trial – even his conviction and hanging were appallingly unsatisfactory. What we expect of international criminal justice is just as perplexing as trying to understand what it is; indeed, one invariably influences the other.

# 2. Order in the courtroom: the unique challenge of maintaining control of a war crimes trial

**Michael P Scharf**

## I. INTRODUCTION

International war crimes trials are inherently messy, especially when former leaders invoke the right of self-representation in order to advance a political agenda that goes beyond defending themselves on the charges against them. Since the turn of the century, we have seen Slobodan Milošević, Vojislav Šešelj and Radovan Karadžić at the International Criminal Tribunal for the former Yugoslavia (ICTY), Charles Taylor at the Special Court for Sierra Leone (SCSL), and Saddam Hussein at the Iraqi High Tribunal (IHT) use self-representation in various ways to disrupt and delay the proceedings.[1]

Of all the modern war crimes trials, Saddam Hussein's behaviour was perhaps the most creatively disruptive. A month after the conclusion of the *Saddam Hussein* trial in September 2006, the author was invited by Luis Moreno Ocampo, the then Prosecutor of the International Criminal Court (ICC), to speak to his staff in The Hague about the lessons from the *Saddam Hussein* trial concerning maintaining order in the courtroom during a war crimes trial. Subsequently, the United Nations Office of Legal Affairs asked the author to present a video lecture on this topic for inclusion in the UN Audio Visual Library of International Law.[2] Drawn from my ICC and UN lectures, this chapter examines some of history's previous messy trials and the strategies judges have employed with varying degrees of success to respond to disruptive conduct by trial participants. It then describes the

---

[1] Christopher Allbritton, 'Saddam's Trial: Behind the Scene', *Time Magazine* (Baghdad, 13 February 2006) 50–51.

[2] Michael Scharf, Video, 'Managing Control of War Crimes Trials' (*United Nations Audiovisual Library of International Law*) <http://untreaty.un.org/cod/avl/ls/Scharf_CLP.html>.

various tactics employed by the judges in *Saddam Hussein* and analyses why they were not more successful. The chapter concludes with a detailed prescription for maintaining order in future war crimes trials.

## II. THE NEED FOR ORDERLY JUSTICE IN WAR CRIMES TRIALS

Disruptive conduct may be defined as any intentional conduct by the defendant or defence counsel in the courtroom 'that substantially interferes with the dignity, order and decorum of judicial proceedings'.[3] There are five main types of disorder: (1) passive disrespect, for example, the refusal to address the judge as 'Your Honour', or refusal to stand when the judge enters the courtroom; (2) refusal to cooperate with the essential ground rules of the judicial proceedings, for example, constantly insisting on making political speeches instead of asking questions during cross-examination; (3) repeated trial interruptions, ranging from insulting remarks to loud shouting or cursing; (4) in a televised trial, attempting to incite acts of mass violence; and (5) resorting to physical violence in the courtroom.[4]

Former leaders and their counsel in war crimes trials are especially likely to engage in such forms of disruption. Because of the political context and widespread publicity, leaders on trial are more likely than ordinary defendants to have concluded that they do not stand a chance of obtaining an acquittal by playing by the judicial rules. Instead, they seek to derail the proceedings, hoping for a negotiated solution (eg amnesty) outside the courtroom; to hijack the televised proceedings, hoping to transform themselves through political speeches into martyrs in the eyes of their followers; and to discredit the tribunal by provoking the judges into inappropriately harsh responses which will make the process appear unfair.

As Robert Jackson, the Chief Prosecutor at the Nuremberg trials, observed over 60 years ago, war crimes trials, whether before international tribunals or domestic courts, seek to establish a credible historic record of abuses and elevate the rule of law over the force of might, thereby facilitating the restoration of peace and the transition to democracy.[5] While

---

[3] Norman Dorsen and Leon Friedman, *Disorder in the Court: Report of the Association of the Bar of the City of New York, Special Committee on Courtroom Conduct* (Pantheon Books 1973) 91.

[4] Ibid.

[5] Robert H Jackson, 'Report to the President from Justice Robert H Jackson, Chief of Counsel for the United States in the Prosecution of Axis War Criminals –

tolerating dissent is a healthy manifestation of a democratic government, 'a courtroom is not an arena in which dissension, particularly of a disruptive nature, may supplant, or even take precedence over, the task of administering justice'.[6] This is especially true in a war crimes trial.

Unlike other forms of acceptable political expression, a disruptive defendant or defence lawyer who interferes with the 'grandeur of court procedure' (as Hannah Arendt once described the judicial process)[7] threatens the proper administration of criminal justice in several fundamental ways. First, disruptive conduct renders it more difficult for the defendant and any co-defendants to obtain a fair trial. Second, it hampers the court's ability to facilitate the testimony of victims and other witnesses. Third, it undermines the public's confidence in and respect for the legal process.

There are those who would argue that a defendant has a right, through his own (or through his lawyer's) disruptive and obstructionist conduct, to an unfair trial, but modern war crimes tribunals have held that the defendant's right to employ disruptive tactics which seek to discredit the judicial process must give way to the tribunal's obligation to protect 'the integrity of the proceedings' and 'to ensure that the administration of justice is not brought into disrepute'.[8] The duty of a war crimes tribunal to ensure that a trial is fair has been interpreted as including concerns that go beyond just those of the accused.

---

June 7 1945' (1945) 39(3) *American Journal of International Law* 178, 184, quoted in Michael P Scharf, *Balkan Justice – The Story Behind the First International War Crimes Trial Since Nuremberg* (Carolina Academic Press 1997) 37 ('We must establish incredible events by credible evidence'); see also Robert H Jackson, 'Opening Statement' (International Military Tribunal, Nuremberg, 6 November 1945), quoted in 'International Military Tribunal – Nuremberg', *Trial of the Major War Criminals Before the International Military Tribunal Nuremberg* (1947) vol II, 98–99.

[6] *United States v Dougherty*, 473 F 2d 1113 (DC Cir, 1972) (Adams J concurring and dissenting).

[7] Hannah Arendt, 'Civil Disobedience' in Eugene V Rostow (ed), *Is Law Dead?* (Simon and Schuster 1971) 212.

[8] See, eg, *Prosecutor v Norman et al* (*Decision on the Application of Samuel Hinga Norman for Self-Representation under Article 17(4)(d) of the Statute of the Special Court*) (Special Court for Sierra Leone, Trial Chamber I, Case No SCSL-04–14-T, 17 Jan 2005) [28].

## III. HISTORY'S MOST TUMULTUOUS TRIALS

### A. From the Chicago Seven to Zacarias Moussaoui

The administration of justice has always endured a degree of disorder, and there have been many notable occasions when trial participants have been particularly unruly and disrespectful to judicial authority. A list of history's most disruptive defendants would include Sir Walter Raleigh (tried in Britain for high treason in 1603), William Penn (tried in Britain for unlawful assembly in 1670), Auguste Vaillant (tried in France for blowing up the Chamber of Deputies in 1894), Michele Angiolillo (tried in Spain for assassinating the Spanish premier in 1897), and Gaetano Bresci (tried in Italy for killing Italian King Humbert in 1899).[9] But by far the most notorious disorderly trial in the twentieth century was the *Chicago Seven* trial of 1969–70.

The *Chicago Seven* trial is particularly relevant to the *Slobodan Milošević* and *Saddam Hussein* trials because former US Attorney General Ramsey Clark assisted the defence in all three trials. In the *Chicago Seven* case, the leaders of the anti-Vietnam war movement – Bobby Seale, David Dellinger, Abbie Hoffman, Jerry Rubin, Rennie Davis, Tom Hayden, Lee Weiner and John Froines – were charged with conspiring, organising, and inciting riots during the 1968 Democratic National Convention in Chicago.[10] The trial drew considerable public notice because of the defendants' notoriety and their courtroom antics.

On the first day of the trial, when the presiding judge, Julius Hoffman, refused to issue a postponement so that Bobby Seale's attorney would have time to recover from a gall bladder operation,[11] Seale said to the judge: 'If I am consistently denied this right of legal defense counsel of my choice who is effective by the judge of this Court, then I can only see the judge as a blatant racist of the United States Court.'[12] This brought a strong rebuke from Judge Hoffman.[13] That same day, Judge Hoffman reprimanded Tom Hayden for giving a clenched fist salute to the jury and Abbie Hoffman for

---

[9] Dorsen and Friedman, above note 3, 91.

[10] Although there were initially eight defendants, Bobby Seale was severed from the case before it went to the jury. See *United States v Seale*, 461 F 2d 345 (7th Cir, 1972) 356 ('*Chicago Seven* case/trial').

[11] See *United States v Seale*, 461 F 2d 345 (7th Cir, 1972) 358.

[12] Ibid 374.

[13] Ibid.

blowing kisses at the jurors.[14] A few days later, the defendants tried to drape the counsel table with a North Vietnamese flag in celebration of Vietnam Moratorium Day, drawing another round of sharp words from the judge.[15]

Throughout the trial, the defendants refused to rise at the beginning or close of court sessions.[16] On two occasions, defendants Abbie Hoffman and Jerry Rubin wore judicial robes in court onto which were pinned a Jewish yellow star, meant to imply that Judge Hoffman was running his courtroom like the courts of Nazi Germany.[17] The defendants frequently called Judge Hoffman derogatory names, accused him of racism and prejudice, and made sarcastic comments to him, such as asking 'How is your war stock doing?' The most serious disorder occurred two weeks into the trial, when Judge Hoffman learned that a few minutes before the commencement of the court session, Bobby Seale had addressed the audience of his supporters in the courtroom, telling them that if he were attacked 'they know what to do'.[18] Judge Hoffman responded by having Seale bound and gagged. Defense counsel William Kunstler then scolded the Court, saying: 'This is no longer a court of order, your Honor; this is a medieval torture chamber. It is a disgrace.'[19]

At the conclusion of the trial, Judge Hoffman issued a total of 159 citations to the defendants and their lawyers for contempt in response to these incidents of disruption and disrespect. The Seventh Circuit Court of Appeals, however, reversed the contempt convictions on the ground that the judge cannot wait until the end of the trial to punish the defendants and their lawyers for misconduct. It also reversed the convictions on the substantive charges, in part due to the prejudicial remarks and actions of the trial judge and inflammatory statements by the prosecutor during the trial.[20] It should come as no surprise that the *Chicago Seven* trial is universally seen as a low point in American courtroom management. Rather than viewing Judge Hoffman as a brave hero fighting anarchy, history remembers him more as an accomplice who unwittingly fanned the flames of disorder. Slobodan Milošević and Saddam Hussein, both of whom were advised by Ramsey

---

14 See Pnina Lahav, 'Theater in the Courtroom: The Chicago Conspiracy Trial' (2004) 16 *Cardozo Studies in Law and Literature* 381, 387.

15 Ibid.

16 *Chicago Seven* case, 461 F 2d 345 (7th Cir, 1972) 386.

17 Lahav, above note 14, 430.

18 Ibid.

19 Ibid.

20 *Chicago Seven* case, 461 F 2d 345 (7th Cir, 1972); *United States v Dillinger*, 472 F 2d 340 (7th Cir, 1972).

Clark, set out to do the same thing to the judges of the ICTY and the IHT respectively.

Just a few months after the *Chicago Seven* trial, the US Supreme Court held in *Illinois v Allen* that an unruly defendant could be excluded from the courtroom during his trial if his disruptive behaviour threatened to make orderly and proper proceedings difficult or wholly impossible.[21] Allen had been tried in a State Court in 1957 for armed robbery of a tavern owner. During his trial, Allan threatened the judge's life, made abusive remarks to the court and announced that under no circumstances would he allow his trial to proceed. The court responded by removing him from the courtroom after appropriate warning, and Allen was convicted in his absence.

The Supreme Court affirmed Allen's conviction, ruling that removal after a warning was permissible and far less objectionable than use of restraints. In a passage that was obviously inspired by the publicity surrounding the *Chicago Seven* trial, the Supreme Court stated:

> Trying a defendant for a crime while he sits bound and gagged before the judges and jury would to an extent comply with that part of the Sixth Amendment's purposes that accords the defendant an opportunity to confront the witnesses at the trial. But even to contemplate such a technique, much less see it, arouses a feeling that no person should be tried while shackled and gagged except as a last resort. Not only is it possible that the sight of shackles and gags might have a significant effect on the jury's feelings about the defendant, but the use of this technique is itself something of an affront to the very dignity and decorum of judicial proceedings that the judge is seeking to uphold.[22]

Yet the Court declined to rule that physical restraints may never be used, saying: 'However, in some situations which we need not attempt to foresee, binding and gagging might possibly be the fairest and most reasonable way to handle a defendant who acted as Allen did here.'[23]

The first major chaotic trial to arise after the Supreme Court's *Allen* decision was that of Charles Manson who, along with three female members of his cult, was tried from June 1970 to March 1971 for the gruesome murder of movie actress Sharon Tate and five others. During the trial, Manson constantly interrupted proceedings by shouting, chanting, turning his back on the judge, assuming a crucifixion pose and singing (actions

---

21 *Illinois v Allen*, 397 US 337 (1970). The Court explained that it was 'essential to the proper administration of criminal justice that dignity, order, and decorum be the hallmark of all court proceedings in our country' at 343.

22 Ibid 344.

23 Ibid.

often parroted by the three women co-defendants).[24] The court responded by repeatedly having the defendants removed from the courtroom. In one instance, the judge removed Manson after he leaped over the defence table to attack the judge with a pencil, shouting: 'In the name of Christian justice, someone should cut your head off.'[25]

More recently, in February 2006, accused Al-Qaeda terrorist Zacarias Moussaoui was thrown out of the courtroom by US District Judge Leonie Brinkema, and then temporarily banned from returning to court, due to his disruptive and belligerent outbursts. 'This trial is a circus … God curse you and America', Moussaoui shouted at the judge as he was led away. 'You are the biggest enemy of yourself', Judge Brinkema replied, ordering that Moussaoui watch the remainder of the proceedings via closed-circuit feed from a jail cell inside the courthouse. Media outlets reported that most legal scholars agreed that Judge Brinkema acted appropriately.[26]

## B. Disorder in The Hague

Slobodan Milošević was the first former Head of State to be tried in an international war crimes trial. Although assisted by an army of defence counsel including Ramsey Clerk, Milošević asserted his right to act as his own lawyer in the televised proceedings before the ICTY, as this would enable him to make lengthy opening and closing statements, and turn cross-examinations into opportunities for unfettered political diatribes. As the trial unfolded, Milošević exploited his right of self-representation to treat the witnesses, prosecutors and the judges in a manner that would earn ordinary defence counsel expulsion from the courtroom. He often strayed from the forensic case into long vitriolic speeches and was frequently strategically disruptive.[27]

---

24 Robert Dardenne, 'The Case of Charles Manson' in Lloyd Chiasson Jr (ed), *The Press on Trial: Crimes and Trials as Media Events* (Praeger/Greenwood 1991) 159, 167.

25 Ibid.

26 Michael P Scharf, 'Did the Dujail Trial Meet International Standards of Due Process?' in Michael P Scharf and Gregory S McNeal (eds), *Saddam on Trial: Understanding and Debating the Iraqi High Tribunal* (Carolina Academic Press 2006) 162, 163; see generally Neil A Lewis, 'Judge Ejects 9/11 Suspect After Outburst' *New York Times* (New York, 15 February 2006) A20; Kelli Arena and Kevin Bohn, 'Al Qaeda Conspirator Barred from Court' (*CNN*, 14 February 2006) <http://www.cnn.com/2006/LAW/02/14/moussaoui.trial/index.html/>.

27 For references by the tribunal of Milošević misusing hearings and cross-examinations as a platform for making political speeches, see: *Prosecutor v Milošević* (*Initial Appearance*) (ICTY, Trial Chamber III, Case No IT-02–54-T, 3

On numerous occasions, the presiding judge, Richard May, tried to reign Milošević in with little success. A defendant who is represented by a lawyer is ordinarily able to address the court only when he takes the stand to give testimony during the defence's case-in-chief. In the usual case, the defendant is limited to giving evidence that is relevant to the charges, and he is subject to cross-examination by the prosecution. While a judge can control an unruly lawyer by threatening fines, jail time, suspension, or disbarment, there is little a judge can effectively do to regulate a disruptive defendant who is acting as his own counsel.

While Milošević's antics did not win him points with the judges, they had a significant impact on public opinion back home in Serbia. Rather than discredit his nationalistic policies, the trial had the opposite effect. His approval rating in Serbia doubled during the first weeks of the trial, and two years into the trial he easily won a seat in the Serb parliament in a nationwide election. In addition, opinion polls indicated that a majority of Serbs felt that he was not getting a fair trial, and that he was not actually guilty of any war crimes.[28] Suspicion surrounding the circumstances of Milošević's death just before the conclusion of his trial has only reinforced these widely held views.

Six months after Milošević's death, another Serb leader, Vojislav Šešelj, decided that he too would utilise the right of self-representation as a means of disrupting his trial before the ICTY. A Belgrade University professor of law-turned paramilitary group leader, Šešelj made his unruly intentions clear on the eve of trial when he published three books in Serbia entitled: *Genocidal Israeli Diplomat Theodor Meron* (about the President of the ICTY), *In the Jaws of the Whore Del Ponte* (about the Chief Prosecutor of the Tribunal), and *The Lying Hague Homosexual, Geoffrey Nice* (about the lead trial prosecutor).[29] Šešelj tried repeatedly to provoke the judges at

July 2001); *Prosecutor v Milošević* (*Status Conference*) (ICTY, Trial Chamber III, Case No IT-02–54-T, 30 October 2001); *Prosecutor v Milošević* (*Open Session*) (ICTY, Trial Chamber III, Case No IT-02–54-T, 10 November 2004); *Prosecutor v Milošević* (*Hearing*) (ICTY, Trial Chamber III, Case No IT-02–54-T, 10 November 2004); *Prosecutor v Milošević* (*Pre-Defense Conference*) (ICTY, Trial Chamber III, Case No IT-02–54-T, 17 June 2004); See also Jerrold M Post and Lara K Panis, 'Tyranny on Trial: Personality and Courtroom Conduct of Defendants Slobodan Milošević and Saddam Hussein' (2005) 38 *Cornell International Law Journal* 823, 832.

[28] Michael P Scharf and Christopher M Rassi, 'Do Former Leaders Have an International Right to Self-Representation in War Crimes Trials?' (2005) 20 *Ohio State Journal on Dispute Resolution* 3, 6.

[29] *Prosecutor v Šešelj* (*Decision on Assignment of Counsel*) (ICTY, Trial Chamber II, Case No IT-03–67-PT, 21 August 2006) [30].

pre-trial hearings and made numerous obscene and improper statements in his pre-trial motions, including one submission which stated: 'You, all you members of The Hague Tribunal Registry, can only accept to suck my cock.'[30]

On the eve of trial in August 2006, the Trial Chamber revoked Šešelj's right to self-representation.

> While it is clear that the conduct of the Accused brings into question his willingness to follow the 'ground rules' of the proceedings and to respect the decorum of the Court, more fundamentally, in the Chamber's view, this behaviour compromises the dignity of the tribunal and jeopardizes the very foundations upon which its proper functioning is based.[31]

The Appeals Chamber agreed that the Trial Chamber could revoke the right to self-representation where the Trial Chamber found that 'appropriate circumstances, rising to the level of substantial and persistent obstruction to the proper and expeditious conduct of the trial exist'.[32] The Appeals Chamber however held that the Trial Chamber had to give the defendant an explicit warning first.

Šešelj's obstructionist behaviour persisted at trial. He requested that judges remove their robes in his presence because the judges 'reminded him of medieval inquisitors'. He moved to have Judge Schomburg disqualified solely because he was from Germany, stating: '[T]he smell of crematoriums and gas chambers comes into The Hague courtroom with him.' He publicly accused the judges and lawyers of bribing witnesses to testify against him, intimidated witnesses on the stand and disclosed the name of confidential witnesses to an outsider so that the outsider could 'disable' them.[33]

In the face of these continuing disruptions, the Trial Chamber issued repeated warnings, and then ruled that counsel could be rightly imposed on Šešelj. The Appeals Chamber disagreed, and reinstated Šešelj as primary counsel. The Trial Chamber later assigned standby counsel.[34]

About this time, the trial of Bosnian Serb leader Radovan Karadžić commenced. On the eve of his trial in 2009, Karadžić too asserted his right

---

30 Ibid [48].

31 Ibid [77].

32 *Prosecutor v Šešelj* (*Decision on Appeal against the Trial Chamber's Decision on Assignment of Counsel*) (ICTY, Appeals Chamber, Case No IT-03-67-AR73.3, 20 October 2006) [21].

33 Rachel K Jones, 'Untangling the Right to Self-Representation in the International Criminal Tribunal for the Former Yugoslavia' (2009) 43 *Georgia Law Review* 1285, 1309–10.

34 Ibid 1311–13.

to self-representation. Karadžić subsequently insisted on not recognising the authority of the Tribunal; he refused to abide by procedures or attend trial sessions.[35] After issuing repeated warnings, the Trial Chamber appointed standby counsel to represent the interests of Karadžić if required.[36] This time, the decision was upheld on appeal.[37]

## C. Disarray in the Dujail Trial

On 11 August 2005, the democratically elected Iraqi National Assembly adopted the Statute of the IHT with some modifications: notably, the Assembly replaced the clause providing for a right of self-representation with a clause that said that all defendants before the Tribunal had to be represented by Iraqi Counsel, who could be assisted by foreign lawyers.[38] The author was part of the team of international advisers that provided training workshops to the IHT judges in the months leading up to the trial. During the training sessions, the author strongly advocated for such an amendment in order to ensure that Saddam Hussein would not be able to use self-representation as a means of hijacking and disrupting the IHT. What the author did not comprehend at the time however, was that this legislative change would not accomplish the goal if the judges decided to follow the unique Iraqi legal tradition of permitting a defendant to cross-examine each witness after his lawyer had done so,[39] in essence enabling them to serve as co-counsel.

---

[35] *Prosecutor v Karadžić* (*Decision on Appointment of Counsel*) (ICTY, Trial Chamber, Case No IT-95–5/18-T, 5 November 2009).

[36] Ibid.

[37] *Prosecutor v Karadžić* (*Decision on Karadžić's Appeal from Decision on Motion to Vacate Appointment of Richard Harvey*) (ICTY, Appeals Chamber, Case No IT-95–5/18-AR73, 12 February 2010) 6.

[38] Qanoon Al-Mahkamat Al-Jeena'eyyat Al-Eraqiyyat Al-Mukhtas (Statute of the Iraqi High Tribunal), art 19(d) <www.law.case.edu/saddamtrial/documents/IST_statute_official_english.pdf (Iraq)>, reproduced in Scharf and McNeal, above note 26, 283; Rule 29 is contained in the IHT Rules of Procedure and Evidence (2005) (English trans), at 313.

[39] There is also some international tribunal precedent for the approach of the IHT. After assigning counsel over the accused's objection, the ICTY permitted the accused, Krajišnik, 'as an exception to the usual regime, to supplement counsel's cross-examination with his own questions': *Prosecutor v Krajišnik* (*Reasons for Oral Decision Denying Mr Krajišnik's Request to Proceed Unrepresented by Counsel*) (ICTY, Trial Chamber, Case No IT-00–39-T, 18 August 2005) [3].

During the *Dujail* trial,[40] Saddam Hussein and the other defendants were constantly disruptive and prone to political theatre.[41] Hussein's disruptive conduct often coincided with the most emotionally compelling testimony of victims. He engaged in frequent angry outbursts, yelling at the judge to 'go to hell' and calling the judge a homosexual, a dog, and a whore-monger. He made wild accusations of mistreatment by his American jailers, insisted on prayer breaks in the middle of witness testimony, went on hunger strikes and repeatedly refused to attend trial sessions. Most troubling, he took advantage of the above-mentioned Iraqi legal tradition that permits the defendant to cross-examine each witness after his lawyer has finished his cross-examination, by making frequent political speeches and impelling his followers – who were watching the television broadcasts of the proceedings – to kill American occupiers and Iraqi government collaborators.

Meanwhile, Hussein's co-defendant, Barzan al-Tikriti, who had served as head of the Internal Security Agency, competed with Hussein for the most offensive insults directed at the bench. On one occasion, he appeared in court wearing only his pyjamas,[42] and another time he insisted on sitting on the courtroom floor with his back to the judge.[43]

For their part, Saddam Hussein's retained lawyers, in particular Lebanese defence attorney Bushra al-Khalil and Jordanian lawyer Salah al-Armouti, frequently made outrageous political speeches and acted in outright contempt of the IHT. They engaged in tactics such as insulting Judge Ra'ouf, holding up photos of US prison abuses at Abu Ghraib,[44] and on one occasion pulling off their defence counsel robes and hurling them at the bench.[45] Saddam Hussein's retained lawyers also staged a walk-out in the middle of a trial session and boycotted the majority of the trial sessions

---

[40] Judgment, Al-Dujail Case, No.1/9 First (2005); English translation available at: <http://law.case.edu/saddamtrial/documents/dujail_opinion_pt1.pdf>.

[41] Michael A Newton and Michael P Scharf, *Enemy of the State: The Trial and Execution of Saddam Hussein* (St. Martin's Press 2008) 106–70 (chapter detailing defendant's disruptive conduct on each day of the trial).

[42] Edward Wong, 'The Reach of War: The Trial; Hussein, Gleeful, Badgers the Judge and Declares a Hunger Strike Over His Treatment' *New York Times* (New York, 15 February 2006) A10.

[43] Robert F Worth, 'Prosecutors of Hussein Press Charges of Execution' *New York Times* (New York, 14 February 2006) A8.

[44] Edward Wong, 'Saddam Admits He Swiftly Doomed 148 Villagers' *New York Times* (New York, 5 April 2006).

[45] Hussan M Fatah, 'For a Shiite, Defending Hussein is a Labor of Love' *New York Times* (New York, 24 June 2006) A4.

including the closing arguments.[46] These acts violated Iraqi law and the Iraqi Code of Legal Professional Ethics, which provide that lawyers practising in Iraqi courts must be respectful toward the court, must appear in court on the set dates, should not try to delay the resolution of a case, and must facilitate the task of the judge.[47]

The first presiding judge, Rizgar Amin, attempted to deal with such disruptive behaviour by ignoring it.[48] Although human rights groups applauded Judge Rizgar's calm demeanour in conducting the trial, the Iraqi population felt that he was losing the 'battle of the wills' against the former dictator, and he resigned under the weight of mass public criticism.[49] The replacement presiding judge, Ra'ouf Abdul Rahman, employed a number of tactics to regain control of his courtroom.[50]

Judge Ra'ouf began his first day as presiding judge by sternly warning defendants and counsel that outbursts and insults would not be tolerated. A few minutes later, he demonstrated his resolve by evicting defendant Barzan al-Tikriti and defence counsel Bushra al-Khalil when they failed to heed his admonishment. When the retained defence counsel responded by boycotting the trial en masse, Judge Ra'ouf appointed public defenders to replace them. Notably, when the retained defence counsel later asked to return, Judge Ra'ouf permitted them to do so. He never imposed fines or other sanctions on them for their misbehaviour, despite the fact that they resorted to such tactics again and again throughout the trial; nor did he revoke the defendants' right to question the witnesses or to address the court, despite the fact that it was frequently abused.

---

[46] See Nehal Bhuta, *Judging Dujail: The First Trial before the Iraqi High Tribunal* (Human Rights Watch 2006) 71 – discussing the role of Defense Office lawyers after privately-retained defence counsel began boycotting the *Dujail* trial in February 2006.

[47] Law of the Legal Profession – No 173 of 1965, art 50, annex ('Lawyer's Professional Code of Conduct') art 9, cited in ibid 70.

[48] See Michael Scharf, 'Who Won the Battle of Wills in the December Proceedings of the Saddam Trial?' in Scharf and McNeal, above note 26, 130.

[49] See Michael Scharf, 'A Changing of the Guard at the Iraqi High Tribunal' in Scharf and McNeal, above note 26, 136–37.

[50] See Michael Scharf, 'The Battle of the Wills – Part Two' in Scharf and McNeal, above note 26, 143–44.

## IV. REMEDIES FOR DISRUPTION

### A. Limiting Self-representation

Permitting a former leader to assert the right of self-representation in a war crimes trial is a virtual licence for abuse. While there is ongoing debate about whether there exists a customary international law right to self-representation, many countries of the world require that defendants be represented by counsel in all cases involving serious charges.[51] The Iraqi National Assembly was prudent to require that defendants before the IHT be represented by Iraqi lead counsel, whom the tribunal could control through various sanctions available under Iraqi law.

It was a huge mistake, however, for the presiding judges of the IHT to allow the defendants to question witnesses following their lawyers' cross-examinations, as this completely undermined the objective of the National Assembly's revisions to the IHT Statute. Instead, the judges should have recognised that departures from traditional Iraqi practices were warranted in an extraordinary trial of this nature, especially as the traditional practice was neither required by Iraqi nor international law.

In the United States, courts have held that a defendant who is represented by a lawyer has no right to act as co-counsel by, for example, cross-examining witnesses or addressing the bench. The rule limiting the defendant's participation is necessary 'to maintain order, prevent unnecessary consumption of time or other undue delay, to maintain the dignity and decorum of the court and to accomplish a variety of other ends essential to the due administration of justice'.[52]

Even in a tribunal such as the ICTY, whose statute provides for the right of self-representation, the Appeals Chamber decision in the *Šešelj* case recognised that such a right is a qualified one: abuse it and you lose it.[53] Drawing from international tribunal precedent, defence counsel should be imposed on a defendant who seeks to represent himself where: (1) the defendant attempts to boycott his trial;[54] (2) the defendant's

---

51 Scharf and Rassi, above note 28, 13–15.

52 *United States v Foster*, 9 FRD 367 (SDNY, 1949) 372.

53 See *Prosecutor v Šešelj* (*Decision on Appeal against the Trial Chamber's Decision on Assignment of Counsel*) (ICTY, Appeals Chamber, Case No IT-03–67-AR73.3, 20 October 2006) [21].

54 *Prosecutor v Barayagwiza* (*Decision on Defense Counsel Motion to With draw*) (ICTR, Trial Chamber I, Case No ICTR-07–19-T, 2 November 2000) [24]; see also *Diaz v United States*, 223 US 442 (1912) 458, holding that a trial could continue where the defendant refused to appear in the courtroom, as to hold

self-representation would prejudice the fair trial rights of co-defendants;[55] (3) the defendant is being persistently disruptive or obstructionist;[56] or (4) self-representation would unreasonably prolong the trial.[57]

Since most war crimes tribunal courtrooms are partitioned by sound-proof glass, a judge may effectively deal with minor disruptions simply by turning off the defendant's microphone. In the case of persistent disruptions, the judge must give a specific warning before revoking the right of self-representation. In addition, the defendant must be accorded at least a chance to reclaim the right if he manifests a willingness to conduct himself consistently with the decorum and respect inherent in the concept of courts and judicial proceedings. One commentator advocates a 'three strikes approach' after which the right would be permanently revoked, while others believe that the Court should have complete discretion to determine whether to give the defendant yet another chance.[58]

## B. Standby Public Defenders

Whether in a situation where a defendant is representing himself, or where he is represented by retained counsel, a war crimes tribunal must have standby counsel ready to step in when needed.[59] Such occasions would include situations where the defendant or his counsel engage in persistently disruptive or obstructionist behaviour, where they become too ill to participate actively in court sessions, or where they stage a walkout or a boycott of the proceedings.

---

otherwise would enable the defendant to 'paralyze the proceedings of courts and juries and turn them into a solemn farce'.

55 *Prosecutor v Norman et al* (*Decision on the Application of Samuel Hinga Norman for Self-Representation under Article 17(4)(d) of the Statute of the Special Court*) (Special Court for Sierra Leone, Trial Chamber I, Case No SCSL-04–14-T, 17 Jan 2005) [28].

56 *Prosecutor v Šešelj* (*Decision on Appeal against the Trial Chamber's Decision on Assignment of Counsel*) (ICTY, Appeals Chamber, Case No IT-03–67-AR73.3, 20 October 2006) [21].

57 *Prosecutor v Milošević* (*Decision on Interlocutory Appeal of the Trial Chamber's Decision on the Assignment of Defense Counsel*) (ICTY, Appeal Chamber, Case No IT-02–54-AR73.7, 1 November 2004) [17].

58 Nicole L Camier, 'Controlling the Wrath of Self-Representation: The ICTY's Crucial Trial of Radavan Karadžić' (2010) 44 *Valparaiso University Law Review* 957, 1008.

59 The concept of standby counsel refers to an attorney who is appointed to assist a self-represented defendant, and to step in as counsel as needed. Ibid 981.

Just as a war crimes tribunal should appoint at least one alternate judge who observes the trial from its commencement in case one of the judges should need to be replaced for health or other reasons, so too should standby public defenders be present from the beginning of the trial. Such counsel should be highly qualified, receive the same international training as prosecutors and judges, and be assisted by international experts. The very presence of standby public defenders can have a deterrent effect on misconduct by a self-represented defendant or by retained defence counsel because they will recognise that their disruptive actions will not successfully derail the trial, which can proceed without pause with standby counsel.

Ironically, the IHT did in fact appoint standby public defenders, but failed to provide timely notice to the media of their appointment, describe their credentials or explain their function. Consequently, several print and broadcast media outlets erroneously reported that Saddam Hussein was not represented by any counsel during those periods in which his retained counsel were boycotting the proceedings. Similarly, human rights organisations, who were publicly critical of the skills and experience of the public defenders, failed to recognise that they were in fact being assisted by international experts obtained and paid for by the International Bar Association.[60]

## C. Expulsion and Other Sanctions

The ICTY Appeals Chamber indicated in the *Milošević* case that the principle of proportionality must always be taken into account in crafting an appropriate response to disruption or delay.[61] With this admonition in mind, a war crimes tribunal should deal with the five categories of defendant misconduct identified above (see subsection II) as follows.

First, passive disrespect should generally be ignored unless it substantially interferes with the proceedings. The essential dignity and decorum of a courtroom does not turn on whether the defendant stands or addresses the judge as 'Your Honour'.

Second, a judge should inquire as to why a defendant is refusing to cooperate with the fundamental ground rules of court proceedings. Often

---

60 See Eric Blinderman, 'Judging Human Rights Watch: An Appraisal of Human Rights Watch's Analysis of the Ad-Dujayl Trial' (2007) 39 *Case Western Reserve Journal of International Law* 99.

61 *Prosecutor v Milošević* (*Decision on Interlocutory Appeal of the Trial Chamber's Decision on the Assignment of Defense Counsel*) (ICTY, Appeal Chamber, Case No IT-02–54-AR73.7, 1 November 2004) [17]–[18].

such behaviour is in response to perceived unfair decisions by the bench.[62] The defendant should be assured that his rights will be protected, and warned that he faces exclusion from the courtroom or other appropriate and proportional actions if obstructive behaviour continues.

Third, a single obscenity or outburst should be met with a warning that continued disruptions of this kind will lead to sanctions, including expulsion from the courtroom. Where the defendant is excluded from his trial, the court should make reasonable efforts to enable him to keep apprised of the progress of the trial and to communicate with his attorney.

Fourth, since a televised trial gives the defendant the opportunity to communicate directly with the population at large, the judge must be particularly vigilant not to permit the defendant to use the courtroom as a stage to incite mass violence.[63] Usually, there is a 20-minute delay in broadcasting to enable the tribunal to bleep out references to confidential witnesses. While it may also be appropriate to excise defence outbursts that seek to incite violence, this approach is of limited efficacy since such statements will most likely be reported in the print media.

Fifth, physical violence in the courtroom cannot be tolerated, and a court may deal with it by immediate expulsion or use of physical restraints.

Following the first incident of disruption, the judge should issue a warning, explicitly describing the sanction that will be imposed if the disruptive conduct continues. The warning should explain that the defendant's conduct is disruptive and will not be tolerated. It should also alert the defendant that future occurrences will result in expulsion from the trial for as long as his disruptive posture is maintained, and that the trial will continue in his absence. The warning should explain that in addition to exclusion, the judge may impose other sanctions on the defendant, such as relocating him to a smaller cell, decreasing the time he gets for recreation, or reducing his access to other prisoners and family.

While the judicial process may well proceed more smoothly without the defendant in the courtroom, his absence may diminish the educative function of the trial. During Saddam Hussein's boycott of the *Dujail* trial for

---

62 In the case of the *Saddam Hussein* trial, this perception was in part caused by the judges' ill-conceived decision to defer pronouncement of most pre-trial motions until after the trial's conclusion.

63 Most war crimes tribunals have employed a 20-minute delay in the broadcast of the trial proceedings to enable them to edit out such dangerous outbursts, but the judge should firmly communicate that such statements will be met with the sanction of exclusion. In the *Dujail* trial, the judge reportedly told Saddam Hussein it was one thing to encourage supporters to kill Americans, but it was utterly unacceptable for him to encourage the killing of Iraqis.

example, print and broadcast media attention quickly dwindled, denying the public a chance to learn about some of the most important documents and testimony admitted into evidence. Thus, there are good reasons to avoid the sanction of expulsion if possible. Consequently, if disruptive conduct persists despite the initial warning, the judge should issue a firmer warning, recess to discuss the matter with the defendant and his lawyer, or briefly adjourn the proceedings to allow for a cooling-off period. Further disruption should result in temporary exclusion, followed by a calibrated response proportionate to the degree and persistence of disruption.

## D. Responding to Contumacious Counsel

With respect to disorderly defence counsel, the judge should clearly set the ground rules of the trial from the beginning, warning that disruptive conduct will not be tolerated and describing the sanctions that will be imposed in response to such transgression. Although the demeanour and conduct of counsel that is deemed acceptable may vary somewhat from country to country, most of the world's legal professions follow the basic principle that a lawyer must be 'respectful, courteous and above-board in his relations with a judge' before whom he appears.[64] Especially in a major war crimes trial, deferential courtroom behaviour is necessary to ensure that the judge's decisions are not perceived to be based on emotional reactions to insult.

Following the lead of the Special Court for Sierra Leone, all war crimes tribunals should adopt a Code of Professional Conduct, which spells out the rules of courtroom decorum applicable to both the prosecution and defence counsel. Consistent with such a code, persistent insults and disrespectful comments should be met with sanctions after an appropriate warning, including fines, jail time, suspension, and even disbarment. Because a judge has inherent power to remove a disruptive defendant from the courtroom, he also possesses the inherent power to deal with a disruptive lawyer in the same way, and to replace him temporarily or permanently with standby counsel.

It is important in this regard to stress that the obligation of a defence counsel is not purely to act as agent for his client, permitted and perhaps even obliged to do for the accused everything he would do for himself were he trying his own case, but also to the court and to the larger interests of justice that the court is serving. As the American Bar Association has explained, '[i]t would be difficult to imagine anything which would more gravely demean the advocate or undermine the integrity of our system of

---

[64] For example, Model Code of Professional Responsibility (1980), EC 7–36.

justice than the idea that a defense lawyer should be simply a conduit for his client's desires'.[65] If a client insists on his attorney asking improper questions, making irrelevant speeches, insulting the bench, or staging walkouts or boycotts, the lawyer must reject those instructions, for he cannot excuse his own professional misconduct on the ground that his client demanded it.

Moreover, the defence counsel should seek to dissuade his client from improper courtroom behaviour, including explaining to him the sanctions that may be imposed by the judge and the probable prejudice to his case if he disrupts the proceedings. A defence counsel who encourages courtroom misconduct may be punished under the rules that establish his own responsibility for maintaining courtroom decorum. If he advises a client to act disruptively (or suggests methods for doing so), the court has authority to discipline counsel.

## V. CONCLUSION: FAIR TRIAL VERSUS INTEREST OF JUSTICE

Revoking the right of self-representation, replacing retained counsel with standby public defenders, or expelling the defendant or retained defence lawyer from the courtroom may initiate a number of practical difficulties. After the revocation of Slobodan Milošević's right of self-representation for example, the defendant refused to cooperate with the assigned counsel, and witnesses for the defendant refused to appear in court or to answer questions until the defendant's control of his case was restored.[66] Vojislav Šešelj responded to the assignment of standby counsel by staging a hunger strike.[67] Similarly, Saddam Hussein not only refused to cooperate with the public defenders during the boycott of his retained counsel, but he attempted (without success) to prevent the public defenders from delivering a closing argument on his behalf.[68]

Such a situation obviously impacts negatively on the defendant's fair trial rights, but the international tribunals have interpreted the duty to ensure that

---

65 American Bar Association, *Standards Relating to the Prosecution Function and the Defense Function 146 – ABA Project on Standards for Criminal Justice* (Institute of Judicial Administration 1971).

66 See generally submissions by the prosecution, referring to the accused being implicated in refusal of witnesses to testify in *Prosecutor v Milošević* (*Open Session*) (ICTY, Trial Chamber III, Case No IT-02–54-T, 10 November 2004).

67 Jones, above note 33, 1309–10.

68 See Blinderman, above note 58.

a trial is fair as including concerns that go beyond just those of the defendant. The narrow fair trial rights of the defendant must be considered in the context of broader interests of justice which require 'that the trial proceeds in a timely manner without interruptions, adjournments or disruptions'.[69]

[69] *Prosecutor v Šešelj* (*Decision on Prosecution's Motion for Order Appointing Counsel to Assist Vojislav* Šešelj with His Defense) (ICTY, Trial Chamber II, Case No IT-03–67-PT, 9 May 2003) [21].

# 3. Making war crimes trials work – balancing fairness and expedition

**Iain Bonomy***

## I. THE STORY SO FAR

The author's vision of justice in the arena of armed conflict was formed during his early years in cinemas showing a weekly diet of Westerns. Life was cheap; the good and the bad were clearly defined and distinguished; justice was exclusively the province of the white man; it was never administered by the Indian. The prisoner captured by the Indian had to be handed over for a fair trial under white man's justice, and the lynch mob was kept at bay until the US Marshal arrived or a judge was brought in. Making these arrangements took a matter of days and the trials themselves never seemed very long. By the end of the film, the viewer was never in doubt that what had happened was fair and expeditious.

Of course as a child the author had no refined notion of due process, but it was already in existence. Indeed, go back more than a century before these days of the American Wild West and there you will find in the United Kingdom discussion of *mens rea* and the burden of proof in terms which are readily understood today.[1] Fast forward to the present day however, and relatively simple notions of what is fair come wrapped in layers of procedural complexity.

The objectives of military action can be ill-defined – e.g. locating and disabling weapons of mass destruction, or regime change? The uncertainty over the objectives, one of which may be legitimate and the other not, seems almost designed to create confusion. Notions of self-defence and the protection of a civilian population from attack seem to be defined in increasingly complex terms, with a view to providing a cloak to cover the

* The author is grateful to his former associate legal officer at the International Criminal Tribunal for the former Yugoslavia (ICTY), Silva Hinek, for her assistance with research for this chapter.

[1] *See* e.g. *R* v *Woodfall* [1558 to 1774] All ER 602.

often confused circumstances in which the innocent die. Alliances of nations, which may in reality be fragmented, give apparent respectability to action that might be viewed as aggression if committed by states seen to form part of, or be on the fringes of, the 'axis of evil' (as former US President George Bush defined states supporting terrorism).

So, distinguishing the 'goody' from the 'baddy' has become increasingly difficult. In the simple days of black and white cinema (which extended even beyond the end of World War II) and victors' justice, the distinction was easy – in the words of ABBA, 'The Winner Takes It All'. The era of confusion and complexity was probably ushered in by the conflict in the former Yugoslavia which extended in some form over lands occupied then by people who now live in six or seven separate states,[2] and could then be seen as seven national groups. It is a tribute to the work of the International Criminal Tribunal for the former Yugoslavia (ICTY) that those tried and convicted include nationals of five of these states.[3] We can of course argue endlessly over the justice of every individual case, as has been the custom to date in the former Yugoslavia, but that does not detract from the fact that a simple review of ICTY statistics points to a determined attempt to bring justice to every national group in the former Yugoslavia.

However, other statistics point up another feature which is a source of great concern and the subject of this chapter. The proceedings are seen as lasting an unconscionable time. Easily the most prolific of modern international criminal tribunals, the ICTY has seen 161 accused indicted, but no clear end is in sight for a number of the accused held since 1995 when the Tribunal was up and running and even the Appeals Chamber had been called into action.[4]

There are a number of simple and obvious explanations for the lapse of a good part of this period. The first task for the original prosecution team was to identify the appropriate responsible accused. Once identified, the accused, many of whom were reluctant to surrender voluntarily and some determined to avoid arrest, had to be detained. Although the ICTY is a United Nations (UN) body with which, in terms of Art 29 of the Statute of the Security Council establishing it, all member states of the UN must

---

2 Bosnia-Herzegovina, Croatia, Macedonia, Montenegro, Serbia, Slovenia and (depending on your political point of view) Kosovo.

3 No nationals of Montenegro or Slovenia have been prosecuted or convicted.

4 *See* eg, *Prosecutor* v *Duško Tadić*, ICTY, Case No. IT-94–1-AR72, Decision on the Defence Motion for Interlocutory Appeal on Jurisdiction, 2 October 1995.

cooperate,[5] instant cooperation was not always forthcoming, particularly from the states of the former Yugoslavia and indeed on occasion from the member states of NATO. To a judge, it seems odd that the various parts of the former Yugoslavia, from the ranks of whose political, military, police and civil leaderships the accused were to come before the ICTY, should have the same status and obligations as any other member state of the UN to 'co-operate' with the ICTY, rather than be subject to direct enforcement action when it came to securing the detention of accused and the recovery of documentation. That may simply be a reflection of modern political reality and a long-term feature of the work of similar tribunals, on which the author is not qualified to comment. As long as there is no international police force to execute the warrants of such tribunals, the position is unlikely to change.

However, the contribution of these various factors to the delay in ICTY proceedings is no greater than the contribution of procedural delay. There remain seven ongoing cases in which the first instance judgments have not yet been issued. These cases, with the dates of detention of the accused, are as follows: Jadranko Prlić and others (all transferred to the ICTY on 5 April 2004); Vojislav Šešelj (24 February 2003); Zdravko Tolimir (1 June 2007); Jovica Stanišić and Franko Simatović (11 June 2003 and 30 May 2003 respectively); Stanišić and Stojan Župljanin (17 March 2005 and 21 June 2008 respectively); Momčilo Perišić (7 March 2005);[6] and Radovan Karadžić (30 July 2008). In the last of these cases, as at the end of August 2011, the prosecution had exhausted only 170 hours of the 300 hours allocated to them for presentation of their case. A quick calculation, on the assumption that the accused will be allocated a similar period of time, indicates that it is unlikely that the evidence will be completed earlier than late 2014. The situation at the International Criminal Court (ICC) is no more encouraging. While three trials have commenced, none has been concluded. The first trial of Thomas Lubanga Dyilo commenced on 26 January 2009, almost three years after he first appeared in court following his surrender, and in spite of the fact that the court was able to confirm the charges on 29 January 2007 following a two-week hearing. The

---

[5] Article 29(1) states as follows: 'States shall co-operate with the International Tribunal in the investigation and prosecution of persons accused of committing serious violations of international humanitarian law.'

[6] Judgment delivered 6 September 2011 when Perišić was convicted of war crimes and crimes against humanity by majority verdict(the Presiding Judge (Moloto) dissenting), and sentenced to 27 years' imprisonment.

closing oral statements were made on 25 and 26 August 2011, as the first judges of the court neared the end of their nine-year term of office.[7]

This fairly modest pace is part of a roller coaster that has characterised the development of international criminal procedure. When eventually the concept of individual criminal responsibility was accepted as the way forward in enforcing international criminal law in the course of the twentieth century, the initial developments thereafter were rapid. Contemporary accounts of both the Nuremberg and Tokyo tribunals and their various offshoots give an impression of the application of creative ingenuity at breathtaking speed.[8] However, the post-World War II trials were followed by a lethargic lack of will to take steps to enforce international criminal law that pervaded the Cold War years. The establishment of the ICTY by Security Council resolution 827 of 25 May 1993 triggered an initial period of political activity – the International Criminal Tribunal for Rwanda (ICTR) quickly followed.[9] The original President of the ICTY, Antonio Cassese, personified the vigour that was then applied to trying to make the tribunals work effectively. Since then, a more modest pace has been adopted in the conduct of international criminal proceedings in general.

Because the proceedings take so long, there is a danger that the world will lose patience. Some states already have; led by the Russian Federation, a number of states have expressed dissatisfaction with the work of the ICTY on a number of occasions when the President and the Prosecutor have attended to report to the Security Council.[10] The will of this group of states

---

[7] There are two other trials: (i) the joint trial of Germain Katanga (transferred to ICC on 17 October 2007) and Mathieu Ngudjolo Chui (transferred to ICC on 7 February 2008) (both Congo), and (ii) the trial of Jean-Pierre Bemba Gombo (transferred to ICC on 3 July 2008) (Central African Republic). There are pre-trial proceedings against Callixte Mbarushimana (Congo) and against William Samoei Ruto, Henry Kiprono Kosgey and Joshua Arap Sang (all Kenya).

[8] *See* Telford Taylor, *The Anatomy of the Nuremberg Trials: A Personal Memoir* (Alfred A Knopf 1998); Arnold C Brackman, *The Other Nuremberg: The Untold Story of the Tokyo War Crimes Trials* (Harper Collins 1989).

[9] ICTR was established by Security Council resolution 955 of 8 November 1994. Other international tribunals have been established under different constitutional arrangements; the International Criminal Tribunal for Sierra Leone (ICTSL) was set up through Security Council resolution 1315 of 14 August 2000 followed by the 'Agreement Between the United Nations and the Government of Sierra Leone on the Establishment of a Special Court for Sierra Leone' of 16 January 2002.

[10] *See* the discussion at the Security Council meeting of 6 December 2010, which can be found at the UN website, and during which the representatives of the Russian Federation expressed concern about the 'continued prolongation of the Tribunals' existence'.

was that the ICTY should be closed down. Loss of patience is one thing, but the length of proceedings could also result in a loss of interest in securing a functioning system of international criminal justice with universal application, and in particular in converting the ICC to that role. It is vital that that dream is not allowed to die: it is seen as a bulwark against what is widely described as a 'culture of impunity' embraced by dictators and despots the world over. The better known of them may be slowly diminishing in number, but recent events in various parts of the world – the Arab Spring is a good example – illustrate that the sources of potential armed conflicts are many and that the possibility of the commission of war crimes and crimes against humanity is ever present. It is therefore imperative that the dream is not abandoned.

The prevalence of such conflicts highlights the utter inadequacy of the system established so far. In the period between World War II and 2008, there were some 313 armed conflicts resulting in about 100 million deaths and the commission of innumerable international crimes.[11] Set against that, the product of the hundreds of millions of dollars invested in international tribunals is paltry.[12] It ranges from the figure given above for the ICTY, through fairly substantial figures for the ICTR,[13] to a handful of cases in other tribunals and in various national jurisdictions, including some such as Belgium and the Netherlands where there is jurisdiction to try crimes committed in foreign war zones. Some encouragement can be drawn from the establishment and development of domestic judiciaries capable of dealing with war crimes and crimes against humanity, such as in the countries of the former Yugoslavia.

In contrast to the widespread concern about the pace and throughput of international criminal tribunals, it is impossible to deny the major contribution made by them to the development of the jurisprudence of international criminal law and the development of practices which satisfy the highest standards of due process. A good example of the beneficial legacy that the ICTY will leave can be seen in the ICTY 'Manual on Developed Practices' prepared in conjunction with the United Nations Interregional Crime and Justice Research Unit (UNICRI) as part of a project to preserve the legacy

---

[11] *See* M Cherif Bassiouni (ed), *The Pursuit of International Criminal Justice: A World Study on Conflicts, Victimization, and Post-Conflict Justice* (Intersentia 2010).

[12] The ICTY website provides that the annual budget of ICTY for the year 2010–2011 is $301,895,900.

[13] The ICTR has completed 32 cases. There are five ongoing trials at the moment (20 accused in total), nine cases are at the appeal stage, and one accused is awaiting trial.

of the ICTY. One half of the balance referred to in the title of this chapter has therefore been secured: trials are demonstrably fair. This chapter is concerned with the other half of the title; how reasonable expedition can be achieved in the relatively near future without in any way prejudicing the fairness of proceedings.

This chapter will now focus on certain features of the system for prosecuting and determining international criminal cases, to try to identify areas where changes may result in greater expedition to complement the jurisprudential contribution. As with all good studies, this one shall start at the very beginning, with the process for appointing judges.

## II. APPOINTMENT OF JUDGES

Judges in tribunals for which the UN are responsible are generally elected by the General Assembly. Judges of the ICC are elected by the States Parties to the Rome Treaty. In both cases, every member state has a vote. Of course there are rules as to eligibility, requiring candidates to be qualified to sit as members of the highest courts of their respective countries and to have certain relevant experience.[14] However, that means that there is a very large pool of potential candidates. No state can propose more than one candidate, and the choice of candidate is for the state; the electorate has no other control over nominations. The result has been that judges have tended to fall into one of three broad categories – professional judges, international law academics, and former diplomats. At the ICTY, the presiding judges in trials have tended to be the professional judges, and at the ICC, the presiding judge at its first trial is a professional judge.[15] On the other hand, the influence of academics and former diplomats in the Appeals Chambers of both has been strong.

It is not easy to identify what particular expertise it is thought that former diplomats bring to the judicial process in international criminal law, in contrast to judges from an academic background whose knowledge of the

---

14 Article 13 of the ICTY Statute deals with qualifications of ICTY judges and states as follows: 'The permanent and ad litem judges shall be persons of high moral character, impartiality and integrity who possess the qualifications required in their respective countries for appointment to the highest judicial offices. In the overall composition of the Chambers and sections of the Trial Chambers, due account shall be taken of the experience of the judges in criminal law, international law, including international humanitarian law and human rights law.' For the ICC, the equivalent provision in the Rome Statute is Art 36.

15 Sir Adrian Fulford, judge of the High Court in England.

subject can play a major role in the development of international criminal law. Overall, the balance, which has resulted at the ICTY in fewer than 50 per cent of the permanent judges being professional judges, is wrong. Although there is and has been considerable scope for the development of substantive international criminal law, the bulk of the decisions taken by the judges relate to procedure, the admissibility of evidence and the determination of guilt. These are the daily diet of the professional judge.

Because the nomination is for the state, it is a matter of chance just what proportion of candidates are professional judges. Which are elected is also largely a matter of chance, since voting patterns suggest that the state of origin of the candidate is probably the principal factor in determining the votes that will be secured. To many judicial minds, that system is basically unsound. This factor has been confirmed for some by their experience of the 'electioneering' or 'canvassing' in which states' candidates are expected to engage. The electorate for UN Tribunals, in the form of the permanent representatives of states to the UN, wish to see the candidate, but on occasions express far more interest in issues of common concern to their states and the candidate's state, to the point of endeavouring to horse-trade.

While recognising that this is a democratic process which accords respect to the equal standing of all states who are members of the UN or are parties to the Rome Treaty, one only needs to describe the system to realise that it must be possible to devise a better one. However, the democratic recognition of the equality of all states and their inevitable involvement at some stage in the voting process means that it may not be possible to eliminate all of the unsatisfactory features of the current system.

An obvious improvement would be the establishment of an appointments commission comprising five members.[16] Inevitably membership of such a commission would be a coveted post, and the unsatisfactory features of diplomatic voting might simply be moved to that election process. On the other hand, qualification to be appointed to the commission could be prescribed in a way that would ensure the election of those well-fitted to the task. A group of that size would be wellplaced to study the qualifications of the candidates, carry out detailed interviews, have regard to the need for the right blend of experience and qualifications in those appointed, and, if appropriate, try to secure a gender and regional representation balance. For all that the author spent an intensive week of electioneering in New York,

[16] A similar system exists in relation to the election of the judges sitting on the UN Dispute Tribunal. *See* General Assembly resolution 62/228 of 6 February 2008, Arts 35–38.

little attempt was made to explore his judicial and legal experience and qualifications for the job, surely the most important factor.

## III. TAILORING THE RULES

The judges of international tribunals have wide ranging rule-making powers. Article 15 of the ICTY Statute provides:

> The judges of the International Tribunal shall adopt rules of procedure and evidence for the conduct of the pre-trial phase of the proceedings, trials and appeals, the admission of evidence, the protection of victims and witnesses and other appropriate matters.[17]

That power is exercised extensively. When the author left the Tribunal in August 2009 the print of the rules was in its forty-third revisal. While there have been critics of the exercise of the power who consider that the judges have impinged upon substantive law and customary international law by assuming too great powers, more valid criticisms of the exercise of the power relate to the failure to exercise it as robustly as is possible, the occasional use of vague or 'diplomatic' language and the framing of unnecessary rules. Examples of the first two of these weaknesses can be found in the amendments in May 2006 to Rule 73 *bis*, relating to the powers a trial chamber may exercise at a pre-trial conference. This chapter will examine these and certain related areas where there is scope for further judicial legislation.

In addition to powers to determine the number of witnesses the prosecutor may call and the time available to the prosecution for presenting their case, in terms of Rule 73 *bis* (D) a trial chamber has power to 'invite' the prosecutor to reduce the number of counts charged in the indictment. The chamber also has power to fix a number of crime sites or incidents comprised in one or more of the charges, in respect of which evidence may be presented by the prosecutor. Precisely what the difference is between a 'count' and a 'charge' is not clear. In terms of (E) the chamber may 'direct' the prosecutor to select the counts on the indictment on which to proceed. What is unclear is what action might be taken by the chamber in the event that the prosecutor fails to select the counts in the indictment and reduce their number.

---

17 The ICC scheme for amending its rules is different as the amendments are subject to an approval by a two-thirds majority of the state parties to the Rome Treaty. *See* Arts 51 and 52 of the Rome Statute.

The number of counts, crimes charged and crime sites are all critical factors in determining the length of the trial. The main reason for war crimes trials lasting so long is the scale of the indictments. Regrettably, the power of the court to control the scale of indictments is expressed in language which is unclear and thus results in a lack of robust application.

The absence of effective power in the court to reduce the scope of indictments has become increasingly problematic, the longer the ICTY has endured. The greater cooperation of the states of the former Yugoslavia, and the greater success of the efforts of the prosecution in recovering evidential material in light of their growing experience in practice, have led to the accumulation of large quantities of additional material, particularly over the last six or seven years, that 'may' have relevance to ongoing trials. With the accumulation of material comes an obligation of disclosure. Disclosure does seem at times to be made by the prosecution on a non-discriminating basis, with the result that enormous volumes of documents are passed intermittently into the hands of the accused, some of whom represent themselves and lack the knowledge and experience to distinguish quickly the wheat from the chaff. One striking example of the impact this can have on a case is the nine-week adjournment of the trial of Radovan Karadžić in spring 2011 to allow time for such material to be considered.

The fact that material is still coming to light and being disclosed is the result of the lack of an effective investigative agency to conduct the ICTY's inquiries. As already noted, it is a standard feature of the constitution of UN-related international tribunals that the member states of the UN are bound to cooperate in the investigation and prosecution of those falling within the jurisdiction of the tribunal. Although that is a mandatory obligation, no legal sanction for failure to comply exists. Any state might find that the circumstances in which it is called upon to cooperate may indicate that cooperation would not necessarily be in the national interests of that state, a recognised basis for refusing to cooperate. That is particularly so where the state in question is one to which the territorial jurisdiction of the tribunal applies, for example, a state of the former Yugoslavia in relation to cooperation with the ICTY. The fact that the states of the former Yugoslavia are treated in the same way as all other members of the UN and are thus relied upon to cooperate rather than being subject to special enforcement procedure has inevitably created barriers to, and delays in, the investigation of crimes. Experience of these obstacles and delays suggests that a different rule should apply in relation to the state or states where the participants in the conflict were based or which were themselves involved in the conflict. There would remain the practical problem that there is not available to the prosecution or the court any enforcement organisation: there is no international police force, so perhaps attention should be given to that in the first instance. These weaknesses of the current system have had a significant bearing on the pace of current ICTY proceedings.

The principal disclosure obligations of the ICTY prosecution are set out in Rule 68(i) and (ii) as follows:

> (i) the Prosecutor shall, as soon as practicable, disclose to the Defence any material which in the actual knowledge of the Prosecutor may suggest the innocence or mitigate the guilt of the accused or affect the credibility of Prosecution evidence;
>
> (ii) without prejudice to paragraph (i), the Prosecutor shall make available to the defence, in electronic form, collections of relevant material held by the Prosecutor, together with appropriate computer software with which the Defence can search such collections electronically;

In practice, disclosure appears to be made under (ii). Although 'exculpatory' material tends to be disclosed separately, it appears to be simply material which 'might' be helpful to the defence rather than material which 'in the actual knowledge of the Prosecutor' is helpful to the defence. The accused is thus left with no option but to trawl through the material to assess its inculpatory and exculpatory potential. Even after 18 months of trial proceedings in the *Karadžić* case, massive volumes of material were still being disclosed without distinguishing clearly between paragraphs (i) and (ii). One possible way of avoiding an adjournment to enable the accused to consider the documents in that situation would be for the court to order withdrawal of any charges affected by the material. Were that remedy available to the court, it is likely that disclosure would be effected in a much more specific way by the prosecution to avoid the loss of any charges.

Just how voluminous disclosure might be in any given case is illustrated by the circumstances of the *Milan Milutinović* case.[18] There the prosecution disclosure exceeded 500,000 pages, which is the equivalent of 893 volumes of Dan Brown's novel, *The Da Vinci Code*. Disclosure in *Karadžić* has exceeded two million pages.

## IV. THE RIGHT TO SELF-REPRESENTATION

An issue which has had a major impact on the length of proceedings is the right, recognised in the jurisprudence of the ICTY, of an accused to represent himself. That flows from the Tribunal's interpretation of Art

18 *Prosecutor* v *Milutinović* ICTY, Case No. IT-05–87-T, 26 February 2009.

21(4)(d) of its Statute.[19] When the Trial Chamber in Slobodan Milošević's case imposed counsel on him,[20] the Appeals Chamber overturned the decision, not on the basis that the right to self-representation was unqualified, but on the basis that the requirements for the imposition of counsel had not been met, in particular that all other options had not been excluded.[21] In the case of Šešelj, the Appeals Chamber overturned the Trial Chamber's imposition of counsel[22] because they considered that the possibility that such a decision would be made by the Trial Chamber on account of the accused's conduct of the case had not been made sufficiently clear to him before the decision was actually made.[23] It is recognised that there are circumstances in which counsel may be imposed, such as obstructive behaviour by the accused. To date, on no occasion has the imposition of counsel survived the attentions of the Appeals Chamber intact. However the significant impact of self-representation on the length of trials has resulted in the judges of the ICTY introducing Rule 45 *ter*, providing simply: 'The Trial Chamber may, if it decides that it is in the interests of justice, instruct the Registrar to assign a counsel to represent the interests of the accused.'

That rule may be seen as an example of the third weakness of the exercise of the judicial rule-making power referred to above. It is certainly viewed as controversial because, if it is simply a declaration of the law as it stands, then it was unnecessary, and if it effectively creates a power, then it is arguably inconsistent with Art 21.4(d) of the Statute. Perhaps the correct way to view it is as a clear statement that the power to impose counsel exists,

---

[19] Article 21(4)(d) provides: '4. In the determination of any charge against the accused pursuant to the present Statute, the accused shall be entitled to the following minimum guarantees, in full equality: (d) to be tried in his presence, and to defend himself in person or through legal assistance of his own choosing; to be informed, if he does not have legal assistance, of this right; and to have legal assistance assigned to him, in any case where the interests of justice so require, and without payment by him in any such case if he does not have sufficient means to pay for it.'

[20] *Prosecutor* v *Milošević*, ICTY, Case No. IT-02–54-T, Reasons for Decision on Prosecution Motion Concerning Assignment of Counsel, 4 April 2003.

[21] *Prosecutor* v *Milošević*, ICTY, Case No. IT-02–54-AR73.7, Decision on Interlocutory Appeal of the Trial Chamber's Decision on the Assignment of Defence Counsel, 1 November 2004.

[22] *Prosecutor* v *Šešelj*, ICTY, Case No. IT-03–67-PT, Decision on Assignment of Counsel, 21 August 2006. *See* also Decision on subsequent appeal (following hunger strike), 8 December 2006.

[23] *Prosecutor* v *Šešelj,* ICTY, Case No. IT-03–67-AR73.3, Decision on appeal Against the Trial Chamber's Decision on Assignment of Counsel, 20 October 2006. *See* also decision on subsequent appeal (following hunger strike), 8 December 2006.

and as providing a focus for an application to apply the power should appropriate circumstances arise.

This clarification and focus is to be welcomed. There are a number of very sound reasons for endeavouring to avoid a trial being conducted by an accused in person, including the following points:

1. Personal hobby horses are not normally the best forensic points.
2. The court may be abused as a political platform.
3. Failure of the accused to have a clear objective view of the case to be met – 'failing to see the wood for the trees' – means the trial is not conducted in the best forensic or legal interests of the accused.
4. The accused may not be able to cope with the volume of material.
5. Any sanctions imposed for breaches of orders may have adverse side effects on the conduct of the trial.

A good example of the last point was the refusal by a number of defence witnesses in the *Milošević* case to attend the trial when the Trial Chamber, albeit briefly until overruled by the Appeals Chamber, withdrew the right of the accused to represent himself and imposed counsel.

It is a common complaint of self-represented accused that they suffer an inequality of arms. There are a number of reasons for that, including the time that has been available to the prosecution to investigate and prepare. Reliance is also placed on the need for the self-represented accused to read all the material as preparation for the conduct of the case. Sitting alone and isolated in the courtroom, he may appear to the outside world to be on his own, but the reality has tended to be somewhat different. Not only is there, as in the case of Karadžić, legal aid for qualified lawyers to work as assistants to self-represented accused, some, such as Milošević, had a network of supporters working in their interest behind the scenes, including a number who were legally qualified. That illusion of isolation, contrasted with the reality of support, led a colleague at the ICTY to redefine the right to self-representation as 'the right to pretend to represent yourself'.

It is an irony of international criminal tribunals that inquisitorial systems, such as that used in the former Yugoslavia, require obligatory legal representation, yet common law systems using adversarial proceedings, where representation might be regarded as more necessary, do not. It is the author's hope that the introduction of Rule 45 *ter* will be an important step towards reversing the trend for political and quasi-political leaders to represent themselves.

## V. MANAGEMENT OF THE PRE-TRIAL PHASE

The focus of this chapter now turns to the practical conduct of proceedings, beginning with the pre-trial phase. The cases before the ICTY have been characterised by lengthy pre-trial phases in which the adversarial system has been allowed to flourish in a pure and unrestrained form. That results in the control of the pace of the proceedings being left largely in the hands of the parties. While the rules provide for judicial intervention at regular status conferences and the compilation of a 'work plan' (a sort of pre-trial timetable), and give a role to a senior legal assistant of the trial chamber to ensure the implementation of the work plan, the pace of the pre-trial phase was traditionally set by the prosecution and, in particular, by their state of preparedness and their method and pace of disclosure.[24] It has been the author's experience that the 'tone' of court proceedings tends to be set in the early stages. Cases which go off the rails procedurally tend to follow a fairly unstable procedural pathway thereafter. A casual approach to the pre-trial phase and disclosure by the prosecution sets a pattern which the defence will seek to replicate. Equality of arms is regularly founded upon as justification for lengthy periods for defence preparation. Counsel are naturally cautious and will generally seek more time for preparation than is necessary. However, the adversarial system is not inconsistent with judicial case management. In fact, active judicial case management is essential to the expeditious conduct of proceedings in large international trials. A robust timetable should be set by the pre-trial judge who thereafter should play a proactive role in managing the disclosure process and ensuring that the inevitable avalanche of pre-trial motions, many of them relating to trial issues which can be decided prior to the commencement of the trial, are presented timeously, answered within a reasonable time and determined expeditiously. The author's experience was that proactive judicial participation in the pre-trial phase resulted in counsel and also self-represented accused 'engaging' with the judge in identifying issues that needed to be addressed in the pre-trial phase and complying with the pre-trial judge's indicative timetable. Forging sound professional working relationships among prosecution and defence counsel and the bench set a positive tone which continued into, and was, generally speaking, maintained throughout, the subsequent trial proceedings.

The inter-relationship between certain rules requires particular vigilance on the part of the pre-trial judge. Disclosure to the defence of the material used to support the indictment and the witness statements obtained by the

---

24 *See* Rule 65 *ter* of ICTY Rules of Procedure and Evidence (ICTY Rules).

prosecution triggers the running of the time limit for a series of preliminary motions such as one to challenge jurisdiction.[25] For certain motions there is an automatic right of appeal, and decisions in others may be appealed with leave of the Trial Chamber. There is thus built into the rules scope for extensive, time-consuming litigation on what may turn out to be fairly peripheral issues, many of which may be capable of deflecting attention from the job in hand of getting the case to trial. Time limits relating to different stages in the proceedings are often expressed in language which gives the court discretion in determining exactly when the action in question must be undertaken, e.g. 'not less than 6 weeks before …'. That allows considerable scope for ordering early action within reason.

## VI. FINALISATION OF WRITTEN WITNESS STATEMENTS

The single most important procedural development during the life of the ICTY has probably been the extent to which the use of written statements has come to be accepted as the norm. It is extremely doubtful that the work of the ICTY could have been completed without that development.[26] Although there are various ways of challenging the evidence of a witness, such as leading the contrary evidence of a more impressive witness, cross-examination remains the principal effective means of challenging evidence so far devised. As long as that is the case and proceedings are conducted on an adversarial basis, witnesses speaking to core issues such as the acts and conduct of the accused will require to be available for cross-examination. No amount of judicial case management can dispense with that. However, the very fact that the witness will be required to attend at the court in the course of the trial proceedings underlines the importance of early preparation of the final version of his statement and disclosure to the defence, so that any necessary consequent investigation can be carried out, if possible, pre-trial. Regrettably, it remains the case today that the final version of a witness statement that is ultimately presented to the court is generally compiled in the days immediately before the witness gives evidence, often resulting in a significant revisal of the statement and adjournment for further investigation.

---

25 *See* ICTY Rule 72.

26 Interestingly, the ICC takes a slightly different approach and restricts the use of non-cross examined witness statements to situations where both parties agree to their use. *See* Rule 68 of the Rules of Procedure and Evidence of the ICC. Cf. ICTY Rules 92 *bis, ter* and *quater*.

The presentation of large volumes of evidence in writing is not without problematic side effects. The statements often contain, and refer to, so much material (some of it often immaterial or irrelevant) that it is impossible to cross-examine the witness on everything. Attention has to be focused on the issues that matter, and the themes for cross-examination prioritised accordingly. In allocating time for cross-examination, the trial chamber should recognise that it is not always possible to predict precisely what may turn out to be the most significant evidence emerging and exactly how much time will be required to explore the prioritised avenues. Where good cause can be shown for extending the time for cross-examination to a party, then the trial chamber should be prepared to accommodate that. Similarly, where some issue is given low priority and not addressed in cross-examination but later turns out to have greater significance than might reasonably have been anticipated, then it should be understood that the party affected may apply at a later stage in the trial for leave to recall a witness for further cross-examination. It may be appropriate to incorporate in any scheduling order limiting time for the presentation of any part of a case provision along these lines. The importance of judicial monitoring of cross-examination cannot be overstated: it is a vital tool in ensuring that trials are both fair and expeditious. While counsel can be expected (on occasion with little encouragement) to recognise the need to prioritise the issues for, and tailor the conduct of, cross-examination and to act accordingly, the professional knowledge, skill and discipline necessary to achieve the aim of a focused and effective cross-examination are not generally distinctive features of the conduct of their cases by the self-represented accused. Many judges now have experience of the need for vigilance in presiding over cross-examination by accused in person to try to exclude the irrelevant, maintain the focus of the accused on the important issues in the case, and indeed to ensure that the trial is a forensic process and not a political platform.

The rules of the ICTY provide for stages in the proceedings which are to a large extent discrete and need not be so. Perhaps the most striking example is that there is no obligation on the defence to file witness and exhibit lists until after the close of the prosecution case; in marked contrast, there is power in the court to order a pre-trial brief at an earlier stage and indeed to record 'points of agreement and disagreement on matters of law and fact' in the course of the pre-trial phase.[27] There is also power for the pre-trial judge to require submissions to be made by the parties where he considers agreement might be reached. Disclosure of defence expert witness statements may also be ordered. There is thus plenty of scope to engage a

27 *See* ICTY Rule 65 *ter* (H).

cooperative defence at an early stage in trying to identify areas of evidence which are not really in dispute, in particular expert evidence.

There is now enormous scope in relation to certain events in the former Yugoslavia for the application of the rule allowing judicial notice to be taken of adjudicated facts.[28] The events at Srebrenica are a good example. Decisions on these and other matters relating to the admissibility of evidence do, however, tend to be postponed to the trial. That is often because the trial chamber is composed of different judges from the pre-trial chamber. In many instances the delay is unnecessary. Early determination assists the parties in the preparation of their respective cases. However, judicial notice of adjudicated facts has not played as large a part in the work of the ICTY as was anticipated. An adjudicated fact is simply a rebuttable presumption which any accused is entitled to challenge no matter how often the facts have been proved and no matter how notorious the events. In an ideal world all accused charged in respect of events at Srebrenica would have been tried together, avoiding the need for facts to be proved on more than one occasion. Because so many accused were at large for so long, it has proved necessary to deal with the cases relating to Srebrenica piecemeal. If the concept of adjudicated facts is to be a feature of international criminal trials, then there is now enough accumulated experience to enable the scope and effect of the rule to be reviewed with an eye to the future.

## VII. SCOPE FOR GREATER JUDICIAL CONTROL OF SIZE OF CASES

The powers of the trial chamber to place limits upon the volume and length of the prosecution case were mentioned above. While there is a degree of vagueness about these, they are in one view fairly extensive powers. Because they have not been extensively used, there has been little opportunity for their width to be authoritatively judicially determined. However, greater use thereof is unlikely to cause injustice in view of the provision in Rule 73 *bis* (F) allowing for variation of any order restricting the presentation of the prosecution case. The rule also includes power to fix the number of witnesses that the prosecution may call and fix the time available for presenting the evidence. It even includes power to call upon the prosecutor to shorten the estimated length of examination in chief of some witnesses. Proactive judicial case management of the pre-trial phase should equip the trial chamber with the information about, and understanding of, the case

---

28 *See* ICTY Rule 94.

necessary to make sound judgments about these matters, fully informed by the pre-trial judge and pre-trial chamber. In light of a full understanding of the case, limits can be set in a number of imaginative ways.[29]

Possibly the single most important recent development towards securing trials which are both expeditious and fair was the decision of the prosecutor at the ICTY to seek to separate the charges in the indictment against Ratko Mladić and to proceed to trial first on those relating to Srebrenica. That raises the possibility of a fairly speedy, focused trial confined to one of the most significant atrocities of the late twentieth century, and could prove to be a pilot for a similar approach in the future where the proceedings against a major military or political leader relate to a series of important episodes. Whatever the outcome of the application, greatly to be welcomed is the belated realisation by the prosecution of the need for more focused proceedings, and that in an essentially adversarial system it is their responsibility to design and craft a case that can be presented fairly and expeditiously.

## VIII. THE TRIAL

It is now accepted that the power referred to above to limit the time for examination and cross-examination of witnesses may be exercised in the course of the trial, subject of course to the important right in Rule 73 *bis* (F) above, conferred on both prosecution and defence to seek additional time to present evidence should that turn out to be in the interests of justice as the trial proceeds.

That is simply one example of the degree of flexibility built in to the rules of procedure to provide for judicial control of the proceedings. Another is to be found in Rule 90(F) of the ICTY which is in the following terms:

> The Trial Chamber shall exercise control over the mode and order of interrogating witnesses and presenting evidence so as to

---

29 *See* for example *Prosecutor* v *Milutinović et al.*, ICTY, Case No. IT-05–87-T, Decision on Application of Rule 73 *bis*, 11 July 2006; *Prosecutor* v *Prlić et al.*, ICTY, Case No. IT-04–74-PT, Decision Adopting Guidelines on Conduct of Trial Proceedings, 26 April 2006; *Prosecutor* v *Prlić et al.*, ICTY Case No. IT-04–74-PT, Revised Version of the Decision Adopting Guidelines on Conduct of Trial Proceedings, 28 April 2006; *Prosecutor* v *Prlić et al.*, ICTY, Case No. IT-04–74-T, Decision on Adoption of New Measures to Bring the Trial to an End Within a Reasonable Time, 13 November 2006; *Prosecutor* v *Prlić et al.*, ICTY, Case No. IT-04–74-AR73.4, Decision on Prosecution Appeal Concerning the Trial Chamber's Ruling Reducing Time for the Prosecution Case, 6 February 2007.

(i) make the interrogation and presentation effective for the ascertainment of truth; and
(ii) avoid needless consumption of time.

Other international criminal tribunals have similar rules.

To ensure that decisions on the management of trial proceedings, such as limiting time, are fair and indeed effective, it is necessary that they should be fully informed decisions. The better informed the court is as to the evidence to be presented, the issues to be addressed by that evidence, and the scope of the evidence, the fairer and more effective the management decisions are likely to be. A well-organised prosecution case will be presented, so far as possible, in sequential chapters. The proper implementation of a rule such as the above requires recognition by the prosecution of the aims of the rule, and regular dialogue between the bench, the prosecution and the defence to ensure that the trial chamber is given every opportunity to prepare fully for each court session and thus to manage the trial in a way that will ensure that the limited court time available is concentrated on the most controversial issues.

Since proactive judicial case management runs the risk that an important issue may not be as fully explored by counsel as they would wish, it may be appropriate, during the trial as in the pre-trial phase, to incorporate into the decision allocating time a provision enabling counsel to apply for further time with an explanation of the basis for doing so, if they consider that the conduct of their case might be prejudiced as a result of the restriction of time.[30] It is important for the court to make clear its constant appreciation that expedition must not be achieved at the expense of fairness.

Fairness also involves balancing the interests of the various accused in multi-accused trials. The author has experienced a willingness on the part of counsel to liaise with one another, identify the counsel with the principal interest in cross-examining a witness, allow him to take the lead and agree that others should confine their involvement to supplementary questions relating to the particular interest of the accused. Of course there will be circumstances, such as that of a cut-throat defence, where the interests of an individual accused demand that cross-examination should be conducted on behalf of accused in a particular order and might even require unusual specific arrangements to be made. Subject to that, it is undoubtedly in the interests of multi-accused to coordinate their approach to ensure the best use of available time.

---

30 See *Prosecutor* v *Milutinović et al.*, ICTY, Case No. IT-05–87-T, Decision on Application of Rule 73 *bis*, 11 July 2006.

The use of written statements to present evidence in chief is a useful tool, if properly used, to focus the evidence on the crucial issues. There is no need to have such statements read in full. The full text of any statement should be available to the public in any event. If considered appropriate, a brief summary might be read; otherwise much of the benefit to the expeditious conduct of the trial may be lost. It is important that evidence in statement form is not over-expansive and is concentrated on what really matters. Judges have to be vigilant to ensure that unnecessarily tendentious or irrelevant material does not slip through the net in a written statement, not fully vetted in advance, because the anxious or even lazy prosecutor has not done the editing that should have been done. The danger is that the defence, particularly unrepresented accused, may be inadvertently encouraged to concentrate cross-examination on material that has little bearing on the significant issues in the case. That in turn can lead to regular judicial intervention with the inherent risk of a deterioration in the atmosphere in court and the efficient and effective conduct of the proceedings.

It is a feature of adversarial proceedings that there is a half-time interval at the close of the presentation of the prosecution case when the accused can argue that there is no case to answer. In an ideal world the prosecutor's review of the evidence in dealing with such a submission should lead to the exercise of a wise discretion to prune from the indictment those parts of the case which are comparatively weak. That has only occasionally occurred in the author's experience. While the rule, not only in international criminal proceedings but also in domestic common law proceedings, obliges the trial chamber to confine any judgment of acquittal to a count where there is no evidence 'capable of supporting a conviction' and does not envisage the trial chamber assessing the quality of the evidence at that stage, it is undoubtedly open to the trial chamber to enter a judgment of acquittal, even where there is some evidence supporting a count, if the trial chamber would not contemplate making a finding of guilt beyond reasonable doubt on the basis of that evidence. It is not uncommon in a number of domestic jurisdictions for presiding judges, who consider that there are significant weaknesses in part of the prosecution case, or indeed consider that parts of the case are far less serious or more peripheral than others, to ask the prosecution in open court if it still intends to proceed with that part of the indictment. A diplomatic hint of that sort need not indicate in any way the view of the judge on the merits of the part of the case in question. The presiding judge's query is confined to the wisdom of proceeding on the whole indictment, thus diverting attention and resources from strongly supported core elements of the case.

## IX. JUDGMENT WRITING

A number of tasks may be undertaken in relation to the drafting of the final judgment well before the completion of the evidence and closing arguments. For example, a template setting out the form in which the judgment should be presented might be prepared. Preliminary consideration might be given to how the chamber should set out the issues that have to be addressed, such as the elements of the various crimes charged. Software now available should make it possible for staff to prepare early compilations of the evidence relating to specific issues in the trial which can be regularly updated. Throughout the trial the legal support staff of the chamber should always have the outline of the final judgment in mind. This should ensure that the evidence can be related to the issues that the trial chamber has to determine in a way that will expedite collation of the relevant evidence as the judgment is drafted.

The scale of the cases is such that the time between conclusion of the proceedings and issuing the judgment is inevitably many months or even in excess of a year. While the judgment is being written, the next case on the stocks must wait patiently for a start date to be assigned. Giving early attention to judgment drafting can facilitate the earlier commencement of new trials. Better programming and pacing of judgment drafting can also facilitate the commencement of a new trial before the trial chamber has issued its final judgment in the preceding case, as has on occasion occurred.

## X. THE APPEAL

Since the author's experience of the conduct of appellate proceedings is limited, his comments are confined to one broad general observation. Subject to the unexpected emergence of significant new material following the trial, it should be possible to set a fairly tight and firm timetable for the appeal proceedings shortly after grounds of appeal have been filed. Indeed the ICTY Rules envisage that.[31] Convicted accused will generally remain in custody, serving their sentences during the appellate proceedings. However, in practice, time limits are regularly extended, leading to prolonged appellate proceedings. It is important that these proceedings should be concluded as quickly as is reasonably possible.

---

[31] *See* ICTY Rules 107–17.

## XI. ROLE OF INTERNATIONAL CRIMINAL TRIALS

This chapter comes at an opportune time to reflect upon the role of international trials (not including any pre-conceived notion such as 'in the securing peace'). Any commentary on the role of international criminal justice will inevitably be influenced by the personal views of the writer about the role of justice and judicial systems in general. In a domestic situation any definition will include as an objective, probably the overriding objective, the protection of the public. That, translated into the international arena, becomes protection of the civilian population, exactly the mandate that the nations of the world were given by the Security Council to authorise their recent intervention in Libya.[32] The international judicial system should be seen in that light – as a means of ensuring the protection of civilian populations of the states of the world, which equates to securing and maintaining peace.

Others might place the emphasis elsewhere. The victim might see justice as a means of redressing the balance. While that objective may explain the origins of very early judicial systems, and increased recognition of the interests of victims is a developing feature of the modern international criminal justice system, their interest is not a sufficient justification for the existence and development of the sophisticated system that we are considering. Redressing the balance for victims is nevertheless a significant objective of the system. Much more questionable, however, is the notion that there is some duty upon those conducting the trial process to try to achieve a complete and accurate historical record of the events of a conflict. These events are part of history. The trial itself is an element in the history of a nation or region. It would be a subversion of the purpose of the judicial process to tailor it to create a historical record or to establish some historical proposition. Considerable time has been spent in some trials exploring the historical background to the development of a conflict. That historical background has in some instances been seen to extend over prior decades and even centuries. There is no clear evidence that such an approach adds value to the trial process and in any way improves the prospects of achieving a just result.

The trial process is also seen as a means of encouraging reconciliation. It is thought that an impartial inquiry into the events of a conflict leading to an authoritative determination of responsibility, culpability and victimisation has a significant role to play in achieving a degree of reconciliation among

---

[32] Security Council resolution 1973 of 17 March 2011.

opponents, with a view to future peaceful co-existence. This has occurred in practice, particularly where responsibility has been accepted by a guilty plea.[33]

The crucial point is that the best prospect for achieving these various ancillary objectives or incidental benefits of the international criminal justice process, viz, restoring and maintaining peace, redressing the victim/perpetrator balance, establishing an accurate historical record and facilitating reconciliation, is the effective, efficient, fair and expeditious conduct of proceedings brought before international criminal tribunals. The important thing is to establish for the international criminal justice system a reputation for effectiveness. That takes time. While the volume of work of the ICTY, ICTR and indeed the ICTSL, is perhaps not as widely appreciated as one would wish, it is well understood in the regions affected. A regularly stated aim of these tribunals and the ICC is to defeat the 'culture of impunity'. It is only when a court is seen to administer justice effectively that its reputation and the associated threat to call the leaders of tyrannical regimes and armed forces to account before it will have any impact or influence on the battle to end the culture of impunity that is so prevalent among such regimes and their opponents around the world.

Maintaining the momentum of the challenge to the culture of impunity requires a coordinated international effort. It has been encouraging to see states such as Norway, the Netherlands, Belgium and Canada undertake prosecutions for war crimes on the basis of their exceptional jurisdiction provisions. It is even more encouraging to see the progress that has been made in the states of the former Yugoslavia, particularly in Bosnia, to build a new and effective judicial system, which includes special arrangements for addressing the crimes of the early 1990s. Australia, the United Kingdom and others have shown themselves willing to continue to investigate the extent to which immigrant residents of their countries should be held to account for their criminal responsibility for events in World War II, although the law of diminishing returns means that that process is now more or less exhausted. Attention is now principally upon the work of the ICC. Supportive states should continue their efforts to encourage those not committed to recognise the importance of the ICC as a major tool for protecting civilian populations and thus securing future peace and justice in the world, and to commit themselves to its work.

---

33 *See* for example *Prosecutor* v *Bralo*, ICTY, Case No. IT-95–17-PT, Plea Agreement, 18 July 2005.

## XII. THE WAY FORWARD

And finally, something that may be music to the academic ear. There must be a better way of gathering, disclosing and presenting the masses of material that relate to the offences which are the subject of international criminal indictments. Having regard to the circumstances in which many of the eyewitnesses of atrocities live and their total unfamiliarity with the legal process, better ways of dealing with their evidence must be found. The extreme, but not entirely ridiculous, suggestion has been made that the equivalent of a television documentary team of investigatory judge/interviewer, clerk/cameraman and sound recordist might video record judicial examination of crime scene witnesses, and possibly others, in situ. That idea is associated with the notion of the presentation of crime scene evidence in a dossier. To date the ICTY has rejected dossiers of written material, mainly because the format proposed included presenting a prosecution summary of the evidence rather than simply presenting it in full. Evidence so gathered might be disclosed to prosecution and defence to enable them to make submissions about which, if any, of the witnesses are required to attend the court for further examination or cross-examination. The pre-trial judge could then decide whether and to what extent the evidence so gathered might be admitted at trial without further examination, and which witnesses should be required to attend. It is important that procedures are identified which will ensure that detailed examination of witnesses is concentrated on the crucial controversial issues which in general will be those of individual criminal responsibility and joint criminal enterprise.

While it is often said that the rules of procedure and evidence applied in international criminal tribunals are an amalgam of the rules of the civil law and common law systems, the procedure of the common law systems tends to dominate because of the essentially adversarial nature of the proceedings. On the other hand, it is clear that as experience of workings of the various tribunals has increased, the advantages to be gained by introducing more of the practices followed in civil law jurisdictions have been better appreciated. The general admissibility of hearsay evidence and the widespread use of written statements in lieu of oral evidence are good examples of practices from civil law systems by which the procedures of these tribunals are enhanced. However there has been no determined systematic attempt to devise a set of rules that reflects the best features of the multiple variations of the rules of both systems, that can be found throughout the world, including particularly imaginative procedures for obtaining, securing and presenting the evidence of witnesses. There is enormous scope for a major academic project aimed at meeting that challenge: those in the field are urged to give further thought to that suggestion.

# 4. Applied rights in international criminal law: defence counsel and the right to disclosure

**Peter Morrissey**

## I. INTRODUCTION

To understand the content and significance of fair-trial rights, it is crucial to understand how they work in the hands of those charged with applying them: counsel for that most desperate of creatures, the defendant in international criminal proceedings. Defence counsel brings a distinctive, pragmatic and utilitarian perspective to the learned study of fair-trial rights in international criminal law. Defence counsel views rights entirely instrumentally. This chapter considers how two important rights – the rights to disclosure of the case and disclosure of the evidence – operate in practice, how they work in the defendant's interest, and how they are applied by counsel and by tribunals. Thus 'rights in action' is the focus.

This approach does seem intellectually unromantic at first; in his *Divine Comedy*, Dante might well have hesitated to admit pragmatic defence counsel to the judicial Heaven of the Sun with Gratian and the great doctors of law. But an instrumental approach to fair-trial rights is justifiable and valuable. First, a pragmatic and historical approach to human rights allows the rights to be explored and assessed, rather than simply admired.[1] More importantly, international criminal justice sets itself high goals, and adopts a system of adversarial criminal procedure to validate its openness, its reliability and its justice. It arms an accused with fair-trial rights, and with representation to apply those rights. That system demands robust and adversarial deployment of the rights of defendants, and is kept healthy by such an approach. Next, a utilitarian approach serves the accused. Armed with rights (such as the disclosure rights discussed here), he may secure a

[1] The author adopts the approach articulated by Michael Ignatieff in *Human Rights As Politics and Idolatry* (Princeton University Press 2001) at p. 55.

fair trial, and an acquittal if a reasonable doubt is raised. Fair trial is the key concept: as the International Criminal Court (ICC) Appeals Chamber recently observed: '[a] fair trial is the only means to do justice. If no fair trial can be held, the object of the judicial process is frustrated, and the process must be stopped.'[2] A fair trial is one where the rights a defendant possesses can be effectively deployed.

Finally, an analysis of the rights in action (necessarily viewed from a primarily defence perspective) could assist tribunals to consider how best to allow the proper benefit of those rights to accused at trial. The fact is that tribunals struggle to sanction breaches of procedural rights; the available sanctions (stay, dismissal, exclusion of evidence) are too blunt,[3] and evidently distasteful to judges committed to the international justice project. But an appreciation of the functional importance of the rights might assist tribunals to settle in-trial controversies without recourse to nuclear-powered options such as stays. As shall appear below, the nuanced approach taken by an International Criminal Tribunal for Rwanda (ICTR) Trial Chamber in *Bizimungu* shows how trial chambers might manage breaches of disclosure rights.

The focus of this short contribution will be on disclosure – disclosure of the case (the 'nature and cause' of the charge) and of the evidence. By looking at these, we may learn something about the rights themselves and also about the role of defence counsel in their application. The author hopes to show that the rights can be meaningfully applied in international criminal courts. Some decisions illustrate the point positively; but even the occasional judicial lapse can provide guidance to those charged with securing a fair trial. By applying the rights diligently, defence counsel give the accused a persuading voice in the courtroom where he is presumed innocent and may very well be innocent. By doing that, counsel advances international justice. The study of rights in action and of defence strategy is necessarily relevant.

---

2 *Prosecutor v Lubanga (Judgment on Appeal of Mr Thomas Lubanga Dyilo against the Decision on the Defence Challenge to the Jurisdiction of the Court Pursuant to Article 19(2)(a) of the Statute of 3 October 2006)* (ICC, Appeals Chamber, Case No ICC-01/04–01/06–722, 14 December 2006) [37].

3 *Prosecutor v Bizimungu (Judgment and Sentence)* (ICTR, Trial Chamber II, Case No ICTR-99–50-T, 30 September 2011) [174]: 'The Chamber recalls that other remedial options include drawing a reasonable inference in favour of the Accused from the exculpatory material, excluding relevant parts of the Prosecution evidence, ordering a stay of proceedings and dismissing charges against the Accused … Of these four options, the Chamber considers that the latter three are both unnecessary and too extreme in the present case … .'

## II. DISCLOSURE OF THE CASE

A crucial procedural right upon which counsel must insist is the right to be informed promptly and in detail of the nature, cause and content of the charge. This right emanates from Art 14(3) of the International Covenant on Civil and Political Rights (ICCPR) and recurs in the Rome Statute at Art 67(1)(a).[4] In short, it is a right to disclosure of the prosecution case. The entire structure of adversarial proceedings at the ICC is based upon it, including the exercise of other fair-trial rights such as the right to confront.[5] At the International Criminal Tribunal for the former Yugoslavia (ICTY), the charges were contained in the indictment; at the ICC, in the colourlessly-named 'Document Containing the Charges'. It is a fundamental fair trial right in most jurisdictions; as the European Court of Human Rights (ECHR) observed in *Dallos v Hungary*:

> In criminal matters the provision of full, detailed information concerning the charges against a defendant, and consequently the legal characterisation that the court might adopt in the matter, is an essential prerequisite for ensuring that the proceedings are fair.[6]

This right is directly related to the right to adequate time and facilities and, in turn, helps to determine what adequate time and facilities mean in a particular case.

This right must be applied at trial against real dangers. Defence counsel fear a vague prosecution case. As shall appear, it exposes them to uncertainty and error, to the expenditure of resources and to the peril that they will not adequately confront the case on which the prosecution finally relies. In

---

4 At the ICTY, Arts 21(4)(a), 21(4)(b) and 21(2) of the Tribunal's Statute (SC Res 827, UN SCOR, 48th sess, 3217th mtg, UN Doc S/RES/827 (25 May 1993) ('ICTY Statute')), were crucial, linking the right to disclosure of the case to the fair trial and the right to adequate time and facilities. See *Prosecutor v Galić (Judgment)* (ICTY, Appeals Chamber, Case No IT-98–29-A, 30 November 2006) [74] n 219.

5 Salvatore Zappalà, 'The Rights of Victims v The Rights of the Accused' (2010) 8 *Journal of International Criminal Justice* 137, 150: 'the structure of the proceedings at the ICC implies that prior to trial the defendant *must* be in a position to organize his or her defence. The right to be informed in detail of the charges and of the evidence supporting them is an essential component of the right to a fair trial.'

6 *Sadak v Turkey (Judgment)* (ECHR, Chamber, Applications Nos 29900/96 and 29903/96, 10 July 2001) [49]; see also *Dallos v Hungary (Judgment)* (ECHR, Chamber, Application No 29082/95, 1 March 2001) [47]–[53]; *Case of Pelissier and Sassi v France (Judgment)* (ECHR, Chamber, Application No 25444/94, 25 March 1999) [52].

flagrant adversarial language: the right allows the defence to see the target and to keep it still. Case disclosure is fundamental to every step taken by the defence. Taking instructions and giving appropriate advice depends on a proper appreciation of the case pleaded: consider the situation which arose in *Erdemović*, where the accused entered an erroneous plea because he did not appreciate the nature and cause of the charges.[7] Subsequently, the formulation of strategy, the allocation of resources, the identification of issues, the concession of non-controversial evidence and the design of cross-examination all depend on disclosure of the case. The structure of the defence case in response is shaped by it. Finally, the right can be used to protect the defendant from a re-casting or expansion of the case pleaded.

What specific disclosure must the defence seek? What is required is a clear articulation of the charges and their elements, on the mode of liability alleged and on the material facts (including the individual criminal acts alleged and the accused's link to them). The prosecution must also demonstrate a 'clear line of reasoning' tying their evidence to the charges pleaded.[8] This latter requirement is fundamental in protecting the accused against late shifts in a prosecution's case theory.

Certainly at a general level, international tribunals do recognise this right. At the ICTY in *Kupreškić*, the Appeals Chamber commented:

> the Prosecution is expected to know its case before it goes to trial. It is not acceptable for the Prosecution to omit the material aspects of its main allegations in the indictment with the aim of moulding the case against the accused in the course of the trial depending on how the evidence unfolds.[9]

The earlier the defence insists upon specifics, the better it might hold the case still and focus energy upon the elements of it. If this is done, tribunals will generally compel the prosecution to disclose, to give particulars or to amend an indictment. For example, at the ICTY in *Krnojelac*, the defence identified for the Trial Chamber a level of vagueness concerning the mode of liability pleaded. When the prosecution declined to amend, the Trial

---

[7] Jarinde Temminck Tuinstra, 'Defending the Defenders: The Role of Defence Counsel in International Criminal Trials' 8(2) (2010) *Journal International Criminal Justice* 463; *Prosecutor v Erdemović (Sentencing Judgment)* (ICTY, Trial Chamber, Case No IT-96–22-T *bis*, 5 March 1998) [7]–[8]; Erdemović re-pleaded to a different charge and received a lesser sentence.

[8] *Prosecutor v Lubanga (Public Redacted Version with Annex I – Decision on the Confirmation of Charges)* (ICC, Pre-Trial Chamber I, Case No ICC-01/04–01/06–803-tEN, 29 January 2007) [39].

[9] *Prosecutor v Kupreškić (Appeal Judgment)* (ICTY, Appeals Chamber, Case No IT-95–16-A, 23 October 2001) [92].

Chamber refused to permit the prosecution to rely on a broad version of Joint Criminal Enterprise.[10] The Appeals Chamber upheld the decision[11] and said:

> the Prosecution's obligation to draw up a sufficiently precise indictment must be interpreted in the light of the provisions of Articles 21(2), 21(4)(a) and 21(4)(b) of the Statute, which state that, in the determination of charges against him, the accused shall be entitled to a fair hearing and, more specifically, to be informed of the nature and cause of the charge against him and to have adequate time and facilities for the preparation of his defence.[12]

As we will see, controversy arises over what is 'sufficient'.

At the ICC, the confirmation process contemplates a final 'document' honed by the confirmation litigation. Endless positioning occurred concerning case disclosure in *Bemba,* until the charges he faced were finally settled in the Second Amended Document Containing the Charges.[13] Predictably, there was significant delay in *Bemba*, as the Pre-Trial Chamber came to terms with a novel process. In fact, the shake-out which inevitably occurs during confirmation might reduce delay, by augmenting the level of certainty and stability in the case faced by an accused.

Nonetheless, defence counsel may insist that disclosure be 'prompt'. Here the instrumental approach of the defence contrasts with the abstract analysis of high level commentary.[14] To a defendant, the value of 'prompt' disclosure lies not simply in hastening the trial but in allowing a settled understanding of the case to be formed at an early stage, and preserved against subsequent expansion or alteration. Of course, the prosecution case cannot be formulated and disclosed until a critical mass of evidence is

---

[10] *Prosecutor v Krnojelac (Judgment)* (ICTY, Trial Chamber II, Case No IT-97–25-T, 15 March 2002) [86].

[11] *Prosecutor v Krnojelac (Judgment)* (ICTY, Appeals Chamber, Case No IT-97–25-A, 17 September 2003) [144].

[12] Ibid [139].

[13] *Prosecutor v Bemba (Decision on the Defence Application for Corrections to the Document Containing the Charges and for the Prosecution to File a Second Amended Document Containing the Charges)* (ICC, Trial Chamber III, Case No ICC-01/05–01/08–836, 20 July 2010) [84]–[86].

[14] See Human Rights Committee, *General Comment No 32, Article 14: Right to Equality before Courts and Tribunals and to a Fair Trial*, 90th sess, UN Doc CCPR/C/GC/32 (7 July 2007): 'The right to be informed of the charge "promptly" requires that information be given as soon as the person concerned is formally charged with a criminal offence under domestic law … or the individual is publicly named as such.' See also Stefan Trechsel, *Human Rights in Criminal Proceedings* (Oxford University Press 2006) 207.

collected; ICC prosecutors must investigate before charging, must seek 'the truth' and must discover and disclose exculpatory material.[15] In practical terms, therefore, this right assumes prominence only once the accused is 'charged', and it is therefore trial counsel, rather than the Office of Public Council for the Defence (OPCD) or ad hoc counsel, who must apply it.

Ultimately, however, the prosecution case must be made to crystallise at the time the indictment is confirmed. At the ICTY, the confirmation process under Art 19 was flawed; it is impractical for any accused to participate meaningfully.[16] But at the ICC, the confirmation process under Art 61 provides a genuine opportunity to identify and fix the case alleged. At this stage the charge consists of two parts: first, the statement of facts (Reg 52(b)) and second, the legal characterisation of the facts (Reg 52(c)).[17] In theory, the 'charge' which the prosecution undertakes to prove is fixed by the confirmation process under Art 61. Thus, the confirmation litigation may seem necessarily and fiercely adversarial. The defence will contest the Documents Containing the Charges vigorously, seeking to fix the ambit of the case and deter the prosecution from subsequent alterations.[18] Unsure of the full strength of their case, prosecutors will resist particularity. Putative victims may also be heard at this stage, seeking to limit defence access to material which, they assert, might endanger or traumatise them.

Of course, the adversarial quality of this litigation is affected by case strategy. The prosecution may opt for a narrow and precisely pleaded case. Alternatively, a defence might choose to 'pick off' the case as pleaded, seeking no further information lest the prosecution patch its case.[19] For the

---

15 Rome Statute of the ICC (adopted 17 July 1998, entered into force 1 July 2002) 2187 UNTS 90, Art 54(1)(a) ('Rome Statute'); see also the expanded explanation of the Disclosure obligation in Art 67(2).

16 ICTY Statute; see also rule 47 of the Rules of Procedure and Evidence (ICTY, Rules of Procedure and Evidence, Doc No IT/32/Rev 18 (first adopted 11 February 1994, as amended to 13 June 2006) (ICTY RPE), which articulates a confirmation process conducted solely between the Prosecutor, the Registrar and the Judge.

17 ICC, Regulations of the Court (adopted 26 May 2004) ('ICC Regulations'), discussed in *Prosecutor v Lubanga (Minority Opinion on the "Decision Giving Notice to the Parties and Participants that the Legal Characterisation of Facts May be Subject to Change in Accordance with Regulation 55(2) of the Regulations of the Court")* (ICC, Trial Chamber I, Case No ICC-01/04–01/06–2054, 17 July 2009) [18].

18 Ibid [20].

19 This occurred in the *Situation in the Republic of Kenya: in the Cases of the Prosecutor v Francis Kirimi Muthaura, Uhuru Muigai Kenyatta and Mohammed Hussein Ali (Decision on the Confirmation of Charges* Pursuant *to Article 61(7)(a)*

defence, it is also a matter of judgement whether to contest the standing and participation of victims; in order to prevent the kind of late ambush which occurred in *Lubanga*, the defence may welcome full victim participation at confirmation. But the confirmation system seems to welcome and use adversarial argument in a manner which, if well managed, could reduce the dangers of uncertain indictments which bedevil the ad hoc tribunals. Certainly the rights enshrined in the Rome Statute should ensure the defence an attentive hearing when insisting on disclosure of the case.

What is to be disclosed? First, the charge itself must be articulated. Here, the defence shares with the tribunal an interest in specificity. However, care must be taken. In *Prosecutor v Galić* the Trial Chamber permitted (and the Appeal Chamber allowed) a rather marked alteration of the 'nature and cause' of the charge of causing terror among the population. Despite an unclear indictment, Galić was said to have had clear notice of the relevant alteration through the prosecution's Pre-Trial Brief.[20] Victims, too, can lure a tribunal to alter the charge or charges, as appears below.

The mode of liability likewise is crucial. The Pre-Trial Chamber in *Bemba* interpreted Art 61(7)(c)(ii) in light of the rights under Art 67:

> If the Chamber were to read article 61(7)(c)(ii) of the Statute in such a manner as to exclude the mode of liability, considerations of fairness would also arise since the Defence would be deprived of its right to be informed promptly and in detail of the nature, cause and content of the charges, in accordance with article 67(l)(a) of the Statute, and of the opportunity to submit observations thereto.[21]

Accused suffer prejudice where a prosecution is permitted to advance alternative and perhaps inconsistent bases of liability. In *Blaškić* the defence made multiple complaints concerning unclear and inconsistent prosecution theories of responsibility.[22] The Appeals Chamber accepted that 'in certain circumstances, an indictment which fails to plead with sufficient detail an

*and (b) of the Rome Statute)* (ICC, Pre-Trial Chamber II, Case No ICC 01/09–02/11–382-Red, 23 January 2012), where the accused Ali (police chief of Kenya) was discharged following a very narrow and targeted attack by defence counsel, at [426].

[20] *Prosecutor v Galić (Appeal Judgment)* (ICTY, Appeals Chamber, Case No IT-98–29-A, 30 November 2006) [74]; see also *Prosecutor v Čermak and Markac (Decision on Motion on Form of Indictment)* (ICTY, Trial Chamber II, Case No IT-03–73-PT, 8 March 2005) [5].

[21] *Prosecutor v Bemba (Decision Adjourning the Hearing Pursuant to Article 61(7)(c)(ii) of the Rome Statute)* (ICC, Pre-Trial Chamber III, *Case* No ICC-01/05–01/08–388, 3 March 2009) [28].

[22] *Prosecutor v Blaškić (Judgment)* (ICTY, Appeals Chamber, Case No IT-95–14-A, 29 July 2004) [231]–[232].

essential aspect of the Prosecution case, may result in the reversal of a conviction'.[23]

However, in that case, the Appeals Chamber was not persuaded that actual prejudice resulted from the Prosecution's double-barrelled approach.[24] As will appear, procedural injustice is difficult to rectify on appeal; trial counsel's job is to evade it during trial.

Furthermore, material facts must be disclosed in accordance with Art 61 and Reg 52(b). At the ICTY, the Appeals Chamber in *Kupreškić* said:

> an accused is entitled to a fair hearing and, more particularly, to be informed of the nature and cause of the charges against him and to have adequate time and facilities for the preparation of his defence. In the jurisprudence of the Tribunal, this translates into an obligation on the part of the Prosecution to state the material facts underpinning the charges in the indictment, but not the evidence by which such material facts are to be proven. Hence, the question whether an indictment is pleaded with sufficient particularity is dependent upon whether it sets out the material facts of the Prosecution case with enough detail to inform a defendant clearly of the charges against him so that he may prepare his defence.[25]

This requirement causes migraines to prosecution and defence alike.

A primary defence concern is to prioritise the facts in issue. Given the mass of evidence which attends most international trials, only a selective challenge is possible: the identification of material facts is fundamental. The defence fear is that the prosecution (and the trial chamber) will ultimately rely on a collection of unpleaded facts to prove an important matter at trial. An indictment where the material facts are inadequately or ambiguously pleaded afflicts the defence, which expends resources meeting half-formed and contradictory theories. Of course, the defence must mix realism with vigour. Trial chambers do tolerate some vagueness in pleading material facts, especially when the accused is not the perpetrator but a commander or leader remote from the crime base. Thus there is no requirement that all relevant evidence be pleaded explicitly,[26]

---

[23] Ibid [239].

[24] Ibid [242].

[25] *Prosecutor v Kupreškić (Appeal Judgment)* (ICTY, Appeals Chamber, Case No IT-95–16-A, 23 October 2001) [88] (footnote omitted).

[26] *Prosecutor v Cermak and Markac (Decision on Prosecution Motion Seeking Leave to Amend the Indictment)* (ICTY, Trial Chamber II, Case No IT-03–73-PT, 19 October 2005). The Trial Chamber held, at [5], that an indictment is 'pleaded with sufficient particularity it if sets out the material facts of the Prosecution case with enough detail to inform the accused of the charges against him, allowing him time to prepare his defence'.

nor need the prosecution prove each material fact beyond reasonable doubt.[27]

Trial chambers need constant reminders of the actual prejudice caused by vague case disclosure of this type. In *Bagosora*,[28] the accused Nsengiyumva faced a flawed indictment: he was convicted on many charges of which the indictment provided almost no notice. The Appeal Chamber overturned convictions on some, but sustained others on the basis that the imperfections were progressively cured. However, Nsengiyumva contended that, regardless of whether the charges were sustainable, his preparation was undermined by the uncertainty caused by the indictment. His grievance was most understandable; as he pointed out, he was acquitted of every charge which *was* adequately pleaded.[29] But appellate justice focuses upon proved prejudice, rather than on rights-breaches, and in a rather curt and general passage, the *Bagosora* Appeal Chamber dismissed the appellant's complaint because he failed to demonstrate prejudice.[30]

There is room to improve the reach of appellate justice when considering procedural breaches like this one. Requiring an appellant to demonstrate 'prejudice' sets a difficult task in the hushed appeal chamber, particularly because an errant trial chamber will not likely articulate how the breach of rights helped convict the appellant. Instead, the prosecution could be asked to show why the accused was not substantially disadvantaged – the qualifier 'substantially' would protect against allegations of rights-breaches of a merely technical nature. To do otherwise is to qualify the fair trial right. But in the trial chamber, defence counsel must insist both upon the imperfect pleading and upon the procedural prejudice it causes. Trial chambers should welcome such interventions, since they cannot be expected to appreciate the actual prejudice caused if it is not pointed out. When it is pointed out, trial chambers should act with decision to insist upon clarity.

On the other hand, trial chambers can be persuaded to offer some protection to an accused who seeks it from a vague indictment. For example, in the pre-trial litigation in *Ojdanić*, the Chamber was prepared to order the amendment of the indictment to better identify the military unit responsible for the crime-base offending.[31] This decision, like others before

---

27 *Prosecutor v Milutinović (Judgment)* (ICTY, Trial *Chamber*, Case No IT-05–87-IT, 26 February 2009) [10]. See also cases in below notes 42–46.

28 *The Prosecutor v Theoneste Bagosora and Anatole Nsengiyumva (Judgment)* (ICTR, Appeals Chamber, Case No ICTR 98–41-A, 14 December 2011).

29 Ibid [211].

30 Ibid [216]–[217].

31 *Prosecutor v Milutinović et al (Decision on Defence Motions Alleging Defects in the Form of the Proposed Amended Joinder Indictment)* (ICTY, Trial

it,[32] fell well short of arming the defence with the ability to adequately contest the identity, liability or subordination of killers, even though this might have constituted a defence to some charged deaths or incidents. Uneasy compromise is inevitable. Applied rights thinking involves asking, 'What facts did we clarify and lock in?', rather than, 'Have we been cheated of justice yet again?' By dragging the material facts into the open, the defence can benefit, both by clarifying the case and minimising the danger of minor facts belatedly assuming major significance.

Proper exposure of material facts is also important to the disclosure of the 'reasoned path to conviction', the case theory which the prosecution pleads. Uncertainty regarding the way in which the facts prove the alleged crime can cause injustice: the sexual offences alleged in *Mattocia v Italy* at the ECHR were blighted by this uncertainty, and the accused was baffled in his challenge to the facts by alterations to the case.[33] Thus, finally, a coherent path of reasoning from alleged facts to criminal liability must be pleaded. The defence must seek early and specific articulation of the 'reasoned path' to prevent alterations such as the type which was attempted in the *Halilović* appeal litigation, considered below.[34]

Once the prosecution case is disclosed, the defence faces the challenge of preventing subtle alterations. The pressures to alter come from two sources. First, the prosecution might see a new opportunity as the evidence unfolds, either because the prosecution evidence turns out poorly, or where the defence calls evidence which changes the battleground. Secondly, victims may request alteration, as occurred in *Lubanga*.[35] Exposure to late alterations in the legal characterisation of a prosecution is prejudicial.

Timely protest and litigation are essential for the preservation of a fixed case. Such a vigilant stance has two benefits: timely protest will be more

---

Chamber III, Case No IT-05–87-PT, 22 March 2006) [10]. See also *Prosecutor v Milutinović et al (Decision on Motion to Amend the Indictment)* (ICTY, Trial *Chamber* III, Case No IT-05–87-PT, 11 May 2006) [5]–[6].

32 *Prosecutor v Milošević (Decision on Defence Preliminary Motion under Rule 72(A)(ii))* (ICTY, Trial Chamber, Case No IT-98–29/1-PT, 18 July 2005) [21]: the Trial Chamber accepted that pleading that Milošević commanded Bosnian Serb forces comprising or attached to the Sarajevo Romanija was specific enough.

33 *Mattocia v Italy (Judgment)* (ECHR, Chamber, Application No 23969/94, 25 July 2000) [70]–[71]; see also Trechsel, above note 14, 201.

34 *Prosecutor v Halilović (Judgment)* (ICTY, Appeals Chamber, Case No IT-01–48-A, 16 October 2007).

35 *Prosecutor v Lubanga (Decision Giving Notice to the Parties and Participants that the Legal Characterisation of the Facts May Be Subject to Change in Accordance with Regulation 55(2) of the Regulations of the Court)* (ICC, Trial Chamber I, Case No ICC-01/04–01/06–2049, 14 July 2009) [24].

effective, and it will also avert the spectre of waiver. Counsel for Tihomir Blaškić fought well to preserve his protest against a woolly indictment. Twice he protested, in timely fashion, to the Trial Chamber; finally he elicited from the judges a reassurance that they would

> not fail to draw all the legal consequences at trial of the possible total or partial failure to satisfy the obligations incumbent upon the Prosecutor, insofar as that failure *inter alia* might not have permitted the accused to prepare his defence … [36]

By taking the point, counsel for Mr Blaškić was able to resist an argument on appeal that he had waived his right.[37] But the perils of waiver were made very clear.[38]

The defence counsel cannot be doctrinaire concerning case disclosure. Some reconceptualisation of the case by the prosecution is permitted; not merely at confirmation but subsequently. A pre-trial chamber may permit amendments, or even recasting of the case, as occurred in *Bemba*.[39] It can occur post-confirmation,[40] or (residually) pursuant to Reg 55, even after the trial has commenced.[41] It is open to victims' organisations, as well as to the prosecution, to make such an application. Some orderly, predictable and open reconceptualisation need not prejudice an accused and may in fact help him. The ICC system is consistent with ECHR jurisprudence and fairer

---

[36] See *Prosecutor v Blaškić (Judgment)* (ICTY, Appeals Chamber, Case No IT-95–14-A, 29 July 2004) [198], quoting from *Prosecutor v Blaskić (Decision on the Defence Request for Enforcement of an Order of the Trial Chamber)* (ICTY, Trial Chamber, Case No IT-95–14-PT, 23 May 1997) 5.

[37] *Prosecutor v Blaškić (Judgment)* (ICTY, Appeals Chamber, Case No IT-95–14-A, 29 July 2004) [222]–[224].

[38] Ibid [222]; see also *Prosecutor v Tadić (Appeal Judgment)* (ICTY, Appeals Chamber, Case No IT-94–1-A, 15 July *1999*) [55]: 'A party is under the obligation to formally raise before the Trial Chamber, either during trial or pre-trial, any issues that require resolution. A party "cannot remain silent on [a] matter only to return on appeal to seek a trial *de novo* … ".'

[39] *Prosecutor v Bemba (Decision Adjourning the Hearing Pursuant to Article 61(7)(c)(ii) of the Rome Statute)* (ICC, Pre-Trial Chamber III, Case No ICC-01/05–01/08–388, 3 March 2009) [19].

[40] Rome Statute Art 61(9).

[41] ICC, Regulations of the Court, Doc No ICC-BD/01–01–04 (adopted 26 May 2004) (ICC Regulations); see also *Prosecutor v Lubanga (Judgment on the Appeals of Mr Lubanga Dyilo and the Prosecutor against the Decision of Trial Chamber I of 14 July 2009 Entitled 'Decision Giving Notice to the Parties and Participants that the Legal Characterisation of the Facts May Be Subject to Change in Accordance with Regulation 55(2) of the Regulations of the Court')* (ICC, Appeals Chamber, Case No ICC-01/04–01/06 OA 15 OA 16, 8 December 2009).

by far. In *Dallos v Hungary*,[42] Mr Dallos found himself convicted by a regional court of a fraud not pleaded. The ECHR forgave this blatant breach of Art 6(3)(a) of the Convention[43] because of the subsequent appellate remedies available to Mr Dallos; better by far for Mr Dallos if he knew the case he faced when building his defence at trial. The ICC permits any revision of the prosecution case with trial safeguards.

That said, however, reconceptualisation is usually overwhelmingly prejudicial to an accused. An excellent illustration of this occurred at the ICC in *Lubanga*, where victim advocates tried to expand the case very late.[44] They succeeded in persuading an errant Trial Chamber majority to add (in effect) several new charges of a different nature to those in the Document Containing the Charges. The dangers to a fair trial were stark; Judge Fulford (dissenting) noted that absent significant new measures to protect the rights of accused persons, an alteration to the legal characterisation of facts, made at trial's end, will inevitably infringe the safeguards in Art 67 and elsewhere.[45] Doubtless the victim-applicants were motivated by a desire to have sexual crimes included in the judgment, but the fair-trial rights of the accused were imperilled. It was the prosecution who pleaded on appeal that:

> New legal characterisations mean that new issues may become relevant, different elements must be proven, and different lines of defence may be available. It would be unfair to the Prosecution and to the accused if they were denied any right to make submissions, to call new evidence, or to re-examine previous witnesses in order to fully explore the new issues and to address the new legal elements.[46]

---

42 *Dallos v Hungary (Judgment)* (ECHR, *Chamber*, Application No 29082/95, 1 March 2001).

43 European Convention for the Protection of Human Rights and Fundamental Freedoms, opened for signature 4 November 1950, 213 UNTS 221 (entered into force 3 September 1953).

44 *Prosecutor v Lubanga (Decision Giving Notice to the Parties and Participants that the Legal Characterisation of the Facts May Be Subject to Change in Accordance with Regulation 55(2) of the Regulations of the Court*) (ICC, Trial Chamber I, Case No ICC-01/04–01/06–2049, 14 July 2009).

45 *Prosecutor v Lubanga (Minority Opinion on the 'Decision Giving Notice to the Parties and Participants that the Legal Characterisation of Facts May be Subject to Change in Accordance with Regulation 55(2) of the Regulations of the Court')* (ICC, Trial Chamber I, Case No ICC-01/04–01/06–2054, 17 July 2009) [33].

46 *Prosecutor v Lubanga (Prosecution's Document in Support of Appeal against the 'Decision Giving Notice to the Parties and Participants that the Legal Characterisation of the Facts May Be Subject to Change in Accordance with*

Although the Appeals Chamber ultimately overruled the Trial Chamber's decision,[47] the warning to defence counsel is clear: beware the derogation of rights to which tribunals may be tempted by victim advocates. In this instance, the accused spent two extra months in custody and the defence was delayed in anxious anticipation of a five-charge expansion of the case confirmed under Art 61.[48] But their persistent opposition was rewarded.

Another major danger of reconceptualisation is that the defence, by misunderstanding the case it faces, may fail to meet a pathway to conviction. An ever-changing prosecution case theory remains a danger right up to judgment and through to appeal. The necessity for vigilant application of this right was highlighted in the *Halilović* appeal judgment.[49] At trial, Halilović was charged under Art 7(3) with the murder of civilians at Grabovica and Uzdol in Herzegovina committed by soldiers of the Army of the Republic of Bosnia and Herzegovina.[50] Halilović was acquitted on the basis that the prosecution failed to prove what the indictment had pleaded: that 'by virtue of his position and authority as Commander of the Operation' Halilović had effective control of the soldiers. The indictment was very clear and very limited, and the Trial Chamber made findings on that basis. But on appeal, the prosecution alleged that the Trial Chamber erred by ignoring another case: the 'case beyond command'[51] which, it was argued, had been advanced by the prosecution at trial.

On this appeal, the defence watched anxiously as the prosecution skilfully wove an alternative case, of which it alleged the defence had notice. The Appeals Chamber analysed the indictment first: of course, no 'case

---

*Regulation 55(2) of the Regulations of the Court' and Urgent Request for Suspensive Effect)* (ICC, Appeals Chamber, Case No ICC-01/04–01/06 OA15, 14 September 2009) [48].

47 *Prosecutor v Lubanga (Judgment on the Appeals of Mr Lubanga Dyilo and the Prosecutor against the Decision of Trial Chamber I of 14 July 2009 Entitled 'Decision Giving Notice to the Parties and Participants that the Legal Characterisation of the Facts May Be Subject to Change in Accordance with Regulation 55(2) of the Regulations of the Court')* (ICC, Appeals Chamber, Case No ICC-01/04–01/06 OA 15 OA 16, 8 December 2009).

48 Ibid [24] contains the relevant procedural history.

49 *Prosecutor v Halilović (Judgment)* (ICTY, Appeals Chamber, Case No IT-01–48-A, 16 October 2007) [75]–[99].

50 *Prosecutor v Halilović (Judgment)* (ICTY, Trial Chamber I, Section A, Case No IT-01–48-T, 16 November 2005) [752].

51 *Prosecutor v Halilović (Judgment)* (ICTY, Appeals Chamber, Case No IT-01–48-A, 16 October 2007) [75]–[99]: the prosecution position was that Halilović might have enjoyed effective control outside his unproved role as a commander.

beyond command' appeared.[52] But the Chamber refused summary dismissal and the prosecution was permitted to trawl the pre-trial briefs, the opening statements, the evidence, the final briefs and the closing statements in support of their contention.[53] In short, the Appeals Chamber took no narrow view of how the prosecution might plead its case, and appeared to countenance the possibility of an implied case. In the event, none was found, because the defence had maintained a strict insistence on the terms of the indictment at every stage.

Thus, it is at trial, rather than on appeal, where the prosecution must be tied to its pleadings. In *Prosecutor v Galić* the Appeals Chamber forgave the prosecution and the Trial Chamber the alteration of the 'nature and cause' of the charge (of causing terror among the population) noted above.[54] Although appeals chambers have refused prosecution appeals against a trial chamber's decision to hold the prosecution to their pleadings, it is unlikely that a due process failure will result in a full retrial. However, due process failures (including disclosure failures) can in theory be addressed on appeal; this occurred in *Blaškić*. But a tribunal will not likely order a re-trial for an accused; it has never occurred internationally.[55]

One weapon in the defence armoury when resisting such goalpost-shifting is the right to an expeditious trial. At the ICTY, chambers facing applications to amend will consider whether the right under Art 21(4)(c) of the Statute to be 'tried without undue delay' is infringed; the ICTR took a similar position.[56] In *Kovačević*, the Trial Chamber denied the prosecution

---

52 Ibid [82]: 'In light of this specificity, the Defence was entitled to understand that this was the only basis advanced by the Prosecution to demonstrate Halilović's effective control over the perpetrators of the crimes.'

53 Ibid [44]; doubtless encouraged by *Prosecutor v Krnojelac (Judgment)* (ICTY, Appeals Chamber, Case No IT-97–25-A, 17 September 2003) [138], which explicitly countenances articulating a case theory in a brief.

54 *Prosecutor v Galić (Appeal Judgment)* (ICTY, Appeals Chamber, Case No IT-98–29-A, 30 November 2006) [74]; see also *Prosecutor v Čermak and Markac (Decision on Motion on Form of Indictment)* (ICTY, Trial Chamber II, Case No IT-03–73-PT, 8 March 2005) [5].

55 However, in *Erdemović*, the Appeals Chamber did remit the matter to a differently-constituted Trial Chamber so that the Appellant could replead upon being properly informed of the nature of the charges to which he was pleading; *Prosecutor v Erdemović (Judgment)* (ICTY, Appeals Chamber, Case No IT-96–22-A, 7 October 1997) [20].

56 See *Prosecutor v Brdjanin and Talic (Decision on Form of Fourth Amended Indictment)* (ICTY, Trial Chamber II, Case No IT-99–36-PT, 23 November 2001) [17]; *Prosecutor v Karemera et al (Decision on Prosecutor's Interlocutory Appeal against Trial Chamber III Decision of 8 October 2003 Denying Leave to File an*

leave to amend the indictment,[57] although the Appeals Chamber reversed this.[58] But in *Halilović*, the Pre-Trial Chamber ruled that, despite the absence of any substantive injustice arising from the amendment, the prospect of delay tilted discretionary judgement against permitting it.[59] The amendment triggered procedural requirements which would have meant that another trial took precedence over that of Mr Halilović, who was indicted in 2001 but released.[60] In *Kolundžija*, the defence successfully resisted a rather logical motion to join Mr Kolundžija to a joint trial on the basis of the consequent delay.[61]

Disclosure battles are thus distinctly adversarial, as these examples demonstrate. But the emergence of victims into the trial process magnifies that adversarial quality, as shown by the victim intervention in *Lubanga* noted above. Defence counsel now faces two hostile opponents in court. Formally, victims may not be parties; as a Pre-Trial Chamber said in 2006: 'victims participating in criminal proceedings cannot be regarded as "either the opponent – or for that matter necessarily the ally – of the prosecution, their roles and objectives being clearly different"'.[62]

---

*Amended Indictment)* (ICTR, Appeals Chamber, Case No ICTR-98–44-AR73, 19 December 2003) [13].

[57] *Prosecutor v Kovačević* (*Decision on Prosecutor's Request to File an Amended Indictment*) (ICTY, Trial Chamber, Case No IT-97–24-PT, 5 March 1998).

[58] *Prosecutor v Kovačević* (*Decision Stating Reasons for Appeals Chamber's Order of 29 May 1998*) (ICTY, Appeals Chamber, Case No IT-97–24-AR73, 2 July 1998).

[59] *Prosecutor v Halilović (Decision on Prosecutor's Motion Seeking Leave to Amend the Indictment)* (ICTY, Trial Chamber, Case No IT-01–48-PT, 17 December 2004) [41].

[60] Of course, where an application for amendment or joinder is made in a timely and coherent manner, it is difficult to resist. The spectre of prejudice by delay suffered by Messrs Cermak and Markac did not persuade the Appeals Chamber to grant them a separate trial from Mr Gotovina, whose case was less advanced: *Prosecutor v Gotovina; Cermak and Markac* (*Decision on Interlocutory Appeal against the Trial Chamber's Decision to Amend the Indictment and for Joinder)* (ICTY, Appeals Chamber, Case Nos IT-03–73-AR73.1; IT-03–73-AR73.2; IT-01–45-AR73.1, 25 October 2006).

[61] *Prosecutor v Kvocka, Kos,* Radic *and Zigic; Kolundžija (Decision on Prosecutor's Motion for Joinder)* (ICTY, Trial Chamber, Case Nos IT-98–30/1-T; IT-95–8-T, 19 October 1999).

[62] *Situation in the Democratic Republic of the Congo (Decision on the Application for Participation in Proceedings of VPRS1, VPRS 2–3-4–5-6*) (ICC, Pre-Trial Chamber I, Case No ICC-01/04–101-tEN_Corr, 17 January 2006) [51], quoting from *Berger v France (Judgment)* (ECHR, App No 48221/99, 3 December

But in most situations, the defence would fail in its duty of diligence to regard victim advocates any other way. Victim advocates owe none of the prosecutorial duties of disclosure and fairness. They are concerned to shield their clients from trauma, to have their story told and accepted, and to secure justice for the victims. The formal primacy of the accused's rights over those of victims is apparent in the Statute.[63]

Thus victim interventions should be policed to the extent that they interfere with case disclosure by the prosecution, as occurred late in *Lubanga*. Other rights may also be deployed. For example, the expeditious trial right can be invoked against discontented victim advocate motions. It is wrong to say that delay is acceptable merely because the Statute now allows for a potential expansion of any given proceedings at the behest of victims; Judge Song's comments[64] should not be read as authorising any such conclusion. The Statute does not say so and having an expeditious trial is a right which protects an accused from oppression.

In conclusion: trial counsel bears the responsibility for credibly deploying this right, against a background of the right to a fair and expeditious trial. This works best when the defence has committed to a strategy governing preparation, filings, cross-examination and the elements of the charged crimes it chooses to contest. Of course, ad hoc counsel can greatly assist the defence before the case theory is implemented,[65] but disclosure of the case per se is trial counsel's battle. Tribunals can respond to diligent insistence upon disclosure rights and upon an expeditious trial, especially if

---

2002) [38] and referring also to *Perez v France (Judgment)* (ECHR, App No 47287/99, 12 February 2004) [68].

[63] See Rome Statute Art 68, describing measures which the Prosecutor may take to protect victims and witnesses and thrice reiterating that such measures 'shall not be prejudicial to or inconsistent with the rights of the accused and a fair and impartial trial'.

[64] *Prosecutor v Lubanga (Judgment on the Appeal of Mr Thomas Lubanga Dyilo against the Decision of Pre-Trial Chamber I Entitled 'Décision sur la Demande de Mise en Líberté Proviso Ire de Thomas Lubanga Dyilo')* (ICC, Appeals Chamber, Case No ICC-01/04–01/06–824, 13 February 2007) 55–57.

[65] For example, regarding Darfur, Sudan, Trial Chamber I permitted the OPCD to file valuable observations on victims' applications concerning the situation in Darfur: *Situation in Darfur, Sudan (Decision Authorising the Filing of Observations on Applications a/0021/07, a/0023/07 to a/0033/07 and a/0035/07 to a/0038/07 for Participation in the Proceedings)* (ICC, Pre-Trial Chamber I, Case No ICC 02/05, 23 July 2007).

the defence can appear consistent and credible (not always simple in international tribunals).[66]

## III. DISCLOSURE OF EVIDENCE

Disclosure of the evidence is equally important to the defence. Evidentiary disclosure is the life-blood of the fact-finding process. Given the inevitable mismatch of resources between prosecution and accused, disclosure is the tool by which the defence achieves equality of arms in the adversarial trial process and, thereby, a fair trial. From an accused's viewpoint, it matters little whether the right to evidentiary disclosure is sourced in the general fair trial right, the specific right to adequate time and facilities or the nebulous right to equality of arms.[67] What the defence faces is a gross mismatch of resources and a prosecution whose attitude to disclosure often seems hostile and obfuscatory. In the hyper-adversarial context of ICC litigation, this right falls to be applied with persistence by counsel; no accused could meaningfully fight the battle unrepresented.

In principle, the accused has an extensive right to disclosure of the evidence, both inculpatory and exculpatory, at international tribunals. As to inculpatory evidence, the Statute provides for disclosure at the confirmation stage under Art 61(3)(b); this must be in sufficient detail to permit the defence to challenge it, if they choose, pursuant to Art 61(6)(b). Thereafter, Art 64(3)(c) permits the Trial Chamber to make directions about evidentiary disclosure and 64(6) empowers them to make relevant orders. Article 67 contains the right to adequate time and facilities and other relevant rights. As to exculpatory evidence, the Rules are deceptively clear. Following the jurisprudence of the ICTY,[68] Art 67(2) of the Rome Statute deals with exculpatory material thus:

---

66 Hafida Lahiouel, 'The Right of the Accused to an Expeditious Trial' in Richard May et al (eds), *Essays on ICTY Procedure and Evidence in Honour of Gabrielle Kirk McDonald* (Kluwer Law International 2001) 204; in *Prosecutor v Kunarac* (*Further Decision on Request for Release of Dragoljub Kunarac*) (ICTY, Trial Chamber, Case No IT-95–23PT, 17 November 1999) adverse comment was made concerning applications for provisional release which betrayed an institutional suspicion of defence motives.

67 See *Edwards v United Kingdom* (2002) ECHR 303, which concerned a failure to disclose potentially exculpatory evidence (the victim saw the offender, but did not identify the accused, thus potentially excluding him). See generally Trechsel, above note 14, 224.

68 Exculpatory material was defined at the ICTY in *Prosecutor v Delalić (Decision on the Request of the Accused Pursuant to Rule 68 for Exculpatory*

> The Prosecutor shall, as soon as practicable, disclose to the defence evidence in the Prosecution's possession or control which he or she believes shows or tends to show the innocence of the accused, or to mitigate the guilt of the accused, or which may affect the credibility of prosecution evidence.

Rules 76 and 77 amplify the right; other provisions create limited exemptions.[69] If the prosecution is in doubt concerning the 'exculpatory' nature of evidence, it must seek guidance, ex parte, from the Court under Rule 83. These procedures are underpinned by several of the specific minimum guarantees found in Art 67: the right to adequate time and facilities, the right to confront and the right to call and examine witnesses on the same terms as the prosecution may. The overriding right to a fair and expeditious trial also informs the fundamental right to disclosure.[70]

At the ICC, the prosecution's obligations are reinforced, by their duty, pursuant to Art 54(1)(a) of the Rome Statute, to investigate incriminating and exonerating circumstances equally, in order to establish 'the truth'. The prosecution's obligation is broader than that which applies in national jurisdictions[71] and, because of Art 54, broader than that applied at the ad hoc tribunals.

Despite these provisions, and despite clear judicial statements concerning the prosecution's disclosure duties,[72] the defence frequently finds itself locked in adversarial battle over disclosure. Indeed, experience suggests that disclosure arguments generate significant delay and marked ill will and distrust between parties. Thus, the application of this right at trial entails examining some of the scenarios that arise. The conclusion is that the defence must engage closely and cooperatively with the prosecution, only

---

*Information)* (ICTY, Trial Chamber, Case No IT-96–21-T, 24 June 1997) [12], as 'material which is known to the Prosecutor and which is favourable to the accused in the sense that it tends to suggest the innocence or mitigate the guilt of the accused or may effect the credibility of prosecution evidence'.

[69] For instance, internal work documents (exempt under rule 81), or 'springboard evidence' (obtained subject to undertakings of confidentiality pursuant to Art 54(3)(e)).

[70] On this connection see, eg, *Prosecutor v Katanga and Ngudjolo Chui (Decision on Article 54(3)(e) Documents* Identified *as Potentially Exculpatory or Otherwise Material to the Defence's Preparation for the Confirmation Hearing)* (ICC, Pre-Trial Chamber I, Case No ICC-01/04–01/07–621, 20 June 2008) [3]–[6] and the extracts cited therein.

[71] See, eg, in the US *Kyles v Whitley*, 514 US 419 (1995) (Souter J).

[72] See, eg, *Prosecutor v Kupreškić (Decision on Communication between Parties and Their Witnesses)* (ICTY, Trial Chamber, Case No IT-95–16-T, 21 September 1998) [3].

litigating once a record is clearly created which allows a chamber to rule favourably.

Concerning inculpatory evidence, timeliness is the first battle. At the ICTY, the prosecution habitually produced important evidence late. Material disclosed late is difficult to investigate, because pre-trial resources are depleted and attention is focused upon the approaching trial. In *Halilović*, pre-trial disclosure was so poor that the Pre-Trial Chamber was persuaded to impose a requirement on the prosecution to seek leave to disclose any further inculpatory material, and to account for unexplained delays.[73] Occasionally a prosecution discloses very late, deep into the trial itself. A spectacular revelation occurred in *Krstić* when, as the accused General testified, the prosecution suddenly produced a tape purporting to record General Krstić issuing explicit and bloodthirsty orders to 'kill them all'. The prosecution had possessed this tape, without disclosing, since the pre-trial phase. The explanation proffered for this disclosure breach was lame at best, and the evidence was sharply excluded:

> The Chamber further notes that the Prosecution was in possession of the evidence before the start of the case-in-chief and decided not to use it. It appears that the Prosecution made the tactical decision to use it during cross-examination rather than in the case-in-chief … .[74]

It is hard to see how the defence could anticipate such a bombshell. Defence counsel must address disclosure in this super-adversarial atmosphere, and the instrumental deployment of statutory rights is the best weapon available to the defence.

A second requirement is that disclosure be comprehensive. Redaction is to be resisted; although security and privacy concerns are relevant, relevance (for example, of contextual material) is a matter best left to the defence to determine. The defence will often base a valuable line of enquiry on peripheral detail in statements: who was present, who was well-placed to overhear orders, who sighted documents, who conveyed messages.

Controversy arises where the prosecution seeks anonymity for its witnesses. Unfortunately, in international criminal proceedings the true identity of witnesses cannot be assumed. In *Lubanga*, the Trial Chamber was compelled to find the following bizarre facts:

---

73 *Prosecutor v Halilović (Decision on Defence Objection to Prosecution Continued Disclosure)* (ICTY, Trial Chamber, Case No IT-01–48-PT, 7 May 2004) [2]–[3].

74 *Prosecutor v Krstić (Decision on the Defence Motion to Exclude Exhibits in Rebuttal and Motion for Continuance)* (ICTY, Trial Chamber I, Case No IT-98–33-T, 4 May 2001) [25ff].

> there is a real possibility that victims a/0229/06 and a/0225/06 (at the instigation or with the encouragement of a/0270/07) stole the identities of Thonifwa Uroci Dieudonné (D-0032) and Jean-Paul Bedijo Tchonga (D-0033) in order to obtain the benefits they expected to receive as victims participating in these proceedings.[75]

In *Lubanga*, the prosecution was harshly criticised for employing intermediaries to procure witnesses of doubtful truthfulness.[76] But the reality is that, without an international police force, prosecutors must rely upon colourful and outlandish sources to procure witnesses. Trial chambers should encourage the defence to insist upon proper disclosure even of the basic facts like identity and personal details. The problem has been apparent since *Tadić* in 1995; there the Trial Chamber allowed a meretricious villain to testify with inadequate disclosure of his identity. Only after litigation did the necessary disclosure occur, disgracing the witness.[77]

Controversy also arises where the prosecution possesses material pursuant to a confidentiality agreement. In *Lubanga* the prosecution possessed 'springboard evidence' elicited pursuant to a confidentiality agreement with the UN under Art 54(3)(e) of the Rome Statute.[78] The defence contended that this, or some of it, was exculpatory or relevant to the preparation of the defence; the prosecution considered itself bound not to disclose. By determined litigation, the defence was able to procure the evidence when the prosecution faced the termination of its case by permanent stay, as we shall see below.[79] The use of such 'springboard evidence' is necessary for the prosecution, which lacks its own police force; but disclosure dilemmas perforce arise. In that situation, the defence may realistically seek disclosure of prosecution material which, although it appears inculpatory in that it contains allegations, is in fact helpful because it reveals inconsistencies or evidence of collusion.

---

[75] *Prosecutor v Lubanga (Public – Judgment Pursuant to Article 74 of the Statute)* (ICC, Trial Chamber I, Case No ICC-01/04–01/06–2842, 14 March 2012) [502].

[76] Ibid [482].

[77] *Prosecutor v Tadić (Appeal Judgment)* (ICTY, Appeals Chamber, Case No IT-94–1-A, 15 July 1999) [57], [65].

[78] *Prosecutor v Lubanga (Decision on the Consequences of Non-Disclosure of Exculpatory Materials Covered by Article 54(3)(e) Agreements and the Application to Stay the Prosecution of the Accused, Together with Certain other Issues Raised at the Status Conference on 10 June 2008)* (ICC, Trial Chamber I, Case No ICC-01/04–01/06, 13 June 2008) 72.

[79] *Prosecutor v Lubanga (Public – Judgment Pursuant to Article 74 of the Statute)* (ICC, Trial Chamber I, Case No ICC-01/04–01/06–2842, 14 March 2012) [10(i)].

Despite gross examples like *Krstić*, the prosecution will generally disclose inculpatory material in a timely and comprehensive manner. Indeed, given the ban at the ICC on 'proofing' of witnesses, detailed statements ought to be expected. Further, defence counsel can give life to this right by seeking all inculpatory statements, even those not relied on; patterns of suggestion by investigators, government officials or 'intermediaries' can be discerned and suspicious patterns of evidence by prosecution witnesses can be shown by the well-prepared defence.[80] This strategy was effectively deployed in *Lubanga*.

Exculpatory evidence is quite different, being inevitably controversial. Defence counsel at trial seeks for disclosure of exculpatory material. As noted above, this is because it is from the prosecution's collected materials that any exculpatory material will come, given that the accused is usually gravely disadvantaged in investigating. In applying this right at trial, the defence must formulate and pursue a consistent strategy.

In broad terms, the defence should identify the type of material likely to be held and secure its release. That strategy must eschew posturing and acrimony, but embrace persistence and a clear record of requests made and information provided in support of those requests. It need not be formalised or rigid; it is designed to compel disclosure and to prevent unexpected evolution of the prosecution case as the trial unfolds. The defence must assess what sort of exculpatory material the prosecutor is likely to hold or control;[81] it must assemble evidence (perhaps circumstantial) that the prosecution does hold it;[82] it must request it, politely but clearly and persistently; it must litigate on the basis that it may not succeed initially; and it must persist. The test facing an accused seeking an order to disclose is quite onerous:

> In accordance with the International Tribunal's jurisprudence, the test to be applied for discovery under Rule 68 has two steps: first, if the Defence believes that the Prosecution has not complied with Rule 68, it must first establish that evidence other than that disclosed might prove exculpatory for the accused and

---

[80] Following disclosure, the defence is able to object to redactions, anonymity, remote hearsay and 'historical record' evidence or evidence designed chiefly to palliate the sufferings of a witness. If there are competing pressures on a trial chamber – adjudicative purity versus compatibility with the great goals of international justice – the defence will insist on the former. Skirmishing on these matters will always occur and need not be analysed here.

[81] A Rumsfeldian assessment of the 'known unknowns' is important here.

[82] See *Prosecutor v Blaškić (Judgment)* (ICC, Appeals Chamber, Case No IT-95–14-A, 29 July 2004) [268].

is in the possession of the Prosecution; and second, it must present a *prima facie* case which would make probable the exculpatory nature of the materials sought.[83]

A trial chamber will not lightly intervene where the prosecution asserts it has nothing to disclose. Furthermore, the ICTY and ICC will presume a measure of competence and good faith in the prosecution.[84] Even so, it will step in if persuaded to do so. The steady, cumulative approach adopted by the defence team in *Lubanga* on the issue of intermediaries serves as an excellent example.

Why does the prosecution often fail to disclose exculpatory material? A well-prepared defence can identify the reasons and act accordingly. One reason is confidentiality: sometimes the prosecution feels obliged not to disclose in order to protect the interests of the information provider. Another reason is the mass of material in prosecution possession, with which they have an imperfect familiarity. Another is a failure to recognise the exculpatory nature of material, sometimes through ignorance of the defence case and sometimes through application of a narrow policy on defining what is 'exculpatory'.

Disclosure failures can occur when the prosecution possesses material pursuant to a confidentiality agreement. As noted above, in *Lubanga*, the defence pressed for disclosure of 'springboard evidence' provided by the UN to the prosecution.[85] This was exculpatory evidence, but the prosecution felt bound not to disclose because of undertakings given to the evidence-provider (the UN). The situation this produced was intolerable, as the Appeals Chamber commented:

> In sum, as of 13 June 2008, the Trial Chamber was faced with a situation in which a large number of documents containing potentially exculpatory information or information relevant to the preparation of the defence was in the possession of the Prosecutor, but could not be disclosed to Mr Lubanga Dyilo. Nor could the Trial Chamber have access to the documents in order to assess

---

[83] Ibid.

[84] See *Prosecutor v Radovan Karadžić (Decision on Accused Motion for Inspection and Disclosure)* (ICTY, Trial Chamber, Case No IT-95–5/18-PT, 9 October 2008) [6]; *Prosecutor v Radovan Karadžić (Decision on Motion on Modalities of Rule 66(A)(ii) Disclosure)* (ICTY, Trial Chamber, Case No IT-95–5/18-PT, 27 April 2009) [5].

[85] *Prosecutor v Lubanga (Decision on the Consequences of Non-Disclosure of Exculpatory Materials Covered by Article 54(3)(e) Agreements and the Application to Stay the Prosecution of the Accused, Together with Certain other Issues Raised at the Status Conference on 10 June 2008)* (ICC, Trial Chamber I, Case No ICC-01/04–01/06, 13 June 2008).

> whether a fair trial could be held even without the disclosure of the documents. As explained above, the Appeals Chamber has no reason to fault the assessment of the Trial Chamber on 13 June 2008 that this situation would continue. If the trial of Mr Lubanga Dyilo had taken place in such circumstances, there would always have been a lurking doubt as to whether the disclosure of the documents in question would have changed the course of the trial.[86]

Here the defence prevailed, although at the cost of resources, time and extended custody for Mr Lubanga. In this case, the defence was able to target the material it expected to find: the Trial Chamber was assisted by having specific material on which to focus, rather than facing a fishing expedition.

A more serious and troubling failure of this type arose later in *Lubanga*, when the issue of intermediaries flared up.[87] From early in the trial, the defence had alleged that false witnesses had been procured by intermediaries[88] and, as the case evolved, the defence developed the allegation that this was systemic and occurred with the connivance of the prosecution itself. In this case the prosecution was in possession of evidence concerning the credibility of its witnesses: the activities of witness-gathering 'intermediaries' became relevant to the credibility of alleged child soldiers pressed into service by Lubanga. Despite initial setbacks, this material was progressively extracted by a persistent defence. The perceived recalcitrance of the prosecution led to a further application for a permanent stay. Although the Trial Chamber refused this extreme remedy,[89] the defence campaign for disclosure was a success. At judgment, the Trial Chamber rejected the evidence garnered by those intermediaries.[90]

Another frequent reason for failure is the prosecution's imperfect familiarity with its material. Cynical defence counsel may jeer, but the fact is that

---

[86] *Prosecutor v Lubanga (Judgment on the Appeal of the Prosecutor against the Decision of Trial Chamber I Entitled 'Decision on the Consequences of Non-disclosure of Exculpatory Materials Covered by Article 54(3)(e) Agreements and the Application to Stay the Prosecution of the Accused, Together with Certain other Issues Raised at the Status Conference on 10 June 2008')* (ICC, Appeals Chamber, Case No ICC-01/04–01/06–1486, 21 October 2008) [97].

[87] See generally *Prosecutor v Lubanga (Redacted Decision on Intermediaries)* (ICC, Trial Chamber I, Case No ICC-01/04–01/06, 31 May 2010).

[88] Ibid [16], quoting earlier transcripts of argument.

[89] *Prosecutor v Lubanga (Redacted Decision on the 'Defence Application Seeking a Permanent Stay of the Proceedings')* (ICC, Trial Chamber I, Case No ICC-01/04–01/06–2690-Red2, 7 March 2011) [197].

[90] *Prosecutor v Lubanga (Public – Judgment Pursuant to Article 74 of the Statute)* (ICC, Trial Chamber I, Case No ICC-01/04–01/06–2842, 14 March 2012) [480], [482]–[484].

prosecutors do miss exculpatory matters quite innocently. Tribunals will not place unreal demands on the prosecution; thus the Appeals Chamber in *Blaškić* recognised that Rule 68 disclosure was potentially burdensome to the prosecution.[91] The prosecution may glean something of the defence case from filings or interviews, but they do not have the benefit of the accused's instructions or of the defence strategy. They cannot guess. Where the allegedly exculpatory material is circumstantial in nature, the prosecution will routinely and innocently miss the clues. Where the material relates to a counter-narrative, the prosecution will miss it; it will miss credibility issues, patterns of witness behaviour and much else. That danger is magnified at the ICC where victims are independently represented and have independent interests. In *Bemba*, the defence asserted that the victims had engaged, in their applications, in a coordinated campaign amounting to 'synchronised swimming': their statements had universally moved to include an allegation of 'pillage', which had not appeared previously.[92] Such a pattern could undermine the credibility of the 'synchronised swimmers', but also confirm the existence of organised witness corruption, which might form a plank in the defence case against other witnesses. But without proper notice, it is hard to see even a diligent prosecution spotting every relevant piece of evidence.

Therefore, the defence must apply the right in a nuanced manner and ensure that specific requests have been carefully pursued with the prosecution before seeking intervention from a trial chamber. Its demands must be realistic and focused. Trial chambers will protect the prosecution from oppression; as the Appeals Chamber said in *Krstić*:

> The Appeals Chamber is sympathetic to the argument of the Prosecution that in most instances material requires processing, translation, analysis and identification as exculpatory material. The Prosecution cannot be expected to disclose material which – despite its best efforts – it has not been able to review and assess.[93]

The defence must therefore endeavour to put the prosecution on notice as to what material it is likely to hold and how that material might be exculpatory. Naturally, forensic dilemmas arise as to how much information the accused

---

[91] *Prosecutor v Blaškić (Judgment)* (ICTY, Appeals Chamber, Case No IT-95–14-A, 29 July 2004) [265].

[92] *Prosecutor v Bemba (Decision on 418 Applications by Victims to Participate in the Proceedings)* (ICC, Trial Chamber III, Case No ICC-01/05–01/08, 15 December 2011) [14]. See also [19]–[20].

[93] *Prosecutor v Krstić (Judgment)* (ICTY, Appeals Chamber, Case No IT-98–33-A, 19 April 2004) [197].

should share. But exculpatory material, in a practical sense, is any material which can affect the trial chamber's assessment of those facts, inferences and conclusions which are necessary to prove the elements of the crimes charged.[94] Such material cannot be categorised; it is totally case-specific and, especially for a diligent prosecutor ignorant of the accused's instructions and strategies, difficult to anticipate. By giving judicious notice to the prosecution of the type of material sought, the defence will alert and persuade fair prosecutors to disclose and corner recalcitrant prosecutors into a position which can be attacked before a chamber. Such notice may also help to persuade a chamber that the material exists and is likely to be exculpatory. This might appear to represent a dilution of the adversarial process, but in reality it serves to promote a proper adversarial contest by permitting the defence to arm itself with the necessary mastery of relevant facts.

Another target of defence disclosure policy should be the overly narrow disclosure policies adopted by some prosecutors; examples of this abound. At the ICTR in *Karemera*, the accused Nzirorera sought a document which was at least partially exculpatory: it showed that his political party and ideology was quite distinct from that of an alleged co-offender, Mr Barayagwiza. The prosecution resisted disclosure because it viewed the evidence as not entirely exculpatory. Counsel for Nzirorera was able to seek redress from the Appeals Chamber.[95]

At the ICC, prosecution disclosure policies have been strongly attacked. Arts 54(1) and (2) clearly oblige the prosecution to conduct a proactive and 'effective' investigation extending to exculpatory material. But in *Katanga*, a plainly frustrated defence filed a motion setting out in detail the grievances occasioned by prosecution practices.[96] Against a background of unequal capacity between the parties in their ability to investigate or build a case,[97] Mr Hooper (counsel for Katanga) asserted that the prosecution investigated inadequately and disclosed poorly, either by over-restrictive provision of material, or by dumping masses of undifferentiated documents on the defence, which might contain exculpatory material. The approach by

---

[94] The phraseology of Art 67(2) is apt to mislead: the defence does not want material suggesting innocence, but material relevant to raising a reasonable doubt.

[95] *Prosecutor v Karemera (Decision on Joseph Nzirorera's Motion for Disclosure of Witness T Material)* (ICTR, Trial Chamber III, Case No ICTR-98–44-T, 16 April 2010).

[96] *Prosecutor v Katanga (Defence Response to the Prosecution's Submissions Regarding Paragraph 8 of the Order of 10 December 2008)* (ICC, Trial Chamber II, Case No ICC-01/04–01/07, 2 February 2009).

[97] Ibid [9ff].

the Katanga defence team is of interest *inter alia* because it subtly focused upon the prosecution's assessment criteria: where the prosecution is denying the undeniable in disclosure battles, the defence might profitably pursue the criteria being applied.

Sometimes the prosecution disputes the exculpatory nature of evidence because it conceives the issues differently to the defence. In *Prosecutor v Cermak*, the prosecution alleged a Joint Criminal Enterprise to forcibly move Serbian civilians in the Krajina region of Croatia. It possessed voluminous evidence of hatred for and activity against the Serbs by local Croatian forces. Counsel for Cermak argued that these forces were in no common enterprise with him and did not answer to him. Here the prosecution contended that the material was not exculpatory at all, but the Chamber disagreed.[98] At the ICC, Rule 83 permits the prosecution to raise the issue *ex parte* with a chamber; in that situation, the defence can arm the chamber with sufficient information to identify what is exculpatory. That is a necessary process, because prosecutors sometimes claim that material, which seems radiantly exculpatory to defence counsel, is in reality irrelevant, mere context or fine quality smokescreen.

Trial chambers manage controversies best where counsel provide focused assistance. As noted earlier, the remedies for prosecutorial procedural failings have been uneven. Traditional common law remedies (stays and exclusions) seem ill-adapted to international criminal law, and disproportionate in nature. On the other hand, the empty censures sometimes visited upon cynical prosecutors often leads to disenchantment among accused. The existence of proper remedies for procedural breaches is important; without such remedies, trial chambers will appear to produce unjust results and inadequate records and ultimately the international criminal justice project will lose legitimacy.

Trial chambers at the ICTY have recently demonstrated an approach to disclosure failures which combines principle with pragmatism in a manner consistent with the thesis of this chapter. In *Ndindiliyimana*, plainly exculpatory statements were disclosed to the defence under Rule 68 – but after the trial had finished. The Trial Chamber responded thus:

> In this regard, the Chamber recalls that a Trial Chamber may, where the Prosecution's violation of its disclosure obligation is so extensive or occurs at such a late stage of the proceedings that it would violate the right of the accused

[98] *Prosecutor v Gotovina; Cermak and Markac (Decision on Interlocutory Appeal against the Trial Chamber's Decision to Amend the Indictment and for Joinder)* (ICTY, Appeals Chamber, Case Nos IT-03–73-AR73.1; IT-03–73-AR73.2; IT-01–45-AR73.1, 25 October 2006).

> to trial without undue delay, or where it would be impossible or impractical to recall Prosecution witnesses without effectively re-opening the case in its entirety, opt to draw reasonable inferences from the disclosed material at the stage of its definitive evaluation of the evidence.[99]

Similarly, in *Bizimungu* the Trial Chamber responded thus:

> Drawing the reasonable inferences due to the late disclosure of this highly relevant, probative and exculpatory material, the Chamber entertains reasonable doubt with respect to the Prosecution evidence in this proceeding concerning the meeting at Mariane's house in the second week of April 1994 and the subsequent killing of Mutabazi. (1532) In the midst of this Chamber's judgment deliberations, the Prosecution held onto this material for over a year before discharging its disclosure obligations. The ensuing prejudice cannot be minimised, and the Chamber's consideration in this regard would not be impacted even if there is merit in the Prosecution's position that Bicamumpaka delayed in raising the issue. (1533) There is no excuse for the late disclosure, particularly considering Prosecution Counsel in Nzabonimana was the same Prosecution Counsel in this proceeding. Accordingly, the Chamber will not consider the meeting at Mariane's house as a basis for conviction in its Legal Findings.[100]

These passages are set out at length because they represent an 'applied rights' perspective – a hands-on approach to giving meaning to these rights in a trial context. Trial counsel can learn from these applications.

The examples set out above also demonstrate that disclosure of the facts is extremely adversarial in international criminal trials. This is not a passing phase: even the most ethical prosecution faces new pressures on its disclosure abilities. One such pressure is caused by the absence of its own investigative resources. The prosecution does not control its own material as domestic prosecutors do; evidence is procured by a colourful and little-understood collection of sources. The intermediaries impugned in *Lubanga* and in *Katanga* are merely examples. When the Trial Chambers requested a clarification of the role of these intermediaries, the prosecution said:

> The prosecutor's mandate to investigate and prosecute the world's most serious offences cannot succeed without the use of trusted and reliable intermediaries; any action by the court that chills the ability of the Prosecutor to protect their

---

[99] *Prosecutor v Ndindiliyimana (Judgment and Sentence)* (ICTR, Trial Chamber II, Case No ICTR-00–56-T, 17 May 2011) 435, n 3627.

[100] *Prosecutor v Bizimungu (Judgment and Sentence)* (ICTR, Trial Chamber II, Case No ICTR-99–50-T, 30 September 2011) [1065], [1192].

identities and security will chill the Prosecution's ability to obtain assistance from other intermediaries in future cases … .[101]

Another novel pressure is the potential for intervention by victims and their advocates. Victims may intervene in a variety of situations pursuant to Art 68(3). It is likely that victims would have standing on many disclosure motions: the Appeals Chamber has expressed divergent views about the ambit of the 'personal interests' of the victim,[102] but victims were heard in the *Lubanga* Regulation 55 Appeal.[103] Disclosure could indeed directly affect a victim's personal interests. The defence must anticipate hostile and persistent submissions from victims, who owe no duties to the accused. The participation of victims creates potential injustices; rights are undermined,[104] defence resources are stretched, time is wasted and disclosure is compromised. In *Lubanga*, the defence at one point faced 43 new applications for victim participation, with a short timespan in which to respond.[105] The defence complained[106] and the palliative measures allowed (extra resources, extension of filing deadlines) serve to highlight the dangers. Clearly such interventions can be fought: for example, in *Bemba* defence counsel had certain patently unreliable alleged victims excluded.[107]

---

101 Lubanga Prosecutions Submissions in Response to Trial Chamber's Oral Request of 10 February 2010 (22 February 2010).

102 Charles P Trumbull IV, 'The Victims of Victim Participation in International Criminal Proceedings' (2008) 29 *Michigan Journal of International Law* 777, 798–800.

103 *Prosecutor v Lubanga (Judgment on the Appeals of Mr Lubanga Dyilo and the Prosecutor against the* Decision *of Trial Chamber I of 14 July 2009 Entitled 'Decision Giving Notice to the Parties and Participants that the Legal Characterisation of the Facts May Be Subject to Change in Accordance with Regulation 55(2) of the Regulations of the Court')* (ICC, Appeals Chamber, Case No ICC-01/04–01/06 OA 15 OA 16, 8 December 2009).

104 Trumbull, above note 102, 823; *Prosecutor v Lubanga (Prosecution's Observations Concerning the* Status *of Applicants VPRS 1 to 6 and Their Participation in the Case of the Prosecutor vs Thomas Lubanga Dyilo)* (ICC, Pre-Trial Chamber I, Case No ICC-01/04–01/06–73, 7 April 2006) [13].

105 Mugambi Jouet, 'Reconciling the Conflicting Rights of Victims and Defendants at the International Criminal Court' (2007) 26 *Saint Louis University Public Law Review* 249, 278.

106 Prosecutor *v Lubanga (Defence Observations Relative to the Proceedings and Manner of Participation of Victims a/0001/06 to a/0003/06)* (ICC, Pre-Trial Chamber I, Case No ICC-01/04–01/06–379, 4 September 2006) 15–16.

107 *Prosecutor v Bemba (Decision on 418 Applications by Victims to Participate in the Proceedings)* (ICC, Trial Chamber III, Case No ICC-01/05–01/08, 15 December 2011). The Trial Chamber said, at [20]: 'In the view of the Chamber,

In doing so, the Chamber had regard to matters of pure credit. But this battle creates grave disadvantages for the defence: it involves a significant diversion of resources and a disclosure of the argument to be put to and about such applicants. These matters endanger the fair trial of accused men.

This is a fight for trial counsel. Although it falls to the defence to insist, at every stage of the process, upon a trial which is not clouded by disclosure failures, trial counsel has the heaviest duty. Prior to his or her engagement, there is no way for an unrepresented accused to navigate this battlefield. Nor can OPCD or ad hoc counsel hope to construct or pursue such a strategy prior to the initial appearance of the accused and commencement of the confirmation process under Art 61.

In conclusion, then, the point of disclosure warfare is to win disclosure, not to disgrace the prosecution or create appeal points. The benefits of unmasking an allegedly recalcitrant prosecution are very limited for an accused man, though satisfying for those few defence counsel who can contribute to policy formation. In *Stakić*, alleged failures of disclosure were swiftly dismissed.[108] In *Furundžija*, the failures were said to be redressed by a later opportunity to cross-examine.[109] Where a genuinely egregious breach occurs, the defence may seek extreme and punitive remedies like the stay of proceedings which flared briefly in *Lubanga*.[110] But such measures are exceptional and unwieldy, because they tend to undermine the high-level rationale of international criminal justice. *Lubanga* was not stayed despite astounding conduct by the prosecution. Defence folklore says there is no sanction for disclosure failures and nothing to deter a malign prosecutor from concealing what he can; however, the rights applied in *Ndindiliyimana* and *Bizimungu* provide a more positive outlook.

---

obvious contradictions as to the circumstances of the loss of property undermine the intrinsic coherence of an application and, as such, affect the credibility of the applicant's account. Accordingly, in the absence of any explanation for the contradictions, the application will be rejected.'

[108] *Prosecutor v Stakić (Judgment)* (ICTY, Appeals Chamber, Case No IT-97–24-A, 22 March 2006) [183]–[193].

[109] *Prosecutor v Furundžija (Judgment)* (ICTY, Appeals Chamber, Case No IT-95–17/1-A, 21 July 2000) [9].

[110] Fausto Pocar, *Letter Dated 29 May 2006 from the President of the International Tribunal for the Prosecution of Persons Responsible for Serious Violations of International Humanitarian Law Committed in the Territory of the Former Yugoslavia since 1991, Addressed to the President of the Security Council* (United Nations 2008) [25], recommended that power to sanction for non-disclosure be used.

Failures of evidentiary disclosure have limited value as appeal points. In *Blaškić*, the Appeals Chamber found significant breaches of the prosecution's disclosure obligations relating to important issues in the case,[111] but found that Blaškić had not proved prejudice.[112] Mr Blaškić, desperate to establish that he did not command the outrageous 'Jokers' in Bosnia, would doubtless have preferred to have the material at trial; to cross-examine on it, exploit it and rely on it in combination with other material, in order to persuade the Chamber of reasonable doubt about a crucial fact. The pallor of the undisclosed evidence, viewed on appeal, seldom captures its potential significance if available to counsel at trial. The message is simple: the defence must persistently chase the material and not be content with gaining an appeal point.

## IV. EXPEDITIOUS TRIAL

It is convenient to mention one aspect of the right to an expeditious trial because it can be used to augment applications for disclosure. Defence counsel is often reluctant to rely on this right, being under-resourced, swamped with material, oppressed by deadlines and wrestling to develop a viable case concept; indeed, the right. But if a defence team is swiftly trial-ready, many advantages flow.

No trial chamber can ignore this right. Expedition and timeliness are fundamental requirements of a fair trial and are recognised in Art 14 of the ICCPR.[113] Requirements of timeliness abound in the Rome Statute of the ICC.[114] Art 67(1)(c) contains the right to trial without undue delay, Art 64(2) requires a trial chamber to ensure that any trial is fair and expeditious, Art 67(1) requires 'prompt' notification of the nature and cause of the charge and there are several other references.[115] This collection of entitlements, for our purposes, can be called the right to an expeditious trial. It is valuable in itself as a cure for oppression,[116] as delay exposes the accused to

---

111 *Prosecutor v Blaškić (Judgment)* (ICTY, Appeals Chamber, Case No IT-95–14-A, 29 July 2004) [295]–[303].

112 Ibid [295].

113 ICCPR (adopted 16 December 1966, entered into force 23 March 1976) 999 UNTS 171.

114 Rome Statute.

115 Ibid. Article 61(1) requires a confirmation hearing within a 'reasonable time'; disclosure of the case and the evidence relied on at confirmation must also occur 'within a reasonable time', at Art 61(3).

116 Lahiouel, above note 66, 198.

forensic and personal hardship and undermines the relevance and effectiveness of the tribunal's proceedings.[117] But for present purposes, the right supports the assertion of other rights, particularly the disclosure rights discussed in this chapter.[118]

One use of the expeditious trial right is to resist a bloated indictment. Overloaded indictments (or 'Documents Containing the Charges') place massive burdens upon any accused, and in particular undermine his or her ability to insist upon the disclosure rights noted above. The oppression may consist of a gross number of charges, or competing modes of liability, or there might be repetitious factual allegations designed to support an inference of participation in control of perpetrators by the accused.

The most glamorous example of an oppressive super-prosecution was in *Prosecutor v Slobodan Milošević*. The accused faced an unmanageable case:[119] as described by one survivor (amicus Gillian Higgins), it featured over 1.2 million pages of disclosure, 46,000 pages of trial transcript, over 85,000 pages of prosecution exhibits, over 100 videos and written filings covering 2,600 separate briefs, motions, replies and responses. The indictment featured 66 counts, charging 23 different types of crime, relying on two distinct modes of criminal liability.[120] He faced a case theory ('Greater Serbia') which appeared puzzling to the judges very late in the trial.[121] In those circumstances, Milošević's right to know the nature and cause of the charge could not be exercised. As to evidentiary disclosure, he faced an unreadable mass, which also beggared his right to adequate time and

---

[117] Ibid 198.

[118] Paradoxically, this right has often been used to the detriment of individual accused. At the ICTY, the 'completion strategy' led to breaches of important trial rights. Thus, in *Prosecutor v Milošević* (*Decision on Interlocutory Appeal on the Admissibility of Evidence-in-Chief in the Form of Written Statements)* (ICTY, Appeals Chamber, Case No IT-02-54-AR73.4, 21 October 2003) [20] ('*Milošević*'), Judge Hunt, in dissent, criticised the admission of written statements by the prosecution under section 92 *bis* as entailing 'a consequential destruction of the rights of the accused enshrined in the Tribunal's Statute and in customary international law'. He went on to say: 'The only reasonable explanation for these decisions appears to be a desire to assist the prosecution to bring the Completion Strategy to a speedy conclusion.'

[119] This was by no means mitigated by his own evident ill-faith at trial.

[120] Gillian Higgins, 'The Impact of the Size, Scope, and Scale of the Milošević Trial and the Development of Rule 73bis before the ICTY' (2007) 7(2) *Northwestern Journal of International Human Rights* 239, 246.

[121] See Gideon Boas, *The Milošević Trial: Lessons for the Conduct of Complex International Criminal Proceedings* (Cambridge University Press 2007) 90–92, for a concise history of the unfolding 'Greater Serbia' case.

facilities. *Milošević* is a powerful precedent for those seeking to limit indictments.

Though *Milošević* represents an extreme case, the danger of a bloated indictment will remain. ICC prosecutors endeavour to pursue a limited, focused case concept.[122] However, like prosecutors at the ICTY, they face multiple pressures to lay a broad swathe of charges[123] and there are often coherent policy arguments to do so.[124] Where an accused is a high-level superior, the prosecution might seek to infer membership of a Joint Criminal Enterprise or superior responsibility, by pointing to patterns of behaviour at diverse crime scenes, as occurred in *Ojdanić*.[125] Mr Krajišnik faced charges arising from over 30 municipalities.[126] Further, at the ICC, the prosecution must take into account the interests of victims when determining whether to initiate or pursue an investigation[127] and thereafter. The Court will also hear submissions from victims concerning their right to participate in proceedings at various stages. This necessarily leads to demands for larger, more inclusive 'Documents Containing the Charges'.[128] But when this occurs, the political purposes of the tribunals are erupting

---

[122] A 2006 prosecution policy document indicated *inter alia* that 'the Office selects a limited number of incidents and as few witnesses as possible are called to testify' – Louis Moreno-Ocampo, '*Report on Prosecutorial Strategy*' (Report, Office of the Prosecutor, 14 September 2006) [5].

[123] O-Gon Kwon, 'The Challenge of an International Criminal Trial as Seen from the Bench' (2007) 5 *Journal of International Criminal Justice* 360, 363, perceived that the OTP loaded indictments heavily because of a perceived responsibility to victims and to the presentation of a complete historical record.

[124] For example, where joint criminal enterprise is alleged, the prosecution needs to prove a widespread sweep of criminal activity from which to infer a coordinated enterprise. Prosecutor David Re successfully put this argument against an application to remove several counts from the indictment in *Prosecutor v Haradinaj (Decision Pursuant to Rule 73bis(D)(1))* (ICTY, Trial Chamber I, Case No IT-04–84-PT, 22 February 2007).

[125] *Prosecutor v Milutinović* (*Judgment*) (ICTY, Trial Chamber, Case No IT-05–87-IT, 26 February 2009) [482]–[494].

[126] *Prosecutor v Krajisnik (Judgment)* (ICTY, Trial Chamber I, Case No IT-00–39-T, 27 September 2006) – the analysis of each municipality occupies 145 pages in the Judgment, at 110–255.

[127] Rome Statute Art 53(1)(c). See also Art 54(1).

[128] Ibid Art 68. See, eg, *Situation in the Democratic Republic of the Congo (Public Redacted Version Decision on the Applications for Participation in Proceedings of VPRS 1, VPRS 2, VPRS 3, VPRS 4, VPRS 5 and VPRS 6* (ICC, Pre-Trial Chamber 1, Case No ICC-01/04, 17 January 2006) [2].

into the adjudicative trial process; it falls to the defence to protect the adjudicative quality of the trial, restricting the issues by reference to relevance.

To persuade a pre-trial chamber to exercise its undoubted discretionary powers to limit an over-expansive case is possible; accused have already succeeded in having charges dismissed at confirmation hearings.[129] One component of such persuasion is prompt insistence upon an expeditious trial, against a background of trial readiness. The chamber will more readily accept an argument based on the right to an expeditious trial if the defence is genuinely ready for an expedited trial. Another component is an informed chamber; the defence must arm the chamber with a familiarity of the case, so that it may weigh up the assurances of the prosecution that the case is neither complex nor oppressive. Thus, at the ICTY in *Milutinović et al*, the defence sought to limit the range of crime-based evidence to be led. In that case, the accused, Ojdanić, was able to persuade Bonomy J (who was well familiar with the factual matrix of the case)[130] that an excessive number of crime sites was being led. The Chamber had wide power, under Rule 73 *bis*, to deal with the issue[131] and was able to limit the number of sites to be proved and simplify the trial. Ojdanić was convicted, but Milutinović was not. In *Milošević* itself, the Trial Chamber was keen to limit the ambit of the case by severing the indictment; the Appeals Chamber's reversal of that step[132] was widely regretted.[133]

Other uses of this right to buttress proper disclosure have been mentioned above. The decisions concerning late amendment in *Kolundžija* and *Halilović* demonstrate how the indictment can be preserved, and the punitive

---

[129] For example, in *Prosecutor v Katanga and Ngudjolo Chui (Decision on the Confirmation of Charges)* (ICC, Pre-Trial Chamber I, Case No ICC-01/04–01/07–717, 30 September 2008) [573]–[581], three charges were not confirmed at the Confirmation Hearing.

[130] Kwon, above note 123, 375.

[131] *Prosecutor v Milutinović et al (Decision on Application of Rule 73bis)* (ICTY, Trial Chamber, Case No IT-05–87-T, 11 July 2006) [2], [6]. The Chamber found, at [6], that: 'Under the terms of these provisions, therefore, the Trial Chamber has four options for direct or indirect action: i. The Chamber can invite the Prosecution to reduce the number of counts charged; ii. The Chamber can fix the number of crime sites; iii. The Chamber can fix the number of incidents; and iv. The Chamber can direct the Prosecution to select the counts upon which to proceed.'

[132] *Prosecutor v Milošević (Decision on Prosecution Interlocutory Appeal from Refusal to Order Joinder)* (ICTY, Appeals Chamber, Case No IT-99–37-AR73; IT-01–50-AR73; IT-01–51-AR73, 1 February 2002) [13]–[15].

[133] Boas, above note 121, 119–21.

disclosure orders in *Halilović* show the extent to which a pre-trial chamber can be persuaded to protect an accused against capricious factual disclosure.

## V. CONCLUSION

International criminal justice may be borne of political and moral considerations, but it deploys the adversarial trial for the benefits of credibility that form of trial enjoys. The trial is adjudicative first; if not, it is no trial. It falls to defence counsel to preserve the adjudicative character of the trial. Thus, a robust, adversarial defence is not truth-defeating and does not conflict with the goals of international justice. In the end, forceful representation, which insists upon the fair trial of the accused, is a necessity for the proper exercise of the court's powers and for its standing as a court dispensing justice. The author endorses the comment of Salvatore Zappalà:

> It is worth clarifying that the rights of the accused are not 'just' human rights guarantees; they are part and parcel of the epistemological mechanism for fact finding in criminal proceedings. Respecting the rules to establish the truth requires full consistency with rights of the accused; these must be seen as an essential component of accurate and truthful fact finding on which punishment is premised … There is no truth outside the process; there is no truth that can be reached without full respect of the rights of the accused.[134]

The centrality of counsel is recognised in the Statute and the Rules.[135] Counsel is subject to a 'unity of identity' with their client which is 'indispensible to the workings of the international tribunal'.[136] Counsel's decisions bind the accused: indeed, the Appeals Chamber at the ICTY has said that 'due diligence will be presumed'.[137] That is how defence counsel

---

[134] Zappalà, above note 5, 145.

[135] For instance, the Rome Statute Art 55(2)(c) provides for representation pre-trial (see also ICC, Rules of Procedure and Evidence, Doc No ICC-ASP/1/3 (adopted 9 September 2002) r 117(2); and at trial – Art 67(1)(d) (see also ICC, Regulations of the Court, rr 74, 75, 76; ICC, Rules of Procedure and Evidence, Doc No ICC-ASP/1/3 (adopted 9 September 2002) rr 20, 21, 22). See also *Prosecutor v Nahimana (Judgment)* (ICTR, Appeals Chamber, Case No ICTR-99–52-A, 28 November 2007) [139]–[140], cited in Tuinstra, above notes 7, 13, 63.

[136] *Prosecutor v Tadić (Decision on Appellant's Motion for the Extension of Time Limit and Admission of Additional Evidence)* (ICTY, Appeals Chamber, Case No IT-94–1-A, 15 October 1998) [65].

[137] Ibid [50].

generally regards their role.[138] The rights of accused persons are not self-executing; in an adversarial trial, it falls to counsel to apply them. The disclosure issues discussed above must be considered in that light.

How adversarial must defence counsel be? To understand the role of defence counsel in the cosmopolitan, intellectually exciting world of international criminal justice, one must visit the dreary UN Detention Unit in Scheveningen. There waits the accused, a prisoner of the ponderous, coercive power of the international community, personified for prisoners by the Dutch guards and the *lekker* cuisine. The accused faces grave charges, heavy sanctions and perpetual obloquy. Merely because he is charged, his name is smeared, his life is disrupted, his liberty is imperilled and suspended. Moreover, he must distrust the very enterprise of international justice and its judicial organs. Are these tribunals not created to 'end impunity'? To 'bring peace and stability to the region'? To create an accurate historical record and to comfort victims? It is difficult to see that an acquittal directly advances any of those moral or pedagogical goals. He must fear the three judges who await persuasion as to his liability.

At trial, he knows that his conviction, punishment and public denunciation is the settled goal of prosecutors avid for justice and also of victims, victims' advocates, human rights organisations, investigators proper and improper and, very often, hostile political forces in his own country or internationally. He sees the prosecution fly at the court like the Archangel Gabriel, armed with a broadly articulated case and inculpatory statements and exhibits containing horrific allegations, electronically organised and presented with righteous confidence by lawyers comfortable and evidently practised in the arena. That case grows and changes as the indictment is amended[139] or new elements or modes of participation are subtly added in filings or evidence. New evidence is disclosed sporadically and its full disclosure is aggressively resisted. Motions proliferate. Victims and their representatives seek to expand the case against the accused[140] and to limit his right to test the evidence in support.

---

138 J I Turner, 'Defense Perspectives on Law and Politics in International Criminal Trials' (2008) 48 *Virginia Journal of International Law* 529, 566.

139 Or, at the ICC, the 'document containing the charges' – see *Prosecutor v Bemba (Decision on the Defence Application for Corrections to the Document Containing the Charges and for the Prosecution to File a Second Amended Document Containing the Charges)* (ICC, Trial Chamber III, Case No ICC-01/05–01/08–836, 20 July 2010).

140 *Prosecutor v Lubanga (Defence Observations Relative to the Proceedings and Manner of Participation of Victims a/0001/06 to a/0003/06)* (ICC, Pre-Trial Chamber I, Case No ICC-01/04–01/06–379, 4 September 2006).

No accused misunderstands the adversarial nature of his trial, whatever his native legal tradition. None but the grand poseurs like Milošević, Šešelj or Barayagwiza misunderstand the need for a legal champion. Counsel is needed because of the complex and adversarial nature of the trial faced by the accused.[141] In this fiercely adversarial system, the accused will not receive a fair trial without forceful representation, a point recognised internationally[142] and domestically.[143] Defence counsel in the modern, cosmopolitan justice system must be adversarial and diligent, and must think long-term about disclosure and about the case strategy which arises from understanding what is disclosed. In short, they must apply the rights of the accused; not to vindicate the Enlightenment, but to assist an accused human being who is subject to a coercive process.[144] Yet, in the end, that goal is wholly consistent with the grand goals of international criminal justice, which does not want suspect convictions, uneven and slanted records, endless plaintive review applications and – in short – the smell of the show-trial. Where an accused is tried fairly, his conviction is sound and safe and the goals of international justice are safely advanced.

Hence this contribution. By analysing disclosure in action, one can see the outline of a proper defence campaign. Such a campaign[145] is hard to

---

141 *Prosecutor v Lubanga (Judgment on Appeal of Mr Thomas Lubanga Dyilo against the Decision on the Defence Challenge to the Jurisdiction of the Court Pursuant to Article 19(2)(a) of the Statute of 3 October 2006)* (ICC, Appeals Chamber, Case No ICC-01/04–01/06–722, 14 December 2006); Jens Dieckmann and Christina Kerll, 'Representing the "General Interests of the Defence" – Boon or Bane? – A Stocktaking of the System of *Ad Hoc* Counsel at the ICC' (2011) 11 *International Criminal Law Review* 105.

142 *Salduz v Turkey (Judgment)* (ECHR, Application No 36391/02, 27 November 2008) [51]: 'the right of everyone charged with a criminal offence to be effectively defended by a lawyer … is one of the fundamental features of a fair trial.'

143 The plight of the unrepresented accused in a domestic trial was set out in *Gideon v Wainwright*, 372 US 335, 342–43 (1963), quoting *Powell v Alabama*, 287 US 45, 68–69 (1932) (Sutherland J).

144 Salvatore Zappalà, above note 5, 140, asserts: 'The primacy of the rights of the accused, which is enshrined in all international human rights instruments and is to a large extent customary international law, must be implemented at three levels. Firstly, it must be recognized within the relevant normative instruments regulating the activities of each given court; secondly, it must be ensured by the judges in the proceedings on a case by case basis; thirdly, there should be some mechanism of redress in case of violations.' But in court, it is defence counsel who will 'ensure' in the instant case, that the rights of the accused are given effect.

145 Meaning a legitimate campaign, not one involving criminal interference with the course of justice.

design in the abstract – the facts of the case swamp general theories of advocacy, especially with the monstrous events giving rise to international criminal trials. But the early formulation of a defence strategy lends focus to all the steps taken in defence of the accused: the surrender of the accused, the participation in interviews, the stance taken at confirmation hearings, the pursuit of disclosure of the case and the evidence, the allocation of resources in building the defence case, the matters to be conceded and contested, and the witnesses to be challenged. The formulation of strategy requires competent counsel, and disclosure of the case and of the evidence, in a timely manner. It is these rights which must be 'applied' by counsel to build the strategy.

# 5. Complexities in prosecuting international crimes: the ICC Libyan warrants

**Mark Ierace**

## I. INTRODUCTION

The 'Arab Spring' that took the world by surprise in 2011 and continues to unfold to an uncertain resolution, has impacted in different and sometimes surprising ways on many states and international institutions. An example is the United Nations (UN) Security Council's unprecedented unanimous referral of the Libyan situation to the International Criminal Court (ICC) then Prosecutor, Luis Moreno Ocampo. In a time frame that recalls the confirmation of the indictment against Slobodan Milošević et al during the Kosovo conflict in 1999, the Prosecutor quickly determined (in contrast to the tempo of his earlier investigations) that a prima facie case existed against at least three high-ranking government figures.

The alleged crimes involved an armed conflict in various mixed urban settings, the besieging of a city (Misrata) and the infliction of terror by the deliberate sniping and indiscriminate shelling of a civilian population, as a means of forcing capitulation. Trials involving such charges, where there is little direct evidence linking high-level perpetrators to a complex crime-base, are technically challenging. They may be protracted by the prosecution's obligation to establish the link circumstantially – by building up evidence of command and control, including the source of fire, accessibility to the implicated weaponry and so on – and to eliminate the reasonable possibility of scenarios such as an acceptable confusion with legitimate targets, or crimes perpetrated by paramilitaries outside the accused's chain of command.

These crimes are markedly dissimilar to those which have been the subject of the Prosecutor's earlier investigations, and in that sense will be novel for his investigators and lawyers. However, they are strikingly reminiscent of the International Criminal Tribunal for the former Yugoslavia

(ICTY) cases of *Prosecutor v Stanislav Galić*[1] and *Prosecutor v Dragomir Milošević*,[2] concerning the siege of Sarajevo.

This chapter considers the Prosecutor's early steps taken in the Libyan situation, with reference to the ICTY Kosovo/Slobodan Milošević indictment, contemporaneous investigations into human rights abuses in Libya initiated by the UN Human Rights Council, investigation and trial techniques employed in the *Galić* and *Milošević* cases that may have some application in any ICC trial arising from the Libyan situation, and the absence of a counterpart war crime of 'terror' in the Rome Statute of the ICC (Rome Statute).[3]

The ICC is the natural beneficiary of the accumulated expertise and experience of the various ad hoc tribunals of the last 18 years. However, its needs are unique, like those of each individual ad hoc tribunal. One of the most challenging aspects of the ICC's uniqueness is that the Office of the Prosecutor (OTP), unlike those of the ad hoc tribunals, must have sufficiently versatile investigative assets to be able to respond to a broad range of types of armed conflicts and civil unrest, sometimes at short notice. This versatility is a critical prerequisite to the OTP's implementation of a successful prosecutorial strategy.

This brief chapter is a critical review of the early stages of the OTP's response to the Libyan situation, which presents such a challenge.

## II. THE SHORT LIBYAN TIME FRAME

The Libyan situation progressed from the commencement of an armed conflict in January 2011, to the point of referral by the UN Security Council to the ICC Prosecutor, Luis Moreno Ocampo, within two months.[4] On 17 March 2011, the Security Council authorised military action to protect civilians.[5] An international coalition accordingly commenced an air and

---

1 *Prosecutor v Galić (Judgment and Opinion)* (ICTY, Trial Chamber I, Case No IT-98–29-T, 5 December 2003).

2 *Prosecutor v Milošević (Decision on Prosecution's Third Motion for Leave to Amend its Rule 65 ter Exhibit List)* (ICTY, Trial Chamber III, Case No IT-98–29/1-T, 23 April 2007).

3 Rome Statute of the ICC (adopted 17 July 1998, entered into force 1 July 2002) 2187 UNTS 90.

4 SC Res 1970, UN SCOR, 6491st mtg, UN Doc S/RES/1970 (2011) (26 February 2011). The referral was confined to events 'since 15 February 2011', at [4].

5 SC Res 1973, UN SCOR, 6498th mtg, UN Doc S/RES/1973 (2011) (17 March 2011) [4]: The resolution authorised member states 'acting nationally or

missile campaign against Libyan government forces and weaponry, relinquishing control to NATO on 27 March.

On 4 May, a little over two months after the referral to the Prosecutor, Moreno Ocampo reported back to the Security Council with a skeletal outline of his investigations thus far,[6] which covered a broad range of criminal allegations:

- a series of incidents involving security forces firing at civilian demonstrators in cities across Libya;
- the systematic arrests, torture, rape, killings, deportations and enforced disappearances of civilians suspected of supporting the uprisings;
- the use of imprecise (area) weaponry such as cluster munitions, multiple rocket launchers and mortars, and other forms of heavy weaponry in crowded urban areas so as to involve the deliberate targeting or reckless endangerment of civilians;
- the deliberate targeting of medical facilities (particularly in Misrata);
- the blocking of humanitarian supplies;
- the use of civilians as human shields;
- the torture of prisoners of war and civilians in the context of the armed conflict;
- the mistreatment of journalists;
- the use of children as combatants.

In addition, the Prosecutor said he was investigating supporters of the rebel forces for the unlawful arrest and possible mistreatment and killings of sub-Saharan Africans.

Twelve days later, Moreno Ocampo filed an application[7] with the Pre-Trial Chamber seeking warrants against Muammar Gaddafi, Saif Al-Islam

---

through regional organizations or arrangements … to take all necessary measures … to protect civilians and civilian populated areas under threat … while excluding a foreign occupation force of any form on any part of Libyan territory … '.

6 ICC, *First Report of the Prosecutor of the International Criminal Court to the UN Security Council Pursuant to UNSCR 1970 (2011)* (ICC 2011) <http://www.unhcr.org/refworld/docid/4dc9034a2.html> ('Prosecutor's First Report to the UNSC'). Moreno Ocampo reported that he had conducted 15 missions to 10 states, conducted 45 interviews 'or individuals have been screened to be interviewed' (as of 26 April 2011) and collected more than 569 documents, 'including visual material … such as videos and pictures', at 5 [30].

7 *Situation in the Libyan Arab Jamahiriya (Prosecutor's Application Pursuant to Article 58 as to Muammar Mohammed Abu Minyar GADDAFI, Saif Al-Islam*

Gaddafi (one of his sons, whom Moreno Ocampo described as Gaddafi's de facto Prime Minister), and his brother-in-law and Intelligence Chief Abdullah Al-Senussi, for two modes of crimes against humanity – murder and persecution.[8]

In contrast to the slow pace of some of his earlier investigations,[9] the Prosecutor had found that there were 'reasonable grounds to believe that the person[s] committed a crime within the jurisdiction of the court', which is the test to be satisfied by the Pre-Trial Chamber if it is to issue warrants,[10] within two months of the referral and four months of the commencement of the armed conflict.

This is a temporal, political and military framework which recalls the interplay in 1999 between the Kosovo conflict[11] and the ICTY Prosecutor, culminating in the confirmation of the indictment against President Slobodan Milošević et al on 4 May 1999, during the NATO bombing campaign of Serbia. In an article published four days later, the ICTY Prosecutor at that time, Louise Arbour, said of this effort: 'I believe that it is an extraordinary achievement for us to have brought to successful confirmation an indictment against the five accused for crimes of this magnitude committed since the beginning of this year.'[12]

Both Arbour and Moreno Ocampo were motivated to advance their investigations quickly in order to have an impact on the continuing armed conflict that generated the charges. For both cases, in spite of the respective

---

*GADDAFI and Abdullah AL-SENSUSSI)* (ICC, Pre-Trial Chamber I, Case No ICC-01/11, 16 May 2011).

[8] Rome Statute, Arts 7(1)(a), (h).

[9] The Prosecutor has been criticised for the time taken with the Darfur and Central African Republic (CAR) investigations. In relation to the CAR situation (the case of Jean-Pierre Bemba), the OTP announced the commencement of an investigation in May 2007, being four years after an NGO (the International Federation for Human Rights) first requested the Prosecutor to investigate, three and a half years after the CAR government itself formally referred the situation to the Prosecutor and almost six months after the Pre-Trial Chamber sought an explanation from the Prosecutor as to why he was taking so long: ICC, *Decision Requesting Information on the Status of the Preliminary Examination of the Situation in the Central African Republic*, Doc No ICC-01/05 (30 November 2006) < http://www.icc-cpi.int/iccdocs/doc/doc320175.PDF>.

[10] Rome Statute, Art 58(1).

[11] The Račak massacre occurred on 15 January 1999, the Rambouillet Conference took place between 6 February and 18 March 1999 and the NATO bombing campaign occurred between 24 March and 11 June 1999.

[12] From the edited text of a statement by Louise Arbour, 'The Indictment of Milošević' *The Guardian* (28 May 1999) <http://www.guardian.co.uk/world/1999/may/28/balkans6>.

NATO bombing campaigns, there was a perceived danger that the targeted suspects would be responsible for war crimes and crimes against humanity of a significantly greater scale, should the armed conflict continue unimpeded.

On 25 February 2011, the day before the Security Council's referral of the Libyan situation to the ICC, the UN Human Rights Council resolved to establish an international Commission of Inquiry to investigate human rights violations in Libya, and to 'establish the facts and circumstances of such violations and of the crimes perpetrated and where possible, to identify those responsible…'.[13] The Commission was appointed on 15 March, comprising Mahmoud Cherif Bassiouni (Chair), Asma Kahder and Philippe Kirsch.

The Commission of Inquiry reported back to the Human Rights Council on 1 June 2011 (hereafter referred to as the Commission's Report),[14] that is, two weeks after Moreno Ocampo's Application for Warrants was filed. The similarity of the mandates of the Prosecutor and the Commission of Inquiry, the coincidence of the time frame of their investigations and the Commissioners' international humanitarian law credentials (among their many accomplishments, Bassiouni was the Chair of the drafting Committee of the Rome Conference, and Kirsch was the first President of the ICC) are factors which naturally invite a comparison between the Commission's investigations and Report, and the Prosecutor's investigation and Application for Warrants.

In the same resolution as that authorising the establishment of the Commission of Inquiry, the Human Rights Council requested that the UN High Commissioner for Human Rights, Navi Pillay, 'provide all administrative, technical and logistical assistance required to enable the abovementioned Commission of Inquiry to fulfil its mandate' and submit a follow-up Report on the human rights situation in Libya.[15] This Report was submitted on 7 June 2011.[16]

---

13 *Situation of Human Rights in the Libyan Arab Jamahiriya*, UNHRC Res S-15/1, 15th sess, UN Doc A/HRC/S-15/1 (25 February 2011) ('UNHRC Res S-15/1').

14 Human Rights Council, *Report of the International Commission of Inquiry to Investigate All Alleged Violations of International Human Rights Law in the Libyan Arab Jamahiriya*, 17th sess, UN Doc A/HRC/17/44 (1 June 2011).

15 UNHRC Res S-15/1, above note 13, [12], [13].

16 Human Rights Council, *Report of the High Commissioner under Human Rights Council Resolution S-51/1*, 17th sess, UN Doc A/HRC/17/45 (7 June 2011) (High Commissioner's Follow-Up Report).

## III. INHERENT INVESTIGATIVE DIFFICULTIES OF THE LIBYAN ARMED CONFLICT

As noted earlier, the ICC Prosecutor must have the capability, including the expertise, to investigate alleged war crimes, crimes against humanity and genocide in a wide range of types of armed conflicts and civil unrest. Any trial arising from the Libyan situation would inevitably involve allegations of crimes committed in the course of armed conflict in key Libyan cities, that is, urban settings; the first armed conflict of this type to be investigated by the OTP. If the case proceeds to trial with elements to be proved by circumstantial (rather than direct) evidence of criminal culpability, a different set of investigative skills will be required from those employed in respect of the other conflicts that the OTP has investigated over the past eight years.

Arbour had the distinct advantage when investigating the Kosovo conflict that, typical of a conflict-specific ad hoc tribunal, her Office had been dealing exclusively with the broader Balkan conflicts for the six years since the ICTY's inception in 1993,[17] so that her investigators and lawyers had established networks and were familiar with the political, ethnic and military landscape. Moreno Ocampo, on the other hand, had no particular reason to turn his attention to Libya until a matter of weeks before the referral to him by the Security Council in early 2011, nor had his Office conducted a prior investigation in the North African region.

Central to a determination of whether crimes have been committed in armed conflict in an urban setting are the principles of distinction and proportionality. Both principles are norms of customary international law, applicable in both international and non-international armed conflicts.[18] The principle of distinction is the fundamental principle of international humanitarian law.[19] It is expressed in Art 48 of Additional Protocol I of the 1949 Geneva Conventions (AP I):

> In order to ensure respect for and protection of the civilian population and civilian objects, the Parties to the conflict shall at all times distinguish between

---

[17] SC Res 827, 3217th mtg, UN Doc S/RES/827 (1993) (25 May 1993).

[18] See, eg, Jean-Marie Henckaerts and Louise Doswald-Beck, *Customary International Humanitarian Law, Vol – 1 Rules* (Cambridge University Press 2005) 3 (Distinction), 46 (Proportionality).

[19] Ibid. The authors express the rule in customary international law as: 'The parties to the conflict must at all times distinguish between civilians and combatants. Attacks may only be directed against combatants. Attacks must not be directed against civilians.'

> the civilian population and combatants and between civilian objects and military objectives and accordingly shall direct their operations only against military objectives.

The principle of proportionality is reflected in AP I, Art 51.5 (b), which elaborates on what types of attacks are indiscriminate and therefore prohibited, pursuant to Art 49:

> an attack which may be expected to cause incidental loss of civilian life, injury to civilians, damage to civilian objects, or a combination thereof, which would be excessive in relation to the concrete and direct military advantage anticipated.

In the High Commissioner's Follow-Up Report, Pillay noted the relevance of these two principles to the legal framework within which the Libyan conflict is to be understood.[20]

A prosecution of crimes allegedly committed in the course of an armed conflict in an urban setting (that is, where there is some intermingling of military assets with civilians and civilian objects) is difficult, particularly where one or more of the protagonist forces is not uniformed. The Prosecutor must focus on incidents that are capable of proof beyond reasonable doubt[21] and not ones that may be clouded by reasonable exculpatory explanations arising from the circumstance of the mixed urban setting. For example, a prosecutor should not allege a breach of the principle of distinction where the evidence cannot exclude a reasonable possibility that the alleged perpetrator was unaware of a targeted victim's civilian status, and had reason to think the victim was a combatant. The same applies to an alleged breach of the principle of proportionality, where the prosecutor cannot exclude a reasonable possibility that an attack that generated civilian casualties was intended for a nearby legitimate military target, and despite reasonable inquiries the perpetrator may have been unaware of the civilians' close proximity or the disproportionately high number of civilians.

---

[20] High Commissioner's Follow-Up Report, above note 16. The general applicability of the principles was noted ('Libya's international human rights and international humanitarian law obligations both apply to the armed conflict that erupted in February/March 2011, including the principles of distinction and proportionality', at [19]), as well as specifically to rebel forces ('relevant rules of customary international humanitarian law apply to such non-State armed groups party to an armed conflict, including the principles of proportionality and distinction', at [20]) and to NATO forces ('relevant rules of customary international humanitarian law apply to NATO military operations carried out in the armed conflict, including the principles of proportionality and distinction', at [21]).

[21] Rome Statute, Art 66.3: 'In order to convict the accused, the Court must be convinced of the guilt of the accused beyond reasonable doubt.'

At his news conference on the day his Application for Warrants was filed, Moreno Ocampo reportedly said his Office had not taken accounts from witnesses inside the country because their safety would thereby be endangered, but nevertheless said: 'We're almost ready for trial'.[22] If Moreno Ocampo was correctly reported, a statement that he considered his Office to be virtually trial-ready without having visited the crime scenes is troubling. There is no substitute for investigators and prosecuting lawyers visiting crime scenes and interviewing local witnesses in situ, pointing out where they were at relevant times, and so on.

Where it is alleged that crimes have been committed in an urban armed conflict, close familiarity with crime scenes and on-site witness interviews are pre-requisites to trial readiness. When Arbour's investigators and lawyers gained access to Kosovo in June 1999, even though her indictment was confirmed, there remained considerable work to be done there (visiting crime scenes, gathering evidence and interviewing witnesses), before her Office was trial-ready. In the author's experience as a Senior Trial Attorney with the OTP in the ICTY, interviewing witnesses at crime scenes can prompt a radical rethink on what can, and cannot, be proved in court.

The Prosecutor's approach contrasts with that taken by the Commission of Inquiry. The Commission's staff conducted Libyan field missions, meeting with dozens of individuals and making '[s]ite visits to specific locations where incidents had occurred. In this respect, the Commission was able to visit some sites in Benghazi and Tripoli, though its access was limited due to the ongoing armed conflict.'[23] This difference in investigative approach between the OTP and UN Human Rights organs, or Commissions of Inquiry, over the issue of witness safety and the need to gather the best evidence on the ground, is not without precedent.

Following the referral by the Security Council of the Darfur situation to the ICC in March 2005, the Prosecutor made six-monthly progress reports to the Security Council, in which he noted he was not carrying out

---

22 Marlise Simons, 'International Court Seeks Warrant for Gaddafi' *New York Times* (New York, 16 May 2011): 'At a news conference at The Hague, the prosecutor hinted that he had received intelligence from other governments, from Libyans outside the country and recently from "a lot of phone calls from inside Libya," but he said his Office was not taking evidence from witnesses inside the country "because they can be killed." There was so much evidence, Mr Moreno Ocampo said, that "we're almost ready for trial."'

23 Commission's Report, above note 14, 16 [8(a)], [(c)]. The Commission also studied 'more than 5,000 pages of documents, more than 580 videos and over 2,200 photographs', at 16 [9]. As of 26 April 2011, the ICC OTP had viewed more than 569 documents, videos and pictures: Prosecutor's First Report to the UNSC, above note 6, 5 [30].

investigations in Darfur itself, out of concern that interviewed witnesses would be placed in jeopardy.[24] The Pre-Trial Chamber was unimpressed and on 27 July 2006 took the extraordinary step of requesting Arbour, by then the UN High Commissioner for Human Rights, and the former ICTY President, Antonio Cassese (who was also the Chair of the International Commission of Inquiry on Darfur), to 'submit in writing their observations on issues concerning the protection of victims and the preservation of evidence in Darfur, Sudan … '.[25]

Neither Arbour[26] nor Cassese[27] considered the Prosecutor's concerns to be a reasonable basis for not having investigators on the ground in Darfur.

---

[24] In his first report (Luis Moreno Ocampo, 'First Report of the Prosecutor to the UNSC Pursuant to UNSC 1593 (2005)' (Report, ICC, 29 June 2005)), the Prosecutor confirmed he had commenced investigations and explained what preliminary steps he had taken. In his second report, nine months after the referral, he said: 'the establishment of an effective system for protection of victims and witnesses is a precondition to the conduct of investigative activities in Darfur … ' and accordingly 'investigation activities have so far taken place outside Darfur' (Luis Moreno Ocampo, 'Second Report of the Prosecutor to the UNSC Pursuant to UNSC 1593 (2005)' (Report, ICC, 13 December 2005) 4). In his third report (Luis Moreno Ocampo, 'Third Report of the Prosecutor to the UNSC Pursuant to UNSC 1593 (2005)' (Report, ICC, 14 June 2006) 1), he said much the same: 'the continuing insecurity in Darfur is prohibitive of effective investigations inside Darfur, particularly in light of the absence of a functioning and sustainable system for the protection of victims and witnesses … '.

[25] ICC, *Decision Inviting Observations In Application of Rule 103 of the Rules of Procedure and Evidence*, Doc No ICC-02/05–10 (24 July 2006) 5 <http://www.iclklamberg.com/Caselaw/Sudan/PTCI/ICC-02–05–10_English.pdf>.

[26] ICC, *Observations of the United Nations High Commissioner for Human Rights Invited in Application of Rule 103 of the Rules of Procedure and Evidence*, Doc No ICC-02/05 (10 October 2006) <http://www.icc-cpi.int/iccdocs/doc/doc259768.PDF> ('*Observations of the UNHCHR*'). '[I]n the High Commissioner's view … it is possible to conduct investigations of human rights violations during an armed conflict in general, and in Darfur in particular, without putting victims at unreasonable risk', at 21.

[27] ICC, *Observations on Issues Concerning the Protection of Victims and the Preservation of Evidence in the Proceedings on Darfur Pending before the ICC*, Doc No ICC-02/05–14 (25 August 2006) 5 <http://icc-cpi.int/iccdocs/doc/doc259762.PDF>. Cassese proposed that interviews could occur in the capital cities of Darfur: 'large-scale and lengthy investigations … could easily be imperilled by ongoing fighting. In contrast, undertaking *targeted and brief interviews* of victims and witnesses in the capital cities of the three states of Darfur … could prove to be safe.' Cassese also set out detailed strategies to minimise the possibility of contamination of oral testimonies by the early taking of evidence in the Court, at 6.5, 11.

Both Arbour's Office and the Commission of Inquiry had firsthand experience of their staff taking witness accounts in Darfur. Arbour argued that there was no evidence that her staff's interactions had placed the victims at a significantly greater exposure to risk of harm than their interacting with other international actors, such as relief workers and medical personnel.[28] She claimed that:

> carefully tailored strategies can operate effectively to conduct investigations. The International Criminal Court's presence on the ground would also importantly contribute, among other international deployments in the country, to a proactive presence increasing the level of protection perceived and enjoyed by the affected population.[29]

## IV. THE SIGNIFICANCE OF DIRECT EVIDENCE

Both the Commission's Report and the Prosecutor's Application for Warrants conclude that there is evidence that war crimes and crimes against humanity were committed in Libya by government forces,[30] but they differ as to whether the evidence (available to them at that time) is sufficient to establish the identity of the high-level perpetrators, that is, those who commissioned the crimes.

At this stage, one cannot analyse the sufficiency of the material on which the Prosecutor sought the warrants because the 54-page summary of the 'evidence and other information' relied upon by the Prosecutor to establish reasonable grounds for belief that the three accused committed the crimes, has been redacted from the public version. Some cursory references in the Application for Warrants to the alleged crimes remain, to the effect that the killings were allegedly carried out by firing on civilians (including those

---

[28] *Observations of the UNHCHR*, above note 26: 'Generally speaking, the risk of reprisal to victims is an inevitable factor to take into consideration for all international actors working in tense environments, and most acutely in a situation of war. From the documentation of such reprisals in Darfur, it does not appear that risks for victims are higher in relation to their interaction with human rights investigators. As has been observed above, civilians in Darfur face retaliation for interacting with very diverse international actors, including relief workers and medical personnel, and the number of documented cases linked to human rights investigators is remarkably low', at 22 [64].

[29] *Observations of the UNHCHR*, above note 26, 2.

[30] Commission's Report, above note 14, 81 [257], [258]; *Situation in the Libyan Arab Jamahiriya (Prosecutor's Application Pursuant to Article 58 as to Muammar Mohammed Abu Minyar GADDAFI, Saif Al-Islam GADDAFI and Abdullah AL-SENSUSSI)* (ICC, Pre-Trial Chamber I, Case No ICC-01/11, 16 May 2011).

demonstrating against the Gaddafi regime and at funerals),[31] that assets used in the attacks were machine guns,[32] 'heavy weaponry'[33] and snipers who targeted civilians leaving mosques,[34] and that civilians and journalists were detained, tortured and subjected to inhuman acts.[35]

The Pre-Trial Chamber granted the warrants sought.[36] Some additional information as to the acts relied upon by the Prosecutor may be gleaned from the Pre-Trial Chamber's response to the Prosecutor's Application. The Pre-Trial Chamber noted that the latest date of the underlying acts detailed in the redacted portion of the Prosecutor's Application for Warrants allegedly occurred on 28 February, so that the alleged crimes all occurred within a two-week window from 15 February.[37]

Whereas the Prosecutor's redacted Application for Warrants is somewhat rhetorical in style, the Commission's Report is measured, analytical, technical and, in its own words, 'cautious'.[38] The Commission counselled the need for further investigation, concluding that it was not, at that stage, 'in a position to identify those responsible, as requested by the Human Rights Council in the resolution establishing its mandate'.[39] In relation to crimes committed in Misrata for example, the Commission stated:

---

[31] *Situation in the Libyan Arab Jamahiriya (Prosecutor's Application Pursuant to Article 58 as to Muammar Mohammed Abu Minyar GADDAFI, Saif Al-Islam GADDAFI and Abdullah AL-SENSUSSI)* (ICC, Pre-Trial Chamber I, Case No ICC-01/11, 16 May 2011) [2], [12] (demonstrators); [14], [15] (funerals).

[32] Ibid [12].

[33] Ibid [14].

[34] Ibid [20].

[35] Ibid [27], [30], [32], [33], [34].

[36] *Situation in the Libyan Arab Jamahiriya (Decision on the "Prosecutor's Application Pursuant to Article 58 as to Muammar Mohammed Abu Minyar GADDAFI, Saif Al-Islam GADDAFI and Abdullah AL-SENSUSSI")* (ICC, Pre-Trial Chamber I, Case No ICC-01/11, 27 June 2011).

[37] Ibid [7]. *Situation in the Libyan Arab Jamahiriya (Prosecutor's Application Pursuant to Article 58 as to Muammar Mohammed Abu Minyar GADDAFI, Saif Al-Islam GADDAFI and Abdullah AL-SENSUSSI)* (ICC, Pre-Trial Chamber I, Case No ICC-01/11, 16 May 2011), refers to crimes committed from 15 February, conformably with the terms of the Security Council's Resolution.

[38] Commission's Report, above note 14, 2: 'The quality of the evidence and the information obtained by the Commission varied in its accuracy and reliability. The Commission opted for a cautious approach in the present report by consistently referring to the information obtained as being distinguishable from evidence that could be used in criminal proceedings, whether national or international. It was also careful to make a distinction between information and reports received and testimony it heard first-hand, as well as facts that it observed first-hand.'

[39] Ibid 8.

> In many of the cases, while the Commission was able to establish that many civilians (including children) have been killed or injured, the Commission was not able to determine the full circumstances of the attacks in order to be able to evaluate whether the attacks were intentional, indiscriminate and/or disproportionate.[40]

The Commission was similarly circumspect as to whether there was generally sufficient evidence to conclude confidently that Gaddafi and his senior subordinates were high-level perpetrators:

> The consistency of patterns of violations creates an inference that they were carried out as a result of policy decisions by Colonel Qadhafi and senior leadership. Further investigation is required in relation to making definitive findings in relation to the identity of those responsible for the crimes committed. The Commission has received some information concerning individual perpetrators of crimes, but on this topic more investigation is also required.[41]

Of course the Commission did not necessarily have access to the same material as did the Prosecutor; the Commission's Report noted that, although there were consultations between the two bodies, 'the Commission and the ICC have been committed to respecting appropriate confidentiality and independence requirements of each body'.[42] This may explain why the Prosecutor, but not the Commission, was able to identify those responsible and with sufficient confidence to seek warrants for their arrest and trial.

Moreno Ocampo suggested he had evidence directly connecting the suspects with the crimes. In his Application for Warrants, Moreno Ocampo stated he had 'direct evidence of the plan to use extreme and lethal violence'.[43] In his press conference the same day, he said: 'The Office was able to gather direct evidence about orders issued by Muammar Gaddafi himself.'[44]

---

40 Ibid 57 [166].

41 Ibid 82 [260].

42 Ibid 17 [18].

43 *Situation in the Libyan Arab Jamahiriya (Prosecutor's Application Pursuant to Article 58 as to Muammar Mohammed Abu Minyar GADDAFI, Saif Al-Islam GADDAFI and Abdullah AL-SENSUSSI)* (ICC, Pre-Trial Chamber I, Case No ICC-01/11, 16 May 2011) [12].

44 Luis Moreno Ocampo, 'International Criminal Court Prosecutor Accuses Gaddafi of Crimes against Humanity' (Press Conference, 16 May 2011) <http://www.guardian.co.uk/law/video/2011/may/16/international-criminal-court-gaddafi-video>.

There have been media reports that the Prosecutor's Office had access to defectors from the Libyan government,[45] so this 'direct evidence' could include (what is sometimes called in international tribunals) 'insider' evidence; in this case, high-level defectors from the Gaddafi regime who are cooperating with the OTP and who witnessed the issuing of unlawful commands by Gaddafi and the other two indictees. Any such evidence is often open to attack by the defence as self-serving, motivated by a desire by senior officials to save their own skins, and therefore inherently unreliable.

Documentary evidence of actual orders issued by Gaddafi would seem to be unlikely, since in his Application for Warrants Moreno Ocampo stated:

> Gaddafi transmits his orders orally either directly or through the Secretariat or Registry, also known as [the] Information Bureau of the Leader; he does not want to leave any written trace of his actions and he closely follows up on the implementation of his orders.[46]

The Commission's Report also concluded that Gaddafi preferred giving orders orally, relying on telecommunications:

> Orders appear to be given by Colonel Gaddafi through satellite phone calls to commanders. It is also likely that some orders may have been issued by SMS but it is mostly personal communication based in voice recognition. This makes more difficult the task of tracing orders and commands.[47]

In his press conference, Moreno Ocampo did not elaborate on the form or sources of this evidence, but was reported as saying that he had 'received intelligence from other governments'.[48] If he has telecommunications intercepts yielding voice recordings of Gaddafi personally issuing such orders, that would be high-quality evidence indeed.

Regardless of the strength of any direct evidence, there will remain an evidentiary need to prove that civilians were in fact killed or wounded by Gaddafi's subordinates consequent to those orders, and that the attacks were widespread or systematic and 'in furtherance of a State or organizational

---

45 Simons, above note 22: 'Investigators for the prosecution have conducted their interviews in a dozen countries and have had access to defectors from the Libyan government, according to the prosecutor's office.'

46 *Situation in the Libyan Arab Jamahiriya (Prosecutor's Application Pursuant to Article 58 as to Muammar Mohammed Abu Minyar GADDAFI, Saif Al-Islam GADDAFI and Abdullah AL-SENSUSSI)* (ICC, Pre-Trial Chamber I, Case No ICC-01/11, 16 May 2011) [7].

47 Commission's Report, above note 14, 28 [54].

48 Simons, above note 22.

policy to commit such attack'.[49] For these reasons, the OTP will need to investigate and call on evidence of specific killings and of the scale of civilian killings generally, that can be conservatively attributed to unlawful acts of which the three accused were the high-level perpetrators, as opposed to killings that were incidental to legitimate attacks on military targets (the principle of distinction) and proportionate to anticipated military gains (the principle of proportionality).

Moreno Ocampo alluded to as much in his Application for Warrants, stating that the 'direct evidence … is corroborated by the scale, scope and duration of the attacks, [and] the pattern of the attacks in various cities … '.[50] However, he also foreshadowed a difficulty in establishing the scale of the alleged crimes, citing an extended cover-up operation by the Security Forces such that the total number of incidents and ensuing casualties remain undetermined. This cover-up involved disrupting communications; confiscating cameras, memory cards and computer and internet devices so as to prevent the dissemination of images; forbidding medical services from attending to the injured; detaining wounded demonstrators; and hiding bodies of killed demonstrators, including exhuming bodies from cemeteries and other burial sites and secreting them.[51]

## V. SIMILARITIES WITH THE ICTY CASES OF STANISLAV GALIĆ AND DRAGOMIR MILOŠEVIĆ

There are marked similarities between the Libyan situation and the ICTY investigation (and evidence in the subsequent trials) of Generals Stanislav Galić and Dragomir Milošević, concerning the siege of Sarajevo. From September 1992, General Galić commanded the 18,000 Bosnian-Serb forces that besieged Sarajevo, targeting civilians with snipers and shelling. When he was relieved of his command in August 1994, he was replaced with General Dragomir Milošević, who continued the campaign until the end of the conflict in December 1995, with the Dayton accords.

The trials also involved a close focus on the principles of proportionality and distinction (the first international criminal trial to do so); an intermingling of military assets with a civilian population, including one side

[49] Rome Statute, Art 2(a).

[50] *Situation in the Libyan Arab Jamahiriya (Prosecutor's Application Pursuant to Article 58 as to Muammar Mohammed Abu Minyar GADDAFI, Saif Al-Islam GADDAFI and Abdullah AL-SENSUSSI)* (ICC, Pre-Trial Chamber I, Case No ICC-01/11, 16 May 2011) [12].

[51] Ibid [28].

deploying non-uniformed forces in a civilian setting. There is also a strong similarity between the military tactics used: the besieging of a city (Misrata and Sarajevo, both at the relevant time having similar populations of around 300–340,000 inhabitants);[52] the infliction of terror by the deliberate sniping and indiscriminate shelling of a civilian population as a means of forcing capitulation, down to the chilling parallels of targeting funerals,[53] ambulances[54] and hospitals;[55] and using anti-aircraft[56] and area weaponry (that is, weapons with a large casualty zone, such as mortars and multiple rocket launchers).

## A. The Absence of the War Crime of Terror from the Rome Statute

The evidence of the infliction of terror was the basis for a specific charge in the *Galić* case; the war crime of Terror against a Civilian Population, pursuant to Art 51 of AP I and Art 13 of Additional Protocol II (AP II),[57] punishable under Art 3 of the Rome Statute. While Crimes against Humanity charges captured the criminality of the physical campaign of sniping and shelling civilians, the terror count reflected the criminality encapsulated in the campaign's primary objective, which was the terrorising of the 340,000 civilian inhabitants of the city.

---

52 Population of Sarajevo: *Prosecutor v Galić* (*Judgment and Opinion*) (ICTY, Trial Chamber I, Case No IT-98–29-T, 5 December 2003) Trial Exhibit P3731; *Expert Report of Ewa Tabeau*, [9]. The population of Misrata: see High Commissioner's Follow-Up Report, above note 16, [42].

53 *Situation in the Libyan Arab Jamahiriya (Prosecutor's Application Pursuant to Article 58 as to Muammar Mohammed Abu Minyar GADDAFI, Saif Al-Islam GADDAFI and Abdullah AL-SENSUSSI)* (ICC, Pre-Trial Chamber I, Case No ICC-01/11, 16 May 2011) [14], [15]; *Prosecutor v Galić* (*Judgment and Opinion*) (ICTY, Trial Chamber I, Case No IT-98–29-T, 5 December 2003) [584].

54 Commission's Report, above note 14, 60 [174]–[176]; *Prosecutor v Galić* (*Judgment and Opinion*) (ICTY, Trial Chamber I, Case No IT-98–29-T, 5 December 2003) [584].

55 Commission's Report, above note 14, 81 [258]; *Prosecutor v Galić* (*Judgment and Opinion*) (ICTY, Trial Chamber I, Case No IT-98–29-T, 5 December 2003) [584].

56 Commission's Report, above note 14, 39 [95], 40 [97]; *Prosecutor v Galić* (*Judgment and Opinion*) (ICTY, Trial Chamber I, Case No IT-98–29-T, 5 December 2003) [244].

57 Article 51(2) of AP I and Article 13(2) of AP II are in identical terms: 'Protection of the civilian population 2. The civilian population as such, as well as individual civilians, shall not be the object of attack. Acts or threats of violence the primary purpose of which is to spread terror among the civilian population are prohibited.'

However, Terror is not a war crime in the Rome Statute, nor are offences under APs I and II. This forms a significant gap in the Rome Statute's catalogue of crimes and in the Court's subsequent jurisdiction. Media reports and graphic amateur video, accessible on the web, suggest that the war crime of Terror against a Civilian Population, by the use of snipers on civilian gatherings, was not only perpetrated in Libya, but also in various states across North Africa and the Middle East in the recent armed conflicts. There have been credible media reports of what appear to be professional snipers targeting civilians in peaceful gatherings in Egypt, Syria, Bahrain and Yemen, with the apparent objective of discouraging others from assembling against the government.

One can perhaps now conclude that it is a tactic which is likely to continue to feature in the suppression of popular uprisings against brutal regimes. This widespread resort by pro-government forces in various states to sniping and shelling so as to inculcate civilian terror, underscores the need for the ICC to have jurisdiction to prosecute this serious crime and to deter its use in future conflicts in so doing.

### B. The *Galić* Photographic Technique

A central challenge to the long-term feasibility of international criminal justice is the cost and protracted length of trials, including pre-trial detention. It is essential that technology is used, where possible, to minimise these factors. The author was involved in developing a simple and inexpensive technique in the *Galić* case that has since been used in many other trials in the ICTY and in ICC investigations. It is of particular use in a trial involving an armed conflict in an urban setting, where the source of sniper or direct shell-fire is a factual issue.

The *Galić* trial[58] was one of the most technically difficult ICTY prosecutions, for two reasons. Firstly, there was the sheer volume, and conflicting nature, of evidence in a largely circumstantial case, extending over Galić's two-year period of command. Thirty-two specific sniping and shelling incidents were scheduled in the indictment, each requiring separate proof in order to illustrate the alleged campaign of the sniping and shelling of civilians. Considerable complex technical evidence was presented in order to establish the source of fire of bullets, artillery and mortar shells, as well as

---

[58] *Prosecutor v Galić* (*Judgment and Opinion*) (ICTY, Trial Chamber I, Case No IT-98–29-T, 5 December 2003). The trial commenced within two years of arrest and the evidence was completed in 17 months (223 court days). The Prosecution examined 380,000 documents (over 2.5 million pages) and over 3,000 were disclosed, at [799].

extensive demographic statistical evidence used to establish conservative minimum numbers of civilians deliberately killed or seriously wounded.

Secondly, within the besieged territory of Sarajevo there were numerous legitimate military targets (there were some 75,000 combatants defending the city),[59] so that some civilian deaths and injuries were inevitably incidental to legitimate attacks, rather than being intended casualties. There was also credible evidence of rogue paramilitary units on either side of the confrontation lines that may have targeted civilians for their own purposes,[60] all of which the Prosecution had to deal with in order to establish the accused's guilt.

The objective of the new technique was to familiarise the Court with specific sniping crime scenes where a view by the Trial Chamber might not occur (as indeed was the case), and to eliminate the possibility that sniping victims could not have been sighted from territory controlled by the accused's subordinate armed forces. A witness (whether a surviving victim or an eye-witness of the shooting) would be videoed identifying the precise position where the victim was shot. A 360° photograph would then be taken from that marked position, which witnesses, counsel and the judges could manipulate on a computer screen by panning and zooming in or out of the image. Defence counsel accepted an invitation to attend the filming of some of the incidents. The witness would be called at trial and would testify on oath that what he or she could be observed to be doing and saying on the video was truthful. Other evidence established which positions visible on the 360° photograph were held by the accused's subordinate forces and were known sources of sniper fire.[61]

This technique has the value of preserving images of crime scenes while the memory of witnesses is fresh and before post-conflict reconstruction changes the lines of sight from key military positions. It is a relatively inexpensive technique, requiring not much more equipment than two home video cameras, a GPS unit and a tripod with a panoramic head. It is simple to learn and capable of being used by investigators themselves in the field.

---

[59] Ibid [244] (regarding paramilitaries on the Bosnian Serb side), [507] (regarding paramilitaries on the Presidency (ABiH) side within the confrontation lines).

[60] Ibid [655]–[657].

[61] Defence counsel accepted an invitation to attend a number of these recordings. The tendered video included an observed GPS marking (the GPS unit was held up to the video camera to record the coordinates), so that the precise position could be re-established by the defence, or by the judges on a site visit, if required. The participating witnesses were subsequently called at trial, affirmed that their answers and actions recorded on the video were truthful, and on that basis the video and photographic images were tendered.

## VI. CONCLUSION

The similarities between the Libyan situation and the ICTY Sarajevo cases are a reminder that it is important, wherever possible, to avoid reinventing the wheel; although the mission of each tribunal is markedly different from the others, all ultimately exist to serve the common cause of international criminal justice. We are in the relative infancy of developing international jurisprudence and establishing standards of best practice in a range of trial-associated skills, and for one tribunal not to exploit the experience of other tribunals seems counter-productive to our shared goal.

In a major step towards the dissemination of such material, in May 2009, the ICTY and the UN Interregional Crime and Justice Research Institute (UNICRI), published the *ICTY Manual on Developed Practices*.[62] This document impressively sets out a blueprint of many aspects of ICTY procedure, including that of the OTP. It contributes towards a culture of communication between investigators, lawyers and others who have worked for the various ad hoc tribunals over the last 18 years, in such a way that their experience in particular types of investigations can be tapped for guidance as to which techniques and strategies did or did not work. It is important for the future of international criminal justice that we continue to develop forms of sharing relevant investigative and trial procedural experience.

---

[62] ICTY and UNICRI, *ICTY Manual on Developed Practices* (UNICRI Publisher 2009).

# 6. International criminal justice and the past

**Gerry Simpson**

> The theory of the transference of the collective will of the people to historical persons may perhaps explain much in the domain of jurisprudence and be essential for its purposes, but in its application to history, as soon as revolutions, conquests or civil wars occur – that is, as soon as history begins – that theory explains nothing.[1]

## I. INTRODUCTION

This chapter examines whether Leo Tolstoy's 'domain of jurisprudence' – in the present case, international criminal justice – has a theory of history at all (albeit sublimated) and whether that theory of history can (or should) explain why or how certain events occur.[2] This problem of history returns us to a moment in the institutional development of international criminal law written about previously by the author, and viewed by him as the field's modern origin: such as the meetings of a commission of legal experts (including Robert Lansing, Ernest Pollock and James Brown Scott) convened by the delegates to the Versailles Peace Treaty at the end of the First World War.[3] It was here for the first time that lawyer-internationalists had to grapple with the tension sketched by Tolstoy half a century earlier.

In 1919, a committee was established at the Versailles Peace Conference to look into the question of war crimes trials for the defeated German elite (including the Kaiser). This represents the first occasion in international

[1] Leo Tolstoy, *War and Peace* (first published 1865–69, Oxford Classics 1998) 1282.

[2] Some of the research for this paper was undertaken by Monique Cormier, an ARC Research Fellow participating in a larger project tentatively entitled *Invoking Humanity: A History of War Crimes*. This is a modified version of a chapter of a book on the law and literature of war currently being written as part of this project.

[3] Gerry Simpson, *Law, War and Crime* (Polity Press 2007).

history when there was a somewhat methodical, official statement and interrogation of what would become some of the central problems in the field.[4] This committee laboured under a curious but revealing title: The Commission on the Responsibilities of the Authors of the War. Their deliberations turned out to be more contentious than the Versailles statesmen might have anticipated. In effect, the Commission began to enact a series of distinctively twentieth century debates between opposing views of history. In one instance, it was the relationship between a belief that history is found or discovered (through archival zealotry, analytical precision or empirical doggedness) on the one hand, and on the other, the view that history is invented or imagined (through literary device, political decision or methodological preference) in a response to what Hayden White calls the 'inexpungeable relativity' of historical representations.[5]

Another historiographical dispute, and one on which this chapter focuses, involved the nature of historical agency. Here, the Commission began to wrestle with the title it had been given (and the first of its tasks) and the whole idea of 'authorship'. In what sense is history or war authored? And who authors it? Or is 'authorship' the wrong metaphor? Of course, this was not just a struggle over metaphor. The debate over the authorship of war, or what we now call the crime of aggression, has continued to this day.

As such, this chapter will hope to tease out some of these problems of history, which turn out also to be problems of law. These dilemmas can be avoided of course, but the consequences tend to be ideological blindness or doctrinal aridity. Better to choose the approach of Nicolas Polites and James Brown Scott at Versailles or Justices Pal and Röling in Tokyo and work out the conceptual underpinnings of what one is trying to do.

---

[4] 'Commission on the Responsibility of the Authors of the War and on Enforcement of Penalties –Report Presented to the Preliminary Peace Conference' (1920) 14(1) American Journal of International Law 95 ('Commission Report'). The dilemmas faced or identified in 1919 were to repeat themselves throughout the modern history of war crimes. The reservations expressed in the Japanese and American dissenting memoranda were to form the basis of the arguments made by the defence at Nuremberg and Tokyo (and by many of Nuremberg's critics). Meanwhile, the American position at Versailles (cautious, sceptical, legalistic and self-interested) was to be repeated in 1998 and subsequently, when the US reverted to its pre-Nuremberg anxiety about international criminal law.

[5] See Hayden White, *Tropics of Discourse – Essays in Cultural Criticism* (John Hopkins University Press 1978) discussed in Keith Jenkins, *Why History* (Routledge 1999) 95.

## II. COHERENCE

Before elaborating a little on this, it is worth exploring how this question of authorship might intersect with larger questions of coherence and legitimacy pursued by others writing in this volume. The problems of coherence and legitimacy tend to dog even the most well-established fields of study or social practices. Indeed, a fully coherent theory of politics or a maximally or comprehensively legitimate form of politics will tend towards totalitarianism. This accounts for the resistance, on the part of critical theorists, to grand theorising; it may even be the distinguishing feature of critical thought.[6] On the other hand, Ronald Dworkin and John Rawls have generated a whole tradition of liberal thinking around such theories, and Thomas Franck has argued for a form of legitimacy in international law, a central idea of which would be the need for 'coherence' among the norms that constitute the system.[7] But is a coherent system of rules actually possible or even desirable?

One way into this debate is via the recent discussions about 'fragmentation' in the international system: broadly speaking, the idea that in an increasingly elaborate international legal order, with a proliferation of institutional structures and sub-structures, there will be a degree of overlap, perhaps outright contradiction. The astonishing increase in the number of judicial bodies alone leads one to wonder where the authoritative pronouncement on, say, whaling, might be found: the Hamburg Tribunal, the International Court of Justice (ICJ), or the States Parties to the Whaling Convention?[8] Some important work has been completed on this topic already, notably the *ILC Fragmentation Report* and the varied academic

---

[6] See, eg, Terry Eagleton's superb essay discussing a biography of Adorno by Detlev Claussen: Terry Eagleton, 'Determinacy Kills' (2008) 30(12) *London Review of Books* 9.

[7] See generally, Ronald Dworkin, *Taking Rights Seriously* (Harvard University Press 1978); Ronald Dworkin, *Law's Empire* (Harvard University Press 1968); John Rawls, *Political Liberalism* (Columbia University Press 1993); John Rawls, *The Law of Peoples* (Harvard University Press 1999); Thomas Franck, *The Power of Legitimacy among Nations* (Oxford University Press 1990).

[8] This precisely is a problem encountered in the dispute between the UK and Ireland over the MOX nuclear processing plant at Sellafield in Northern England. This dispute implicates three quite distinct functional regimes: *The Law of the Sea Convention* Annex VII (the establishment of the Hamburg Tribunal), *The Treaty on European Union* and *The Treaty Establishing the European Atomic Energy Community* (Euratom) and a *North Atlantic Protection of Marine Life Treaty* (OSPAR Treaty).

commentaries that accompanied it.[9] The most recent major study is Dr Margaret Young's new book on the interaction of regimes.[10]

In international criminal justice we have encountered fragmentation and conflict, both at the normative and institutional level. The ICJ and the International Criminal Tribunal for the former Yugoslavia (ICTY) heard cases simultaneously on the question of genocide in Bosnia: the ICC engaging with questions of state responsibility, while the ICTY raised questions of international criminal responsibility.[11] It is not inconceivable that we might have ended up with two judicial decisions: one finding that Slobodan Milošević was individually responsible for the crime of genocide, the other holding the Serbian State bore no direct responsibility for committing the crime of genocide in Bosnia (which was indeed the decision reached at the ICJ).[12] A version of this problem arose in the very first case heard by the ICTY. In *Tadić*, the Tribunal, in assessing when an outside power becomes responsible for the activities of rebels that it supports, rejected the 'effective control' standard enunciated by the ICJ in *Nicaragua* and sought to replace it with a more flexible 'overall control' test.[13]

---

9 Martii Koskenenniemi, *Report of the Study Group of the International Law Commission – Fragmentation of International Law: Difficulties arising from the Diversification and Expansion of International Law,* UN Doc A/CN.4/L.682 (13 April 2006) ('*ILC Fragmentation Report*'). See, eg, Christian Leathley, 'An Institutional Hierarchy to Combat the Fragmentation of International Law: Has the IC Missed an Opportunity?' (2007) 40 *New York University Journal of International Law and Politics* 259; Sahib Singh, 'The Potential of International Law: Fragmentation and Ethics' (2011) 24 *Leiden Journal of International Law* 23. '[L]aw-making treaties are tending to develop in a number of historical, functional, and regional groups which are separate from each other and whose mutual relationships are in some respects analogous to those of separate systems of municipal law': Wilfred Jenks, quoted in the *ILC Fragmentation Report*, UN Doc A/CN.4/L.682.

10 Margaret Young, *Trading Fish, Saving Fish: The Interaction of Regimes in International Law* (Cambridge 2011).

11 The author discusses this further in his book: Simpson, above note 3, Chapter 3.

12 See *Prosecutor v Slobodan Milošević (Amended Indictment)* (ICTY, Case No IT-02–54-T, 22 November 2002); *Application of the Convention on the Prevention and Punishment of the Crime of Genocide (Bosnia and Herzegovina v Serbia and Montenegro) (Judgment)* [2007] ICJ Rep 43.

13 *Prosecutor v Dusko Tadić (Judgment)* (ICTY, Appeals Chamber, Case No IT-94–1-A, 15 July 1999) [115]–[162] (*Tadić*); *Military and Paramilitary Activities in and Against Nicaragua (Nicaragua v United States of America) (Judgment)* [1986] ICJ Rep 14 (*Nicaragua*).

One answer to this problem is to bemoan the absence of coherence (or worry about legal inequality and/or unpredictability) and insist that institutional or judicial pronouncements be brought into conformity with each other: either through institutional or normative hierarchy, or horizontal judicial deference. The other is to welcome fragmentation as a sign of increasing sophistication.

International criminal justice seems poised between the two, and this may reflect the lawyer's inbuilt preference for uniformity (or generality and consistency) on one hand, and fierce professional independence and sense of institutional autonomy on the other.

## III. DOING HISTORY

Arthur Koetsler once said in a striking phrase: 'But who will be proved right? It will only be known later.'[14] This reminds us of Chou-En Lai's famous comment in 1972 that it was far too early to tell what would be the likely effects of the French Revolution.[15] Yet international criminal law attempts to do a very difficult thing – to fix contemporary history. This is a huge undertaking, and international criminal tribunals have already played a major role in establishing the parameters of official history. Of course, the history of the Holocaust is partly defined by Raul Hilberg and Primo Levi but it is also a product of a peculiar moment of innovation at Nuremberg.[16] In a similar vein, the history of the Balkans is part Misha Glenny, part ICTY.[17]

The question of whether international criminal justice *should* do this has been thoroughly ventilated in Philip Roth's *Operation Shylock*, about the first *Demjanjuk* trial, in Laurence Douglas's *Memory of Judgement* and in David Hirsch's *Cosmopolitan Justice*.[18] Hannah Arendt worried in *Eichmann in Jerusalem* that history was likely to deform law, that didactic

---

[14] A Koestler, *Darkness at Noon* (Penguin Books 1946) 99.

[15] Quoted in Simon Schama, *Citizens: A Chronicle of the French Revolution* (1st edn, Vintage 1990) 1.

[16] Raul Hilberg, *The Destruction of the European Jews* (3rd edn, Yale University Press 2003); Primo Levi, *If This is a Man* and *The Truce* (Stuart Woolf tr, Abacus by Sphere Books 1987).

[17] Misha Glenny, *The Balkans, 1804–1999: Nationalism, War and the Great Powers* (Granta 1999).

[18] *State of Israel v Demjanjuk* [1988] CrimA(Jer) 347/88; on 12 May 2011, the Munich District Court found Demjanjuk guilty of 29,000 counts of accessory to murder at Sobibor camp; Philip Roth, *Operation Shylock – A Confession* (Simon &

jurisprudence was a contradiction, and that telling a story was bound to interfere with larger purposes of giving the accused a fair trial.[19] So, in *Eichmann* there is a sense (recognised by the judges, who tried to limit this tendency) that the trial was the story of the Holocaust, a history lesson for the edification of the Israeli State and the global community (and this recalls Guyora Binder's comment that we must avoid finding war crimes trials edifying).[20] Certainly, we now know that there is a balance to be struck between history and law, between extraneous evidence and best evidence, and between context and act; but that balance is not the subject of this chapter.

So, the larger question is not whether to make history but rather what sort of histories to make, or what sorts of histories are made by international criminal tribunals. Are methodological preferences built into the project of international criminal justice (such as an overvaluing of traditional linear narratives over fragmentary social histories)? Or ideological biases (a preference perhaps for histories that reflect well on liberal values of multiculturalism over the regressive tendencies of nation, *ethnie*, or religion)? Or more transparently political biases (a tendency to write histories that somehow accord with the political requirements of the Great Powers)? There is a great deal to debate here. For the time being, this chapter will attend to three aspects of the problem of history. First, a discussion on the 'subjects' of history (focusing on Versailles): is international criminal justice committed to an idea about individual agency in history, and is this idea defensible? Second, some reflections on the relationship between linear history and chaotic history: is there a tendency in international criminal tribunals to convert history into narrative, or to theorise history by producing over-determined accounts of it? Third, some fairly tentative comments on the relationship between history and hegemony: if the victors really do write the histories, then are international criminal tribunals simply facilitating this process?

---

Schuster 1993); Lawrence Douglas, 'The Memory of Judgement: The Law, Holocaust and Denial' (1999) 7 *History and Memory* 100; Lawrence Douglas, *The Memory of Judgment: Making Law and History in the Trials of the Holocaust* (Yale University Press 2001); David Hirsch, *Law Against Genocide – Cosmopolitan Trials* (Glasshouse Press 2003).

[19] Hannah Arendt, *Eichmann in Jerusalem: A Report on the Banality of Evil* (Penguin Books 2006).

[20] *Attorney-General of the Government of Israel v Eichmann* (1961) 36 ILR 5. See generally Guyora Binder, 'Representing Nazism: Advocacy and Identity at the Trial of Klaus Barbie' (1989) 98 *Yale Law* Journal 1321.

## A. Method: The Subjects of History

Leo Tolstoy's novel *War and Peace* might be read in a number of different ways. Two distinct interpretations present themselves. One is that it is a book dedicated to recovering the historical agency of individual human beings; it is the story of Prince Andre (or Napoleon) forging a personal and world history at an extraordinary time.

However, in the postscript to *War and Peace*, Tolstoy clearly adopts the position that this transference of the collective will to individual persons simply will not do as 'history'. We can perhaps imagine him thinking that individual responsibility operates in only two fictional landscapes: the world of literature and the domain of jurisprudence (ie courts). Authors or judges take a set of historical materials and, for the sake of moulding an attractive and readable story with compelling characterisations in one case and forging an image of personal responsibility in the other, they transform these materials into a story with human agency at its heart.

Novels and trials require characters but history, perhaps, does not.

History, according to his postscript, is endowed with a large 'H' by everyone from Georg Hegel to Francis Fukayama and Philip Bobbitt via Karl Marx. It is history as the motion of forces, or a machine in which mere individuals are tossed around or digested, or a collective will against which individual men and women are powerless. Their stories remain compelling as fiction or biography, but in complex historical studies or theories of international relations or historical sociology, they face demotion. It is an account of history that takes little notice of individual endeavour and imagination: instead, in the materialist camp, historical change is attributed to geography (Jarrod Diamond, *Guns, Germs and Steel*), or technological advances (Philip Bobbitt, *Shield of Achilles*) or, from an idealist perspective, the working through of history's master plan.[21] Hegel might be taken as an archetype of the latter tendency. As he stated in *Lectures on the Philosophy of History*, delivered between 1822 and 1831, 'those manifestations of vitality on the part of individuals and peoples ... are, at the same time, the means and instruments of a higher and broader purpose of which they know nothing ... '.[22]

---

[21] Jared Diamond, *Guns, Germs and Steel: The Fates of Human Societies* (2nd edn, Norton 2005); Philip Bobbitt, *The Shield of Achilles: War, Peace and the Course of History* (Knopf 2002).

[22] Georg Wilhelm F Hegel, 'Lectures on the Philosophy of History' (John Sibree tr) in Monroe C Beardsley (ed), *The European Philosophers from Descartes to Nietzsche* (Modern Library 1960) 559.

In contrast, international criminal justice must, by definition, be wedded to the idea that men make history of their own choosing. No theory of individual responsibility could live without it,[23] as Art 7 of the Rome Statute of the ICTY makes clear: 'A person who planned, instigated, ordered, committed or otherwise aided and abetted in the planning, preparation or execution of a crime … shall be individually responsible for the crime.'

As the ICTY stated in *Tadić*:

> The basic assumption must be that in international law as much as in national systems, the foundation of criminal responsibility is the principle of personal culpability: nobody may be held criminally responsible for acts or transactions in which he has not personally engaged or in some other way participated.[24]

Note, for example, the way in which this tension between the two readings of *War and Peace*, or between its postscript and its main text, undergoes a revival every time someone is brought to court. The arrest of Ratko Mladić brought the standard posturing about responsibility, with Mladić's supporters arguing that he was simply doing Serbian State business in Srebrenica while the ICTY indicted him as an individual, individually responsible for ordering and participating in a crime of genocide.[25] The media obsession with Mladić, Milošević and Ante Gotovina might lead one to suspect that international criminal law sometimes seems to be in the grip

---

[23] There may be an association, too, between structural accounts of criminality and the idea that amnesties might be a useful way to reconstruct the peace. At Westphalia in 1648, individual responsibility – indeed, any account of the Thirty Year War that found fault with any of the adversaries – was off the table. What replaced it was a commitment of international criminal law's opposite – oblivion: 'That there shall be on the one side and the other a perpetual Oblivion, Amnesty, or Pardon of all that has been committed since the beginning of these Troubles, in what place, or what manner soever [sic] the Hostilitys [sic] have been practis'd [sic], in such a manner, that no body, under any pretext whatsoever, shall practice any Acts of Hostility, entertain any Enmity, or cause any Trouble to each other … but that all that has pass'd [sic] on the one side, and the other, as well before as during the War … shall be bury'd [sic] in eternal Oblivion' – *Peace Treaty between the Holy Roman Emperor and the King of France and Their Respective Allies (Treaty of Westphalia)* Munster, 24 October 1648, II <http://avalon.law.yale.edu/17th_century/westphal.asp>.

[24] *Prosecutor v Dusko Tadić (Judgment)* (ICTY, Appeals Chamber, Case No IT-94–1-A, 15 July 1999) [186].

[25] 'Mladić, who has refused to recognise the authority of the war crimes tribunal in The Hague, denied being a killer, adding that all Serbs bore a shared guilt for voting for President Slobodan Milošević, the architect of the Balkan wars': Peter Beaumont and James Meikle, 'Ratko Mladić Denies Ordering Srebrenica Massacre, Says His Son' *The Guardian* (online Sunday, 29 May 2011).

of a 'great man' theory of world events. But it would have to be conceded that this is offset in two ways at the Tribunal: by indicting small fish (the *Tadić* move) and by creating or appropriating doctrines that situate individuals in broader networks of collective responsibility (say, through conspiracy doctrine at Nuremberg or using modes of liability such as joint criminal enterprise or command responsibility at the ICTY).[26] Each of these projects is a way of reaching down and out to the broader contexts in which crime takes place. The prosecution of minor players demonstrates that crimes against humanity are often opportunistic (*Tadić*), sadistic (*Jelisić*) or spontaneous (many of the killings on the Eastern Front, as horribly demonstrated by Christopher Browning in *Ordinary Men*).[27]

Notwithstanding these two complications, it is possible that the ICTY, for example, whether or not it has over-emphasised the personal responsibility of leading Serb nationalists, has certainly understated the role of structural or economic forces in creating the conditions for ethnic warfare (though there is a passing reference to this in para 70 of the *Tadić* Trial Chamber judgment). There has been an enormous amount of work done on the relationship between atrocity and political economy, but little of this permeates the work of the tribunals.[28] Some former officials and commentators have remarked upon an apparent relationship between structural adjustment policies that the World Bank insisted Yugoslavia adopt at the end of the 1990s, and the subsequent economic meltdown that may have led to

---

26 *Prosecutor v Dusko Tadić (Judgment)* (ICTY, Appeals Chamber, Case No IT-94–1-A, 15 July 1999) [185 *et seq*]; *Prosecutor v Kordic and Cerkez (Judgment)* (ICTY, Trial Chamber, Case No IT-95–14/2, 26 February 2001) [371].

27 *Prosecutor v Dusko Tadić (Judgment)* (ICTY, Trial Chamber, Case No IT-94–1-T, 7 May 1997); *Prosecutor v Goran Jelisić (Judgment)* (ICTY, Trial Chamber, Case No IT-95–10-T, 14 December 1999); Christopher Browning, *Ordinary Men: Reserve Police Battalion 101 and the Final Solution in Poland* (Aaron Asher Books 1992).

28 *Prosecutor v Dusko Tadić (Judgment)* (ICTY, Trial Chamber, Case No IT-94–1-T, 7 May 1997) [70]. Of course, by definition it may be that criminal trials screen out the social. After all, it is hardly incumbent on a magistrate to enquire into the social and economic causes of crime when convicting a serial burglar. But two responses come to mind. One is that international tribunals *do* seem interested in establishing some historical ground for their decisions by, say, tracing the reasons for the disintegration of the Yugoslav Federation. Second, international tribunals – whether they like it or not – are producing pseudo-official histories of international or internal armed conflicts and genocides. It is disingenuous to say one is simply acting as a judge or a prosecutor when a particular constellation of highly contested political forces has resulted in one's appointment.

the rise of Milošević and his clique. Indeed, a whole sub-field may need to develop around genocide and political economy.

The Commission delegates at Versailles faced a different problem: the question as to whether in the case of war – the hard case of criminal liability – there could *ever* be a question of personal responsibility. The politicians who established the Commission adopted the view that the war had been authored by the Kaiser and his associates, and hoped the Commission experts would confirm this through a fairly unproblematic reading or, better, restatement of the legal and historical material. But as Alun Munslow puts it, 'facts never speak for themselves'.[29] Wars, and especially their causes, have to be interpreted.

The Commission at Versailles was divided. The *Memorandum of Reservations* issued by the Americans took a radically different approach (arguing for sovereign immunity, against command responsibility and against the category of 'crimes against humanity') from that of the majority, but even the majority opinion is based around a contradictory reading of the material.

The Commission begins by agreeing with the politicians that the Germans (and the Kaiser and his associates in particular) had initiated the war in order to further their loathsome ambitions for territorial expansion.[30] Later, though, when it comes to assigning legal responsibility, the Commission becomes coy about the stability of historical interpretation, stating that the question of authorship was not a juridical question at all. History, as it were, belonged to the historians; and war to the political or moral philosophers:

> any inquiry into the authorship of the war must, to be exhaustive, extend over events that have happened during many years in different European countries, and must raise many difficult and complex problems which might be more fitly investigated by historians and statesmen than by a tribunal appropriate to the trial of offenders against the laws and customs of war ... Any tribunal appropriate to deal with the other offences to which reference is made might hardly be a good court to discuss and deal decisively with such a subject as the authorship of war.[31]

This is a rare moment of diffidence from an international institution willing to deny itself space and prerogatives in a certain field. The most recent example of this is Judge Koojimans's separate opinion in *Congo v Uganda* where he regrets international law's inability to come up with a thick

---

29 Jenkins, above note 5, Introduction, xiii.

30 See the discussion below.

31 *Commission Report*, above note 4, 119.

description of the war in the Great Lakes (and here again we recall that the applicants wanted a condemnation for Ugandan aggression):

> To explain the intervention of one State into the affairs of another is rarely simple or uncontroversial … Moreover the results are likely to be tentative, partial, and complex. And therefore less than totally satisfying.[32]

In the era of juridification and 'inquiry-itis', it is refreshing to witness these denials of expertise.

The 1919 Commission's findings hardly represent a full-blown embrace of history as discourse or indeterminacy, but they do manifest an unusually pluralistic approach to history or, at least, the impossibility of law offering definitive accounts of such histories. Indeed, the Commission may be conducting its own internal history war, anticipating later debates among historians of the Great War.

The Commission both accepts and then implicitly rejects a particular theory of war and political change that overstates the agency of elites. This used to be called the 'Great Man' theory of history and it has powerful associations with the orthodox concept of history as 'a factual account of the past'. Histories of this type (often in fact historical biographies) are regular best-sellers. As Terry Eagleton puts it, they are a form of human interest story, 'a middle-class alternative to material history, one in which the supreme creation known as the individual may hold sway … '.[33]

International criminal law seems, at least temperamentally, implicated in this sort of history. Jenkins writes that 'millions of people have lived in the past but few of them have appeared in history', and the same goes for the history of war crimes trials.[34] Mental states (a deliberate pun), not imperial rivalry or the malfunctioning of the political economy, produce war. When the Versailles experts rejected the juridical account of authorship and declared the causes of war to be multiple, perhaps even unknowable, but certainly structural, they were also rejecting a history that depended on assigning responsibility for war to certain individuals as would happen in the formula 'Hitler invaded Poland'.

---

32 *Armed Activities in the Congo*, Separate Opinion at 1. The case: <http://www.icj-cij.org/docket/files/126/10435.pdf>. Separate opinion: <http://www.icj-cij.org/docket/files/126/10441.pdf>.

33 Eagleton, above note 6, 9.

34 Jenkins, above note 5, 9.

In summary, history can be authored in at least two different senses.[35] In the first version (the Lloyd-George/Clemenceau view after the Great War which to some extent carries through to international criminal law), individuals with some sort of criminal intent capture powerful states and transform some political configuration or other, through force of will or malevolent charisma. In the second version, there is a supreme author of some sort – either God, or the working through of some pre-determined Hegelian historical arc (a form of historicism), or the appearance of a revolutionary class capable of acquiring power, or an economic form promising happiness for humanity and finality for history. In this second version, criminal intent is hardly relevant. In fact, men and women simply find themselves committing errors by ending up on the wrong side of history itself. As Lenin, in his speech at the 8th Soviet Congress on 30 December 1920, said of Nikolai Bukharin, 'he went to one room and found himself in another…'.[36] To conduct criminal trials in the service of extreme versions of such histories is to preside over a show trial, and to this end, Maurice Merleau-Ponty called the Moscow Show Trials 'dramas of subjective innocence and objective treason'.[37]

Of course, collective responsibility and individual liability both suffer from the same defect: they exonerate a large number of people. If everyone is responsible then perhaps no one is. If individuals are capable of leading a state to disaster – think here of Airey Neave shouting at a tramload of grim-faced and sullen Germans outside the Palace of Justice in Nuremburg as they surveyed the devastation wrought by Allied bombing: 'It was Hitler that did this to you!' – then perhaps only the (dead) leader is responsible.[38] For many of the leading Nazis at Nuremberg there was only one defence: 'Hitler did it, I was just a cog'. The great order follower himself, Adolf Eichmann, rested his defence on a variant of this, and his chronicler, Hannah Arendt, gave voice to this idea of Eichmann as a cog, but at the

---

[35] History is also written or authored in the strong sense of being subject to the laws of representation: the writer, incapable of transmitting the past, instead writes or 'authors' history.

[36] Nathan Leites and Elsa Bernaut, *Rituals of Liquidation – The Case of the Moscow Trials* (Free Press 1954) 153.

[37] Maurice Merleau-Ponty, *Humanism and Terror: An Essay on the Communist Problem* (Beacon Press 1969) 202. The French poet, Paul Eluard remarked: 'I am too busy defending the innocent who proclaim their innocence, to have any time left to defend the guilty who proclaim their guilt': Slavoj Zizek, 'The Empty Wheelbarrow – Intellectuals Have to Be Most Critical When Leaders Insist Their Choice is Clear' *The Guardian* (online, 19 February 2005).

[38] Airey Neave, *Nuremberg – A Personal Record of the Trial of the Major Nazi War Criminals in 1945–6* (Hodder and Stoughton 1978) 44–45.

same time held him responsible in history and law. Her alternative indictment – an effort to come to terms with history's dual impulse – found towards the end of *Eichmann in Jerusalem*, could be summed up in this way: '[I]t could have been anyone but it *was* actually you so too bad for you.'[39] Or, as Marx put it (reversing the emphasis but maintaining the duality): ' [Men] make their own history, but they do not make it just as they please in circumstances they choose for themselves; rather they make it in present circumstances, given and inherited.'[40]

## B. Linear Histories

> [T]he Russians and French seemed unable to grasp the implications of the concept [of conspiracy]; when they finally did grasp it, they were genuinely shocked … the Soviets seemed to have shaken their heads in wonderment – a reaction, some cynics may believe, prompted by envy.[41]

History's relationship to the past has been obscure for some time. There certainly is greater acceptance that histories are accounts of the past or interpretations of a set of materials about an existing past. With the demise of the single authoritative history, fresh questions have arisen about how to fashion an authentic account from these materials, or how to rework the materials altogether. There are now serious doubts about whether any sort of non-fictional history is possible.[42] Jean-François Lyotard called this the 'condition of postmodernity' – there is no centre capable of sustaining a single authoritative pronouncement about the past.

New forms have emerged in the wake of these intellectual currents. Orlando Figes has managed to popularise a history from below: anecdotal but authoritative, recuperative, non-linear, decentralised.[43] Sven Lindqvist

---

39 Arendt, above note 19, 277–79.

40 Karl Marx, 'The Enlightenment Brumaire of Louis Bonaparte' in Terrell Carver (ed), *Marx: Later Political Writings* (Cambridge University Press 1996).

41 Bradley Smith, quoted in Allison Marston Danner and Jenny S Martinez, 'Guilty Associations: Joint Criminal Enterprise, Command Responsibility and the Development of International Criminal Law' (2005) 93 *California Law Review* 75, 115.

42 It is this impossibility that leads Dave Eggers for example to describe *What is the What* as a novel rather than a biography. Though the book is based on the life of a young Sudanese refugee and war victim now based in the US, both the novelist and the young Sudanese man agreed that this memory of his early life in Sudan was likely to be too faulty to allow for accuracy: Dave Eggers, *What is the What* (Paw Prints 2008).

43 Orlando Figes, *A People's Tragedy* (Pimlico 1997).

organises his histories in a way that formally displaces linearity and instead offers the reader a number of ways into and through history.[44]

Yet international criminal law and its official bodies are often obliged to offer a theory of history that excludes or flattens some of the quirks or anomalies. Indeed, this goes back, again, to 1919 where the Commission:

> having examined a number of official documents relating to the origins of the World War … determined that the responsibility for it lies *wholly* upon the Powers which declared war in pursuance of a policy of aggression, the concealment of which gives to the origin of this war the character of a dark conspiracy against the rest of Europe.[45]

There is probably not a single historian working today who would find this a complete or even plausible explanation of the origins of the Great War. It is certainly parsimonious. However, its great advantage from the perspective of international criminal law, is that it offers an account of war that meshes with the juridical requirement that wars be the product of an individual's criminal mind or a small elite's criminal conspiracy.

AJP Taylor once said, 'States don't commit crimes, they make mistakes'. The Commission's version of the causes of war leaves little room for 'mistakes'. According to the Commission, the conspiracy began in early 1914 and the assassination of Archduke Ferdinand was a pretext for putting in place an irreversible mobilisation for war. Perhaps we can pause for a moment and consider what is missing from this account. There is nothing about the poisonous and mistrustful nature of nineteenth century European diplomacy (and this was something that US President Woodrow Wilson was agitated about at the time and sought to supplant with an open system of centralised arrangements based on the League of Nations).[46] There was no reference to the inter-imperial rivalry that had disfigured Anglo–German and Franco–German relations in the late nineteenth century (something that Lenin, of course, had written about at the same time), nor about Germany's fear of encirclement or the instability caused by the decline of the Ottoman Empire. There was nothing about the principle of self-determination and the way it had raised expectations of geo-political transformation in Central Europe (the proximate cause of the war was assassin Gavril Princip's gesture of nationalism, of course). Finally, there was no reference to an arms race that had led to a very precarious security system in Western

---

44 Sven Lindqvist, *A History of Bombing* (Granta 2002).

45 *Commission Report*, above note 4, 98 (emphasis added).

46 See the author's discussion in Gerry Simpson, 'International Law in Diplomatic History' in James Crawford and Martti Koskenniemi, *Cambridge Companion to International Law* (Cambridge University Press 2012).

Europe and one which may have encouraged pre-emptive action on the part of Imperial Germany.

At Nuremberg, this tendency continued. Famously, the whole indictment was conditioned by the need to think of the origins of the Second World War as lying in another 'dark conspiracy'; this time one designed and executed by a small cabal of leading Nazis around the figure of Adolf Hitler. This theory of conspiracy – an American idea – permeated and, arguably, deformed the whole trial.[47] Its sheer and largely undisturbed linearity certainly penetrated the final judgment. At the very least, it failed to reckon with the capricious, improvisational and (sometimes) accidental aspect of the aggression and the accompanying genocides.[48] There was an associated failure to understand the special nature of the Holocaust. Instead, it was viewed as an incidental by-product of the central narrative engine: conspiracy to wage war.[49] The Indictment (based on Edward Bernays' imported theory of conspiracy) states that the Nazi accused had:

> during a period of years preceding 8 May 1945, participated as leaders, organizers, instigators, or accomplices in the formulation or execution of a common plan or conspiracy to commit ... Crimes Against Peace, War Crimes, and Crimes against Humanity... and, in accordance with the provisions of the Charter, are individually responsible for their own acts and for all acts committed by any persons in the execution of such plan or conspiracy.[50]

The Tribunal took a similar view, stating:

> The seizure of power by the Nazis, the use of terror, the destruction of the trade unions, the attack on Christian teaching and on churches, the persecution of the Jews, the regimentation of youth – all these are said to be steps deliberately taken to carry out the common plan.[51]

---

47 This is not to deny the controversy that surrounded the conspiracy charge nor the limited role it was to play in the findings of the court in relation to specific individuals. Comparatively few conspiracy charges were upheld by the court (only eight of the accused were convicted of conspiracy to wage aggressive war; as a mode of liability it was insignificant in relation to the crimes against humanity and war crimes indictments).

48 The relationship of policy to killing could be accidental; there is no suggestion that there was anything accidental about the actual killing.

49 See Arendt, above note 19, 256.

50 International Military Tribunal, 'Indictment', in I *Trial of the Major War Criminals,* 27, 29 (1947).

51 *IMT Judgment* (1946) at 43. The Tribunal of course held that the Prosecution had not shown that the pre-1939 deportations, expulsions and persecutions were connected to the conspiracy to wage aggressive war. Did they suddenly become so in 1939?

Two consequences of this are well-documented. Initially, the Jewish victims of the war had to be inserted into this grand narrative as part of national groups (eg 'Poles') or as enemy populations. The Jewishness of the victims was subordinated to their status as nationals of invaded and occupied states. This meant that the Tribunal had to view events in the East as rationally connected to the aggressive war: 'war crimes were committed when and wherever the Fuehrer and his close associates thought them to be advantageous. They were for the most part the result of cold and criminal calculation.'[52]

But this does not sound at all like the 'bloodlands' described in Timothy Snyder's recently-published book of the same name where the killings often took place in an atmosphere of irrational savagery and where such killings were often a hindrance to the larger 'war effort'.[53] This meant, in turn and secondly, that the relationship of the Holocaust to the aggression was poorly understood. The idea that a regime could be so savage as to undertake genocide in ways that *impeded* the war effort was never properly confronted.

Later trials continued in this vein. The author has written elsewhere of the trial of Klaus Barbie in Lyon, where the prosecution and court went to great lengths to present the war as a single struggle between French resistance and Nazi aggression and torture. This linearity occluded, of course, the recent history of fascism and anti-Semitism in France (the *Dreyfus Case*, for example),[54] the Vichy regime's collaboration with the Nazis and the use of torture by French colonial forces in Algeria.[55]

The debate between two ways of thinking about history was at the heart of the half-century long struggle to find an acceptable framework for the crime of aggression. These problems infected both the jurisdictional rules surrounding aggression (Who should have authority to decide or determine? Was it a matter for what Judith Shklar called 'tribunality'?[56] Or should it be a matter of fate, the consequences of which could be handled by

---

[52] *IMT Judgment* (1946) at 44.

[53] Timothy Snyder, *Bloodlands – Europe Between Hitler and Stalin* (Basic Books 2010).

[54] See, eg, Michael Burns, *The Dreyfus Affair: A Brief Documentary History* (Bedford/St Martin's 1987).

[55] Simpson, above note 3, 90.

[56] Judith N Shklar, *Legalism – Law, Morals, and Political Trials* (Harvard University Press 1961).

the UN Security Council?[57]) and the effort to draft an acceptable definition of the crime itself.[58]

At first blush aggression is a simple matter: Germany invaded Belgium in 1914, Belgium's neutrality was guaranteed by the Great European Powers, ergo the German state had committed an act of aggression. Philip Bobbitt reminds us though that aggressors are not always those who strike first (as is the case with the international law definitions). Again, a nuanced history might produce a different account: 'the move to war is an act of the state not of boys … [I]t is the state against whom the aggression has been mounted, typically, that makes the move to war.'[59] Giving him the benefit of the doubt, might it be that the boys are international lawyers feeding off over-simplified narrative histories, while the men are structuralists thinking of war as a form of destiny produced either by the structure of international relations or the proclivities of human nature?

Others may have a better idea of how the ICTY has constructed its histories. It may have made a more self-conscious effort to prepare the historical ground for some of its various decisions than, say, earlier tribunals have done, but the historical narratives it has produced have a neatness that other historical accounts would resist.

The work of Figes and Lindqvist are examples of what *can* be done with historical materials in order to reflect the often decentralised, ambiguous and obscure causes of historical events. If one takes into account the defence arguments, international tribunals *do* produce plural histories. To read the transcripts of the *Milošević* trial, and in particular Milošević's defence submissions, is to form some sense of how a breed of extreme

---

[57] In fact, international law played an odd role in the crisis of 1914. It provided a fake *casus belli* on one hand, and a plausible source of mediation on the other. International (criminal) law is implicated in all of this in many (relatively underappreciated) ways. The Austrians, on German advice, had proposed an ultimatum with a series of demands to which it was felt the Serbians could not possibly concede. In fact, and surprisingly, the Serbians did accept all the demands except one. The single exception now seems strangely legalistic. The Austrians had proposed a judicial inquiry to determine who were the guilty parties. The Serbs agreed to this but insisted that the inclusion of Austrian officials be kept within 'the limits assigned by international law' (*Commission Report,* above note 4, 101). Later, on 29 July 1914, Czar Nicholas had suggested to his cousin, the Kaiser that the dispute be submitted to the recently established Permanent Court of Arbitration in The Hague. That request received no reply.

[58] *Amendments to the Rome Statute of the International Criminal Court on the Crime of Aggression,* RC/Res.6, 13th plen mtg, UN Doc RC/11 (adopted 11 June 2010).

[59] Bobbitt, above note 21, 8.

Serbian nationalism became so compelling to a large number of Serbs. This unauthorised or dissident history also represents the unauthorised legacy of the Tribunal.[60]

## C. Hegemonic Histories

The previous two sections have examined ways in which international criminal tribunals might favour histories that emphasise individual agency over structural causation, and linear arrangements of history over those that tend towards ambiguity or fragmentation. A third, and closely associated, possibility is that the histories produced by war crimes trials will, at any particular time, tend to accord with the contemporaneous self-image of the Great Powers. This may be an attribute of the two deformities traced earlier. By emphasising individual agency, courts reproduce a dominant account of the international system in which its crimes (hundreds of thousands of preventable deaths every month) are understood as accidents or by-products of international political economy, or sovereignty, or the free trade in machetes, while its accidents (the system occasionally results in periods of madness, such as Charles Taylor in Liberia) or singular political acts (Rafic Hariri in Lebanon) are understood as 'crimes'. International criminal justice then becomes an exercise in displacing, in our attentions, the profitable but lethal trade in weapons with model Naomi Campbell's complaint about the inconvenience of giving evidence in the *Taylor* case.[61]

If the weapons trade was thought of as a crime, this would cause inconvenience (unemployment) and loss of political capital (a drop in support among key constituencies) in large Western states such as the United Kingdom. In any event, the intermeshing of military and political elites within most states makes it impossible to contemplate a transformation along these lines. The dominance of the international criminal law model may also allow us to evade responsibilities closer to home. The deaths caused by a particular arrangement of international economic life or a particular consumer desire, are screened out of any discussion of legal responsibility or 'fault' in the international system, while international tribunals put 'an end to impunity' by insisting that old men are brought to The Hague to face trial.

---

60 Simpson, above note 3, 79–104.

61 Lizzy Davies and Matthew Weaver, 'Naomi Campbell Tells War Crimes Tribunal of Diamonds Gift' *The Guardian* (Online, 5 August 2010) <http://www.guardian.co.uk/lifeandstyle/2010/aug/05/naomi-campbell-liberia?intcmp=239>.

In a similar vein, international criminal justice tends to produce highly schematic or simplified histories in which the antecedents of conflict or genocide are elided. If the commission of war crimes has anything to do with the activities of the Great Powers, it is surprising that these activities are so invisible in the reasoning of international tribunals and the writings of international lawyers. Intervention, colonial misadventure or exploitation, economic ruthlessness, the manipulation of local elites, the engagement in proxy wars – the stuff of historical accounts of war – is largely missing from the history produced by international criminal justice. Instead, the focus tends to be on the indigenous cause of violence (the illegitimate seizure of power by local overlords, the abusive projection of that power by 'nationalists' or 'tyrants', the torture and oppression of local populations, the delusions of those local populations, and so on). Just as the focus on individual agency will sidestep the background influences on political maldevelopment, so too will linear history tend to obscure the foreground but antecedent violence of the Great Powers.

The histories produced are not self-evidently hegemonic. Indeed, international criminal justice seems overwhelmingly committed to promoting the rule of law or the idea of humanity *against* hegemonic ambition or sovereign vanity.[62] Nevertheless, the good faith of practitioners and their allegiance to the rule of law hardly disposes of the question of a political project's merit. As EH Carr said:

> When modern writers on international politics find the highest moral good in the rule of law, we are equally entitled to ask, What law? And Whose law? The law is not an abstraction. It cannot be understood independently of the political foundation on which it rests and of the political interests which it serves.[63]

In the abstract, the rule of law, for all its virtues in a stable, liberal democracy, is a form of rule that is likely to favour entrenched elites over resistance groups, vested interests carrying out lawful activity over civil disobedience, official actors over unofficial actors, and property-owners over protestors. In the international system, where the distribution of power, goods and advantage is so vastly, indefensibly and asymmetrically skewed, where the law is largely written by and on behalf of a powerful minority of states and where institutions are funded by, established at the behest or

62 The writings of Cherif Bassiouni exemplify this approach. See, eg, Cherif M Bassiouni, 'From Versailles to Rwanda in Seventy-Five Years: The Need to Establish a Permanent International Criminal Court' (1997) 10 *Harvard Human Rights Journal* 11.

63 E H Carr, *The Twenty Years' Crisis* (Palgrave Macmillan 2001) 179.

instigation of (or, at least, with the tacit approval of) and often directed by sovereign elites, it is little wonder that the rule of law is regarded either as illusory and distant (in its radical guise) or concrete and violent (in its existing instantiation). In one of the most important sentences ever written about international law, China Mieville reminds us that 'the chaotic and bloody world around us *is the rule of law*'.[64] International criminal justice might be (self) regarded as chipping away, imperfectly and with due regard to its inherent 'politicalness', at all of this injustice (this seemed to be a motif of the conference proceedings from which this book is derived), or it might be thought of as another example of injustice.

The other idea or rhetoric that energises international criminal justice and mobilises its practitioners and supporters is the idea of humanity. Certainly, humanity is invoked a great deal in its doctrines ('crimes against humanity' for example), in its institution's preambular statements and in its rhetorical justifications. People who work in international criminal courts would prefer to see themselves as working for 'humanity' rather than an appendage of the Justice Department or the Russian Ministry for Justice. But what if Pierre-Joseph Proudhon and Carl Schmitt – 'he who invokes humanity, cheats' – are right?[65]

Bear in mind here that the perfect system would be one whose norms could be regularly invoked by the Great Powers and whose practitioners were both 'independent' of the Great Powers but also incapable of laying a finger on them or their personnel (because of the structure of international politics or because of the jurisdictional requirements of the relevant court or tribunal). The appearance of neutrality and the good faith of prosecutors, judges and investigators are vital to all of this. It might be possible to be scrupulous and deeply politicised at the same time, which after all is how international criminal justice begins. Largely decent and often brilliant lawyers like Hartley Shawcross, Francis Biddle or Robert Jackson have applied a set of norms that seemed to advance justice and provide a form of retribution for those who had committed ghastly acts. Yet, the history told by the International Military Tribunal (IMT) or International Military Tribunal for the Far East (IMTFE) (with notable exceptions Justices Pal and Röling to this general rule) has nothing to say about the fire-bombings of Tokyo, Dresden and countless German medieval towns undamaged by European wars for a millennium but obliterated by Allied Bomber Command in raids that were radically disconnected from the war effort and, in

---

[64] China Mieville, *Between Equal Rights* (Haymarket Books 2006) 319.

[65] Carl Schmitt, *The Concept of the Political* (University of Chicago Press 1996) 54.

retrospect, almost pathological in their motivation.[66] It did not comment on the way in which the Allies had participated in the dismemberment of Czechoslovakia, on Soviet atrocities under Stalin, or on the relationship between *lebensraum* and the model of British colonialism (expertly explored in Mark Mazower's *Hitler's Empire*).[67] Nuremberg is, by any standard, a pretty strange history of the Second World War: a devastating critique of Nazism but also an apologia produced by men with the best intentions who might have been better off heeding the warnings of the Versailles dissenters.

At the time of writing, the International Criminal Court (ICC) might be falling into the same trap in its investigations in Libya. The Libyan regime was a friend of the West for over a decade, during which its human rights record was shabby to say the least. A 2008 Human Rights Watch Report describes a state in which there were 'arrests and incarceration of political prisoners, some of them disappeared; [and] the torture of detainees … '.[68] Indeed, gross violations of human rights were a regular feature of life in Libya in the 40 years preceding the armed intervention. It was only when it began to defend itself against an armed rebellion that international criminal tribunals became interested. In a system made up of sovereign-states, this is a strange moment to accuse a state of crimes against humanity. It might enhance the standing of the ICC greatly if it decided not to respond to a Security Council authorisation. The alternative is a risk that, at the moment and in some quarters, the ICC looks like NATO's judicial arm.

Robert Cooper, a former adviser to former UK Prime Minister Tony Blair, said:

> The challenge … is to get used to the idea of double standards. Among ourselves, we operate on the basis of laws … But when dealing with more old-fashioned

---

[66] For a penetrating examination see AC Grayling, *Among the Dead Cities: The History and Moral Legacy of the World War II Bombing of Civilians in Germany and Japan* (Walker & Company 2006).

[67] See Mark Mazower, *Hitler's Empire – Nazi Rule in Occupied Europe* (Penguin Books 2008).

[68] Human Rights Watch, *Libya: Rights at Risk* (2008); Amnesty International, *Libya of Tomorrow: What Hope for Human Rights* (Amnesty International Publications 2010) 9, describing 'fears that members of the EU and the USA, rather than using the opportunity to encourage reforms, are turning a blind eye to the human rights situation in order to further their national interests, which include cooperation in counter-terrorism, the control of irregular migration, trade and other economic benefits'. According to Amnesty International, fighting in eastern Libya in the late 1990s had been accompanied by large-scale, deliberate and indiscriminate attacks on civilians, at 19.

> kinds of states ... we need to revert to the rougher methods of an earlier era – force, preemptive attack, deception ... [69]

If this really is the story of the future, then international criminal tribunals will have to perform very delicate diplomatic and legal manoeuvres in order to steer a course between complicity and effectiveness on one hand, and marginalisation and credibility on the other. International judicial institutions, after all, simply do not have the same status, autonomy or cultural power as their municipal equivalents in the US, UK and Australia.

There is of course an entirely different story to be told about international criminal justice and the way it can be or might be used to unseat these hegemonic histories. Nonetheless, to a visitor from Mars perusing the historical record as set out in international tribunals for the past 60 years, the impression given would be that, with the exception of Bosnian Muslims and Croats tried at the ICTY, war crimes, crimes against humanity and genocide are carried out only by those states (or rebels groups) opposed to the interests of the North Atlantic elite. Millions have died as a direct consequence of Great Power intervention (in Vietnam, Cambodia, Afghanistan, Guatemala, El Salvador) or as an indirect consequence of coups and military action (Iraq, Iran). Not a single national of a permanent Security Council member has been tried before an international criminal court since 1945: 'Every discipline is, I suppose, as Nietzsche saw most clearly, constituted by what it forbids its practitioners to do.'[70] As a result, international criminal justice is probably best defined by what it cannot do, by what it is prevented from doing and by what it refuses to do.

---

[69] Robert Cooper, 'The Postmodern State' in Mark Leonard (ed), *Reordering the World: The Long-term Implications of September 11th* (Foreign Policy Centre 2002).

[70] White, above note 5, 126–27. Certain specific crimes remain 'forbidden'. We still cannot seem to think of certain consumption patterns as possible crimes. To take two examples from recent literature, think of Anne Manne's important and horrifying essay on gendercide (the systematic or widespread and state-tolerated killing of female children): Anne Manne, 'Gendercide' *The Monthly* (Online, June 2010); or Mike Davis's book about manmade famine: Mike Davis, *Late Victorian Holocausts: El Nino Famines and the Making of the Third World* (Verso 2001). So many people die preventable deaths and yet international criminal law has nothing much to say about this. Indeed, the relationship between international criminal law and capitalism remains under-rehearsed, to say the least.

# 7. International criminal justice in historical context: the post-Second World War trials and modern international criminal justice

**Robert Cryer**

## I. INTRODUCTION

A great deal was written about international criminal law in the years following the Second World War, and over the last two decades. Indeed, it is only being mildly facetious to say that the primary interaction between international criminal law and environmental law is not the possibility of creating a crime of ecocide,[1] but the extent to which the collective efforts of international criminal lawyers have served to contribute to deforestation. The literature on the Nuremberg trials alone must have consumed countless forests, and once the literature on the ad hoc international tribunals and International Criminal Court (ICC) are also taken into account, the indictment is a grave one indeed. It is not the intention of this chapter to add to those charges by providing another linear chronological history of international criminal law, or a history of the post-Second World War (hereafter referred to as post-War) trials. Many such studies have already been undertaken, and need not be repeated here.[2]

[1] 'British Campaigner Urges UN to Accept Ecocide as International Crime' *The Guardian* (London, 9 April 2010) <http://www.guardian.co.uk/environment/2010/apr/09/ecocide-crime-genocide-un-environmental-damage>.

[2] For examples of the former type see, eg, Timothy LH McCormack, 'From Sun Tzu to the Sixth Committee: The Evolution of an International Criminal Law Regime' in Timothy LH McCormack and Gerry Simpson (eds), *The Law of War Crimes: National and International Approaches* (Kluwer 1997) 311; Robert Cryer, *Prosecuting International Crimes: Selectivity and the International Criminal Law Regime* (Cambridge University Press 2005) ch 1. For examples of the latter see William A Zeck, 'Nuremberg: Proceedings Subsequent to Goering et al' (1947–

Rather, this chapter will look into some of the links between the post-War cases and more modern aspects of international criminal law. It is emphatically not the author's intention to make the case that all aspects of those trials are instructive. Indeed, the disjunctures between then and now will be investigated. There are important similarities but also differences, which affect the way we need to look back at those trials. To treat like cases alike may be one form of justice, but to treat unlike cases as like may not be. This chapter will attempt to approach the trials in two different ways: as precedents for modern international criminal law, and as examples of the themes that arise in international criminal law.

## II. THE STATUS OF THE POST-WAR TRIALS AS PRECEDENTS

It is, of course, trite to note that case law is not binding as a matter of general international law, be it from national or international tribunals.[3] As William Fenrick said at the outset of the prosecution's work in the International Criminal Tribunal for the former Yugoslavia (ICTY), it may also be true that

> it will not be possible, and it would not be desirable, simply to dust off the Nuremberg and Tokyo Judgments, the United Nations War Crimes Commission series of *Law Reports of Trials of War Criminals* and the US government's *Trials of War Criminals Before the Nuremberg Military Tribunals Under Control Council Law 10* and presume that one has a readily available source of answers for all legal problems.[4]

That said, the considerable influence that the Nuremberg and Tokyo International Military Tribunals (IMTs) have had on modern international

1948) 26 *North Carolina Law Review* 350; Matthew Lippman, 'The Other Nuremberg: American Prosecutions of Nazi War Criminals in Occupied Germany' (1992–1993) 3 *Indiana International and Comparative Law Review* 1; Matthew Lippman, 'Prosecutions of Nazi War Criminals Before Post-World War II Domestic Tribunals' (1999–2000) 8 *Miami International and Comparative Law Review* 1.

[3] For some comments on point see Robert Cryer, 'Neither Here nor There? The Status of International Criminal Jurisprudence in the International and UK Legal Orders' in Michael Bohlander and Kaiyan Kaikobad (eds) *International Law and Power: Perspectives on Legal Order and Justice: Essays in Honour of Colin Warbrick* (Brill 2008) 183.

[4] W J Fenrick, 'Some International Law Problems Related to Prosecutions Before the International Criminal Tribunal for former Yugoslavia' (1995–1995) 6 *Duke Journal of Comparative and International Law* 103.

criminal law (evaluated elsewhere) cannot be overstated.[5] Here, focus falls on the other post-War trials, a number of which have been a mainstay of debate in the modern era.

The ICTY in particular has made extensive reference to the post-War case law, and has engaged in detailed discussion of which trials ought to be given specific precedential value.[6] This was a significant issue in the *Erdemović* case.[7] Here, the Prosecutor sought to establish that on the basis of the post-War jurisprudence, duress did not amount to a defence to international crimes involving the killing of innocents. This only convinced Judge Li,[8] the other judges remaining rightly sceptical. What is interesting for our purposes though, is the different approach taken by the joint opinion of Judges McDonald and Vohrah on the one hand, and President (as he then was) Cassese on the other. The joint opinion of the former took the view that the decisions of the American tribunals operating under Control Council Law No. 10 were to be given no greater weight in determining customary international law than other post-War trials.[9] On the flip side, Cassese took the view that because those tribunals were applying international law in their view, this gave them greater authority than other cases that were not regarded as doing so.[10]

Probably the most significant discussion of the issue came in the *Furundžija* case, at trial level (in which Cassese also sat). There, the various levels of authority were sensibly run through:

> For a correct appraisal of this case law, it is important to bear in mind, with each of the cases to be examined, the forum in which the case was heard, as well as the law applied, as these factors determine its authoritative value. In addition, one should constantly be mindful of the need for great caution in using national case

---

[5] See Adam Basak, 'The Influence of the Nuremberg Judgment on the Practice of the Allied Courts in Germany' (1977–1978) 9 *Polish Yearbook of International Law* 161; Christian Tomuschat 'The Legacy of Nuremberg' (2006) 4 *Journal of International Criminal Justice* 830; Neil Boister and Robert Cryer, *The Tokyo International Military Tribunal: A Reappraisal* (Oxford University Press 2008) ch 10.

[6] The story is told well in Kevin Jon Heller, *The Nuremberg Military Tribunals and the Origins of International Criminal Law* (Oxford University Press 2011) 375–77.

[7] *Prosecutor v Erdemović* (*Appeal Judgment*) (ICTY, Appeals Chamber, Case No IT-96–22-A, 7 October 1997).

[8] Ibid Dissenting Opinion of Judge Li, [6]–[12].

[9] Ibid Joint Separate Opinion of Judges McDonald and Vohrah, [52]–[54].

[10] Ibid Dissenting Opinion of President Cassese, [21].

> law for the purpose of determining whether customary rules of international criminal law have evolved in a particular matter.[11]

The Trial Chamber thereby explained its approach as involving consideration of US cases that were set up under Control Council Law No. 10, and, unless they were applying domestic law, UK cases based on the Royal Warrant of 14 June 1945, and those in the French occupation zone.[12]

Although it misses many other States' jurisprudence, the statement contains an important caveat. The various trials were genuinely heterogeneous: after the War there were some international trials, some mixed tribunals, and some purely domestic trials, undertaken by various States on different bases, such as international or domestic law, and at times the applicable standards differed. For example, the US post-War trials tended to be based on Control Council Law No. 10, and applied international law; on the other hand, Norway took the approach that the Norwegian Criminal Code was the basis of its domestic trials; and French cases were based on the idea that for a war crime to be proved, a violation of the municipal law of France had also to be proved.[13] The UK also tended to use domestic principles of liability and defences, while also relying on international law for the substantive content of war crimes.[14] We should therefore be cautious about treating them as a unified whole from which lessons can be drawn. In addition, the nature of citation and the reasons for it ought to give pause for thought.

To take one example,[15] Kevin Jon Heller has engaged in a meticulous study of the influence of the US Nuremberg subsequent proceedings, identifying examples of citation of those cases in later decisions. Rightly, this is leavened by reference to the times that the jurisprudence was referred to inaccurately or incompletely, or simply ignored.[16] But the issue of influence is not a matter solely of counting quotes. As the legal realists, among others, have discussed, citation occurs for various reasons. It can

---

[11] *Prosecutor v Furundžija* (Trial Judgment) (ICTY, Trial Chamber, Case No IT-95–17/1-T, 10 December 1998) [194].

[12] Ibid [195]–[197].

[13] *Wagner* III *Law Reports, Trials of War Criminals* (LRTWC) 23, 50–54.

[14] *Essen Lynching* I LRTWC 88; *Chusaburo* III LRTWC 76, 79–80.

[15] This section draws upon a blog post at EJIL Talk! and the discussion following it: Robert Cryer, 'The Nuremberg Military Tribunals, Naturalism, Authority and Causation' (EJIL Talk! 3 November 2011) <http://www.ejiltalk.org/the-nuremberg-military-tribunals-naturalism-authority-and-causation/>.

[16] Heller, above note 6, 377, 378, 381–82.

come from a genuine belief in the precedential authority of a pronouncement, or the purely pretextual (and for many reasons in between).[17] Where reference is made to bolster a position that has been adopted on other grounds, the case has not been influential per se: it has been co-opted, rather than treated as authority. Given that Heller identifies a number of misstatements and selective citation of the jurisprudence of subsequent proceedings, it can be questioned whether at least some of those references can be explained away as misunderstandings, rather than tactical.

Hence, there are grounds to question Heller's optimism about the authority granted to the findings of the US subsequent proceedings. This can be shown by the (accurate) critique that he has made of the US Court of Appeals for the Second Circuit's decision in *Presbyterian Church of Sudan v Talisman Energy*.[18] This case asserted a purposive standard for the *mens rea* of aiding and abetting on the basis of one acquittal at the Nuremberg subsequent proceedings, when the vast preponderance of those decisions applied a knowledge-based standard. Heller asserts that '[i]f this study had existed a few years ago, the court might have reached a very different conclusion'.[19] This might be the case, but, as Heller has repeatedly shown elsewhere,[20] citation by courts in the US and other countries is often based on reasons far removed from a genuine investigation into the sources of international law and the relevant degree of authority that ought to be attached to them.

This issue is not limited to the Nuremberg subsequent proceedings however, but also applies to the citation of various cases, for example. In *Erdemović*, President Cassese cited a number of Italian cases (such as *Masetti*) which had never been reported (in English, Italian or any official or unofficial law reports), would not likely have been known to the parties, or pled as such. As many common lawyers know, particularly those taught the law in part through the decisions of Lord Denning, there is an extent to which adventitious citation of cases (or indeed State practice) is used as a

---

17 William W Fischer, Morton Horwitz and Thomas Reed (eds), *American Legal Realism* (Oxford University Press 1993).

18 *Presbyterian Church of Sudan v Talisman Energy* 582 F 3d 244 (2nd Cir. 2009).

19 Heller, above note 6, 5.

20 For an example, see Kevin Jon Heller, 'The Fourth Circuit Joins the International Law Improv' (*Opinio Juris* 21 September 2011) <http://opiniojuris.org/2011/09/21/the-fourth-circuit-joins-the-international-law-improv/>.

tactic to support a decision reached on other grounds than authority.[21] Beyond this further problems arise, as precisely what went on in those difficult days after the War is not always as clear as might be hoped.

## III. EPISTEMOLOGY, REPORTING AND THE POST-WAR TRIALS

When looking back to the post-War trials, certain practical or epistemological issues arise. There is an extent to which we only have a partial understanding of the post-War jurisprudence. To explain this further, it is important to separate three different types of trials: those that were fully reported, those that were reported in some form, and those that were not. Where reports were not available and remain so, the extent to which those cases can enter into the debate on the content of international criminal law is limited. To take an example from the era which straddled the post-War trials and the modern revival of international criminal law, in the International Law Commission's draft code of crimes against the peace and security of mankind, references to post-War cases outside of the Nuremberg (and to a little extent Tokyo) IMTs and the US subsequent proceedings were, to say the least, sparse.[22]

The question of reporting does not map as clearly as might be expected across the national and international trials. For example, the Nuremberg IMT's judgment was reported in the *American Journal of International Law*, and both the US and UK published full transcripts of the entire trial. On the other hand, the Tokyo IMT's judgment was not made readily available in full form until one of the judges, Bert Röling, decided to publish it commercially in 1977. The transcripts were only made similarly available in 1981, when they were published as the result of the efforts of two private scholars. Sets were not easily accessible,[23] which partly explains the paucity of academic interest in the Tokyo IMT, in spite of the very

---

[21] It is notable that the first judgment of the ICC decided to apply the law as decided upon in the pre-trial chamber, rather than what at least one of the judges thought it ought to be, as a matter of treaty law, never mind what custom said. *Prosecutor v Lubanga* (Trial Judgment) (ICC, Case No ICC-01/04–01/06, 14 March 2012) [976]–[1016].

[22] See eg, (1983) *Yearbook of the International Law Commission*, 137ff.

[23] At the risk of self-promotion, see now Neil Boister and Robert Cryer (eds), *Documents on the Tokyo International Military Tribunal* (Oxford University Press 2009).

interesting issues that it raised. Some of the controversies that were discussed in the judgments (in particular the Hiroshima and Nagasaki bombings, and the responsibility of the Emperor) may have caused the delay in publication of a full record of the proceedings. This critique applies in particular to the judgment of Judge Pal, which was actively suppressed by the (US) occupation authorities in Japan owing to its vitriolic critique of the Allies, and was only published privately by him in the 1950s.[24]

The lack of reporting does not fall directly across national lines. The US published the Nuremberg IMT proceedings, and in its 'green book' series made available practically all of the transcripts, evidence and judgments of the subsequent proceedings in Nuremberg. Yet other US trials, especially those conducted in the Far East, were either only published in digested form in the *Law Reports, Trials of War Criminals* prepared by the United Nations War Crimes Commission (UNWCC) or were not reported at all. This includes important decisions such as that in the *Toyoda* case, which had a great deal to say about command responsibility.

The 15 volumes of the *Law Reports, Trials of War Criminals* were the most comprehensive attempt to report the post-War cases. This series attempted to draw together important cases brought by the Allied powers, to create a record of the nascent law of war crimes. As Lord Wright, chairman of the Commission said:

> I need not repeat what has so often been emphasised that to construct a system of common or customary law must necessarily involve a system of law reporting. The failure to appreciate the existence, character or scope of the law of war has almost entirely resulted from the absence of adequate reporting of decisions taken regarding acts coming under the law of war. It may be hoped that with the materials now available, it may be possible to evolve a homogeneous, scientific and constructive body of law though there is still no legislature to contribute to that result. That, however, is for the future.[25]

However, the selection of cases for inclusion in the *Reports* was, although not entirely unprincipled, far from systematic. On the positive side, the intention of the *Reports* was to report those cases that raised or settled important issues of international or municipal law.[26] There is no doubt that the Commission did its best to select such cases, but in many ways this would require considerable levels of prescience as to what would prove

---

[24] Radhabinodh Pal, *IMTFE Dissentient Judgment of Justice Pal* (Sanyal and Company 1953).

[25] XV LRTWC xv.

[26] I LRTWC x.

important later. For example, considerable attention is paid to offences committed after an armistice, yet Lord Wright noted that:

> It has not been the intention in this series to report concentration camp cases in general. The Belsen trial, a British one, was very fully reported in Volume II, but there have been many other concentration camp cases ... There were, in addition, numerous *lesser* trials in which the offences charged were those committed by people employed by the Nazis in the various concentration camps. The Dachau concentration camp case has been exceptionally treated. It is principally noteworthy because of its discussion of the nature and effect of common design.[27]

It is difficult to imagine that the same could be said nowadays. Even more than this though, the sheer process of selection means that some trials that would fall under the category of 'important' will have been missed, and thus overlooked. The statistics speak for themselves. Lord Wright himself noted that the *Reports* were only indicative rather than comprehensive: as he stated, the number of Trial Records received when compared to the number reported was, by country, '809 United States ... 28; 524 British ... 27; 256 Australian ... 5; 254 French ... 11; 30 Netherlands ... 7; 24 Polish ... 4; 9 Norwegian ... 5; 4 Canadian ... 1; 1 Chinese ... 1'.[28] Factually, the numbers quoted are undoubtedly under-representative; for example, Australia reported 256 trials to the Commission, but convened at least three times that number. The Commission understandably limited itself to those trials that had been reported to it, and a number of countries on the Commission simply did not do so. Again, Lord Wright's comments are important here:

> It will be observed that not all the countries whose courts have conducted war crime trials in recent years, nor all members of the Commission, are represented in the selection of trials reported in these volumes. The aim has been to make the series as internationally representative as was possible, but the achievement of this purpose has always depended upon and been limited by the transcripts actually submitted by various governments. All members of the Commission were invited to forward records of their trials, but not all did so for various reasons, and this lack of records explains the absence from these volumes of reports of trials held by the courts of certain countries.[29]

The *Reports* contained no Russian trials, including the first war crimes trials of the Second World War, the Kharkov trials. China undertook a large number of trials (probably in the thousands), but did not report them to the

---

27 XI LRTWC ix.
28 XV LRTWC xvi.
29 Ibid xvii.

UNWCC. It is thus extremely difficult to know how many other cases have never seen the light of day, at least outside of the countries where they were heard. This leads to a significant problem: although international criminal law has pretensions to universality, it is worthwhile reflecting on what post-War international criminal law looked like to Russian or Chinese scholars and judges. The vision of the post-War trials in the Western world is probably a culturally limited one.[30] It would be extremely interesting to look into how international criminal law was seen by non-Western cultures at the time, but so far, there has been little comparative research on point.

Beyond this, the *Law Reports, Trials of War Criminals* are vastly incomplete for purely practical reasons. Rather like later war crimes commissions, such as the 808 and 935 commissions, the UNWCC was short on governmental support and money at the best of times.[31] After the War, things became even worse. Therefore the publication of the last ten volumes of the *Reports* was funded by money put aside in a time-limited trust.[32] The nature of the trust meant that it was not possible for any cases decided after March 1949 to be reported. So, in spite of the intention of the Commission to place the *Ministries* case in the fifteenth volume (intended as a summary of the law applied in all the reported cases), it was not reported in the series, as the judgment had not been handed down in time.[33] In this particular case, the US 'green book' reports covered it, but many other cases were largely ignored as a result of practical limitations. Beyond this, it must be remembered that the *Reports* were, in essence, digests. Judgments were reprinted as excerpts and not in full, and in the many cases where there was not a judgment, the decisions on the law in the cases were inducted, often on the basis of what amounted to little more than supposition. Hence, at best, looking to the *Reports* to provide a true picture of what actually occurred in the trials, is as unreliable as looking to Justinian's digest to determine the practice of the courts in ancient Rome.[34]

---

30 On a similar note, William Schabas notes that, although most literature asserts US dominance in the Nuremberg IMT, '[i]f we had access to as much scholarship and as many memoirs in Russian, perhaps we might see the trial through a different lens', William Schabas, *Unimaginable Atrocities: Justice, Politics and Rights at the War Crimes Tribunals* (Oxford University Press 2012) 10.

31 See generally M Cherif Bassiouni, 'The United Nations Commission of Experts Established Pursuant to Security Council Resolution 780' (1994) 88 *American Journal of International Law* 784.

32 V LRTWC vi–vii.

33 XIV LRTWC ix.

34 As was said at the time, outside the reports of the Nuremberg IMT, 'only miscellaneous publications exist' in relation to the other trials and 'none of these

This is not the end of the story though; it would be fallacious to assume that reporting practices were entirely untainted by politics. As mentioned above, it is difficult not to be cynical about the fact that Judge Pal's dissent was not published in Japan during the US occupation.[35] As a counterpoint, although the US whisked some of the members of the notorious Japanese chemical and biological weapons Unit away to the US (Unit 731), promising immunity in exchange for their research findings, the USSR prosecuted members of that Unit in the early 1950s, and ensured that the proceedings were published in English, to make a political point.[36]

It might be asked whether the lack of comprehensive reporting is a fundamental problem. On the one hand it is, as we do not have a complete understanding of all of the post-War trials and the law they applied, but on the other hand, it is not. The link between the post-War trials and modern international criminal justice is in part a function of the image that modern international criminal lawyers have of those trials. This is partial, as shown above, but it is also factually the case. It is therefore worth looking at some of the common themes and disjunctions that characterise past and present international criminal justice.

## IV. COMMON THEMES

### A. Positivism, Naturalism, the Role of Judges and Customary Law

The first striking similarity between the post-War trials and modern international criminal justice until the creation of the ICC, is the level of trust put in the hands of the judges about the definitions of crimes and the principles of liability. In the Nuremberg and Tokyo IMTs' Statutes, the principles of liability were largely left to the judges, the only exceptions being defences, where Art 7 of the Nuremberg Tribunal's Statute (to which Art 6 of the Tokyo Tribunal's Statute to all intents and purposes conformed) removed two of the defences most likely to be asserted: Act of State and Superior

---

publications will … be adequate for intense scholarly study', Franz Neuman, 'The War Crimes Trials' (1949) 2 *World Politics* 135, 135–36.

[35] See above note 24 and accompanying text.

[36] See *Materials on the Trial of Former Servicemen of the Japanese Army Charged With Manufacturing and Employing Bacteriological Weapons* (Foreign Languages Press 1950) and Boister and Cryer, above, note 5, 63–64. There is no question that there was a large element of hypocrisy in the proceedings, in that the USSR had extracted what they had wanted from the defendants prior to putting them on trial.

Orders. The precise details of the law of war crimes were also left to the judges; Control Council Law No. 10 and the UK's Royal Warrant are also laconic documents, which allowed judges the greatest degree of flexibility to determine the law on many issues. This led to what might be termed 'presentational positivism', which finds a frequent place in international criminal law: what is essentially a naturalist idea is presented in positivist terms (usually owing to the *nullum crimen sine lege* principle), albeit with naturalism peeking out at times.[37]

The judgment of the Nuremberg IMT was, in many ways, more positivist than the most stereotypical nineteenth century commentator could have possibly hoped.[38] After all, part of its judgment was that their authority was limited to that which the London Charter expressly granted them:

> The jurisdiction of the Tribunal is defined in the Agreement and Charter, and the crimes coming within the jurisdiction of the Tribunal, for which there shall be individual responsibility, are set out in Article 6. The law of the Charter is decisive, and binding upon the Tribunal.[39]

In spite of this, the Tribunal was clearly concerned that this might not be enough to overcome the plea that the law imposed by the Charter on the Tribunal was in fact *ex post facto*, thus contrary to the *nullum crimen sine lege* principle. Hence they took a more ambivalent and perhaps naturalistic approach by asserting that the *nullum crimen* principle was not actually a binding rule of law, but a non-binding principle of justice, which consequently was dismissible if there existed a more convincing rule of (natural) justice:

> In the first place, it is to be observed that the maxim *nullum crimen sine lege* is not a limitation of sovereignty, but is in general a principle of justice. To assert that it is unjust to punish those who in defiance of treaties and assurances have attacked neighbouring states without warning is obviously untrue, for in such circumstances the attacker must know that he is doing wrong, and so far from it

---

37 This section builds upon Robert Cryer, 'The Philosophy of International Criminal Law' in Alexander Orakhelashvili (ed), *Research Handbook on the Theory and History International Law* (Edward Elgar 2011) 232, 239–57.

38 Although on the imagined views of commentators of that period, see David Kennedy, 'International Law and the Nineteenth Century: The History of an Illusion' (1997) 17 *Quinnipiac Law Review* 99.

39 'Nuremberg IMT Judgment: Judgment and Sentence' (1947) 41 *American Journal of International Law* 172, 216.

> being unjust to punish him, it would be unjust if his wrong were allowed to go unpunished.[40]

That said, it is not clear that the Tribunal convinced itself on point; it felt obliged to make its views known, against the backdrop of the apparently binding nature of the Charter and non-binding nature of the *nullum crimen sine lege* principle.[41] As a result, it engaged in a rather unconvincing discussion of a number of unratified treaties and non-binding recommendations, to attempt to ground its interpretation of the 1928 Kellogg-Briand Pact (the Pact of Paris) as creating criminal liability in authority rather than reason or natural law.[42] Nonetheless what can be seen here is the relationship between natural and positive law that can often be seen in international tribunals' judgments: the inspiration is not infrequently natural law, but the argumentation tends to be framed in a (more or less transparent) positivistic idiom.[43]

This was picked up on by one of the US subsequent tribunals in the *List* trial, which relied heavily on customary international law, and a dynamic concept of it which was not inconsistent with the way the Nuremberg IMT dealt with Crimes against Peace:

> Any system of law that is obviously subject to growth by the crystallisation of generally prevailing custom and practice into law under the impact of common acceptance or consent, must not be confined within the limits of formal pronouncement or complete unanimity ... Any system of jurisprudence, if it is to be effective, must be given an opportunity to grow and expand to meet changed conditions. The codification of principles is a helpful means of simplification, but it must not be treated as adding rigidity where resiliency is essential. To place the principles of International Law in a formalistic strait-jacket would ultimately destroy any effectiveness that it has acquired ... It is true, of course, that customary International Law is not static. It must be elastic enough to meet the

---

40 Ibid 217; see Beth van Schaack, '*Crimen Sine Lege*: Judicial Lawmaking at the Intersection of Law and Morals' (2008–2009) 97 *Georgetown Law Journal* 119, 125–30.

41 'Nuremberg IMT Judgment' ibid 217.

42 Ibid 218–20.

43 Stanley Paulson, 'Classical Legal Positivism at Nuremberg' (1975) 4 *Philosophy and Public Affairs* 132, 138 goes further, to say that the Nuremberg IMT rejected classical legal positivism, as otherwise it would have been necessary to reject international law. It is not necessary for our purposes to make such a strong claim, as here we are discussing positivism as a method of international law, not whether or not international law can be defended on positivistic grounds. For those who are counting, however, it can: see eg Ian Brownlie, *The Rule of Law in International Affairs* (Nijhoff 1998) ch 1.

> new conditions that natural progress brings to the world. It might be argued that this requires a certain amount of retroactive application of new rules and that by conceding the existence of a customary International Law, one thereby concedes the legality of retroactive pronouncements. To a limited extent the argument is sound, but when it comes in conflict with a rule of fundamental right and justice, the latter must prevail.[44]

This link to naturalism as an animating force can also be seen in the *Justice* trial in which the US Tribunal, after engaging in discussion about the Nuremberg IMT Charter and the necessity of custom being flexible within a largely positivistic framework (with particular reference to Charles Cheney Hyde, an old school positivist), cited with approval Lord Wright, an avowed naturalist:

> [I]nternational law is progressive. The period of growth generally coincides with the period of world upheavals. The pressure of necessity stimulates the impact of natural law and of moral ideas and converts them into rules deliberately and overtly recognised by the consensus of civilised mankind. The experience of two great world wars within a quarter of a century cannot fail to have deep repercussions on the senses of the peoples and their demand for an international law which reflects international justice. I am convinced that international law has progressed, as it is bound to progress if it is to be a living and operative force in these days of widening sense of humanity.[45]

The same could be said about the way in which the ICTY has approached custom, within the mandate granted to it. This is especially the case with respect to war crimes. Art 3 of the ICTY Statute granted the ICTY jurisdiction over violations of the laws and customs of war. Importantly, the list of war crimes is not closed, so the ICTY has interpreted this as a reference to all of the law of armed conflict applicable in former Yugoslavia at the relevant times (other than Grave Breaches of the Geneva Conventions, which are criminalised in Art 2 of the Statute).[46] This meant that the ICTY had a very broad mandate to determine what those rules were, and whether or not they were customary. Similarly, owing to the fact that the ICTY Statute only contains very brief provisions concerning principles of liability and defences, and the Secretary-General expressed the wish that the gaps be

---

44 VIII LRTWC 49, 54.

45 VI LRTWC 51, citing Lord Wright, 'War Crimes under International Law' (1946) 62 *Law Quarterly Review* 51.

46 *Prosecutor v Tadić* (Judgment on Interlocutory Appeal on Jurisdiction) (ICTY, Appeal Chamber, Case No IT-91-1-AR72, 2 October 1995), [71]–[93].

filled in by the Tribunal in its jurisprudence,[47] the ICTY has a similarly broad role on point. Although the Rome Statute was somewhat more limited in relation to the International Criminal Tribunal for Rwanda (ICTR), it also granted considerable autonomy to the judges to develop the law.

Probably the first example of this autonomy in the ICTY was the *Tadić* case,[48] the majority opinion in which is generally accepted to have been the work of then-President of the ICTY, Antonio Cassese.[49] The influence of the case on the law of non-international armed conflict has been profound, with some of its more controversial propositions now being considered commonplace or, at the very least, the starting point of debate.[50] Although it is decidedly advancing the law on point, the decision is careful to make reference to traditional sources doctrine,[51] the intention of the drafters of the Statute,[52] and State (and international organisational) practice,[53] which could give succour to the traditional positivist. However it also contains statements such as:

> the impetuous development and propagation in the international community of human rights doctrines, particularly after the adoption of the Universal Declaration of Human Rights in 1948, has brought about significant changes in international law, notably in the approach to problems besetting the world community. A State-sovereignty-oriented approach has been gradually supplanted by a human-being-oriented approach. Gradually the maxim of Roman

---

[47] Statute of the ICTY, Art 7; *Report of the Secretary-General Pursuant to Paragraph 3 of Security Council Resolution* 808 (1993) 3 May 1993 UN Doc S/25704, [58].

[48] *Tadić* above note 46.

[49] Theodor Meron, 'Cassese's Tadić and the Law of Non-International Armed Conflicts' in Lal Chand Vohrah et al (eds), *Man's Inhumanity to Man: Essays on Honour of Antonio Cassese* (Kluwer 2003) 533.

[50] See, eg Anthony Cullen, *The Concept of Non-International Armed Conflict in International Humanitarian Law* (Cambridge University Press 2010) ch 4; Eve La Haye, *War Crimes in Internal Armed Conflicts* (Cambridge University Press 2007) 136.

[51] *Tadić* above note 46 [99], although it is worth bearing in mind that it was a 'progressive' approach.

[52] Ibid [88].

[53] Ibid [100]–[118], [120]–[124]. This aspect of the opinion could be considered part of the modern positivist phase of the judgment, on which see Bruno Simma and Andreas Paulus, 'The Responsibility of Individuals for Human Rights Abuses in Internal Conflicts: A Positivist View' in Steven Ratner and Anne-Marie Slaughter (eds), *The Methods of International Law* (The American Society of International Law 2000) 23.

law *hominum causa omne jus constitutum est* (all law is created for the benefit of human beings) has gained a firm foothold in the international community as well.[54]

Cassese has traced his own intellectual journey from his positivist roots to a more humanitarian-informed approach.[55] Although the majority in *Tadić* was careful to attempt to bolster their case with references to relevant (and at times less relevant) State practice,[56] Cassese has all but admitted this was cover for 'humanising' the law applicable to non-international armed conflicts.[57] He was also content to make arguments on the basis of reason (a tenet of secular naturalism) where authority was lacking. This was entirely intentional, as Cassese later said in relation to *Tadić*: 'We were breaking new ground. You go beyond the black letter of the law because you look at the spirit of law.'[58]

Analogous considerations can also be seen in various other cases before the ICTY. In the *Kupreškić* case,[59] the issue was the lawfulness of reprisals against the civilian population, albeit largely tangential to the major issues before the Tribunal.[60] The Chamber came to the conclusion that such reprisals were unlawful, on the basis of a very controversial reading of a

---

[54] *Tadić* above note 46, [97].

[55] Antonio Cassese 'Soliloquy' in Antonio Cassese, *The Human Dimension of International Law: Selected Papers* (Oxford University Press 2008) lix, lx–lxv.

[56] Christopher Greenwood, 'International Humanitarian Law and the *Tadić* Case' (1996) 7 *European Journal of International Law* 265; Colin Warbrick and Peter Rowe, 'The International Criminal Tribunal for Yugoslavia: The Decision of the Appeals Chamber on the Interlocutory Appeal on Jurisdiction in the *Tadić* Case' (1996) 45 *International and Comparative Law Quarterly* 691; Geoffrey R Watson, 'The Humanitarian Law of the Yugoslavia War Crimes Tribunal: Jurisdiction in *Prosecutor v Tadić* (1996) 36 *Virginia Journal of International Law* 687, 709–28.

[57] Tamás Hoffmann, 'The Gentle Civilizer of Humanitarian Law – Antonio Cassese and the Creation of the Customary Law of Non-International Armed Conflicts' in Carsten Stahn and Larissa van den Herik (eds), *Future Perspectives on International Criminal Justice* (TMC Asser Press 2010) 58, 68.

[58] 'The Judge: Interview with Antonio Cassese' in Heikelina Verrijn Stuart and Marlise Simons, *The Prosecutor and the Judge: Benjamin Ferencz and Antonio Cassese: Interviews and Writings* (Amsterdam University Press 2009) 47, 53.

[59] *Prosecutor* v *Kupreškić* (Trial Judgment) (ICTY, Trial Chamber, Case No IT-95–16-T, 14 January 2000); see generally Christopher Greenwood, 'Belligerent Reprisals in the Jurisprudence of the International Criminal Tribunal for the Former Yugoslavia' in Horst Fischer, Claus Kreß and Sascha Rolf Lüder (eds), *International and National Prosecution of Crimes Under International Law* (Berlin 2001) 359.

[60] This is not unusual. The majority of the seminal discussion in the *Tadić* case was also, as is often overlooked, *obiter*.

small and not necessarily representative amount of State practice. Bolstered by an interpretation of the Martens clause in its 1907 formulation (and tracing the argumentation that appeared in an earlier piece by Cassese),[61] the Chamber took the view that such reprisals were unlawful, because in spite of scepticism on the part of some States:

> Until a more complete code of the laws of war has been issued, the High Contracting Parties deem it expedient to declare that, in cases not included in the Regulations adopted by them, the inhabitants and the belligerents remain under the protection and the rule of the principles of the law of nations, as they result from the usages established among civilized peoples, from the laws of humanity, and the dictates of the public conscience.[62]

The Trial Chamber in *Kupreškić* interpreted the Martens clause in a way that attempted to introduce natural law. As Tamás Hoffmann notes, this amounted to 'the equation of morality with custom'.[63] What needs to be added to such comment is that although this may be the case, the argumentation is notionally or presentationally positivist. The argument of the Chamber was that custom accepted the position, and again some State practice was (mis)quoted. Lest this be thought to be modern, let us return to the post-War era, and look at the view of the Martens clause taken by Lord Wright in his summing up of the overall jurisprudence of the post-war Courts:

> The language of the [Martens] clause ... has sometimes been described as embodying the law of nature or natural law. That expression has been used during so many centuries from the days of the Romans and in so many different connotations and also has been invoked for the purposes of maintaining so many evil and disastrous practices and rules, that its use may perhaps be better abandoned. In truth and in fact, the true view of the law of nature has been the law which aims, however imperfectly, at giving effect to the sense of justice and of right and wrong and which is naturally inherent in all human beings except only the abandoned and vicious.[64]

Perhaps with a considerable degree of historical precedent, judges at the ICTY have certainly leaned more towards natural law/morality in some decisions. The same can be said about the Special Court for Sierra Leone at

---

[61] Antonio Cassese, 'The Martens Clause: Half a Loaf, or Pie in the Sky?' (2000) 11 *European Journal of International Law* 187.

[62] 1907 Hague Convention IV Respecting the Laws and Customs of War on Land (1910) UKTS 9 Cd.5030.

[63] Hoffmann, above note 57, 76.

[64] XV LRTWC xiii.

times, particularly in the *Norman* Child Soldiers opinion.[65] In this, the Appeals Chamber provided a very brief review of State practice to come to the conclusion that enlisting or using child soldiers (ie aged under 15) was a war crime prior to its positive codification in the Rome Statute in 1998.[66] Given that the majority relied in part on the fact that the prohibition reflected 'important values',[67] it could be thought that they were engaging in some naturalistic speculation, and seeking to equate a (somewhat contested) morality with existing law.

This decision was subject to a bitter dissent by Judge Robertson, on the basis that:

> It must be acknowledged that like most absolute principles, *nullum crimen* can be highly inconvenient – especially in relation to conduct which is abhorrent or grotesque, but which parliament has not thought to legislate against. Every law student can point to cases where judges have been tempted to circumvent the *nullum crimen* principle to criminalise conduct which they regard as seriously anti-social or immoral, but which has not been outlawed by legislation or by established categories of common-law crimes. This temptation must be firmly resisted by international law judges, with no legislature to correct or improve upon them and with a subject – international criminal law – which came into effective operation as recently as the judgment at Nuremberg in 1946. Here the Prosecution asserts with some insouciance that 'the principle of *nullum crimen sine lege* is not applied rigidly, particularly where the acts in question are universally regarded as abhorrent and deeply shock the conscience of humanity.' On the contrary, it is precisely when the acts are abhorrent and deeply shocking that the principle of legality must be most stringently applied, to ensure that a defendant is not convicted out of disgust rather than evidence, or of a non-existent crime.[68]

As van Schaack has noted, the chambers have at times:

> Elid[ed] the morally wrong and the legally criminal, invoke[d] the natural law tradition found in all international law. This tradition is particularly cogent in ICL [(International Criminal Law)] ... which has its origins in the belief that the

---

65 *Prosecutor* v *Norman* (*Decision on Preliminary Motion Based on Lack of Jurisdiction (Child Recruitment)*) (Special Court of Sierra Leone, Appeal Chamber, Case No SCSL-2004–14-A, 31 May 2004). Again, it is important to note that these cases occur generally against the background of most of the cases not being so clearly on one side or the other. Only a detailed deconstruction of all the cases could give a definitive discussion on point, but lies far beyond the remit of this chapter.

66 Ibid [17]–[24].

67 Ibid [28]–[29].

68 Ibid Dissenting Opinion of Judge Robertson [12]; see van Schaack, above note 40, 162–63.

> law must conform to a universal transnational morality and conception of justice. Many ICL cases proceed as though a transcendent law exists that has yet to be reduced to positive law but that can be discovered and invoked in criminal proceedings.[69]

Alongside the vague nature of international criminal law and as with the ad hoc tribunals, this has led to allegations that they are legislating from the bench on the basis of morality.[70]

But the historical continuity has now perhaps broken down. When the Rome Statute was being drafted, it was clear that some delegates wished to hem in the discretion of the judges, hence (unlike in the ICTY) *inter alia* there was a closed list of war crimes.[71] In the more general parts of the Statute though, a highly positivistic approach is also visible.[72] To take Art 22 as an example, while the recitation of the *nullum crimen sine lege* principle in para 1 is not especially controversial, the second paragraph is indicative of a very stern view of the appropriate ambit of judicial discretion: 'the definition of a crime shall be strictly construed and shall not be extended by analogy. In case of ambiguity, the definition shall be interpreted in favour of the person being investigated, prosecuted or convicted.' The contrast with the post-Second World War trials can hardly be stronger, and in addition, the British Judge Advocate in the *Peleus* trial averred almost precisely the opposite, that the Court should not be embarrassed about any ambiguity in international law in convicting the accused, as everyone simply knew that the orders in the case (to shoot the shipwrecked) were unlawful.[73]

---

[69] Van Schaack above note 40, 157. Some scepticism might be expressed that natural law is present in all international law, but that debate need not (and probably could not) be settled in a chapter with this focus (or in one chapter at all).

[70] See eg Shane Darcy and Joseph Powderly (eds), *Judicial Creativity in International Criminal Tribunals* (Oxford University Press 2011); Mia Swart, 'Judicial Lawmaking at the ad Hoc Tribunals: The Creative Use of the Sources of International Law and "Adventurous Interpretation"' (2010) 70 *Zeitschrift for ausländisches öffentliches Recht und Völkerrecht* 459.

[71] See Cryer, above note 2, ch 5; Bruce Broomhall, 'Article 22' in Otto Triffterer (ed), *Commentary on the Rome Statute of the International Criminal Court: Observer's Notes: Article by Article* (2nd edn, Hart 2008) 713, 714.

[72] On positivism and codification of the criminal law see Jeremy Horder, 'Criminal Law and Legal Positivism' (2002) 8 *Legal Theory* 221.

[73] I LRTWC 11.

Art 22 is not the only place in which such an approach is manifest. It is also present in Art 21, which provides the applicable sources of law and thus provides the bedrock of the approach the Court is entitled to take.[74] Art 21 reads that:

> The Court shall apply:
>
> (a) In the first place, this Statute, Elements of Crimes and its Rules of Procedure and Evidence;
>
> (b) In the second place, where appropriate, applicable treaties and the principles and rules of international law, including the established principles of the international law of armed conflict;
>
> (c) Failing that, general principles of law derived by the Court from national laws of legal systems of the world including, as appropriate, the national laws of States that would normally exercise jurisdiction over the crime, provided that those principles are not inconsistent with this Statute and with international law and internationally recognized norms and standards.[75]

This provision was intended to relate to the *nullum crimen* principle, and does so by setting up a clear hierarchy of sources.[76] At the top are the Statute, Rules of Procedure and Evidence, and (although they are only guidance) the Elements of Crimes.[77] A preference for written law (emanating from the drafters) is clearly visible. Even customary law (which is not to form the basis of criminal liability itself, owing *inter alia* to the exclusive nature of the lists of offences in Arts 6–8 and the strictures of Art 22) and 'applicable treaties' are relegated to second place. Custom (controversially)

---

74 See also van Schaack, above note 40, 189.

75 See generally Margaret McAuliffe deGuzman, 'Article 21' in Triffterer above note 71, 701. For a critique of the provision in practice see Robert Cryer, 'Royalism and The King: Article 21 of the Rome Statute and the Politics of Sources' (2009) 12 *New Criminal Law Review* 390.

76 deGuzman, above note 75, 702.

77 On the normative status of the Elements see William Schabas, *The International Criminal Court: A Commentary on the Rome Statute* (Oxford University Press 2010) 258–68.

and general principles are relegated to secondary and tertiary roles respectively, although judicial discretion and perhaps natural law[78] could enter into the equation for both.[79]

Even where definitions of crimes could be agreed in Rome, this was not enough for some delegations[80] who wanted greater specificity in the definition of offences, either for principled, political or presentational reasons.[81] This led to Art 9 of the Rome Statute which provided for the drafting of Elements of Crimes: a very detailed set of requirements for conviction which practically amount to a 'check-list' of the necessary parts of offences that needed to be proved. Although many States found the process useful,[82] William Schabas has commented that these Elements were an extraordinary example of an 'obsessive' legal positivism on the part of some of the drafters.[83] Again, the contrast with earlier tribunals is striking, but can be explained on the basis that the drafters were aware that the ICC was an 'unsafe' tribunal which could exercise jurisdiction over their own nationals, whereas the ad hoc tribunals were not expected to do this.[84] This affected their approach to the *nullum crimen* principle, which in this instance was a metonym for their more general if rarely-expressed political/philosophical approach.[85]

A third area in which the highly positivist approach to the law (in contrast to earlier international criminal tribunals such as the Nuremberg and Tokyo IMTs) can be seen is in relation to the crime of aggression. As is well known, at Rome the drafters could not agree upon a definition of that crime, hence the provision for jurisdiction over that offence in Art 5(1) of the Statute, but with the proviso that the Court was not to exercise jurisdiction over that offence unless and until the Statute was amended to include a definition of aggression.[86] The preference for written law over

---

78 Ian Brownlie, *Principles of International Law* (7th edn, Oxford University Press 2008) 16.

79 deGuzman, above note 75, 708–10; see also Fabián O Raimondo, *General Principles of Law in the Decisions of the International Criminal Courts and Tribunals* (Nijhoff 2008) 149–57.

80 In particular, the United States.

81 For some of them see Schabas, above note 77, 258–61.

82 Roy S Lee, 'Introduction' Roy S Lee *et al* (eds), *The International Criminal Court: Elements of Crimes and Rules of Procedure and Evidence* (Transnational 2001) lv, lv–lviii.

83 William Schabas, 'Interpreting the Statutes of the *ad hoc* Tribunals' in Vohrah *et al* (eds) above note 49, 847, 887.

84 Cryer, above note 2, chs 5–6.

85 As might be surmised from the above, the two are not usually so separate.

86 Schabas, above note 77, 109–15.

custom,[87] judicial discretion and arguably (if one is to believe the Prosecution at the Tokyo IMT) natural law, is clear. The recent adoption of a definition of aggression that may be included in the Rome Statute (if it achieves sufficient ratifications) is an instantiation of this approach, not a confounding of it.[88] Approaches which allowed the participants to draw on naturalism were considered acceptable in the post-War era, but were not acceptable for the ICC which might assert jurisdiction over the nationals of the drafters.

The appellate judges of the ICC have largely adopted the positivistic inclinations of the drafters. In part, owing to Art 21, they did not have much of a choice.[89] Nonetheless, the ICC is fully aware that, as a court of voluntary rather than compulsory jurisdiction, if it is to attract ratifications to the Statute, cooperation and financial support, it must not scare States too much, whose approach to international law tends towards the positivist, at least in its presentational form.[90] It is true that when pre-trial chambers and trial chambers have dealt with the law, they have not always been as positivistically inclined,[91] but the Appeals Chamber has been fairly consistent on point, at least at this early stage.

---

87 Aggression is a crime in customary international law, *R v Jones, Milling et al* [2006] UKHL 16, [2007] 1 AC 136.

88 On the debate see Roger S Clark, 'Amendments to the Rome Statute of the International Criminal Court Considered at the First Review Conference on the Court, Kampala, 31 May–11 June 2010' (2010) 2 *Göttingen Journal of International Law* 689; Robert Heinisch, 'The Crime of Aggression After Kampala: Success or Burden for the Future?' (2010) 2 *Göttingen Journal of International Law* 713. For a broad set of reflections see the symposium in (2012) 10 *Journal of International Criminal Justice* 3–288.

89 Although they have at times gone beyond what even Art 21 requires in this regard, Cryer, above note 75.

90 Michael Struett, 'The Politics of Discursive Legitimacy: Understanding the Dynamics and Implications of Prosecutorial Discretion at the International Criminal Court' in Steven Roach (ed), *Governance, Order, and the International Criminal Court: Between Realpolitik and a Cosmopolitan Court* (Oxford University Press 2009) 107.

91 Although they have at times been exactly that, see Cryer above note 75,156. On the other hand, in the first full decision of the trial chamber, the difference between the majority, who tended to rely on the Statute and *travaux preparatoires*, in a fairly traditional positivistic manner, Judge Odio Benito, on the other hand spoke far more of progressive development of the law and more nebulous concepts of the 'object and purpose' of the Statute to rather get around its plain meaning. *Lubanga*, above note 21, Separate and Dissenting Opinion of Judge Odio Benito, [6]–[7].

## B. Victor's Justice

It is a frequently made charge against the post-War trials that they were 'victor's justice', a phrase that tends to have a pejorative implication, the emphasis being more on the first word than the latter. This is in spite of the fact that Justice Jackson, the US prosecutor at Nuremberg, had anticipated such a charge, and in his *tour de force* of an opening speech asserted that

> the record on which we judge these defendants today is the record on which history will judge us tomorrow. To pass these defendants a poisoned chalice is to put it to our lips as well ... [a]nd let me make clear that while this law is first applied against German aggressors, the law includes, and if it is to serve a useful purpose it must condemn, aggression by any other nations, including those which sit here now in judgment.[92]

Indeed Judge Pal in the Tokyo IMT raised a similar argument against the tribunal, finishing his opinion (in which he voted in favour of acquittal of all of the defendants) with the statement that:

> The vindictive and oratorical pleas of the prosecutors in the language of emotionalized generalities did entertain rather than educate. We may not altogether ignore the possibility that perhaps the responsibility did not lie only with the defeated leaders. Perhaps the guilt of the leaders was only their misconception, probably founded on illusions. It may indeed be that such illusions were only egocentric. Yet we cannot overlook the fact that even as such egocentric illusions, these are ingrained in human minds everywhere. It is very likely that: 'When time shall have softened passion and prejudice, when Reason shall have stripped the mask from misrepresentation, then Justice, holding evenly her scales, will require much of past censure and praise to change places'.[93]

Such criticisms had some purchase, as Allied conduct was not, in essence, subject to similar scrutiny to that of the Axis powers.[94] To say so is not to argue in any way that there was moral equivalence between the parties to the Second World War, but to accept that few hands are fully clean at the end of a large-scale conflict. Sadly, from the post-Nuremberg era until the early 1990s, the promise that the law would be applied without fear or favour was

---

[92] *Trial of Major War Criminals Before The International Military Tribunal, Nuremberg,* 49, 85.

[93] Boister and Cryer, above note 23, 1426.

[94] Robert Cryer, Hakan Friman, Darryl Robinson, and Elizabeth Wilmshurst, *An Introduction to International Criminal Law and Procedure* (2nd edn, Cambridge University Press 2010) 114.

essentially honoured only in the breach.[95] Perhaps it was thought that there would be no question of victor's justice in the UN's creation of the ICTY and ICTR, because the UN is meant to be an impartial organisation. However, the ICTY and ICTR have not been immune from claims that their practice, if not their founding documents,[96] have reflected a selective, victor's justice approach, with all the hypocrisy implied.

Although the formal documents of the ICTY and ICTR do not limit their jurisdiction, practicalities have done so. When members of civil society (who may or may not have been reflective of cosmopolitan world opinion) called on the ICTY for the prosecution of NATO officials, hackles were raised on both sides. In spite of initial apparent sympathy (or at least tolerance) from the Prosecutor, such calls led to a rather unconvincing report that argued against further investigation. Nonetheless, the report hardly read like an independent review,[97] and looked to many to be a political call, covered by a (transparent) pretext on the basis that the NATO permanent five members of the Security Council were hostile to any such examination of their conduct, and would have turned off political support, cooperation and money taps if the ICTY continued with such investigations.[98] As William Schabas, among others, has said, it is difficult to see this as anything other than a decision taken on political, rather than objective grounds.[99]

The ICTR has also been subject to similar charges. The Prosecutors of that Tribunal have been chary of looking into crimes committed by the Rwandan Patriotic Front (RPF). The vast majority of victims and witnesses were in Rwanda and, after the *Barayagwiza* decision, if not before,[100] the government of Rwanda has in both word and deed made it clear that its commitment to the Tribunal is contingent on it not looking into RPF offences.[101] The rhetoric of international criminal justice has been a major aspect of the debate about Rwanda from the start. However, that reaction of the ICTR has understandably been subject to critiques that not only refer to

---

95 See Cryer, above note 2, 50–51.

96 Which rather differentiate them from their post-War counterparts, see eg Schabas, above note 30, 74–76.

97 See Cryer, above note 2, 215–20.

98 Danilo Zolo, *Victors' Justice: From Nuremberg to Baghdad* (Verso 2009) 149–58; Schabas, above note 30, 77–79.

99 Schabas, ibid 77–78.

100 William A Schabas, 'Prosecutor v Barayagwiza' (2000) 94 *American Journal of International Law* 563, 565. Victor Peskin, *International Justice in Rwanda and the Balkans: Virtual Trials and the Struggle for State Cooperation* (Cambridge University Press 2008) 170–72.

101 Peskin, above note 100, 208–31; Schabas, above note 30, 78–80.

the same issues (ie victor's justice), but also adopt the same idiom as the critiques of the post-War trials either of victor's justice, or of Nuremberg itself.[102]

The picture is a little more mixed in the hybrid tribunals, when, for example, the Sierra Leone Government perhaps assumed that the Special Court would prosecute the Revolutionary United Front and Armed Forces Revolutionary Council (two rebel groups), but the Prosecutor proceeded against members of the Civil Defence Forces (CDF), including a sitting government minister (Sam Hinga Norman). Although Norman died before judgment was reached, this perhaps serves as a counter-example, although it cannot be ignored that in the CDF trial, Judge King, to all intents and purposes, voted to acquit the remaining defendants on the basis that they were fighting, in his view, on the side of the angels.[103]

William Schabas has also criticised the creation of the Special Tribunal for Lebanon, on the basis that the 2005 killing of Rafiq Hariri, a leader friendly to the West with international connections, gave rise to a hybrid tribunal, when many other more serious events have not led to a similar level of international involvement.[104] It might be thought that being a member of the international elite increases the protection granted by international criminal law, in the sense that offences against such persons are more likely to be the subject of international attention (and prosecution) than others, or that offences committed by such people are less likely to be prosecuted (as long as they remain part of it; once they are not, the same does not apply, as demonstrated by Saddam Hussein's experience). That said, the extent to which this factor has a direct effect must remain at the level of speculation.[105]

There have been considerable criticisms of the ICC for its focus on Africa in the first decade of its operational life. In spite of the initial support for the ICC in the majority of States in Africa, the fact that the initial focus of the ICC has been on Africa has led to critiques on point. Criticism came first of

---

[102] Zolo, above note 98, *passim*; Luc Reydams, 'The ICTR Ten Years On: Back to the Nuremberg Paradigm?' (2005) 3 *Journal of International Criminal Justice* 977; Peskin, above note 100, ch 9.

[103] *Prosecutor v Fofana and Kondewa* (Appeal Judgment) (Special Court of Sierra Leone, Appeal Chambers, Case No SCSL-04–14-A, 28 May 2008), partially Dissenting Opinion of Judge George Gelaga King, [26]–[31], 90–94.

[104] Schabas, above note 30, 80.

[105] Such luminaries as Ian Brownlie have weighed in on point, asserting that '[t]he overall problem remains. Political considerations, power, and patronage will continue to determine who is to be tried for international crimes and who not'. Brownlie, above note 78, 604.

all from an 'interested' observer, the Representative of Sudan at the Security Council when the situation in Darfur was referred to the ICC by the Security Council. At the relevant Security Council meeting he asserted that the referral

> exposed the fact that this criminal court was originally intended for developing and weak States, and that it is a tool for the exercise of the culture of superiority and to impose cultural superiority. It is a tool for those who believe that they have a monopoly on virtues in this world, rife with injustice and tyranny ... [106]

This was later picked up by a spokesman for the African Union, who criticised the Prosecutor on the basis that: 'We Africans and the African Union are not against the International Criminal Court. That should be clear ... We are against [Prosecutor Moreno] Ocampo who is rendering justice with double standards.' Noting that all current investigations related to African States, he rhetorically asked: 'Why not Argentina, why not Myanmar ... why not Iraq?'[107]

There are practical answers to many of these critiques (at least for the first two situations, and probably the third),[108] and, in addition, there have been self-referrals of a number of situations in Africa that might mitigate the critique.[109] Whatever the merits of the arguments in this situation, the fact is that the idiom of the argument is a form of victor's justice, be it explicit (such as the treatment of Saddam Hussein),[110] or in the more (perhaps Marxist, or realist) implicit manner, that the 'winners' (those States that 'won' the economic peace in the post-War era) have greater power over and protection from international criminal law. Whether accurately applied or not, this critique has considerable resonance both then and now, and interestingly from both left- and right-wing commentators.[111]

---

106 UN SCOR, UN Doc, 60th sess, 5158th mtg, UN DOC S/PV/5158 (31 March 2005), 12 (Mr Erwa).

107 'African Union Accuses ICC Prosecutor of Bias' *Reuters* (New York, 30 January 2011) <http://af.reuters.com/article/topNews/idAFJOE70T01R20110130?pageNumber=1&virtualBrandChannel=0>.

108 See Robert Cryer, 'Selectivity in International Criminal Law' in Faria Medjouba (ed), *Building Peace in Post-Conflict Situations* (British Institute of International and Comparative Law 2011) 153, 185–86.

109 Ibid 186–87.

110 Zolo, above note 98, 159–66.

111 Ibid; Gerry Simpson, *Law, War and Crime: War Crimes Trials and the Reinvention of International Law* (Polity 2007) 16–18 (albeit noting that the critique is often a crude one) (broadly from the left); Chantal Delsol, *Unjust Justice: Against the Tyranny of International Law* (Intercollegiate Studies Institute Books 2008) (from the right).

## C. Money

The influence of money is perhaps international criminal law's dirty little secret, previously and in the present day. Money can influence the decisions to initiate prosecutions, the time taken to continue such prosecutions, and, perhaps more cynically, who to prosecute. One of the very rare times in which the issue was discussed openly was in South Africa, in the *AZAPO* case. Here the Court opined that:

> the Constitution seeks to … facilitate the transition to a new democratic order, committed to 'reconciliation between the people of South Africa and the reconstruction of society'. The question is how this can be done effectively with the limitations of our resources and the legacy of the past … The country has neither the resources nor the skills to reverse fully these massive wrongs … Those negotiators of the Constitution and leaders of the nation who were required to address themselves to these agonising problems must have been compelled to make hard choices … They were entitled to permit the claims of … school children and the poor and the homeless to be preferred.[112]

For the most part, the question of funding has been dealt with at the diplomatic level. This had an impact in the post-War era: the questions of whether or not a second international trial in Nuremberg ought to occur came down in part to the question of whether the United States was willing to finance it.[113] Funding or the lack thereof was used as a means of controlling the US subsequent proceedings, and led to resignations and reductions in the number of defendants.[114] Economic considerations (in the broader sense) also impacted upon the decisions to prosecute, and the de-Nazification process.[115] Similar considerations applied to the non-prosecution (and release) of certain Japanese industrialists and politicians.[116]

---

112 *Azanian People's Organization (AZAPO) and others v President of the Republic of South Africa* (1996) 4 SA 562 (CC) [42]–[45].

113 Donald Bloxham, *Genocide on Trial: War Crimes Trials and the Formation of Holocaust History and Memory* (Oxford University Press 2001), 29–30; Telford Taylor, *Final Report to the Secretary of the Army on the Nuremberg Trials Under Control Council Law 10* (US Government 1949) 26.

114 Heller, above note 6, 36–38.

115 See, eg Bloxham, above note 113, 30–31; Heller, above note 6, 21–22; Tom Bower, *Blind Eye to Murder, Britain, America and the Purging of Nazi Germany – A Pledge Betrayed* (Little, Brown and Company 1997).

116 Meirion Harries and Susie Harries, *Sheathing the Sword: The Demilitarisation of Japan* (Hamish Hamilton 1987) ch 20; Than Tun, 'Comments' in C Hosoya,

In the modern era of international criminal justice, the influence of finance is also there. The critiques of the cost of the international criminal tribunals (the ICTY and ICTR), of which there have been many,[117] led to two related phenomena. The first (albeit not chronologically) is the 'completion strategy'. This began in 2003, when the Tribunal(s) amended their rules to allow for referral of cases to national jurisdictions for prosecutions and set timetables (none of which have been kept to) for the ending of investigations, trials and appeals.[118] There is no question that the completion strategies were inspired, in no small degree, by the increasing unwillingness of the UN to continue to fund the Tribunals. The analogy between the creation of Rule 11 *bis*, to allow national prosecution of those who would otherwise have been tried internationally, and the post-War experience, cannot pass by unnoticed; neither can the fact that money has played a considerable (although not always determinative) role in both instances in deciding how many people are prosecuted.

The second phenomenon is what is known as 'tribunal fatigue'. This refers to the fact that the Security Council became unwilling to create any further ad hoc international criminal tribunals in the 1990s.[119] When the Special Court for Sierra Leone was being created, funding was therefore a 'red-line' issue for the Security Council, who insisted, over the concerns of the Secretary-General, that the financing of the Court be based on voluntary contributions.[120] The Court determined that this fact alone did not mean that the judicial work of the Tribunal was biased,[121] but there is no question that

N Ando, Y Onuma and R Minear (eds), *The Tokyo War Crimes Trial: An International Symposium* (Kodanasha 1986) 101, 102.

117 For a representative example, see Ralph Zacklin, 'The Failings of Ad Hoc International Tribunals' (2004) 2 *Journal of International Criminal Justice* 541, 545.

118 See, eg Darryl A Mundis, 'The Judicial Effects of the "Completion Strategies" on the ad hoc International Criminal Tribunals' (2005) 99 *American Journal of International Law* 142; Larry D Johnson, 'Closing an International Criminal Tribunal While Maintaining International Human Rights Standards and Excluding Impunity' (2005) 99 *American Journal of International Law* 158.

119 David Scheffer, *All the Missing Souls: A Personal History of the War Crimes Tribunals* (Princeton University Press 2012), 118. The fact that in relation to the ICTY there had been a considerable row about the sources of funding between the Security Council and the General Assembly cannot be overestimated here either.

120 Robert Cryer, 'A Special Court for Sierra Leone?' (2001) 50 *The International and Comparative Quarterly* 435, 438–39.

121 *Prosecutor v Norman* (Decision on Preliminary Motion Based on Lack of Jurisdiction (Judicial Independence)) (Special Court of Sierra Leone, Appeal Chamber, Case No SCSL-2004–14-AR72(E), 13 March 2004).

the matter of money has impacted on the work of the Court on, for example, the pace of work,[122] and the number of indictees.[123] In addition, the larger donors (in particular the UK) had a position on the management committee of the Court, and they were firmly kept 'in the loop' as to the activities of the Prosecutor at early and critical moments.[124]

Looking at the operation of the ad hoc tribunals, the fact remains that although their funding is formally a matter of the UN budget, some States (in particular the US) have provided very considerable financial, logical and other support in kind to the ICTY, crucial in the early days when its finances were perilous.[125] As such, some put the fact that NATO States were not fully investigated over their actions with respect to Kosovo down to the support given to the Tribunal by those States.[126] The memoirs of David Scheffer, the US's most senior official on war crimes at the time, do little to dispel such fears.[127] The provision of cooperation is also often cited as part of the reason why the ICTY has not turned upon its sponsors.[128] This is almost certainly true, but money has its place here too. The US has provided rewards for the arrests of various indictees from the ICTY, and it is no secret that the transfer of Slobodan Milošević occurred largely because of the pressure put on Yugoslavia by the US, who promised to block loans from the International Monetary Fund (IMF) unless and until he was handed over to the ICTY.[129]

When it has come to the ICC, it would be naïve to think that money has played no role. The extent to which the Assembly of States Parties retains a considerable degree of control over the Office of the Prosecutor through the approval of the ICC's budget deserves further scrutiny. Suffice it to say here, as has been said elsewhere: 'The extraordinary specificity which has characterized the early budgets of the ICC ought to be sufficient to calm the

---

[122] Scheffer, above note 119, 338–39. See generally, Sara Kendall, 'Donor's Justice: Recasting International Criminal Accountability' (2011) 24 *Leiden Journal of International Law* 585.

[123] Kendall, ibid 594, 602–4.

[124] David M Crane, 'The Bright Red Thread: The Politics of International Criminal Law – Do We Want Peace or Justice? The West African Experience' in Leila N Sadat (ed), *Forging a Convention for Crimes Against Humanity* (Cambridge University Press 2011) 59, 67–74.

[125] Scheffer, above note 119, 33–35.

[126] Zolo, above note 98, 149.

[127] Scheffer, above note 119, 291–92.

[128] Ibid.

[129] CSR Report RS21686, *Conditions on US Aid to Serbia,* by Steven Woehrel, 2.

most tremulous critic of the Rome regime of prosecutorial discretion.'[130] There is no line in the budget for spurious investigations, and the Prosecutor has also targeted investigations to take into account the resources of the court. Witnesses before the Court have also noted the impact of resources on investigations by the ICC.[131]

It is against the background of the relevance of financial constraint that the Security Council referrals of the Darfur and Libya situations need to be viewed. Resolution 1593, which sent the Darfur situation to the ICC, required (in a manner which is hardly compatible with the relevant allocation of budgetary authority between the Security Council and the General Assembly) the UN–ICC Relationship Agreement; Art 115 of the Rome Statute demanded that no UN funding be given to finance the investigations following the referral.[132] Lest this be thought apolitical, consider the statement of the US representative at the meeting which adopted the resolution:

> We are pleased that the resolution recognizes that none of the expenses incurred in connection with the referral will be borne by the United Nations ... This principle is extremely important and we want to be clear that any effort to retrench on that principle by this or other organizations to which we contribute could result in our withholding funding or taking other action in response.[133]

In other words, the willingness of the US to allow the situation in Darfur to go before an international criminal tribunal was tempered by the fact that it was unwilling to grant legitimacy to the ICC by allowing it to grant funds. Some might think that this was owing to the fact that the US did not actually want the atrocities in Darfur to be effectively investigated.[134] This seems unlikely, given that the US was willing to fund a separate Darfur Tribunal itself rather than see the matter go to the ICC.[135] The implication that the US view can plausibly be interpreted as linking funding to the extent to which a

---

130 Olympia Bekou and Robert Cryer. 'The International Criminal Court and Universal Jurisdiction: A Close Encounter?' (2007) 56 *The International and Comparative Law Quarterly* 49, 57.

131 *Prosecutor v Lubanga* (Trial Judgment) (ICC, Case No ICC-01/04–01/06, 14 March 2012), [358].

132 See Robert Cryer, 'Sudan, Resolution 1593 and International Criminal Justice' (2006) 19 *Leiden Journal of International Law* 195, 206–8.

133 UN SCOR, UN Doc, 60th sess, 5158th mtg, UN DOC S/PV/5158 (31 March 2005), 4 (Mrs Patterson).

134 This view was once expressed to me verbally by a very well-known international criminal lawyer, who however has not committed that view to print. As such I will preserve their anonymity, and simply say that it is not my own.

135 Cryer, above note 132, 201–2.

tribunal could act contrary to its interests, is salutary. Again, it is possible to believe that the US's views have changed, in that rather than abstaining from the vote (as it did for Resolution 1593), it voted for the referral of the situation in Libya from February 2011 to the ICC in Resolution 1970. However, that Resolution also required the UN to refrain from funding the investigations and prosecutions that followed from it. This is no more lawful than the equivalent parts of Resolution 1593, but shows that in international criminal law, money, *inter alia*, still talks.

## V. DISJUNCTURES

Having canvassed a selection of the similarities between the post-War era and modern international criminal justice, it is important not to move from this to claim identity between the issues that have arisen. As the clichés go, although it might be the case that those who forget history are condemned to repeat it,[136] it is also the case that 'the past is a foreign country: they do things differently there'.[137] As such it would be simplistic to assume that everything was the same without further investigation. Indeed, there are some significant differences between then and now, although on closer examination, some of these differences seem smaller than might initially be thought.

### A. The Peace/Justice Debate

Perhaps the absence of the peace/justice debate in the post-War climate is the most striking difference between it and the current day, where it rages as one of the most divisive issues in international criminal justice. In both the European and Pacific spheres, the idea of a negotiated peace was an anathema to the Allies. By the time the tide had begun to turn against the Axis, there was no question of anything other than a reckoning for the Nazis, at least in the European sphere. Hence, on 1 November 1943, the US, UK and USSR, acting on behalf of all of the Allied States, issued the Moscow Declaration which

> declar[ed] … at the time of the granting of any armistice to any government that may be set up in Germany, those German officers and men and members of the Nazi party who have been responsible for, or have taken a consenting part in the

---

[136] George Santanaya, *Life of Reason, Reason in Common Sense* (Scribner 1905) 284.

[137] L P Hartley, *The Go-Between* (Hamish Hamilton 1953) 1.

> atrocities, massacres and executions, will be sent back to the countries in which their abominable deeds were done in order that they may be judged and punished according to the laws of the liberated countries and of the free governments which will be erected therein ... *the above declaration is without prejudice to the case of the major criminals whose offences have no particular geographical location and who will be punished by a joint declaration of the governments of the Allies.*[138]

The only issue to be decided was what to do with the major war criminals. Opinion was split, along the lines of whether they should be tried or just shot. Whether or not this would lead to prolonging the war was not a major concern to governmental figures,[139] other than to a few marginal and troubling people such as Lord Hankey.[140]

Similarly, in the Pacific sphere on 26 July 1945, the US, China and the UK issued the Potsdam declaration, which provided:

> There must be eliminated for all time the authority and influence of those who have deceived and misled the people of Japan into embarking on world conquest, for we insist that a new order of peace, security and justice will be impossible until irresponsible militarism is driven from the world.

Principle 10, however, was the crucial provision: 'We do not intend that the Japanese people shall be enslaved as a race or destroyed as a nation, but stern justice shall be meted out to all war criminals including those who have visited cruelties upon our prisoners.'[141] Some argue that this delayed the Japanese surrender, on the basis that the Allies had refused to grant immunity to the Emperor.[142]

A rare example of the peace/justice issue being raised formally was by the defence counsel in the Tokyo IMT. In a motion to the Court, the defence

---

138 Declaration of Moscow 1 November 1943, 9 (US) *Department of State Bulletin* 310 (No. 228, 6 November 1943) (emphasis added).

139 Outside of government, though, such luminaries as George Orwell asserted that it would be better to allow Hitler and Mussolini to scuttle off into obscurity, to show their fundamental cowardice and venality. See George Orwell, 'Who Are the War Criminals?' *The Tribune* (22 October 1943), reprinted in Sonia Orwell and Ian Angus (eds), *George Orwell The Collected Essays, Journalism and Letters: Volume 2 1940–1943 My Country, Right or Left* (Penguin 1970) 363, 369.

140 Lord Hankey, *Politics, Trials and Errors* (Pen in Hand 1950). It is not necessary to deconstruct his work to find racism; it is there on the surface. See, eg 66–67, where he considers stationing black soldiers in the Rhineland to be a provocative act on the part of the Allies.

141 Tokyo IMT Transcript, 48, 417; Annex A-1 of the Judgment.

142 Arnold Brackman, *The Other Nuremberg: The Untold Story of the Tokyo War Crimes Trials* (William Morrow 1987) 34.

asked to send a list of questions to 'the world's highest authorities on morals and right conduct, and ... the chief exponents of human wisdom'.[143] These included:

> Whether it would not gravely embarrass statesmen everywhere in the conduct of affairs that they should have to reckon continually with the possibility of their acts being given a criminal interpretation and their having to defend themselves against imputations based on suppositions, inferences and hypercriticism? Whether the law of nations can safely permit the conduct of affairs to be embarrassed this way? ... Will not the knowledge that they may be treated as gross criminals, render the statesmen of the future as desperate and cruel as brigands and pirates?

Perhaps unsurprisingly, the Tribunal did not accede to the request.

Perhaps the closest matter to the modern peace/justice debate in the post-War climate was the possibility of trying the Emperor of Japan. He was left off the indictment largely on the basis that the US considered it expedient to do so, reasoning that his position would assist the effectiveness of the reforms that were intended to be undertaken during the occupation.[144] The broad policy, however, was initially set at prosecution. That said, as mentioned above, reconstruction was clearly an issue in the later prosecution policy in Japan, in that a number of industrial and political figures were exempted from prosecution owing to the fact that they would be useful in the reconstruction of Japan, and later to bolster its role as a bulwark against communism for the US in the Pacific sphere.[145]

Similarly, the relatively quick release of many Nazis, the decision to all intents and purposes to exempt many German industrialists from prosecution (other than the notable *Farben* and *Krupp* cases)[146] and much of the de-Nazification processes, were more on the basis of reconstruction versus justice, rather than peace versus justice. This is something largely absent from debates today, at least expressly. It might be possible to argue that the failure of the West to push further for the indictment of RPF crimes comes

---

[143] Who were, 'His Holiness Pius, the Twelfth of that name, Pope and Bishop of Rome, Mahatma Ghandi of India, the Reverend Karl Berth of Switzerland, John Dewey, Esq, of the USA, André Gide, Esq, of France, Robert Maynard Hutchins, Esq, of the USA, Aldous Huxley, Esq, of England, Roscoe Pound, Esq, of the USA, Hu Shuh, Esq, of China, and Herbert George Wells, Esq, of England, Rabbi Stephen Wise of the USA' IMTFE Papers 148 (15), 12 June 1946, Motion.

[144] See Boister and Cryer, above note 6, 65–69.

[145] See above note 116 and accompanying text.

[146] *Krauch* X LRTWC 1; *Krupp* X LRTWC 69 respectively.

from a willingness to prefer the reconstruction of Rwanda, by the autocratic, albeit effective regime of Paul Kagame, to the pursuit of justice at all costs. Even that might be subject to the response that France (not without controversy) has indicted various high level Rwandan officials for various crimes. This, however, is also subject to the rejoinder that it proves that 'the West' is far from a monolithic entity with a consistent and coherent set of interests and policies.

The Rwanda situation does perhaps have some other similarities with the Second World War era, in that the RPF (which became the government of Rwanda) called for trials rather than negotiations in mid-1994,[147] after the tide had turned against their opponents, in this case the genocidal Habyarimana regime. The same cannot be said for the Yugoslav situation, although the decision to create an international tribunal was taken in 1993, in Security Council Resolutions 808 and 827. The Tribunal was at best on an insecure footing in its early years, with some advocating it be abolished in favour of peace up until the Dayton Accords.[148] Of course, this could be put down to the fact that the outcome of the conflict was uncertain until then, but this would overlook the fact that the Tribunal was created two years before the Accords, and in accordance with the wishes of at least one of the parties (the Bosniaks); it had already obtained its own momentum by that time and thus become an actor in its own right. Nonetheless, the peace/justice issue had been raised at some level there. The issue has not gone away – prior to the Iraq and Libya conflicts, both Saddam Hussein and Colonel Gadhafi were offered a negotiated exit and exile rather than prosecution, although neither availed themselves of the option, with fatal consequences.

With the ICC, the peace/justice (real or imagined) duality has been raised, both in the negotiations for the Court, and with respect to its practice. In spite of a US 'non-paper' on amnesties distributed at Rome, the ICC's Statute very carefully avoids pronouncing directly on the legality of amnesties, in spite of its distinct hints that they are frowned upon.[149] This is not

---

[147] Virginia Morris and Michael Scharf, *The International Criminal Tribunal for Rwanda* (Transnational 1998) 62.

[148] Anthony D'Amato, 'Peace v Accountability in Bosnia' (1994) 88 *American Journal of International Law* 500 *contra* the correspondence in (1994) 88 *American Journal of International Law* 717; (1995) 89 *American Journal of International Law* 93; (1995) 89 *American Journal of International Law* 94. See generally Anonymous, 'Human Rights in Peace Negotiations' (1996) 18 *Human Rights Quarterly* 249.

[149] See, eg Darryl Robinson, 'Serving the Interests of Justice: Amnesties, Truth Commissions and the International Criminal Court' (2003) 14 *European Journal of*

quite the same though as deciding whether or not an investigation or prosecution ought to be undertaken.

The peace/justice issue is implicit in Art 16 of the Rome Statute, which permits the deferral for a (renewable) year-long period of investigations and proceedings if the Security Council requests it in the interests of countering a threat to international peace and security.[150] The basis for this was the ambivalence between peace and justice present in Rome, which has since plagued aspects of the ICC's practice.[151] In response to the indictment of Omar al-Bashir, the African Union, until that time mostly supportive of the Court, claimed that the indictment would undermine the peace process, and implored the Security Council to invoke Art 16. The Council refused to do so, merely

> *[t]aking note* of the African Union (AU) communiqué of the 142nd Peace and Security Council ... [which asked that the Security Council issue a deferral request compliant with Art 16 of the Rome Statute] ... *having in mind* concerns raised by members of the Council regarding potential developments subsequent to the application of the Prosecutor of the International Criminal Court of 14 July 2008, and *taking note* of their intention to consider these matters further ... [152]

The African Union responded to this by issuing its Resolution 1828,[153] demanding that its members refuse to cooperate with the Arrest Warrant.[154] The same pattern was repeated in 2011 with respect to the indictment of Muammar Gadhafi, in spite of the African Union's initial support for the sending of the situation in Libya to the ICC;[155] that issue is, of course, now moot. What is important to note though is that the discussion of the interplay of peace and justice, even against the background of the existence

---

*International Law* 481; Michael P Scharf, 'The Amnesty Exception to the Jurisdiction of the International Criminal Court' (1999) 32 *Cornell International Law Journal* 507; ICC Office of the Prosecutor, *Policy Paper on the Interests of Justice*, September 2007, 3–4, 8–9.

[150] See generally, Schabas, above note 77, 325–34.

[151] See generally, Nicholas Wadell and Phil Clark (eds), *Courting Conflict? Justice, Peace and the ICC in Africa* (Royal Africa Society 2008).

[152] SC Res 1828, UN SCOR, 5947th mtg, UN Doc S/RES/1828 (31 July 2008) 2.

[153] 31 July 2008.

[154] *Decision on the Report of the Second Meeting of States Parties To The Rome Statute on the International Criminal Court (ICC)* AU Assembly, 14th Sess, AU Doc Assembly/AU/Dec.270 (XIV) (2010).

[155] *Decision on the Implementation of the Assembly Decisions on the International Criminal Court,* AU Assembly, 17th Sess, Au Doc Assembly/AU/Dec.366 (XVII) (2011).

of the ICC (which notionally is meant to counter the possibility of impunity), has become far more public and contentious than it was during and after the Second World War. As mentioned above, this may however be because the discussions were amongst the protagonists without third parties such as the UN or ICC, and later on in the conflict, where the outcome of the conflict was sufficiently clear for certainties to be publicly expressed. The difference between the past and present may be more fictitious than real, in that the fundamental issue is whether or not victory is assured, rather than whether principles are determinative. If this is the case, then the victor's justice critique again becomes relevant.

## B. Cooperation

A large difference in the context between the post-War trials and modern international criminal justice is the concentration on issues of cooperation between States and international tribunals prosecuting international crimes. When the post-War trials were ongoing, the issue was not regarded as much of a problem. The territories of Germany and Japan were occupied or completely controlled by the Allies, such that it was simply a matter of taking the suspects into custody and finding the evidence in a way which would not surprise any domestic police officer. It is true that with respect to the IMTs and the Control Council Law No. 10 trials, in retrospect some States kept some information from one another. A particularly egregious example regarded the above-mentioned Unit 731 of the Kwantung Army, who had engaged in chemical and biological weapons use, where the US and USSR both kept incriminatory information from the prosecutors for their own reasons (that they wanted the results of their studies).[156] For the most part though, evidence and defendants were both available and shared.[157]

This perhaps led to a failure to appreciate until the modern era the difficulties that cooperation in prosecuting international crimes involves. Unlike the post-War trials, the defendants and evidence are usually to be found in States who are not subject of occupation or *debellatio*. As a result of this, cooperation cannot easily be compelled. Whether an international tribunal has primacy or operates on the basis of complementarity (as the ICC does), the difficulties of obtaining State cooperation are fierce, in particular when high profile suspects are at issue. It took more than 15 years

---

[156] Tsuneishi Kei-Ichi, 'Reasons for the Failure to Prosecute Unit 731 and its Significance' in Yuki Tanaka, Tim McCormack and Gerry Simpson (eds), *Beyond Victor's Justice? The Tokyo War Crimes Trial Revisited* (Nijhoff 2011) 177.

[157] For an explanation of the good and bad reasons, see Heller, above note 6, 24.

for cooperation with respect to Ratko Mladić to lead to his appearance before the ICTY, which unfortunately typifies the lack of cooperation between international criminal courts and tribunals. Radovan Karadžić evaded that Tribunal for many years, as both he and Mladić were almost certainly protected by sympathetic Serbian officials.

In her characteristically strongly worded memoir, former ICTY and ICTR Prosecutor Carla del Ponte explains and criticises the amount of time she spent attempting to cajole recalcitrant States, not just in the former Yugoslavia, to cooperate with these Tribunals.[158] Victor Peskin has also convincingly demonstrated the difficulties which successive prosecutors of the ad hoc tribunals have had with cooperation.[159] The problems experienced by the ICTR with respect to Rwandan cooperation are also well known: if the ICTR acts in a manner in which the Rwandan Government does not like, it simply refuses all cooperation.[160]

Sadly, the same is largely true for the ICC. In relation to Uganda, the Prosecutor has concentrated on crimes committed by the Lord's Resistance Army, rather than the Ugandan Peoples' Defence Forces, in part because of the unlikelihood of any cooperation being forthcoming with respect to investigations against governmental forces or their political superiors. The same applies, *mutatis mutandis* to the investigations in the Democratic Republic of Congo, which have focused on crimes by rebels, in part because the Government is willing to assist in the investigation of its domestic enemies, but not in the investigation of their own conduct. The situation is worse where the Security Council has referred the situation. In Sudan, any pretextual cooperation dried up the moment al-Bashir was indicted.[161] This shows that Paulo Benvenuti was right to predict a 'complementary paradox', where the ICC would be asking for cooperation from a set of State apparatuses that have already been shown to be 'unwilling or unable' to prosecute offences themselves genuinely.[162] Like the peace/justice debate,

---

[158] Carla del Ponte and Chuck Sudetic, *Madame Prosecutor: Confrontations with Humanity's Worst Criminals and the Culture of Impunity* (Other Press 2008).

[159] Peskin, above note 100.

[160] See generally 'Prosecuting the Leaders: Promises, Politics and Pragmatics' (2009) 1 *Göttingen Journal of International Law* 45.

[161] Robert Cryer, 'Darfur: Complementarity as the Drafters Intended?' in Carsten Stahn and Mohamed el Zeidy (eds), *The International Criminal Court and Complementarity: From Theory to Practice* 1097 (Cambridge University Press 2011) 1097.

[162] Paolo Benvenuti, 'Complementarity of the International Criminal Court to National Criminal Jurisdictions' in Flavia Lattanzi and William Schabas (eds), *Essays on the Rome Statute of the International Criminal Court* (il Sirente 1999) 21, 50.

such discussions, or even the issues that would require such discussion, were essentially absent in the era leading up to the post-War trials.

## C. Fair Trials and Human Rights

In the post-War era, human rights considerations did not play a huge role in the practice of the relevant participants. The rights of defendants were not considered of paramount importance. Even a humanitarian icon such as Benjamin Ferencz (who was Lead Prosecutor in the *Einsatzgruppen* trial) described his approach to investigating war crimes in occupied Germany as follows:

> We had a very simple procedure … I went out in a jeep and a pistol and a carbine in the back of a car. When I entered a town where crimes had been committed, I would look for a person in authority … I would line up all the people who had been in the area and put them against a wall. They were told to sit down and write exactly what happened and they were told that anyone who lied would be shot. This was the 'pre- Miranda' rule.[163]

The Nuremberg and Tokyo IMTs and some domestic tribunals had rules of procedure and evidence, but for the most part they were permissive rather than attendant to the formal rights of the defence.[164] Much therefore depended on the approach of the relevant presiding officer/president of the tribunal that was trying a particular defendant. While some, such as Sir Geoffrey Lawrence, the President of the Nuremberg IMT, acquitted themselves well on point, Sir William Webb, on a set of rules of procedure that were largely similar in the Tokyo IMT, did not.[165] The level of fair trial rights granted in domestic prosecutions ranged from reasonable (in the case of the US Control Council Law No. 10 trials)[166] to non-existent.[167]

What ought to be remembered is that, as implied by Ferencz's statement, the post-War trials occurred against a background prior to the modern

---

163 Benjamin Ferencz, 'The Experience of Nuremberg' in Dinah Shelton (ed) *International Crimes, Peace and Human Rights: The Role of the International Criminal Court* (Transnational 2000) 3, 4.

164 See eg APV Rogers, 'War Crimes Trials Under the Royal Warrant, British Practice 1945–1949' (1990) 39 *The International and Comparative Law Quarterly* 780, 789–90.

165 Matthew Lipmann, 'Nuremberg Forty-Five Years Later' (1991) 7 *Connecticut Journal of International Law* 1, 39; Boister and Cryer, above note 6, ch 4.

166 Although their processes did not pass without negative comment, see, eg Zeck, above note 2, 364–69 (Zeck, however, disagreed with the critics).

167 A notable example was the above-mentioned Unit 731 Trials, where the prosecution statements read like a parody of Stalinist-era show trials.

climate of human rights, and most were completed before the pronouncement of the (non-binding) Universal Declaration of Human Rights (UDHR).[168] Things are mostly different now. The ICTY prides itself on being an exemplar when it comes to fair trial rights (although whether it succeeds in doing so is another question). It frequently refers to the jurisprudence of the European Convention on Human Rights and the Human Rights Committee, and tends to be generous in its interpretation of fair trial rights. Even if not every decision that it has taken has been perfect, many critics of the more recent jurisprudence of the ICTY have accused it of being too solicitous of the claims of defendants,[169] although some critiques have gone the other way.[170] Either way, the common denominator has been the language of fair trial rights as interpreted by the relevant human rights bodies. There was very little international jurisprudence on point in the post-War era, other than the embryonic law on flagrant denial of justice in the law of State responsibility, particularly with respect to trials of war crimes and the like[171] and not referred to by the courts themselves.

What is interesting is that when the ICTY and ICTR were developing their procedures (for many years, works in progress) they did not generally refer to the post-War trials. This is understandable, in that most of those trials were undertaken subject to domestic and often military procedures, and in the context of the extant law on fair trials. There is one counter-example to this, which occurred in *Tadić*, the first trial before the ICTY. In the early parts of the trial proceedings, the question arose of whether or not anonymous witnesses ought to be used. The Trial Chamber asserted that it was acceptable to do so, on the basis that their trials were to be analogised to military proceedings where the law of human rights as applied by tribunals sitting in peacetime could not be applied without modification.[172] However,

---

[168] Whatever its status now, few if any would have argued at the time that the UDHR amounted to positive law in 1948. The most that could be said for such a view was that it amounted to an interpretation of the human rights clauses in the UN Charter, but those were programmatic, rather than absolute.

[169] Göran Sluiter, 'Compromising the Authority of International Criminal Justice: How Vojislav Šešelj Runs his Trial' (2007) 5 *Journal of International Criminal Justice* 529.

[170] *Prosecutor v Milošević* (Dissenting Opinion Of Judge David Hunt On Admissibility Of Evidence In Chief In The Form Of Written Statement) (Appeal Chamber, ICTY, Case No IT-02–54-T, 21 October 2003) [21]–[22].

[171] Jan Paulsson, *Denial of Justice in International Law* (Cambridge University Press 2005) 180–83.

[172] *Prosecutor v Tadić* (Decision on the Prosecutor's Motion Requesting Protective Measures for Victims and Witnesses) (Trial Chamber, ICTY, Case No IT-94–1, 10 August 1995).

in part owing to their evolving self-image, and also the unmasking of an anonymous witness as a perjurer in that trial, the ICTY rapidly repositioned itself as a tribunal self-consciously orientated towards fair trial rights, a position maintained to this day.[173]

Since the ICC was set up by States whose nationals could possibly appear before it, it was predictable that fair trial rights would take a more central role than in the post-War era, where the idea of the Allies using those processes to prosecute their own nationals would not have passed a test of salience in the minds of those who signed off the summary processes.[174] When it came to the ICC though, the Rome Statute itself provides for a detailed list of fair trial rights in Art 67, which largely tally with those provided for in the International Covenant on Civil and Political Rights (ICCPR).[175] Taking a 'belt and braces' approach, in addition to the Rules of

---

173 See generally Stefan Trechsel, 'Rights in Criminal Proceedings under the ECHR and the ICTY Statute – A Precarious Comparison' in Bert Swart, Alexander Zahar and Göran Sluiter (eds), *The Legacy of the International Criminal Tribunal for the Former Yugoslavia* (Oxford University Press 2011) 149.

174 To be even-handed, the dissenters in the *Yamashita* case raised precisely this issue: see *US v Yamashita* IV LRTWC 1, 49, 57–61, 73.

175 These are that:

'1. In the determination of any charge, the accused shall be entitled to a public hearing, having regard to the provisions of this Statute, to a fair hearing conducted impartially, and to the following minimum guarantees, in full equality:

(a) To be informed promptly and in detail of the nature, cause and content of the charge, in a language which the accused fully understands and speaks; (b) To have adequate time and facilities for the preparation of the defence and to communicate freely with counsel of the accused's choosing in confidence; (c) To be tried without undue delay; (d) Subject to article 63, paragraph 2, to be present at the trial, to conduct the defence in person or through legal assistance of the accused's choosing, to be informed, if the accused does not have legal assistance, of this right and to have legal assistance assigned by the Court in any case where the interests of justice so require, and without payment if the accused lacks sufficient means to pay for it; (e) To examine, or have examined, the witnesses against him or her and to obtain the attendance and examination of witnesses on his or her behalf under the same conditions as witnesses against him or her. The accused shall also be entitled to raise defences and to present other evidence admissible under this Statute; (f) To have, free of any cost, the assistance of a competent interpreter and such translations as are necessary to meet the requirements of fairness, if any of the proceedings of or documents presented to the Court are not in a language which the accused fully understands and speaks; (g) Not to be compelled to testify or to confess guilt and to remain silent, without such silence being a consideration in the determination of guilt or innocence; (h) To make an unsworn oral or written statement in his or her defence; and (i) Not to have imposed on him or her any reversal of the burden of proof or any onus of rebuttal.

Procedure and Evidence which were drafted with human rights standards in mind,[176] Art 21 of the Rome Statute requires it to be interpreted with regard to internationally protected human rights.[177] The difference between this and the post-War trials could hardly be more stark. That said, it is telling that in the ad hoc tribunals, the drafters (whose nationals were probably unlikely to be defendants before the tribunals) were willing to provide only skeletal human rights protections, and allowed the judges to develop the rules themselves. The fact that the judges did so broadly on the basis of human rights standards is testament to their sensibility rather than that of the drafters.

Even so, it might be questioned whether the focus of the modern tribunals on some fair trial rights have undermined other such rights, in particular the right to a trial within a reasonable time. The Tokyo trial was considered lengthy at the time, taking two years to consider the huge basis of the charges, relating to an alleged conspiracy to commit aggression since 1928, and its attendant war crimes over approximately fifteen years. The ICC has taken about the same amount of time to deal with its first case, *Lubanga*, which was based on a single count, relating to war crimes. Were a defendant to be acquitted before the ICC, it would likely be against the backdrop of lengthy pre-trial detention, which is perilous from a human rights point of view.[178]

## D. Military or Civilian Trials?

As has been implied above, part of the reason for the difference in the approach to fair trial standards is the self-image and composition of the relevant tribunals at the time. The Nuremberg and Tokyo trials were styled as international military tribunals. In the international military tribunals, the personnel were overwhelmingly military in their backgrounds. Most of the

---

2. In addition to any other disclosure provided for in this Statute, the Prosecutor shall, as soon as practicable, disclose to the defence evidence in the Prosecutor's possession or control which he or she believes shows or tends to show the innocence of the accused, or to mitigate the guilt of the accused, or which may affect the credibility of prosecution evidence. In case of doubt as to the application of this paragraph, the Court shall decide.'

[176] Silvia Fernández de Gurmendi and Håkan Friman, 'The Rules of Procedure and Evidence of the International Criminal Court' (2000) 3 *Yearbook of International Humanitarian Law* 289, 300ff.

[177] On which see deGuzman, above note 75.

[178] Stefan Trechsel, *Human Rights in Criminal Proceedings* (Oxford University Press 2005) ch 6.

judges and prosecutors had seen service in the First or Second World Wars, even if they had not recently been on active duty.

At the domestic level the predominance of military personnel (or those who had seen service) was clear in the majority of States, as exemplified by the UK-run *Almelo* trial. Brigadier GA McL Routledge, eBE, Me, MM, Commander 107 HAA Bde' presided over a bench consisting of Colonel GA de Brauw, Royal Netherlands Army, Lieutenant-Colonel HAA Parker, Lake Superior Regt, Canadian Forces, and Squadron-Leader HB Simpson, HQ 83 Group, RAF. They were assisted by a judge advocate, CL Stirling, Esq, CBE, Barrister-at-Law, Deputy Judge Advocate General of the Forces. Before them was the prosecutor, Major AEE Reade, Intelligence Corps, Major Legal Staff, Headquarters, British Army of the Rhine. The defence were represented by Major DLE Paterson, RA, 244/61 Medium Regiment, RA (Law Clerk).[179] This was usual for most of the post-War trials; the only atypical aspect of the trial was that the bench was multinational, rather than only made up of nationals of one of the Allied States.[180] Equally, in the UK trials if the defendant was a naval officer or member of the air force, it was possible to apply for such a person to be appointed to the bench.[181]

The US Control Council Law No. 10 Trials were similarly populated. The judges were mostly US State court judges, but who had been appointed and approved by the Military Governor of Germany,[182] and most of whom had seen direct military service.[183] Military personnel undertook the role of the prosecution in the US trials in the vast majority of cases.[184] In Australia, Canada, China and France, prosecutions occurred before military rather than civilian courts.[185] In the Netherlands, special mixed military/civilian panels heard war crimes cases.[186] Poland and Norway used civilian courts, so the practice was not utterly unambiguous on point,[187] but the trend towards military proceedings at this time is clear.

---

179 I LRTWC 35.

180 As APV. Rogers notes: 'British trials of war criminals, other than the major war criminals, were dealt with by British military courts', above note 164, 786. In one other British case a Greek national sat on the panel: *The Peleus* (1945) 13 ILR 248.

181 Rogers, above note 164, 790.

182 Zeck, above note 2, 351.

183 Heller, above note 6, chs 2–4.

184 As is well known, the Chief of Prosecution was Brigadier General Telford Taylor. On the military role, see ibid.

185 Lippman (Domestic Tribunals), above note 2, 3–4.

186 Ibid 5–6.

187 Ibid 6–7.

It is less certain in the modern era of human rights that the generalised use of such military procedures would be acceptable now. This is true even though in many States the military justice system is now required to live up to the same human rights obligations (in particular fair trial standards) as civilian courts.[188] The opprobrium that has attended the US use of military tribunals in Guantanamo Bay cannot be ignored,[189] although it is possible that the criticism has come about owing to the denial of fair trial standards before those tribunals rather than their status as military tribunals per se.

In the modern era, outside of the US military tribunals and particularly at the international level where trials of non-nationals are involved, the predominant mode of trial is civilian. The ICTY, ICTR, and ICC are staffed, largely although not entirely,[190] by civilians. Although some have seen military service, the judges are, in vast majority, from civilian walks of life. Indeed, for the ICC, judges are expected to have some experience in international law, human rights law or criminal law.[191] There is no requirement that they have any experience or understanding of military matters.

The question of whether or not there ought to be some such requirement or expectation for judges has proved controversial. Some judges, such as Antonio Cassese[192] and Theodor Meron, have spoken of the role of the ICTY in the 'humanisation' of humanitarian law.[193] Against this, commentators such as Michael Schmitt who come from a (liberal) military approach have questioned whether, with respect to war crimes trials, the pendulum has swung too far from military necessity to humanity. As he has said:

> International tribunals have taken some control over the process ... [of the interpretation and application of international humanitarian law (IHT)] ... from the hands of states. Although their decisions are of technically limited reach, the reality is that they exert significant influence on the general interpretation of IHL. While tribunals have usually proved useful in confirming or interpreting IHL norms, it must be remembered that they do not operate from the same perspective as states, for they do not directly bear the consequences of their

---

188 Peter Rowe, *The Impact of Human Rights Law on Armed Forces* (Cambridge University Press 2006) ch 3.

189 The arguments are canvassed in the agora in (2007) 101 *American Journal of International Law* 35, 35ff.

190 William Fenrick, for many years a high-level advisor in the Office of the ICTY Prosecutor, was a military lawyer with many years' experience.

191 ICC Rome Statute, Art 36.

192 Hoffmann, above note 57; Cassese, above note 58.

193 Theodor Meron, *The Humanization of International Law* (Nijhoff 2006) chs 1–2; Theodor Meron, *The Making of International Criminal Justice: A View From the Bench* (Oxford University Press 2011) ch 4.

> judgments as to the appropriate balance between military necessity and humanity. Accordingly, their reasoning is less focused on the balance. This explains, to a degree, the discernible preference for normative solutions emphasizing humanity at the expense of military necessity.[194]

Schmitt's argument is careful, and ought not to be rejected as being special pleading. Indeed, it has also been argued by others (again from a liberal military perspective) that military personnel are better placed than civilians to make determinations on certain military matters, such as questions of what amounts to proportionate civilian casualties when compared to the relevant expected military advantage,[195] as enshrined *inter alia* in Art 8(2)(b)(iv) of the Rome Statute. The counterpoint to this though was raised by Michael Bothe, with respect to the decision of the Prosecutor not to investigate allegations relating to NATO bombings in the Kosovo conflict. His point was that in the era of civilian control over the military, it is inappropriate to grant exclusive license to determine such questions to the military.[196] Similar critiques have been made at the domestic level, especially where the situation that falls to be determined is one where specialist knowledge or judgment is called for.[197]

These critiques have purchase. It is no coincidence that Bothe's comments occurred against the background of the ICTY prosecutor's report (written by William Fenrick)[198] about the NATO bombings with respect to Kosovo, which *inter alia* proposed that the relevant standard for proportionality be that of the 'reasonable military commander' rather than anyone else.[199] This is a (relatively) rare example of the ICTY's practice being criticised on the basis that it related too much to military practice rather than judicial standards, but this critique, having also been made recently by scholars such as Schmitt, has a greater historical pedigree than might be

---

194 Michael Schmitt, 'Military Necessity and Humanity in International Humanitarian Law: Preserving the Balance' (2010) 50 *Virginia Journal of International Law* 795, 838.

195 See also Rogers, above note 164, 800.

196 'The Protection of the Civilian Population and NATO Bombing on Yugoslavia: Comments on a Report to the Prosecutor of the ICTY' (2001) 12 *European Journal of International Law* 531, 535.

197 See Edward Griew, 'Objections to Feely and Ghosh' [1984] *Criminal Law Review* 341.

198 This in itself shows that the modern tribunals are not entirely stocked with NGO activists.

199 Final Report to the Prosecutor by the Committee Established to Review the NATO Bombing Campaign Against the Federal Republic of Yugoslavia 8 June 2000 (2000) 39 *International Legal Materials* 1257, [50].

thought. To take one example, in the *Ministries* case, the tribunal asserted that '[w]e must not forget that guilt is a personal matter; that men are to be judged not by theoretical, but by practical standards'.[200]

The equivalent argument was made by Antonio Cassese in *Erdemović*, where he asserted that the law ought not to set intractable standards of conduct.[201] He was however dissenting in this case, the majority asserting an unforgiving standard of the expectations that international criminal law ought to have on human behaviour, which, for all others than heroes, could not be lived up to.[202] As is often the case, the truth of the matter probably lies between the two poles. For example, it might be the case that the *High Command* case was gentle towards the defendants when it came to superior orders, but the (largely military) panel also showed a sophisticated understanding of the role played by commanding officers in occupations and staff officers, and showed no sympathy to those that had failed in their duties, or those who stood outside the strict line of command.[203] The problem of reconciling the military and humanitarian aspects of the law of armed conflict has been a repeated theme throughout the law of armed conflicts, and one which is unlikely to disappear, not least as the issues remain those of balance rather than absolute judgment on either side.

## VI. CONCLUSION

Coming to the end of this selective and impressionistic *tour d'horizon* of the past and present approaches to the prosecution of international crimes, it is difficult to be anything other than ambivalent. There are many overlapping issues that link the post-War trials and modern international criminal law which relate to some of the most fundamental aspects of international criminal justice. There are also many developments, and maybe retrogressions, to the extent to which a comparison of the relevant trials cannot be reduced to platitudes on one side or the other.

The Nuremberg and (to a lesser extent) Tokyo IMTs were the *fons et origio* of the jurisprudence of modern international criminal law, but the other post-War trials also have their place in our understanding of the law. In spite of the lessons that those trials have to offer, their practices have not led to a systematic approach to the case law of the post-War period; this is for a variety of reasons, including the fact that the majority of the post-War trials

200 *US v von Weiszacker* XIV TWC 1, 527.
201 *Erdemović*, above note 7, [47].
202 Ibid.
203 *US v von Leeb* X TWC 1, 74, 84ff.

were not fully reported. This is true of procedure, applicable law and the nature of international crimes.

As a result, perhaps what can be noted about both the post-War trials and the work of more modern international criminal tribunals is the extent to which the forms of justice (or lack thereof) are adopted in an ad hoc fashion, reflecting pragmatic solutions to specific problems rather than principled reflection.[204] International criminal law remains a work in progress, where some fundamental issues remain undecided. These instantiate themselves in individual cases, such as the question of whether defendants in Libya ought to be prosecuted domestically or before the ICC, and are still unresolved rather than being the subject of abstract discussion between States. The post-War experience holds valuable lessons for us, but the trials also need to be seen in context, both good and bad. Some issues were seen as already settled, and the law that was applied was not always so; it is also unfortunate that we do not have sufficient reportage of those trials that could provide positive and negative examples of how to run trials of international crimes. The most important lesson we can learn from the post-War trials is the importance of telling the world what was done in their name. Owing to the universalist rhetoric of international criminal law, we should expect and demand no less.

---

[204] One exception is probably the *Lubanga* trial, where the Trial Chamber was willing to bring the future of the prosecution to an end rather than acquiesce in the Prosecutor's strategy.

# 8. Terrorism and international criminal law: questions of (in)coherence and (il)legitimacy

**Ben Saul**

## I. INTRODUCTION

The global reaction to the terrorist attacks of 11 September 2001 ('9/11') has driven a rapid, complex and uncoordinated process of counter-terrorism norm-creation and implementation. These law-making processes have taken place on a variety of registers: vertical norm development;[1] stronger transnational criminal cooperation; new measures in regional public law;[2] the emergence of new 'soft law' standards;[3] the mobilisation of non-State actors;[4] the horizontal, cross-border borrowing and transplant of domestic legal norms across national legal systems;[5] and the vertical uplifting of national norms onto the regional or international plane.[6] Quite a few of these processes 'operate below the level of highly publicized diplomatic conferences and treaty-making, but in aggregate ... regulate and manage

[1] Including consensual processes such as treaty negotiation and domestic implementation and also mandatory processes such as binding UN Security Council resolutions adopted under Chapter VII of the Charter of the United Nations.

[2] Particularly in the European Union.

[3] Through UN bodies, international organisations and *sui generis* entities like the Financial Action Task Force.

[4] Such as the global financial sector's role in countering terrorist financing and money laundering.

[5] Thus, Australia adopted a civil 'control order' regime for suspected terrorists, based on a UK model: see Criminal Code Act 1995 (Commonwealth), sched, division 104. Likewise, various common law States have been attentive to developments in comparable jurisdictions regarding the definition of terrorism, extended periods of investigative detention, surveillance, powers to proscribe terrorist organisations and so on.

[6] As when the definition of terrorism in the Arab Convention on the Suppression of Terrorism 1998 was modelled on Art 86 of the Egyptian Penal Code 1992.

vast sectors of economic and social life through specific decisions and rulemaking'.[7]

The development of 'hard and soft, global and regional law'[8] addressing terrorism illustrates 'the diversity of law-making approaches that international law now offers and [shows] that the choice of process depends upon context, political preference and purpose'.[9] The field of counter-terrorism is now thick with law. But that does not mean that the law is coherent or legitimate. The birth of new rules, institutions and processes can be anarchic. New norms overlay older, pre-existing legal forms and regimes, potentially generating normative, procedural and institutional ambiguity, fragmentation and collision.

In this context, this chapter first assesses the state of international anti-terrorism law in relation to three notions of *coherence*: its *internal coherence* as a discrete legal regime; its *relational coherence* in respect of other specialised legal regimes; and its *consistency of application* as a key characteristic of coherence. The law's coherence may affect its legitimacy; but legitimacy is also affected by other factors. This chapter next considers two such factors: the determinacy of the law, and the legitimacy of legal processes and institutions surrounding it.

This chapter finds that problems of coherence first arise in the sense that anti-terrorism law does not form a discrete or relatively autonomous regime, but comprises a cluster of general and special norms from disparate sources and of varying normative quality. That form of incoherence is not of itself necessarily problematic. But it gives rise in turn to a more serious, second kind of incoherence: ongoing problems of conflict and coordination between norms and institutions deriving from different specialised substantive fields or distinct legal systems. A third kind of overarching incoherence is the unequal or inconsistent treatment of similarly situated 'terrorist' violence, carrying legitimacy, effectiveness, coordination and compliance costs for anti-terrorism law.

In addition to coherence, other factors also affect the law's legitimacy. Legitimacy is understood here as 'the normative belief that a rule or institution ought to be obeyed'.[10] Two further factors affecting legitimacy are considered: the determinacy of legal norms, and process or institutional

---

[7] Benedict Kingsbury, Nico Krisch and Richard B Stewart, 'The Emergence of Global Administrative Law' (2005) 68 *Law and Contemporary Problems* 15, 17.

[8] Alan Boyle and Christine Chinkin, *The Making of International Law* (Oxford University Press 2007) 10.

[9] Ibid 8–9.

[10] Boyle and Chinkin, above note 8, 24. Legitimacy is independent of whether a rule is just: Allen Buchanan, 'The Legitimacy of International Law' in Samantha

legitimacy (that is, the moral right to rule possessed by a given institution).[11] On the first count, a fatal indeterminacy lies at the core of international anti-terrorism law: the failure to define the notion of terrorism itself. Such indeterminacy has not been cured by pragmatic cooperation which side-steps the intractable problem of definition, nor by an unconvincing effort by the UN Special Tribunal for Lebanon to concoct a customary international criminal law definition in 2011.

The indeterminacy of the global counter-terrorism project is magnified by failures of global law-making processes and institutions, bringing a further kind of illegitimacy. The Security Council's arrogation of prospective law-making is replete with legitimacy problems, as are certain efforts by some other UN security bodies (such as the Counter-Terrorism Committee under Resolution 1373, the Resolution 1267 Sanctions Committee, and the UN Office on Drugs and Crime). The UN Special Tribunal for Lebanon too has raised eyebrows because of its hyper-active judicial activism, overstepping judicial boundaries and trampling on basic rights. New, informal actors like the Financial Action Task Force (FATF) also bring process legitimacy concerns. This chapter charts these developments, as well as prospects for mitigating or remedying incoherence and illegitimacy.

## II. THE COHERENCE OF INTERNATIONAL ANTI-TERRORISM LAW

The idea of 'coherence' is used in three different senses in evaluating aspects of international anti-terrorism law. First, the chapter asks whether international anti-terrorism law can be said to constitute an *internally coherent regime* – that is, a relatively discrete body of law which hangs together as a specialised area of international law (just as one speaks of international environmental law, world trade law or some other specialised substantive area). Secondly, the chapter considers the *relational coherence* of anti-terrorism law – that is, the degree to which it collides or harmonises with other specialised areas of international law when it interacts with them in a fragmented international law system. Thirdly, the chapter considers Franck's notion of *coherence as consistency*[12] – that is, whether like cases are treated alike (rather than capriciously or arbitrarily) in the application of

---

Besson and John Tasioulas (eds), *The Philosophy of International Law* (Oxford University Press 2010) 79, 81.

[11] Buchanan, above note 10, 79–80.

[12] Thomas Franck, 'Legitimacy in the International System' (1988) 82 *American Journal of International Law* 705, 741.

anti-terrorism norms, thereby legitimating and helping to induce compliance with such norms.

## A. Regime Coherence: International Anti-Terrorism Law as an Emerging 'Field'

While transnational terrorism has long presented special problems for public international law, prior to 9/11 the conventional view of leading international lawyers was that there is no 'international anti-terrorism law' as such. Terrorism was regarded not as 'a discrete topic of international law with its own substantive legal norms', but as 'a pernicious contemporary phenomenon which ... presents complicated legal problems'[13] across various areas of international law. Being both vague and undefined, the term 'terrorism' was long thought to serve 'no operative legal purpose'.[14] Rather, terrorism was considered 'merely a convenient way of alluding to activities ... widely disapproved of and in which either the methods used are unlawful, or the targets protected, or both'.[15]

On that view, existing *general norms* of international law were thought capable of dealing with terrorism, such as principles of non-intervention, the non-use of force, State responsibility, the law of armed conflict, international human rights law, and international criminal law. While those principles might face occasional difficulty in their specific or practical application to the factual phenomenon of terrorism in given contexts, it was nonetheless thought that they largely covered the field. Such principles could be applied without differentiation or specificity to any type of transnational violence, however described, whether named terrorism, insurgency, rebellion, militancy, extremism and so on. As such, it was felt that there was little need for a more specific, discrete field of 'international anti-terrorism law' by which to regulate a defined subset of such violence.

---

[13] Roslyn Higgins, 'The General International Law of Terrorism' in Roslyn Higgins and Maurice Flory (eds), *Terrorism and International Law* (Routledge 1997) 13–14; see also Richard Baxter, 'A Skeptical Look at the Concept of Terrorism' (1974) 7 *Akron Law Review* 380, 380; Gilbert Guillaume, 'Terrorism and International Law' (2004) 53 *International and Comparative Law Quarterly* 537; M Cherif Bassiouni, 'A Policy-Oriented Inquiry into the Different Forms and Manifestations of "International Terrorism"' in M Cherif Bassiouni (ed), *Legal Responses to International Terrorism* (Martinus Nijhoff 1988) xv, xvi; Richard Friedlander, 'Terrorism' in Rudolf Bernhardt (ed), *Encyclopaedia of PIL*, vol 4 (North Holland 2000) 845.

[14] Baxter, above note 13.

[15] Higgins, above note 13, 28.

Where general norms were occasionally found to be inadequate, they were supplemented by numerous 'sectoral' treaties on transnational criminal cooperation, adopted since the 1960s, which targeted the common methods of violence used by terrorists (such as hijacking, hostage-taking, endangering maritime facilities and so on),[16] but did not create a new international crime of terrorism, or an 'international anti-terrorism law'.[17] At a practical level, such normative frameworks were supplemented by technical assistance and transnational cooperation facilitated by various specialised agencies.[18] The Security Council also occasionally (and selectively) stepped in to deal with very specific, concrete cases of terrorism, such as its activism over the Lockerbie incident in the 1990s, or terrorist bombings in Lebanon in the 2000s.[19]

This pragmatic approach enabled the repression of terrorism while side-stepping the irreconcilable problem of defining it, at a time when States were unable to agree on the legitimacy of violence committed by self-determination movements or by State forces. The result has been a functional transnational cooperation against terrorism, even if there remain regulatory gaps because of the reactive, ad hoc nature of treaty-making (for example, terrorist attacks by small arms, as happened in Mumbai in 2008, are not prohibited by treaty law). In consequence, many international lawyers believe that '[m]ost of the normative work has been accomplished',[20] notwithstanding an ongoing deadlock in United Nations (UN) negotiations for a new (Draft) Comprehensive Anti-Terrorism Convention since 2000.

The traditional view of the above 'extra-legal' status of the concept of 'terrorism' has come under strain with distance from 9/11. In February 2011 the UN Special Tribunal for Lebanon found that there exists a customary international law crime of transnational terrorism;[21] the first time that

---

16 For a list and the texts of the key anti-terrorism treaties, see: United Nations, 'Text and Status of the United Nations Conventions on Terrorism' (*United Nations Treaty Collection*) <http://treaties.un.org/Pages/DB.aspx?path=DB/studies/page2_en.xml>.

17 See Ben Saul, *Defining Terrorism in International Law* (Oxford University Press 2006) ch 3.

18 Such as the International Maritime Organization, International Civil Aviation Organization, International Criminal Police Organization and the United Nations Office on Drugs and Crime.

19 See Ben Saul, 'Definition of "Terrorism" in the UN Security Council: 1985–2004' (2005) 4 *Chinese Journal of International Law* 141.

20 Guillaume, above note 13, 547.

21 *Interlocutory Decision on the Applicable Law: Terrorism, Conspiracy, Homicide, Perpetration, Cumulative Charging* (Special Tribunal for Lebanon,

terrorism has been so recognised by a (hybrid) international tribunal. That decision came on the heels of the hitherto marginal academic view of the late Antonio Cassese after 9/11 that terrorism is an international crime.[22] As discussed further below, the Tribunal's decision has been overwhelmingly condemned as methodologically flawed and substantively incorrect by scholars,[23] though it is still likely to exert normative influence.

There is thus a basic disagreement about the conceptual and normative status of terrorism in contemporary international law. As Higgins observes, '[w]hether one regards terrorism ... as new international law, or as the application of a constantly developing international law to new problems is at heart a jurisprudential question'.[24] Jurisprudential disagreement extends not only to the threshold question of *defining terrorism* and its status in *international criminal law*, but also to the impact of the phenomenon of terrorism on the development of norms across international law as a whole.

It is clear that post-9/11 developments have certainly altered the law as it applies to terrorism, and the conventional view of the extra-legal status of 'terrorism' can no longer hold sway. As noted in the introduction, the global reaction to 9/11 has driven a complex and often uncoordinated process of counter-terrorism norm-creation and implementation, across a variety of registers and institutions. At the same time, it is not accurate to suggest that something like an 'international anti-terrorism law' has emerged as a solidified, coherent 'self-contained regime',[25] with its own autonomous

---

Appeals Chamber, Case No STL-11–01/I/AC/R176bis, 16 February 2011) ('*Interlocutory Decision on the Applicable Law*').

[22] Antonio Cassese, *International Criminal Law* (Oxford University Press 2003) 120–31; Antonio Cassese, 'Terrorism Is Also Disrupting Some Crucial Legal Categories of International Law' (2001) 12 *European Journal of International Law* 993, 994.

[23] Ben Saul, 'Legislating from A Radical Hague: The UN Special Tribunal for Lebanon Invents An International Crime of Transnational Terrorism' (2011) 24 *Leiden Journal of International Law* 677; Kai Ambos, 'Judicial Creativity at the Special Tribunal for Lebanon: Is There a Crime of Terrorism under International Law?' (2011) 24 *Leiden Journal of International Law* 655; Matthew Gillett and Matthias Schuster, 'Fast-track Justice: The Special Tribunal for Lebanon Defines Terrorism' (2011) 9(5) *Journal of International Criminal Justice* 989; Stefan Kirsch and Anna Oehmichen, 'Judges Gone Astray: The Fabrication of Terrorism as an International Crime by the Special Tribunal for Lebanon' (2001) 1 *Durham Law Review* 32; Stefan Kirsch, 'Die Erfindung von "Terrorismus" als Völkerrechtsverbrechen durch den Sondergerichtshof für den Libanon' (2011) 10 *Zeitschrift für Internationale Strafrechtsdogmatik* 800.

[24] Higgins, above note 13, 13.

[25] International Law Commission, *Fragmentation of International Law: Difficulties Arising from the Diversification and Expansion of International Law*, 58th

substantive norms and institutions for implementing them and brokering disagreements of application and interpretation. International law concerning terrorism remains a work in progress – a half-way house between the ordinary application general rules and a fully formed specialised regime. There is not 'any "joined up" international law approach to combating terrorism'.[26]

Rather, there exists an untidy accretion of norms and institutional actors addressing terrorism, emanating from disparate sources, possessing variable juridical qualities, produced and governed by a range of processes and institutions, and of uneven legitimacy. The best that can be said of the story so far of terrorism and international law is as follows. First, there is by and large uncontroversial sectoral treaty law addressing particular forms of terrorist violence through transnational criminal cooperation, largely without naming it as terrorism. Some such treaty regimes have undoubtedly emerged as parallel customary law rules, for instance as regards hijacking and hostage-taking on aircraft, or endangering diplomats.

There is not yet, however, any customary international law definition or crime of terrorism which unifies the different regulatory threads adopted to combat it so far.[27] At best, there is mandatory obligation imposed on States by the Security Council to criminalise terrorist acts in domestic law,[28] without any binding direction being given as to the definition of what terrorism is. The legal implications of these measures are considered later in this chapter.

Secondly, there is genuinely new customary international law regulating terrorist financing. A variety of international, regional, national and intergovernmental regulatory and cooperative measures have been adopted.[29] At

---

sess, UN Doc A/CN.4/L.682 (13 April 2006); see also Bruno Simma and Dirk Pulkowski, 'Of Planets and the Universe: Self-contained Regimes in International Law' (2006) 17 *European Journal of International Law* 483.

26 Boyle and Chinkin, above note 8, 8. Moeckli also tentatively raises the question of whether there is an emerging international law of terrorism: Daniel Moeckli, 'The Emergence of "Terrorism" as a Distinct Category of International Law' (2009) 44 *Texas International Law Journal* 157.

27 The UN Special Tribunal for Lebanon's claim that there now exists a customary international crime of transnational terrorism is discussed further below.

28 SC Res 1373, UN SCOR, 4385th mtg, UN Doc S/RES/1373 (28 September 2001) ('Resolution 1373').

29 See generally Commonwealth Secretariat, *Combating Terrorist Financing: A Model of Best Practice for the Financial Sector, the Professions and Other Designated Business* (2nd edn, Commonwealth Secretariat 2006); Ilias Banketas, 'The International Law of Terrorist Financing' (2003) 97 American Journal of International Law 315; Jean-Marc Sorel, 'Some Questions About the Definition of

the international level, two inter-locking regimes have contributed to customary law formation: the International Convention for the Suppression of the Financing of Terrorism 1999, and Security Council Resolution 1373 (2001). The latter required all States to prospectively criminalise and prevent terrorist-financing through domestic law[30] – in effect universalising the Terrorist Financing Convention and going beyond the Council's situation-specific, limited sanctions regimes.[31]

Supplementing these measures are the 'soft law' standards of the FATF, including 40 Recommendations (1990, revised 1996 and 2004) on money laundering, and nine Special Recommendations on terrorist financing (2001). Such standards have exerted a powerful influence on global financial practices concerning terrorism, and are further reinforced by the practices of other relevant financial actors.[32] The combination of converging norms from formal treaty law, quasi-legislative Security Council measures, informal FATF standard setting and wide State practice conforming to such norms, establishes new customary law in the area.

Thirdly, in various specialised branches of international law (the law on the use of force, international humanitarian law and international human rights law), the problem of terrorism has triggered the clarification of various ambiguities or discretionary areas within existing norms, resulting in particular applications of general rules without producing autonomous terrorism-specific rules as such. Such interpretive developments have tended to confirm the general applicability of the existing law, and obviated the need for new, special law. The various areas of international law have proven to be flexible, accommodating and resilient in responding to the particular challenges presented by terrorism.

---

Terrorism and the Fight against its Financing' (2003) 14 *American Journal of International Law* 365; Anthony Aust, 'Counter-terrorism: A New Approach – The International Convention for the Suppression of the Financing of Terrorism' (2001) 5 *Max Planck Year Book of UN Law 287;* Roberto Lavalle, 'The International Convention for the Suppression of the Financing of Terrorism' (2000) 60 *Zeitschrift für auslandisches offentliches Recht and Volkerrecht* 491.

[30] Resolution 1373 [2(e)].

[31] Such as sanctions against Al-Qaeda and its associates under SC Res 1267, UN SCOR, 4051st mtg, UN Doc S/RES/1267 (15 October 1999) ('Resolution 1267') and SC Res 1390, UN SCOR, 4452nd mtg, UN Doc S/RES/1390 (28 January 2002) ('Resolution 1390').

[32] Including the Group of 8, Asia-Pacific Economic Cooperation (APEC) and private sector actors such as the Wolfsberg Group of Banks and the Basel Committee on Banking Supervision. Relevant primary documents from these organisations are reproduced in Ben Saul, *Documents in International Law: Terrorism* (Hart 2012).

Thus, in international humanitarian law, assertions after 9/11 that new rules of humanitarian law were necessary to deal with terrorism were not met favourably by most States. Instead, there has been a sharpening of general principles: the characterisation of certain terrorist violence as crossing the threshold of a non-international armed conflict;[33] the interpretation of civilian 'direct participation in hostilities' in the targeting of 'terrorists';[34] the lawful bases of, and limits on, security detention of 'terrorists' in international or non-international conflicts;[35] and the minimum guarantees of a fair trial in prosecuting terrorists suspects.[36]

---

[33] See, eg, *Hamdan v Rumsfeld*, 548 US 557 (2006) – where the violence between the US and Al-Qaeda in Afghanistan was classified as a non-international conflict under common Art 3 of the 1949 Geneva Conventions (Geneva Convention for the Amelioration of the Condition of the Wounded and Sick in Armed Forces in the Field, 75 UNTS 31 (Geneva Convention I); Geneva Convention for the Amelioration of the Condition of Wounded, Sick and Shipwrecked Members of Armed Forces at Sea, 75 UNTS 85 (Geneva Convention II); Geneva Convention Relative to the Treatment of Prisoners of War, 75 UNTS 135 (Geneva Convention III); Geneva Convention Relative to the Protection of Civilian Persons in Time of War, 75 UNTS 287 (Geneva Convention IV) ('1949 Geneva Conventions' collectively)); UK Ministry of Defence, *The Manual of the Law of Armed Conflict* (Oxford University Press 2004) [1.33.4]. Recent examples include the conflicts between the US and Al-Qaeda in Afghanistan, Sri Lanka and the Liberation Tigers of Tamil Eelam (LTTE), or Israel and Hezbollah in Southern Lebanon.

[34] A standard expressed in 1949 Geneva Conventions, Additional Protocol I (1977), Art 51(3) ('Additional Protocol I') and reflecting customary law in all armed conflicts. On the interpretive efforts post-9/11, see Nils Melzer, *Interpretive Guidance on The Notion of Direct Participation in Hostilities under International Humanitarian Law* (International Committee of the Red Cross 2009); *Public Committee against Torture in Israel v Government of Israel* [2005] HCJ 769/02 (Israeli Supreme Court) (*Targeted Killings* case); Nils Melzer, *Targeted Killing in International Law* (Oxford University Press 2008); David Kretzmer, 'Targeted Killings of Suspected Terrorists' (2005) 16 *European Journal of International Law* 171.

[35] See generally Ryan Goodman, 'The Detention of Civilians in Armed Conflict' (2009) 103 *American Journal of International Law* 48; Marco Sassòli, 'The Status of Persons Held in Guantánamo under International Humanitarian Law' (2004) 2 *Journal of International Criminal Justice* 96; but see also John Bellinger, US State Department Legal Adviser, 'Prisoners in War: Contemporary Challenges to the Geneva Conventions', Speech delivered at the University of Oxford, United Kingdom, 10 December 2007 (identifying ambiguities in detention in non-international conflicts).

[36] See, eg, *Hamdan v Rumsfeld*, 548 US 557 (2006); James Stewart, 'The Military Commissions Act's Inconsistency with the Geneva Conventions: An Overview' (2007) 5 *Journal of International Criminal Justice* 26; Human Rights

In the law on the use of force, the movement in the law after 9/11 is possibly more extensive, but it can still be characterised as either the clarification or modification of general norms in ways which are not terrorism-specific but applicable to any equivalent armed violence. Thus, there is some new practice endorsing the right of a victim State to use cross-border force in self-defence against an autonomous terrorist (or other armed) group, in certain circumstances. Practice remains however variable, contested and equivocal. In addition, there is contested practice concerning whether the law now permits self-defence against a State which does not direct or 'effectively control' a terrorist (or other armed) group, but which has some looser relationship to it: from tolerating its presence, to more actively supporting its activities.[37] There is an ongoing, unfinished process of clarification of the law in the area, but which might equally apply to the conduct of any armed group, not just 'terrorist' ones.

The same is true of a third area of movement in the law on the use of force after 9/11: pre-emptive, preventive, or anticipatory self-defence. While it is clear that US President Bush's articulation of an *anticipatory* self-defence doctrine in 2002 did not gain acceptance,[38] it may be that the law was not left untouched. The process of repudiating the 'Bush doctrine' may have involved the international community moving away from the traditionally strict approach (where an armed attack must have already *occurred*) to confirm a middle ground of *pre-emptive* self-defence where an attack is *imminent* (but not, as under the Bush doctrine, indeterminate).[39]

---

Committee, *Communication No 2005/2010* (20 September 2010) (*David Hicks v Australia*) (alleging various violations of the International Covenant on Civil and Political Rights (ICCPR) and IHL in the trial of Australian citizen David Hicks before a US military commission).

[37] See Tal Becker, *Terrorism and the State; Rethinking the Rules of State Responsibility* (Hart 2006); Robert Barnidge, *Non-State Actors and Terrorism: Applying the Law of State Responsibility and the Due* Diligence *Principle* (TMC Asser Press 2008); Kimberley Trapp, 'Back to Basics: Necessity, Proportionality, and the Right of Self-Defence Against Non-State Terrorist Actors' (2007) 56 *International and Comparative Law Quarterly* 141; Pierre-Marie Dupuy, 'State Sponsors of Terrorism: Issues of International Responsibility' in Andrea Bianchi (ed), *Enforcing International Law Norms against Terrorism* (Hart 2004) 3.

[38] For an overview of the debate, see Abraham Sofaer, 'On the Necessity of Pre-emption' (2003) 14 *European Journal of International Law* 209; Michael Boethe, 'Terrorism and the Legality of Pre-emptive Force' (2003) 14 *European Journal of International Law* 227.

[39] *Follow-up to the Outcome of the Millennium Summit – A More Secure World: Our Shared Responsibility: Report of the UN High Level Panel on Threats,*

In another specialised area of law, international human rights law, the challenge of terrorism has presented special problems for the spectrum of rights: life, liberty and security, non-discrimination, freedom from torture, freedom of movement, privacy and so on. Human rights law has struggled to retain its normative purchase in regulating and constraining both terrorist and counter-terrorist violence,[40] and has sometimes been instrumentally used to justify 'trade-offs' between the rights of terrorists and of the community as a whole. Yet, like the other branches of law discussed above, the post-9/11 response to terrorism has tended to clarify rather than revolutionise or unravel the law.

In particular, there has been an ongoing refinement in national and regional courts of judicial reasoning concerning justifications for limiting rights and balancing them against public security imperatives, whether in relation to powers of detention, the imposition of control orders, new surveillance powers, the availability and standard of judicial review, and so on. In the assessment of public emergencies, there has been an increasingly sophisticated articulation of the relevant principles, the respective roles of the judiciary and the executive, and the substantive characterisation of terrorism as an emergency.

Further, in military operations abroad, the extraterritorial applicability of human rights law has been increasingly confirmed in relation to the use of force and detention powers. In domestic criminal trials, closer scrutiny has been brought to bear on the minimum requirements of a fair trial,[41] including concerning the disclosure of security-sensitive information to an affected person,[42] as well as a more nuanced risk analysis of preventive

---

*Challenges and Change*, 59th sess, Agenda Item 55, UN Doc A/59/565 (2 December 2004) [188]: '[A] threatened State, according to long established international law, can take military action as long as the threatened attack is *imminent*, no other means would deflect it and the action is proportionate.'

40 See, eg, Joan Fitzpatrick, 'Speaking Law to Power: The War against Terrorism and Human Rights' (2003) 14 *European Journal of International Law* 241; Daniel Moeckli, *Human Rights and Non-Discrimination in the 'War on Terror'* (Oxford University Press 2008); Ben Goold and Liora Lazarus (eds), *Security and Human Rights* (Hart 2007); Oren Gross and Fionnuala Ní Aoláin, *Law in Times of Crisis: Emergency Powers in Theory and Practice* (Cambridge University Press 2006).

41 For an overview, see Martin Scheinin, *Report of the Special Rapporteur on the Promotion and Protection of Human Rights and Fundamental Freedoms while Countering Terrorism*, 63rd sess, Agenda Item 67(c), UN Doc A/63/223 (6 August 2008).

42 See, eg, *A v United Kingdom* (European Court of Human Rights, Grand Chamber, Application No 3455/05, 19 February 2009); *Secretary of State for the*

criminal law approaches. As noted earlier, attention has also focused on the paramount importance of non-discrimination in anti-terrorism measures, including in the treatment of non-citizens and religious or minority groups. The scope of the prohibition of torture has been more finely teased out by the aggressive interrogation practices of certain States, without diminishing the rule itself or carving out exceptions for terrorist suspects. In international refugee law, the temptation to exclude suspected 'terrorists' automatically from protection has been balanced by more nuanced recognition of the legal principles at stake.[43] Despite the serious human rights violations committed in the war on terror, the relentless probing of the adequacy of human rights law in the name of counter-terrorism has paradoxically served to strengthen, rather than unravel, its normative power over time.

The examples above drawn from specialised areas of international law illustrate how the response to terrorism has driven a process of clarification, and occasional modification, of general norms, without creating new terrorism-specific rules or an anti-terrorism regime as such. The final development discernible in post-9/11 counter-terrorism practice is the most straightforward: in some areas there is simply a continuing application of unaltered general norms to the problem of terrorism – areas where, indeed, it is 'business as usual'.

To add to the earlier discussion of human rights law, there has been no large scale refashioning of that area of law in response to contemporary terrorist threats. Human rights law has survived acute challenges relatively intact. For example, attempts to justify torture, whether through creative interpretations of the definition of it, or direct assaults on its prohibition, were ultimately rebuffed by the international community.[44] So too has the international community robustly turned against 'irregular renditions' as a means of gathering intelligence and circumventing the regular legal processes (of extradition, deportation or transfer of detainees in armed conflict). Hawkish opponents of the structure and principles of human rights law have failed to articulate sound reasons for departing radically from it.

---

*Home Department v AF* [2009] UKHL 28 (10 June 2009); *Binyam Mohamed v The Secretary of State for Foreign and Commonwealth Affairs* [2010] EWCA Civ 65 (10 Feb 2010); *Canada (Prime Minister) v Khadr* [2010] SCC 3; Ben Saul, 'The Kafka-esque Case of Sheikh Mansour Leghaei: The Denial of the International Human Right to a Fair Hearing in National Security Assessments and Migration Proceedings in Australia' (2010) 33 *UNSW Law Journal* 629.

[43] See Ben Saul, 'Protecting Refugees in the Global "War on Terror"' (2008) 1 [Indian] *Juridical Review* 13.

[44] See *generally* Ben Saul, 'Torturing Terrorists After September 11: Dershowitz' Torture Warrant' (2004) 27 *International Journal of Law and Psychiatry* 645.

This should come as no surprise: human rights law itself contains highly flexible mechanisms for accommodating a wide range of public security threats and other emergency situations. The law permits necessary and proportionate *limitations* on many rights in order to secure legitimate public safety objectives; in more extreme cases, derogation (suspension) of certain rights is possible. Judiciaries are also sensitive to the expertise and necessary discretion of executive governments in making security assessments and accord appropriate deference to the executive in many cases. Indeed the problem with human rights law is often not that it is too restrictive in responding to terrorist threats, but that it is sometimes not restrictive enough: too ambiguous, too discretionary, too deferential to executive judgments, too fearful of getting it wrong and exposing the public to terrorist attack.

To summarise so far, the international approach to regulating terrorism is ad hoc and fragmented, involving a combination of special measures and general norms. The accretion of sectoral treaty norms over time has generated a kind of modest, incremental normative system in respect of common methods of terrorist violence, but its coverage remains patchy and incomplete. As will be seen below, those norms sometimes interact, and sometimes inhabit their own normative world. It is fair to conclude that presently there does not exist a coherent, over-arching, relatively autonomous 'regime' structure or accompanying institutions and processes. One could conclude that there is a certain incoherence, at least in the sense of messiness, about law dealing with terrorism.

Does all of this complexity, this messiness, this incoherence, matter? It depends on one's perspective. On one hand, one might simply take a deep breath and roll with the punches: the jumble and disarray of anti-terrorism law is a fact of history and contemporary life, and one should learn to live with it. After all, that is what international lawyers are for: to bring order to the chaos by cataloguing where the practice has brought us, and to help regulators and the regulated to navigate through the shoals. On the other hand, incoherence also has a price: a multiplicity of laws bumping around on a given subject may bring efficiency costs and compliance problems, particularly for less well-resourced States and other actors dazzled by the kaleidoscope of obligations coming at them thick and fast from all directions. That is the other purpose of international lawyers: to identify legal disorder, to propose reforms to simplify it and to encourage public confidence that the law's expectations can be understood.

The successful conclusion of a 'framework' UN Draft Comprehensive Terrorism Convention might go some way towards consolidating and progressively developing a field of global anti-terrorism law and enhancing the effectiveness and clarity of counter-terrorism efforts. Such a framework convention would establish conceptual agreement on the definition of terrorism, and thus provide core normative coherence to the cluster of disparate norms coalescing within a nascent anti-terrorism law regime. It could also potentially set out principles for resolving conflicts between anti-terrorism norms (including the sectoral treaties) and other international norms (particularly as regards international criminal law, humanitarian law, Security Council measures and human rights law). Despite the best efforts of sponsor States such as India, the Draft Convention continues to languish, in part because of the unproductive and sometimes unprincipled political positions taken by various blocs of States – positions which often have nothing to do with the effective protection of civilians from terrorist violence, or with pursuing a coherent normative response to it.

## B. Relational Coherence: Problems of Isolation and Fragmentation

A second dimension of coherence concerns the fragmented relationship between international anti-terrorism norms and other areas of international law. A number of controversies have arisen which illustrate the tensions involved and the efforts to reconcile apparent or actual incoherence (stemming from the fragmentation) between different legal regimes or norms.

### 1. International Humanitarian Law (IHL)

It was noted earlier that the Security Council required States to criminalise terrorism (pursuant to Resolution 1373), and many States have also proscribed certain terrorist organisations (either by reference to Resolutions 1267 or 1373), with criminal consequences following for those connected in some way to such groups. One adverse consequence of the criminalisation of terrorism and the banning of terrorist organisations is the potential for interference in the logic and practical effectiveness of the special regime of IHL and its underlying humanitarian purposes in situations of armed conflict.

Namely, if non-State parties to an armed conflict find themselves branded and delegitimised internationally as criminal terrorist organisations, the incentive for those groups to comply with IHL largely evaporates. It then makes sense to such groups to fight as dirtily and for as long as possible to avoid defeat, since defeat and capture bring severe criminal punishment rather than temporary administrative detention and eventually (at the end of the conflict) amnesties, demobilisation and social reintegration.

The demise of the Tamil Tigers in the Sri Lankan civil war in 2009 is a case in point: the LTTE's bitter struggle to the end was partly fanned by their acute legal ostracism and fear of what might follow defeat. In contrast, where non-State groups are not criminalised as terrorists but treated as belligerents in an armed conflict, there is greater reason to comply with humanitarian principles, both to enhance the group's own legitimacy and to stake a claim to more dignified treatment as belligerents upon capture. That is not to paint an ideal picture of what drives compliance or produces non-compliance, but in armed conflict even small steps of logic may save lives.

There are also more specific conflicts between anti-terrorism norms and IHL. The administrative detention (without charge) of dangerous civilians (definitely suspected of hostile activities) is permitted in international armed conflict. The picture is less clear in non-international conflicts,[45] but it is arguably implicit in common Art 3 that such detention may be necessary, even if there are no express powers authorising it.[46] In general, administrative detention must be authorised by law, necessary for security reasons, proportionate to that objective and subject to periodic independent review. The conditions of detention must also be humane.

After 9/11, however, a problem arose where the United States administratively detained 'unlawful combatants', subjected them to criminal trial, and then asserted a right to continue to administratively detain the person regardless of their conviction or acquittal. Such a claim appears to flow logically from the *lex specialis* of IHL, which permits administrative detention of any dangerous civilian. It follows that national authorities may adjudge that a person remains dangerous even after the expiration of a criminal sentence (if, for instance, they have not rehabilitated), or where they are acquitted (given that the criminal standard of proof is more difficult to meet than the lower threshold for security detention).

The problem with such a formalistic interpretation of IHL is that it deprives the criminal trial of any purpose: detention may continue, regardless of the outcome of the trial and the expiation of guilt through serving a criminal sentence is rendered nugatory. The march of human rights law has increasingly put pressure on such a view of IHL, even if security imperatives push the other way. In respect of the Guantanamo cases, States such as Australia made representations to the US that their nationals must be either prosecuted or released, and appeared to take the view that the initiation of a criminal process transforms the legal basis of detention. Once that step is taken, there is no going back to security detention: at that point the law enforcement model displaces the IHL security model, even if the conflict remains on foot.

---

45 See Goodman, above note 35; Sassòli, above note 35.

46 Bellinger, above note 35.

A third instance of colliding regimes concerns competition between the military targeting of 'terrorists' under IHL as opposed to their liability to arrest and criminal prosecution under a law enforcement approach. Criminal law and non-criminal law responses to terrorism are not mutually exclusive regimes, but may overlap in their application to terrorism. A person may be both a criminal suspect and a participant in an armed conflict under IHL. Where such a person participates in hostilities without authorisation under IHL, a State may lawfully target such a person for the duration of their participation in hostilities,[47] and there is no obligation on the State to attempt to arrest the person before targeting them. It is well accepted that IHL operates *lex specialis* in respect of the ordinary application of human rights law: lawful killings under IHL are not 'arbitrary' deprivations of the right to life.

The problem is that the meaning of 'direct participation in hostilities', and the duration of such participation, is in flux.[48] The unsettled scope of IHL in this context spills over into the interaction with the criminal law, for an expansive view of 'direct participation' may permit the killing of a person who would otherwise be subject only to arrest and prosecution on a narrow view of the concept. In practical terms, such interpretive uncertainty affects those many members of terrorist organisations who do not physically fight but perform support functions, such as financing, recruiting, training, arming or supplying the organisation. The line between exposure to arrest or assassination blurs in the prevailing legal incoherence.

Recent efforts by the International Committee of the Red Cross to clarify the meaning of 'direct participation' have gone some way towards building international consensus on the content of the rule. But as with many principles of international humanitarian law there is an inherent vagueness at the heart of the notion of 'direct participation' – at once necessary to accommodate flexibly the range of ways in which violence is perpetrated in armed conflict, but simultaneously confounding because of its relative lack of precision.

## 2. International human rights law

Problems of coherence have also arisen in the interaction between international anti-terrorism norms and international human rights law. At the outset, there is the conceptual potential for anti-terrorism law to newly criminalise political freedoms. Depending on the scope of the definition of

---

[47] Additional Protocol I, Art 51 (reflecting customary law in any armed conflict).

[48] See above note 34.

terrorism and the acceptability of any exceptions to it, the criminalisation of terrorism risks empowering the State –including autocratic ones – at the expense of other political claims to the use of violence. Terrorism may often jeopardise the human rights of civilians; but if terrorism is defined more widely as any violence against the State, then the criminalisation of terrorism itself strips away the human freedom to resist oppressive or authoritarian regimes with force. Political freedom often springs from domestic political crimes against an *ancien régime*, but international law should not be complicit by assisting States (through transnational criminal cooperation) to criminalise and repress legitimate resistance (which does not deliberately harm civilians).

Secondly, particular controversy has dogged the relation between various UN Security Council measures and regional human rights law. First, the Security Council's anti-terrorism sanctions regime under Resolution 1267 (2001), dealing with Al-Qaeda and its associates worldwide,[49] has been indirectly challenged through regional courts in Europe. In the *Kadi* case in 2008, the European Court of Justice (ECJ) annulled European Union measures which implemented the Security Council's sanctions regime against Al-Qaeda,[50] on the basis that the EU measures infringed the applicant's fundamental human rights under European Community law, and in circumstances where the UN's own procedures did not provide a fair procedure.[51] In particular, the EU measures infringed the right to be heard before a court, the right of effective judicial review and legal remedy, and the right to property.[52]

The ECJ did not purport to judicially review Security Council measures directly, but rather exercised its jurisdiction to review the European Community law implementing them. The case turned on the dualist relationship between EU law and UN law: one binding EU institutions within the 'autonomous legal system' of the EU,[53] the other binding individual EU member States on the international plane as States Parties to the UN Charter. The ECJ was primarily exercising the scope of its jurisdiction as

---

49 Stemming from Resolution 1267, Resolution 1390 and related resolutions.

50 *Kadi and Al Barakaat v Council of the European Union and Commission of the European Communities* (Joined Cases C-402/05 P and C-415/05 P) [2008] ECR I-6351.

51 Ibid [323].

52 Ibid [331]–[372].

53 Ibid [316].

conferred by EU law, and asserting itself as a 'self-contained regime'[54] of the strictest kind:

> the review by the Court of the validity of any Community measure in the light of fundamental rights must be considered to be an expression, in a community based on the rule of law, of a constitutional guarantee stemming from the EC Treaty as an autonomous legal system which is not to be prejudiced by an international agreement.[55]

EU States were left facing the possibility of non-compliance with their obligations under the UN Charter. In terms, the UN sanctions regime does not require Member States to exclude procedural fairness to persons listed by the UN. But where EU law refuses to implement Security Council sanctions against a person who has not been afforded procedural fairness, or where procedural fairness is afforded and sanctions are found to be unjustified, EU States would find themselves in breach of the UN Charter.[56] The ECJ gave EU States only a little breathing space by allowing three months before the annulment of the EU law, in part out of consideration of the importance of the Security Council obligations.[57]

At one level, the *Kadi* decision embodies a collision between competing obligations arising under separate legal regimes, potentially producing incoherent fragmentation. UN sanctions face the prospect of splintering into States that automatically enforce them, and those prepared to second-guess them through regional (or indeed national) legal procedures. Those that provide local procedures in turn could differ among themselves in the standards applied. Among other things, this may encourage forum shopping

---

54 See generally Eckart Klein, 'Self-Contained Regime', *Max Planck Encyclopedia of Public International Law* (Oxford University Press 2009).

55 *Kadi and Al Barakaat v Council of the European Union and Commission of the European Communities* (Joined Cases C-402/05 P and C-415/05 P) [2008] ECR I-6351, [316].

56 The obligations violated would include Art 25 of the Charter of the United Nations (requiring UN Member States to carry out decisions of the Security Council acting under Chapter VII) and Art 103 (providing that Charter obligations prevail over other international obligations, including treaties creating the EU legal system).

57 *Kadi and Al Barakaat v Council of the European Union and Commission of the European Communities* (Joined Cases C-402/05 P and C-415/05 P) [2008] ECR I-6351, [373].

and safe haven.[58] It also undermines the mandate, authority and effectiveness of the Security Council[59] – although the Council's failure to respect due process itself is productive of illegitimacy.

Yet, the news is not quite so bad. On a different view of fragmentation, *Kadi* is productive – an instance of constructive feedback and cross-institutional dialogue, resulting from a rights-based 'push-back' against a UN security apparatus slightly drunk on its own power. The ECJ's decision has grounded, articulated and amplified widespread concerns, including lawyerly unease, about the manifest procedural and structural inadequacies of the UN's sanctions regime. That feedback has in turn stimulated reform, including the creation of a UN Ombudsman to modestly enhance the level of protection. A more charitable view of the fragmentation of international law is that diversity and polycentricism can be good things.[60]

The Ombudsman procedure still falls well short of the due process expectations of human rights law.[61] As the ECJ noted, the UN sanctions regime is essentially a diplomatic, political model of decision-making,[62] all the while performing what are essentially judicial tasks without according judicial protections. In a second *Kadi* decision decided in 2010,[63] the European Union General Court (EGC) determined that the revised Resolution 1267 procedures still do not provide an effective, independent, impartial judicial procedure. It may also have raised the bar on degree of disclosure of security-sensitive information required to facilitate a fair hearing,[64] fuelling the conflict of regimes.

The cross-institutional dialogue continues, and it may be some time before it becomes known who is prepared to blink first. The EU could of course amend its internal constitutional law to give explicit recognition to the primacy of Security Council obligations, thus giving regional legal effect to the international law obligations of individual member States

---

58 Peter Fromuth, 'The European Court of Justice Kadi Decision and the Future of UN Counterterrorism Sanctions' (2009) 13(20) *American Society of International Law Insight*.

59 Lisa Ginsborg and Martin Scheinin, 'Judicial Powers, Due Process and Evidence in the Security Council's 1267 Terrorist Sanctions Regime: The *Kadi II* Conundrum' (2011) *European Union Working Paper* RSCAS 2011/44, 7.

60 Joost Pauwelyn, 'Fragmentation of International Law', *Max Planck Encyclopedia of Public International Law* (Oxford University Press 2009) [17]–[18].

61 Ginsborg and Scheinin, above note 59, 4.

62 *Kadi and Al Barakaat v Council of the European Union and Commission of the European Communities* (Joined Cases C-402/05 P and C-415/05 P) [2008] ECR I-6351, [323].

63 *Kadi v European Commission* (T-85/09) [2010] ERC I-2729.

64 See the discussion in Ginsborg and Scheinin, above note 59.

under Arts 25 and 103 of the UN Charter. Certainly that is the approach of various States outside Europe, which simply give effect to Council sanctions without concern for domestic due process, invoking the Charter as a simple source of obligation, or trump, to do so. Equally, it is open to the Security Council to do the right thing by affected individuals and entities, by moving beyond an antiquated political, diplomatic protection model and acknowledging the legal personality and rights of affected individuals and entities.[65]

The real focus would then become figuring out the precise content of due process protections in a way which does not jeopardise vital security interests. Plainly, human rights law itself offers a model of accommodation: procedural protections may legitimately vary according to context, including where necessary to protect security interests. What is unacceptable is the perpetuation of an 'extra-legal' security model which substitutes legality for politics, and basic rights for paternalistic diplomatic protection or weak Ombudsman oversight.

A different case before a different regional court, *Al-Jedda v United Kingdom* in the European Court of Human Rights (ECHR) in 2011,[66] also illustrates the tensions arising between anti-terrorism measures and human rights protection, and between Security Council measures and regional legal systems. That case demonstrates, however, a different approach from that of the ECJ in *Kadi* to resolving or managing such tensions.

In *Al-Jedda*, the ECHR found that the UK's security internment of detainees in Iraq, ostensibly pursuant to a Security Council resolution, had breached the UK's obligations concerning freedom from arbitrary detention under Art 5 of the European Convention on Human Rights. Security Council resolution 1546 authorised the UK to 'take all necessary measures to contribute to the maintenance of security and stability in Iraq', which the UK interpreted as authority to detain shorn of ordinary human rights protections.

The ECHR observed that in interpreting Security Council resolutions, 'there must be a presumption that the Security Council does not intend to impose any obligation on Member States to breach fundamental principles of human rights', absent 'clear and explicit language' to the contrary.[67] Further, 'the interpretation which is most in harmony with the requirements of the Convention and which avoids any conflict of obligations' must be

---

65 Alternatively, European States sitting on the Council could block any listing where there would be an inadequate level of disclosure to enable effective review: ibid.

66 *Al-Jedda v United Kingdom* [2001] Eur Court HR 1092.

67 Ibid [102].

chosen.[68] On the facts the ECHR determined that the Council resolution in question did not unambiguously require States to utilise indefinite internment with charge and judicial guarantees, in breach of international human rights law.[69] As such, no conflict arose between the Council measure and the European Convention,[70] and there was hence no need to consider the effect of Art 103 of the Charter in resolving conflict by prioritising Charter obligations over others.

The case nonetheless suggests a starkly different approach to the ECJ in *Kadi* in managing competing obligations arising under different legal regimes. By determining whether the Council resolution displaced European Convention rights, the ECHR's premise was that the European Convention *is* subject to and conditioned by other relevant international law, including the potential displacement of a Convention right by Art 103 of the Charter.[71]

The ECHR's approach thus appears to attempt to harmonise the requirements of European States' obligations under the European Convention and the UN Charter, respecting that Charter obligations may sometimes prevail. The European Convention is thus understood not as an autonomous legal system (like the ECJ claims for the European Community), but as a subsidiary regime within the legal hierarchy determined by international law itself. Institutionally, the ECHR's jurisdiction is not limited to a 'pure' application of the European Convention, but encompasses competence to interpret and apply the European Convention within the wider system of international law which creates and mandates it, even if doing so introduces external, unwritten limitations into the express words of the Convention.

Because there was no inconsistency of regimes on the facts of that case (that is, the Security Council resolution did not in fact exclude human rights in detention), the limits of harmonisation were not tested any further. The ECHR has previously suggested that a State acting pursuant to an international obligation may still be held responsible under the European Convention where 'the protection of Convention rights was manifestly deficient: in such a case, the interest of international cooperation would be

---

[68] Ibid.

[69] Ibid [105].

[70] Ibid [109].

[71] Nowhere in its judgment does the ECHR say so expressly, although it records the UK's contention that '[t]he Convention was part of international law and derived its normative force from international law', and the UK's invocation of an earlier ECHR decision that the Convention should not undermine or conflict with Security Council measures: ibid [91] (referring to *Behrami and Saramati* at [147]–[149]).

outweighed by the Convention's role as a "constitutional instrument of European public order" in the field of human rights'.[72] The ECHR has admittedly accorded special deference to binding Security Council measures, which 'are fundamental to the mission of the UN to secure international peace and security' and 'rely for their effectiveness on support from member states'.[73] As such, it found in the *Behrami* and *Saramati* cases that

> the Convention cannot be interpreted in a manner which would subject the acts and omissions of Contracting Parties which are covered by UNSC Resolutions and occur prior to or in the course of such missions, to the scrutiny of the Court. To do so would be to interfere with the fulfilment of the UN's key mission in this field including … with the effective conduct of its operations. It would also be tantamount to imposing conditions on the implementation of a UNSC Resolution which were not provided for in the text of the Resolution itself … .[74]

Yet, even State action pursuant to Security Council measures may still be reviewable on human rights grounds in certain circumstances. Such review was excluded in the cases of *Behrami* and *Saramati* because of the high degree of control exercised by the United Nations over the missions to which the individual States contributed. By contrast, where the Council delegates authority to States to act with a greater degree of autonomy, there may be greater scope for the ECHR to review State conduct.

A harder question then arises. Suppose the facts of *Al-Jedda* were different and the Security Council resolution did in fact require States to displace their international or regional human rights law treaty obligations. The ECHR would then be faced with a choice. It could simply invoke Art 103 of the UN Charter and give it direct effect in the interpretation and implantation of the European Convention, resulting in the resolution trumping a Convention right to the extent of the inconsistency. Those most concerned to preserve the unity of international law might favour such an approach.[75]

Alternatively, it could determine that the purported displacement of a given Convention right so compromised that right, not otherwise

---

72 *Behrami and Behrami v France* and *Saramati v France Germany and Norway* (joined cases) (European Court of Human Rights, Grand Chamber, Application Nos 71412/01 and 78166/01, 2 May 2007) [145], citing *Bosphorus Airlines v Ireland* (European Court of Human Rights, Grand Chamber, Application No 45036/98, 30 June 2005).

73 Ibid [149].

74 Ibid.

75 See, eg, Pauwelyn, above note 60 [14].

adequately protected through UN processes, so as to engage the Convention's protective role as a 'constitutional instrument of European public order'. It would surely depend on the importance of the right at stake, and the security interests in question. The latter approach does not set up the European Convention as an autonomous legal regime in a dualist relation to international law (as the ECJ did in *Kadi*), but nor does it subordinate its own authority to a monist acceptance of the exclusive primacy of the UN Charter. It is a finer textured approach: Charter obligations will ordinarily be respected, but the Security Council should watch out if it oversteps and transgresses those fundamental rights which should not be set aside even in the interests of security.

## C. Coherence as Consistency: Relativity and Selectivity

One other kind of incoherence affecting international anti-terrorism law deserves brief mention. If inconsistency or selectivity of application is harmful to the coherence and legitimacy of any legal rule, then the application of anti-terrorism laws presents acute problems of incoherence and illegitimacy. On the one hand, the inconsistent treatment of like situations is a feature of many areas of international law, particularly where questions of violence or security arise (or fail to arise) in the high politics of the Security Council.

But the inconsistency involved in the application of law to terrorism is especially pernicious. As the next section shows, the notion of terrorism itself is unsettled and indeterminate, so the application of anti-terrorism norms involves a magnification of inconsistency. Not only are the norms applied unevenly and incoherently, but the norms themselves are uneven and incoherent. Naturally the Security Council condemns some terrorist acts but not others, depending on geo-politics, the interests of the Permanent Five, and so on. But UN member States also disagree on what 'is' terrorism for the purpose of applying the rules at all, deepening the incoherence of Council practice and the national practices which flow from it.

National authorities are deeply inconsistent in their application of anti-terrorism norms, often by way of utilising broad prosecutorial discretions not to treat conduct as terrorism even where it fits the formal definitions of it encoded in national law. Thus, so far as the Australian authorities are concerned, armed militants attacking the Afghan Government in a civil war are 'terrorists', whereas armed militants attacking Gaddafi's Libyan Government are 'rebels' rising up for freedom against an oppressive State. Australian military forces attacking foreign governments (as in Iraq) are not treated as terrorists, but various non-State forces (such as the Taliban or

Tamil Tigers) are – even though the Australian legal definition formally regards any political violence against any State as terrorism, with no exception for State violence or armed conflicts governed by IHL.

The deeply politicised selectivity of application brings the law into disrepute: no one can trust that it will be applied to the matters it formally claims authority to regulate. All animals are equal, but some animals are more equal than others. In such a legal universe, the law dissipates into the political preferences of the prevailing law enforcement authorities. This can readily happen because international anti-terrorism laws, being so indeterminate, offer so little restraint. At the same time, there is a prevailing sentiment, driven by the Security Council's practice after 9/11, that security matters more than human rights.

One of the most pernicious kinds of inconsistency in the field of anti-terrorism norms concerns self-determination violence. Some States (led by the Organisation of the Islamic Conference and the Non-Aligned Movement) have persistently objected that violence in pursuit of the just cause of self-determination does not constitute terrorism. The modest version of this claim is that terrorism ought to be left to be regulated by other areas of international law; the more extensive version (which is increasingly less fashionable) is that liberation violence can never be regarded as criminal at all.

The problem of how anti-terrorism norms should deal with self-determination violence is complicated by an awkward relationship to IHL and the inconsistent treatment of self-determination violence within IHL itself. Parties to Protocol I recognise self-determination struggles as international armed conflicts.[76] As such, the forces of parties to such conflicts may qualify as combatants (under more relaxed conditions of combatancy recognising the needs of guerilla warfare),[77] and enjoy immunity for lawful acts of war.[78] Combatants cannot be characterised as terrorists for acts compliant with IHL; Protocol I thus decriminalises conduct formerly regarded as terrorist. Liberation forces must comply with the detailed provisions of IHL, including prohibitions on terrorist-type acts against non-combatants, and the restrictions on permissible means and methods of war.[79]

---

[76] Additional Protocol I, Art 1(4).

[77] Ibid Art 44(3).

[78] Leslie Green, *The Contemporary Law of Armed Conflict* (2nd edn, Manchester University Press 2000) 64.

[79] *Elizabeth* Chadwick, *Self-Determination, Terrorism and the International Humanitarian Law of Armed Conflict* (Martinus Nijhoff 1996) 2, 6–9, 204–6.

While many of the protective provisions of Protocol I have entered customary law, Art 1(4) – which 'internationalises' self-determination struggles – has not. As such, States not party to Protocol I may continue to treat national liberation struggles as non-international armed conflicts.[80] That in turn permits States to deny combatant status to liberation forces and to treat them as criminals,[81] including as 'terrorists'. In the absence of combatant immunity, those States may wish that such persons should fall within an international crime of terrorism (defined, say, as violence to intimidate populations or coerce governments).

The differential treatment of similarly-situated liberation movements undermines the consistency and coherence of IHL. But it also frustrates efforts to conclude and apply equally any international crime of terrorism. There is thus some intellectual force in the claims of some States that the struggle for self-determination must be differentiated from terrorism. Dealing with all liberation violence within the framework of IHL would assist in depoliticising and defining terrorism[82] and in making the law more consistent and coherent.

States are naturally 'reluctant to accept a form of international legislation which might eventually undermine their own power structure'.[83] Yet, denial of combatant status to movements resisting the forcible denial of self-determination implicates international law in oppression. The *erga omnes* right of self-determination is of fundamental international concern.[84] Yet under the guise of non-intervention in the affairs of States not party to Protocol I, international law protects oppressive regimes from popular destabilisation, preferencing State sovereignty over more reasonable claims of popular sovereignty.

If international law takes self-determination seriously, it should not criminalise – as terrorists – those who forcibly resist its denial. Rather, international agreement on any crime of terrorism must be conditioned on the exclusion of liberation movements in armed conflict from the scope of general anti-terrorism law. Fighters who target military objectives in accordance with the laws of war would thus not be liable to prosecution as 'terrorists', but would be accorded combatant immunity. Any breaches of

---

[80] Green, above note 78, 64.

[81] Ibid 64.

[82] Chadwick, above note 79, 204.

[83] Antonio Cassese, *International Law in a Divided World* (Clarendon 1994) 92.

[84] *Legal Consequences of the Construction of a Wall in the Occupied Palestinian Territory* (Advisory Opinion) [2004] ICJ Rep 136 [88], [155]–[156]; *East Timor (Portugal v Australia)* (Judgment) [1995] ICJ Rep 90, 102 [29].

the laws of war could be comprehensively punishable as war crimes[85] or crimes against humanity.

## III. THE LEGITIMACY OF INTERNATIONAL ANTI-TERRORISM LAW

The coherence of law is an important aspect of the law's legitimacy,[86] but it is not the end of the story. A messy, disorderly or less-than-coherent legal regime can still be a legitimate one, or perceived to be so. Other factors bear upon the law's overall legitimacy. One important factor is *determinacy*. As Franck puts it, determinacy is 'the ability of a text to convey a clear message' and a 'readily ascertainable meaning', thus conveying the expectation of a rule and ultimately exerting a compliance pull.[87] The question arises whether international anti-terrorism laws are sufficiently determinate to ground their claim to be legitimate as 'law'.

A second important factor bearing upon a law's overall legitimacy is the *legitimacy of legal processes and institutions*. This aspect of legitimacy refers to 'that quality of a rule which derives from a perception on the part of those to whom it is addressed that it has come into being in accordance with right process'.[88] The further question which arises is whether the processes of making international anti-terrorism law, and the institutions for its application, can be considered legitimate, so as to legitimate the enterprise of anti-terrorism law as a whole.

### A. Determinacy and Legitimacy

The central indeterminacy impairing the legitimacy of international anti-terrorism is the lingering absence of an agreed definition of terrorism as such. Until 9/11, the well-known indeterminacy of the term 'terrorism' was legally insignificant since it did not have operative consequences under international law. After 9/11, however, by Resolution 1373 (2001) (adopted under Chapter VII of the UN Charter), the Security Council required all

---

85 Including under specialised prohibitions on acts of terror, spreading terrorism and measures of terrorism under IHL: see Geneva Convention IV, art 33(1), Protocol I: Art 51(2), Protocol II: Arts 13(2), 4(2)(d); see also Statute of the International Criminal Tribunal for Rwanda, Art 4(2)(d); Statute of the Special Court for Sierra Leone, Art 3(d).

86 Franck, above note 12, 735–51.

87 Ibid 713.

88 Ibid 706.

States to criminalise 'terrorist acts' in domestic law. That resolution did not define terrorism for the purpose of national criminalisation. The predictable result was the decentralised and haphazard national implementation of the resolution. Many States unilaterally defined terrorism to suit their own political purposes, including to camouflage assaults on fundamental rights, or to deviate from procedural protections enjoyed by criminal suspects.

The Security Council also provided direction to States concerning inchoate terrorist offences and extended modes of criminal participation. Resolution 1373 requires States not only to criminalise the 'perpetration' of terrorist acts, but also participation in the 'financing, planning, [or] preparation' of such acts.[89] It is not entirely clear how such concepts relate to the forms of legal responsibility recognised in international criminal law (for example, as reflected in Art 25 of the Rome Statute of the International Criminal Court (ICC)).[90] Certainly some States have expansively interpreted Resolution 1373 to criminalise, for instance, acts preparatory to the commission of a terrorist act even where no specific terrorist act has been agreed upon;[91] as well as mere membership of a 'terrorist' organisation.[92]

Paradoxically, the indeterminacy of the definition of terrorism, and the scope of criminal responsibility for it, appealed to many States since it preserved their sovereign freedom of action to deal with 'terrorists' according to their own self-interested understanding of it. Indeterminacy thus helped to legitimate the law from a statist perspective, since the international norm primarily empowered States to counter terrorism as a threat to States themselves, even if it also constrained States from sponsoring terrorism against their people or other States. This considerable alignment of the Security Council's measures with the sovereign interests of many States undoubtedly accounts for the relative lack of State resistance to the Council's apparently radical, intrusive, quasi-legislative measures.

From a different standpoint, however, such indeterminacy at the heart of the international anti-terrorism project is a sign of the law's chronic illegitimacy: how can a norm even be said to exist if the scope of its

---

89 In addition, in (non-binding) SC Res 1624, 5261st mtg, UN Doc S/RES/1624 (14 September 2005) 3, the Security Council called upon States to '[p]rohibit by law incitement to commit a terrorist act or acts', prevent incitement, and deny safe haven or entry to inciters, and similar developments have occurred at the regional level.

90 Including commission and joint commission; ordering, soliciting, or inducing; aiding, abetting or assisting; joint criminal enterprise; and attempt.

91 Criminal Code Act 1995, ss 101.2(1–3), 101.4(1–3), 101.5(1–3), 101.6(1–2).

92 Criminal Code Act 1995, s 102(3).

obligation is so radically indeterminate? Decentralised UN law-making is one thing; the excessive delegation to States acting unilaterally of the Council's security powers to deal with terrorism is quite another. If the Security Council does not identify (through definition) the terrorist threat attracting its Chapter VII powers, there can be little confidence that the Council's measures are in fact within the ambit of those powers. The Council may be acting *ultra vires* by requiring States to combat a threat which is so indeterminate (for lack of definition) that it is uncertain whether the threat meets the threshold for action in Art 39 of the Charter, even allowing the widest discretion.

The Council's subsequent measures have only gone part way in addressing this core legitimacy problem. Faced with an increasingly vociferous backlash from international, regional and national human rights bodies and from civil society, in Resolution 1566 (2004) the Security Council eventually signalled its own conception of terrorism, by recalling that:

> criminal acts, including against civilians, committed with the intent to cause death or serious bodily injury, or taking of hostages, with the purpose to provoke a state of terror in the general public or in a group of persons or particular persons, intimidate a population or compel a government or an international organization to do or to abstain from doing any act, which constitute offences within the scope of and as defined in the international conventions and protocols relating to terrorism, are under no circumstances justifiable by considerations of a political, philosophical, ideological, racial, ethnic, religious or other similar nature, and *calls upon* all States to prevent such acts and, if not prevented, to ensure that such acts are punished by penalties consistent with their grave nature ...[93]

The definition of terrorism presented by the Council is only a working definition which does not require States to conform their anti-terrorism legislation to it. Nonetheless, that resolution is understood by States as establishing 'soft' guide-posts in the implementation of earlier Resolution 1373. Resolution 1566 presents a fairly narrow and rights-respecting concept of terrorism.[94] It does not criminalise any conduct which is not already criminal under existing transnational crime treaties; rather, it reclassifies as 'terrorism' those existing criminal wrongs where they are also designed to

---

[93] SC Res 1566, 5053rd mtg, UN Doc S/RES/1566 (8 October 2004) [3] ('Resolution 1566').

[94] Ibid – defining conduct as terrorism only: (a) when it is committed to harm people, (b) when it has the purpose of provoking a state of terror, intimidating a population, or compelling a government or an international organisation, and (c) where such conduct *also* constitutes an offence under the existing sectoral anti-terrorism treaties.

terrorise, intimidate or compel. There is no further 'special intent' or motive requirement of a political, religious or ideological purpose, although the addition of that further element would help to differentiate terrorism from private violence which seeks to intimidate or compel.[95]

Over time, that guideline definition in Resolution 1566 has the potential to stimulate increasing uniformity among national anti-terrorism laws adopted under Resolution 1373. The Security Council's Counter-Terrorism Directorate has utilised that definition in its dialogue with States, encouraging further convergence, although historically the Counter-Terrorism Committee tolerated widely divergent national approaches to definition. Sufficient State practice in conformity with the guideline definition – that is, the *actual* universal domestic criminalisation of terrorism as so defined – may evidence the emergence of a customary international law crime. There is, however, a long way to go before there is such evidence of a global normative consensus.

Franck observes that indeterminacy may be cured if there exists a forum or process for subsequently rendering the norm determinate: 'a legitimate forum mitigates the textual elasticity of the rule by introducing process determinacy'.[96] The paucity of international tribunals with jurisdiction to consider 'terrorism' has historically precluded the development of jurisprudence giving content to a legal concept of terrorism: the League of Nations' proposed international criminal court to adjudicate terrorist crimes never came into effect.[97]

More recently, however, the UN Security Council's Special Tribunal for Lebanon, established to prosecute terrorist bombings against Lebanese democracy, has distinguished itself by its effort to articulate a general international law notion of terrorism. The Appeals Chamber's finding in 2011 that there exists a customary international law crime of terrorism in peacetime[98] might be thought to assist in the legitimation of international

[95] See Ben Saul, 'The Curious Element of Motive in Definitions of Terrorism: Essential Ingredient or Criminalising Thought?' in Andrew Lynch, Edwina MacDonald and George Williams (eds), *Law and Liberty in the War on Terror* (Federation Press 2007) 28–38.

[96] Franck, above note 12, 724.

[97] See Ben Saul, 'The Legal Response of the League of Nations to Terrorism' (2006) 4 *Journal of International Criminal Justice* 78.

[98] *Interlocutory Decision on the Applicable Law*, above note 21, [85], where the elements of the crime were found to be as follows: '(i) the perpetration of a criminal act (such as murder, kidnapping, hostage-taking, arson, and so on), or threatening such an act; (ii) the intent to spread fear among the population (which would generally entail the creation of public danger) or directly or indirectly coerce

anti-terrorism law by lending determinacy to the term 'terrorism'. Customary law reflects widespread and representative State practice and is the expression of universal State consent *par excellence*. Its legitimacy is therefore harder to fault, at least in formal terms and from a State-centric perspective. If there exists customary law against terrorism, then such norms must be deeply embedded in international social life, and certainly thicker that the more wobbly diktats issuing from a Security Council composed of only 15 States and breaking new ground.

The Appeals Chamber was not recognising direct liability for an international crime of terrorism within the Tribunal's jurisdiction, but rather identified such crime for the purpose of interpreting the scope of domestic terrorism offences under Lebanese law (as provided for under the Tribunal's Statute). Its assessment of customary law is, however, highly controversial and has been overwhelmingly condemned by scholars.[99] Neither the prosecution nor the defence argued that terrorism is a customary international crime. The close analysis below of the sources relied upon by the Appeals Chamber[100] demonstrates that its conclusion was mistaken: there is no customary international crime of transnational terrorism. In consequence, it cannot be accepted that the Tribunal has provided determinacy, and thus legitimacy, to the notion of terrorism in international criminal law.

As regards treaties referred to by the Tribunal, an obvious but decisive starting point is that numerous efforts by the international community since the 1920s have not produced agreement on a general international crime of terrorism.[101] While there are numerous sector-specific treaties which address particular criminal means or methods used by terrorists, none of those treaties – individually or collectively – contains a comprehensive definition of terrorism[102] or establishes a general international crime of

---

a national or international authority to take some action, or to refrain from taking it; (iii) when the act involves a transnational element.'

[99] See generally above note 23.

[100] Including regional anti-terrorism treaties, General Assembly resolutions, Security Council Resolution 1566, the UN Draft Comprehensive Anti-Terrorism Convention, the Terrorist Financing Convention 1999, 37 national laws and nine national judicial decisions.

[101] See Saul, above note 17, chs 3–4; Guillaume, above note 13; Higgins, above note 13, 13–14.

[102] Martin Scheinin, Special Rapporteur, *Promotion and Protection of Human Rights – Report of the Special Rapporteur on the Promotion and Protection of Human Rights and Fundamental Freedoms while Countering Terrorism*, 62nd sess, Agenda Item 17, UN Doc E/CN.4/2006/98 (28 December 2005) [28] ('*Report of the Special Rapporteur*').

transnational 'terrorism'. At most, specific offences in some treaties may have entered into customary law, such as aircraft hijacking or hostage-taking.[103]

In the absence of a general crime of terrorism in treaty law, no parallel customary rule can arise out of those treaties. The sectoral approach was adopted precisely because States could not reach agreement on 'terrorism' as such. The decades of deadlock – continuing in the negotiations for a UN Draft Comprehensive Terrorism Convention since 2000 – demonstrate a lack of consensus amongst the international community on defining and criminalising terrorism. Even the 1999 Terrorist Financing Convention (sometimes pointed to as a generic definition of terrorism) only defines and criminalises terrorist *financing*, not terrorism per se.

The Appeals Chamber also invokes the treaties of certain regional organisations to support its conclusion that there exists an international consensus on a customary international crime. Yet, an accurate reading of those conventions establishes exactly the opposite: enormous variation in regional conceptions of terrorism and no consensus on a common definition.[104]

Some regional treaties focus on specific terrorist methods, without defining terrorism;[105] others contain (often wide or conflicting) generic definitions,[106] or define terrorism only to criminalise ancillary conduct;[107] and yet others do not create offences at all, but serve other purposes (such as

---

[103] *United States v Yunis,* 924 F 2d 1086, 1092 (DC Cir, 1991); *Burnett et al v Al Baraka Investment and Development Corporation et al*, 274 F Supp 2d 86 (DC Cir, 2003).

[104] Ben Saul, above note 17, ch 4.

[105] *Organisation of American States (OAS) Convention to Prevent and Punish Acts of Terrorism Taking the Form of Crimes against Persons and Related Extortion that are of International Significance* (adopted 2 February 1971, entered into force 16 October 1973, 1438 UNTS 194); *Inter-American Convention against Terrorism* (adopted 3 June 2002, in OAS General Assembly res 1840 (XXXII-O/02).

[106] *Arab League Convention on the Suppression of Terrorism* (adopted 22 April 1998; entered into force 7 May *1999*); *Organisation of the Islamic Conference (OIC) Convention on Combating International Terrorism* (adopted 1 July 1999, annexed to res 59/26-P); *Organisation of African Unity (OAU) Convention on the Prevention and Combating of Terrorism* (adopted 14 July 1999, entered into force 6 December 2003); *EU Framework Decision on Combating Terrorism* (2002/475/JHA), 13 June 2002, *Official Journal* L164/3, 22 June 2002, entered into force 22 June 2002.

[107] Council of Europe Convention for the Prevention of Terrorism (adopted 16 May 2005, ETS No 196); *South Asian Association for Regional Cooperation (SAARC) Additional Protocol* 2004 (adopted 6 January 2004) *to the SAARC Regional Convention on Suppression of Terrorism* (adopted 4 November 1987,

extradition or law enforcement cooperation).[108] Some of the treaties do not enjoy wide participation by members of the regional organisation (as with the Organisation of the Islamic Conference (OIC)), and even where States are parties, the treaty may not have influenced national practice much at all (as with the Organisation of African Unity (OAU)).

Concerning UN resolutions, the Appeals Chamber invokes a series of General Assembly resolutions to support its position. Yet, the core of those resolutions, the 1994 Declaration on Measures against International Terrorism,[109] must be viewed cautiously. The Declaration itself emphasises the need to progressively develop and codify the law on terrorism,[110] far from reflecting existing rules. Many States argued that there was still a need to define terrorism and/or to adopt a comprehensive treaty criminalising it,[111] and to distinguish self-determination struggles[112] – including the 118 States of the Non-Aligned Movement and 56 OIC States.[113] At most the Declaration reflects a political agreement on the wrongfulness of terrorism which

---

entered into force 22 August 1998); *African Union Protocol* 2004 (adopted 8 July 2004) *to the OAU Convention*, ibid.

108 *Inter-American Convention against Terrorism* 2002, above note 105; *Council of Europe Convention on the Suppression of Terrorism* (adopted 27 January 1977, entered into force 4 August 1978, ETS No 90); *SAARC Regional Convention*, ibid; *Commonwealth of Independent States (CIS) Treaty on Cooperation in Combating Terrorism* (adopted 4 June 1999, entered into force 4 June 1999).

109 *Measures to Eliminate International Terrorism*, GA Res 49/60, 84th plen mtg, UN Doc A/RES/49/60 (9 December 1994) annex ('*Declaration on Measures against International Terrorism*'). The declaration states that '[c]riminal acts intended or calculated to provoke a state of terror in the general public, a group of persons or particular persons for political purposes are in any circumstance unjustifiable, whatever the considerations of a political, philosophical, ideological, racial, ethnic, religious or any other nature that may be invoked to justify them', at [3].

110 *Declaration on Measures against International Terrorism*, [12].

111 UNGAOR (49th Session) (6th Cttee), 14th mtg (20 Oct 1994), UN Doc. A/C.6/49/SR.14, [5] (Sudan), [13] (India), [27] (Algeria), [71] (Nepal); 15th mtg (21 October 1994), UN Doc. A/C.6/49/SR.15, [4] (Sri Lanka), [9] (Iran), [18]–[19] (Libya).

112 Ibid, 14th meeting, 20 Oct 1994, [6] (Sudan), [20] (Syria), [24] (Pakistan); 15th meeting, 21 October 1994, [9] (Iran), [18]–[19] (Libya).

113 Non-Aligned Movement (NAM), XIV Ministerial Conference, Final Document, Durban, 17–19 August 2004, [98–99], [101–102], [104]; NAM, XIII Conference of Heads of State or Government, Final Document, Kuala Lumpur, 25 February 2003, [105–106], [108], [115]; NAM, XIII Ministerial Conference, Final Doc, Cartagena, 8–9 April 2000, [90–91]; OIC resolutions 6/31-LEG (2004), [5]; 7/31-LEG (2004), preamble, [1–2]; 6/10-LEG(IS) (2003), [5]; 7/10-LEG (IS) (2003), [1–2]; OIC, Islamic Summit Conference (10th Session), Final Communiqué, Malaysia, 16–17 October 2003, [50]; OIC (Extraordinary Session Foreign

falls short of evidencing a customary international crime, particularly against a background of continuing, inconclusive UN treaty negotiations on point since 2000.

Moreover, the Declaration's definition of terrorism (requiring a political purpose) is, in any case, different to that in the UN Draft Comprehensive Convention (which does not require a political motive); different again from that in Security Council resolution 1566 (which is limited to underlying sectoral offences, and does not catch all forms of terrorism); different from the definitions in recent treaties such as the 1999 Terrorist Financing Convention; and different from those many different definitions in national laws and regional treaties (as shown below). All of this suggests that the legal definition of terrorism, and such criminal liability as may attach to it, remains deeply contested.

In relation to national laws, the Appeals Chamber claimed that 'the national legislation of countries around the world consistently defines terrorism in similar if not identical terms to those used in the international instruments'.[114] This is plainly not accurate and national laws do not evidence any customary law agreement on a shared definition and crime of terrorism. In the first place, the Appeals Chamber conflates national laws which address *domestic terrorism* with those concerning *international terrorism*, when only the latter are relevant in evidencing the Appeals Chamber's supposed crime of *transnational* terrorism.

Secondly, the Appeals Chamber relies on national definitions of terrorism used for *criminal offence* purposes with definitions used for *non-criminal* purposes, when only the former may be evidence of a customary international *crime* of terrorism. Thirdly, while the Appeals Chamber argues that the many national laws converge on a common definition of terrorism,[115] that reductive assertion conceals the reality of fundamental conceptual disagreements about terrorism which are clearly evident even on the face of those 37 laws – let alone in the more than 160 other divergent national laws which are not mentioned by the Appeals Chamber. Such divergence has not been cured by the UN Security Council's edict in Resolution 1373 (2001) requiring States to criminalise terrorism; rather, the Security Council has seemingly tolerated a wide variety of national law approaches to terrorism without creating uniformity.

---

Ministers), Declaration on International Terrorism, Kuala Lumpur, 1–3 April 2002, [8], [11], [16] and Plan of Action, [2–3]; all of the above documents are reproduced in Ben Saul, *Documents in International Law: Terrorism* (Hart 2012), Part 6.

114 *Interlocutory Decision on the Applicable Law*, above note 21, [91]; see also [91]–[98] regarding national laws.

115 Ibid [97].

Fourthly, the Appeals Chamber invokes some national (and regional) laws which patently violate international human rights law, such as by being too vague to satisfy the principle of legality and freedom from retroactive criminal punishment under Art 15 of the ICCPR.[116] Such unlawful acts are not accompanied by any *opinio juris* to the effect that rights-violating definitions of terrorism are now permissible forms of international anti-terrorism law: they remain simply unlawful.

The final category of sources invoked by the Appeals Chamber – nine national judicial decisions – also do not support its contention that terrorism is a customary law crime.[117] The Appeals Chamber misreads, exaggerates or misrepresents each decision. One case did not concern terrorism at all,[118] while in various other cases, the customary law status of terrorism was not an issue in their disposal.[119] One decision explicitly refrains from ruling on the point.[120] One matter was a civil case and did not involve criminal liability,[121] while others concerned national law contexts such as extradition[122] or exclusion from refugee status.[123] One decision identifies 'the essence' of terrorism for the limited purpose of interpreting a domestic immigration law statute, but acknowledges that 'there is no single definition

---

[116] ICCPR (adopted 16 December 1966, entered into force 23 March 1976, 999 UNTS 171). For human rights critiques of national laws, see, eg, 'Concluding Observations of the UN Human Rights Committee': United States of America (15 September 2006) UN Doc. CCPR/C/USA/CO/3, [11]; Algeria (18 August 1998) UN Doc. CCPR/C/79/Add.95, [11]; Egypt (9 August 1993) UN Doc CCPR/C/79/Add.23, [8]; Democratic Peoples' Republic of Korea (27 August 2001) UN Doc. CCPR/CO/72/PRK, [14]; Portugal (Macao) (4 November 1999) UN Doc. CCPR/C/79/Add.115, [12]; Peru (25 July 1996) UN Doc. CCPR /C/79/Add.67, [12]; *Report of the Special Rapporteur*, [27]–[28], [45]–[47], [56], [62]; all of the above documents are reproduced in Ben Saul, *Documents in International Law: Terrorism* (Hart 2012), Part 4.

[117] *Interlocutory Decision on the Applicable Law*, above note 21, [86].

[118] Enrique *Lautaro Arancibia Clavel case,* Argentinean Supreme Court, No. 259 (2004), 24 August 2004.

[119] *Cavallo* case, Mexican Supreme Court, No. 140/2002, 10 June 2003; *US v Yunis*, 924 F 2d 1086 (DC Cir, 1991); *EHL* case, Cass. 15 février 2006, RG P.05.1594.F, Pas. 2006, No. 96; RDP2006, 795, cited in *Rapport annuele la Cour de cassation de Belgique 2009.*

[120] *Zrig v Canada (Minister of Citizenship and Immigration)* [2003] 3 FC 761, [180].

[121] *Almog v Arab Bank*, 471 F Supp 2d 257 (EDNY, 2007).

[122] *EHL* case, above note 119.

[123] *Al-Sirri v Secretary of State for the Home Department* [2009] EWCA Civ 364.

that is accepted internationally' and that '[o]ne searches in vain for an authoritative definition'.[124]

At best, some of the decisions accept that certain forms of terrorism may have attracted international consensus[125] (for instance, hijacking or hostage-taking), but that falls far short of support for the existence of a comprehensive, universal crime of terrorism as such. In those few cases which mention customary law, the methodology of analysing custom formation is minimal to say the least and 'rest[s] upon a very inadequate use of the sources'.[126]

While one decision appears to squarely identify a customary crime of terrorism,[127] it then proceeds to define such crime quite differently from the notion presented by the Appeals Chamber – specifically by requiring a political, religious or ideological motivation. On that view, terrorism is simply *not* terrorism unless it is defined to include the motive element. This is not a trivial or marginal difference of opinion. The Appeals Chamber's assessment of the customary crime of terrorism is directly at odds with the judgment it invokes in its support. The Appeals Chamber also ignores other national judicial decisions which cast doubt on the customary law status of terrorism.[128] Overall, the Tribunal's deeply unsatisfactory analysis fails to substantiate its claim that terrorism is a customary international crime, and its definition consequently cannot supply determinacy and legitimacy to anti-terrorism law.

## B. Institutional Legitimacy

A further factor in evaluating the legitimacy of international anti-terrorism norms is whether the processes or institutions of the law's creation and application can be perceived as legitimate. A number of institutional focal

---

124 *Suresh v Canada* [2002] 1 SCR 3, 53 [94].

125 *Zrig v Canada (Minister of Citizenship and Immigration)* [2003] 3 FC 761; *US v Yunis*, 924 F 2d 1086 (DC Cir, 1991).

126 Ian Brownlie, *Principles of Public International Law* (6th edn, Oxford University Press 2003) 22 (speaking of the value of national decisions generally).

127 *Bouyahia Maher Ben Abdelaziz et al*, Italian Corte di Cassazione Judgment of 17 January 2007, No. 1072 (2006) XVI *Italian Yearbook of International Law* 322.

128 *US v Yousef et al*, 327 F 3d 56 (US Crt App, 2nd Cir) (4 April 2003) 34, 44, 46, 53–60, affirming *Tel-Oren v Libyan Arab Republic* 726 F 2d 774 (DC Cir, 1984) 795 (Edwards J), 806–07 (Bork J); *Ghaddafi case*, French Court of Cassation (Criminal Law Chamber), Appeal Nr. 00–87215, Judgment of 13 March 2001, published in (2001) No. 64, *Bulletin Criminel*, 218–19; *Madan Singh v State of Bihar* [2004] INSC 225 (2 April 2004).

points are relevant. First, the Security Council has been criticised for taking the lead on post-9/11 international law making, particularly in adopting 'quasi-legislative' measures – with general, prospective effect, not linked to a concrete security situation.[129] The binding security powers of the Council under Chapter VII are certainly an attractive route for creating new law: a small executive club of States can expeditiously 'make' the law, and it sticks, in contrast to the frustratingly incremental 'soft law' standard-setting of a General Assembly riven by bloc politics, or the slow pace and compromises of multilateral treaty-making. In one sense, Council action carries a certain legitimacy precisely because of the fact that it is able to act against a grave threat, in contrast to the inertia or deadlock in codification through the General Assembly.

But the concern lies precisely in shifting prospective law-making from the ordinary, inclusive, relatively transparent and consensual processes of treaty negotiation to the less transparent, participatory and representative forum of the Security Council. The latter entails a more 'top down' and less consensual approach to law-making in the area, not to mention the exclusion of civil society participation. As others have observed, 'where law is made through a long-established process that gives effect to state consent there is less likelihood of its being deemed illegitimate'.[130]

Even though there has been general compliance by States with the Council's regime, compliance has sometimes been grudging and variable, and its legitimacy questioned. Thus there have been suggestions that the regime parochially[131] privileges western security interests, reorientates

---

[129] See Stefan Talmon, 'The Security Council as World Legislature' (2005) 99 *American Journal of International Law* 175; Nicholas Rostow, 'Before and After: The Changed UN Response to Terrorism since September 11th' (2002) 35 *Cornell International Law Journal* 475, 479; Eric Rosand, 'Security Council Resolution 1373, the Counter-Terrorism Committee, and the Fight against Terrorism' (2003) 97 *American Journal of International Law* 333; Paul Szasz, 'The Security Council Starts Legislating' (2002) 96 *American Journal of International Law* 901; Jane Stromseth, 'The Security Council's Counter-Terrorism Role: Continuity and Innovation' (2003) 97 *American Journal of International Law Proceedings* 41.

[130] Christine Chinkin, cited in Shaha El-Sheemy, *International Law-Making: Problems of Coherence and Fragmentation – A Summary of the Chatham House International Law Discussion Group Meeting Held on 23 March 2007* (The Royal Institute of International Affairs 2007) 3 <http://www.chathamhouse.org/sites/default/files/public/Research/International%20Law/il230307.pdf>.

[131] Regarding the parochialism and legitimacy, see generally John Tasioulas, 'The Legitimacy of International Law' in Samantha Besson and John Tasioulas (eds), *The Philosophy of International Law* (Oxford University Press 2010) 97, 105–12.

international attention away from more pressing problems, diverts resources from development to national security, and so on. The indeterminacy surrounding the definition of terrorism in Council measures would never have survived the cautious, lawyerly approach to drafting treaty provisions in a multilateral negotiation, and evidences the pitfalls of a politicised, diplomatic approach shorn of legal attention to detail.

The legitimacy of Council measures has been particularly problematic in its attitude to human rights issues in counter-terrorism. State consent through ordinary law-making processes is not the end of the legitimacy story: conformity with fundamental rights is also relevant.[132] The Counter-Terrorism Committee initially rejected calls to take human rights considerations into account when responding to State reports about national action against terrorism in implementing Resolution 1373, and resisted the appointment of a human rights expert to its ranks. Matters have since improved, but it is hard to escape the impression that the Council considers security as mainstream in a hierarchy of values where human rights are marginal, rather than intimately bound up with security.

Such an approach has marked various UN institutions entrusted with counter-terrorism functions. Notwithstanding the indication in Resolution 1566 that terrorist offences should be linked to the existing sectoral treaties, in practice the Counter-Terrorism Committee and the UN Office on Drugs and Crime have encouraged States to extend legal liabilities for terrorism beyond those which are formally provided for in sectoral anti-terrorism treaties and Security Council measures.[133] The involvement of such technical experts in the law-making process is hardly politically neutral, despite claims to that effect. An elite UN expert urging the removal of the political offence exception to extradition, where it is not provided for in 'hard' treaty law, has profound implications for political freedom in countries where it

---

[132] See, eg, Allen Buchanan, 'The Legitimacy of International Law' in Samantha Besson and John Tasioulas (eds), *The Philosophy of International Law* (Oxford University Press 2010) 79, 94–6.

[133] See, eg, United Nations Office on Drugs and Crime, *Legislative Guide to the Universal Legal Regime against Terrorism* (UNODC 2008); United Nations Office on Drugs and Crime, *Draft Model Legislative Provisions against Terrorism* (UNODC 2009). In particular, States have been urged to criminalise a range of preparatory offences in relation to all sectoral treaty offences, even where the treaties themselves do not authorise it. Likewise, extended extraterritorial jurisdiction and the removal of the political offence exception to extradition have been encouraged in relation to all terrorist type offences, beyond the terms of many of the treaties themselves.

may be necessary *in extremis* to use proportionate violence in defence of human rights.[134]

Such privileging of security over rights has even seeped into institutions which ought to know better. In the decision of the UN Special Tribunal for Lebanon mentioned earlier, for instance, an international crime of terrorism was recognised notwithstanding that it would give rise to retrospective criminal liability, contrary to general principles of law, international criminal law, and human rights law.[135] It was hardly foreseeable to a person in Lebanon in 2005 that terrorism as such was an international crime, or that such crime would be used ostensibly in 'interpreting' domestic offences, but in reality to impose new liabilities.

The Appeals Chamber may well be right that the conduct it identified *should be* an international crime. It may indeed be abhorrent that a wider net of terrorist conspirators in Lebanon could otherwise get away with – on a positivist technicality – assassinating a former Lebanese Prime Minister or killing many others. One might even argue on natural law grounds, channelling Nuremberg, that no competent person in Lebanon in 2005 could seriously have believed that terrorist bombing was a terrorist crime, but using a machine gun or knife was not. Even so, the *lex ferenda* should not be misrepresented by judges as the *lex lata*, however compelling the moral case for punishing the wicked after the fact, even in circumstances where the positive law then in force turns out to be deficient.

Incorrect decisions based on poor reasons and sloppy methodology, or violating human rights law, are not good for international law or public confidence in its institutions and processes. Further, to the extent that an international tribunal held up rights-disrespecting national and regional definitions of terrorism as global gold standards in its analysis of custom formation, encouragement and legitimacy has been given to despots to demonise and convict their opponents as terrorists. The punitive instinct of the tribunal could benefit from a strong dose of human rights sensitisation, in a field where States are already pushing the limits too far. The risks of overreach and overreaction are particularly acute in a tribunal established by the Security Council under its security powers; on a subject as politicised as terrorism; and against the background of a tense and highly charged Lebanese politics.

Over time, elsewhere in the UN system various human rights bodies have increasingly asserted themselves against excessive State anti-terrorism

---

134 See Saul, above note 17, ch 2.

135 See Saul, above note 23.

measures,[136] including those which earlier may have received a nod of approval from the Counter-Terrorism Committee. On a number of occasions, for instance, the UN Human Rights Committee has criticised national definitions of terrorism for being too vague or ambiguous and thus failing to satisfy the principle of legality underlying freedom from retroactive criminal punishment.[137] Definitions have also been criticized as having discriminatory or prejudicial effects against particular racial or religious groups. Such scrutiny has helped to identify and wind back excessive national anti-terrorism laws, and to re-balance public security imperatives with human rights, subject to the limitation that UN human rights bodies can only make recommendations whereas the Security Council's counter-terrorism measures invoke binding Chapter VII powers.

One area where human rights are still struggling to make headway concerns the Security Council's Resolution 1267 sanctions regime against Al-Qaeda. As noted earlier, that regime has been heavily criticised for the lack of due process in the listing and delisting of persons and entities, including as regards notification, disclosure of evidence, standard of proof, the right to judicially challenge a decision, and shortcomings in the politicised, diplomatic, non-judicial mode of decision-making. The process has been collaterally attacked and found to be deficient in proceedings before various European courts.

---

[136] Including the UN Human Rights Committee, various Special Rapporteurs, the Human Rights Council and the UN High Commissioner for Human Rights. See, eg, Human Rights Committee, *General Comment No 29: States of Emergency (article 4)*, 1950th mtg, UN Doc CCPR/C/21/Rev.1/Add.11 (31 August 2001); Commission on Human Rights Res 2003/37, 58th mtg, UN Doc E/CN.4/2003/L.11/Add.4 (23 April 2003) and Commission on Human Rights Res 2005/80, 60th mtg, UN Doc E/CN.4/2005/L.10/Add.17 (21 April 2005); Human Rights Council Res 7/7 (2008), Human Rights Council Res 10/9 (2009), Human Rights Council Res 10/11 (2009), Human Rights Council Res 10/15 (2009), Human Rights Council Res 10/22 (2009). Report of independent expert (Robert K Goldman) on the protection of human rights and fundamental freedoms while countering terrorism, 7 February 2005. Reports of the Special Rapporteur (Martin Scheinin) on the promotion and protection of human rights and fundamental freedoms while countering terrorism: Report to the Commission on Human Rights, 28 December 2005; Reports to the General Assembly, 16 August 2006, 15 August 2007, 6 August 2008; Reports to the Human Rights Council, 29 January 2007, 21 November 2007, 4 February 2009. Office of the UN High Commissioner for Human Rights, Report to the UN Human Rights Council on the protection of human rights and fundamental freedoms while countering terrorism, 2 September 2009. All of the above documents are reproduced in Ben Saul, *Documents in International Law: Terrorism* (Hart 2012), Part 4.

[137] ICCPR, opened for signature 16 December 1966, 999 UNTS 171 (entered into force 23 March 1976), Art 15.

Gradual improvements to the process, culminating in an Ombudsman process, have only partly remedied the defects and failed to shake off the deep perceptions of illegitimacy which dog these State-favouring institutional processes. The Council appears insistent on invoking security concerns to trump human rights, even though human rights law itself provides flexible means of accommodating security concerns without extinguishing rights as the Council does. It is also resistant to the push for a 'global administrative law' to counterbalance or even out the effects of new forms of coercive but unconventional global norm-setting and regulation in which there is an 'accountability deficit'.[138] It is particularly concerned about accountability, transparency, participation, reasoned decision, legality, and effective review[139] – conditions which are only embryonic in the Council's committees.

A further institutional process raising legitimacy questions is the FATF's role in setting standards on terrorist financing. The FATF is not an international organisation with legal personality, a constitution, or a basis in treaty law, but is a loose inter-governmental partnership of 32 States and two regional organisations.[140] As such, it has a small, unrepresentative membership and there are transparency and accountability deficits in its decision-making. It has exerted a powerful influence on norm creation beyond its membership, since its members include most of the world's largest economies and its standards have become conditions of doing business with non-members. There are thus irresistible commercial incentives for non-members to conform to FATF standards.

That FATF recommendations are formally enacted through domestic legal systems[141] does not change the reality that their substantive origin and normative force are located within the FATF as a centre of quasi-legislative gravity that cannot easily be resisted. The FATF is perhaps an example of how globalisation 'has changed the modalities of international law by often emphasizing regulation above law … manifest in the growth of soft-law, directives, and standards … [over] constraint and bindingness'.[142] Such developments have not been accompanied by a growth in administrative

---

138 Kingsbury, Krisch and Stewart, above note 7, 16.

139 Ibid 17.

140 The European Commission and the Gulf Cooperation Council.

141 A claim to legitimacy accepted by a UK parliamentary inquiry: European Union Committee, 'Money Laundering and the Financing of Terrorism' (Report No 19, UK House of Lords, 14 July 2009) [27].

142 Frederic Megret, 'Globalization and International Law', *Max Planck Encyclopedia of Public International Law* (Oxford University Press 2009) [36].

accountability and transparency which one might expect from legitimate legal processes.

## IV. CONCLUSION

The field of counter-terrorism is packed with law, but coherence and legitimacy are often lacking. Such problems are a product of historical accretion, the exigencies of new threats, political expediency, and a collision of competing value systems and priorities in international social life. The law too often subordinates individual rights to abstract security interests. Global anti-terrorism law did not spring fully formed, but is an imperfect, chaotic work in progress.

The processes and institutions for managing incoherence will gradually muddle through some of the problems of ambiguity, indeterminacy, conflict and fragmentation. Sometimes the dialogue will be constructive, and at other times it will be pistols at ten paces. The processes and institutions themselves are affected by their own legitimacy problems. None of this is to suggest that illegitimate law might not still possess some instrumental value.[143] Much work nonetheless needs to be done to adjust the superstructures which produce and circulate the law. The reform project is urgent not least because the law continues to subordinate liberty to State interests, without necessarily making the world safer.

---

143 Tasioulas, above note 131, 99.

# 9. The International Criminal Court and the complexities of international criminal justice

**James Potter***

## I. INTRODUCTION

A recent significant development in international criminal justice is the adoption of amendments to the Rome Statute of the International Criminal Court (Rome Statute)[1] dealing with the crime of aggression. These amendments were adopted at the International Criminal Court's ('the Court') inaugural Review Conference which took place in Kampala from 31 May 2010 to 11 June 2010.[2] This chapter looks at the Kampala outcome and focuses on the issue of state consent to the amendments.

It is clear that international criminal justice demands that justice be applied to all. In the famous words of American Prosecutor Robert H Jackson during the Nuremberg trials: 'We must never forget that the record on which we judge these defendants today is the record on which history will judge us tomorrow. To pass these defendants a poisoned chalice is to

---

* The author previously worked as a Principal Legal Officer at the Office of International Law in the Commonwealth Attorney-General's Department and from 2007 to 2010 participated as a member of the Australian delegation to the crime of aggression negotiations. However, the views expressed in this chapter are the views of the author and do not necessarily represent the views of the Australian Government.

1 Rome Statute of the International Criminal Court, opened for signature 17 July 1998, 2187 UNTS 90 (entered into force 1 July 2002) ('Rome Statute'). Unless otherwise noted, references to Articles in this paper are references to Articles in the Rome Statute.

2 Assembly of States Parties to the Rome Statute of the International Criminal Court, Review Conference of the Rome Statute of the International Criminal Court, RC/Res.6, Official Records, 13th mtg, RC/11 (11 June 2010) 17–22 ('Crime of Aggression Resolution').

put it to our own lips as well.'[3] At the same time, the Court is an international body created by treaty law which has been endowed with jurisdiction within the limits agreed by states in the Rome Statute. To what extent then should the principle that justice be applied equally to all be limited by the notion of state sovereignty and consent to the Court's jurisdiction over the crime of aggression? This issue came to the forefront during the negotiations on the crime of aggression amendments.

This chapter will look firstly at the role of state consent in the Rome Statute system of jurisdiction over international crimes, including the push by some states, at the Rome Conference which established the Court, to grant universal jurisdiction to the Court. In light of this background, the chapter will then look at the issue of the consent of the alleged aggressor state to the crime of aggression amendments, which was one of the key issues forming part of the compromise package adopted at the Review Conference. It will consider the outcome reached at Kampala in relation to state consent and the impact of this result on the legitimacy of the Court's jurisdiction over the crime of aggression.

## II. ROLE OF CONSENT AND UNIVERSAL JURISDICTION

It is clear that international law depends to a large degree on the notion of state consent for its validity. According to voluntarist theories of international law, the 'will of States is the basis of international law and hence … the law is dependent on the consent of States'.[4] This notion is reflected in the fundamental rule of treaty interpretation under customary international law, as reflected in Art 34 of the Vienna Convention on the Law of Treaties,[5] that a state is not bound by obligations to which they have not consented (*pacta tertiis*). It is also evident in consent-based elements of customary international law, such as the requirement for *opinio juris* and the ability of a state which does not agree with an emerging rule of customary international law to 'opt-out' by becoming a persistent objector to that rule.

---

[3] *Trial of the Major War Criminals before the International Military Tribunal – Nuremberg 14 November 1945–30 November 1945* (International Military Tribunal, 1947) vol 2, 101.

[4] Oscar Schacter, *International Law in Theory and Practice* (Martinus Nijhoff 1991) 10.

[5] Vienna Convention on the Law of Treaties, opened for signature 23 May 1969, 1155 UNTS 331 (entered into force 27 January 1980) Art 34.

Thus, a non-State Party can have no obligations under the Rome Statute unless it consents to such obligations. This was acknowledged by the United Nations Security Council in resolutions referring the situations in Darfur and Libya to the Court, which both 'recogniz[ed] that States not party to the Rome Statute have no obligation under the Statute'.[6] Although these resolutions decided that non-States Parties Sudan and Libya should cooperate with the Court, thereby imposing a binding obligation on them to do so pursuant to Art 25 of the Charter of the United Nations ('UN Charter'),[7] they both recognised that absent this power, Sudan and Libya could have no obligations under the Rome Statute as they had not consented to it.

However, the issue of the Court's jurisdiction over individuals must be looked at differently. Although states are the primary entities subject to international law, international criminal law does impose liability on individuals by directly criminalising their actions in certain circumstances. In this regard, a distinction can be drawn between international crimes and crimes which do not constitute international crimes, but which states have agreed by international treaties to criminalise in their domestic laws. The former type of crimes constitutes breaches of international rules entailing the personal criminal liability of the individuals concerned,[8] such as war crimes, crimes against humanity and genocide. The latter category of crimes includes crimes such as terrorism or drug trafficking. The Court's original subject matter jurisdiction consisted of crimes in the former category of international crimes proper,[9] the perpetrators of which may, due to the universal interest in repressing these crimes, be prosecuted by any state.[10]

It is regarded by most commentators as well established that under customary international law universal jurisdiction exists over war crimes (at

---

[6] SC Res 1593, UN SCOR, 60th sess, 5158th mtg, UN Doc S/RES/1593 (31 March 2005) [2]; SC Res 1970, UN SCOR, 66th sess, 6491st mtg, UN Doc S/RES/1970 (26 February 2011) [5].

[7] Charter of the United Nations.

[8] Antonio Cassese, *International Criminal Law* (2nd edn, Oxford University Press 2008) 11.

[9] Note however that there have been proposals, dating back to the Rome Conference itself, to include crimes in the latter category, such as drug-trafficking offences and terrorism, in the Court's subject matter jurisdiction. Assembly of States Parties to the Rome Statute of the International Criminal Court, Official Records, 8th sess, Doc No ICC-ASP/8/20 (18–26 November 2009) annex II ('Report of the Working Group on the Review Conference') 53–6.

[10] Cassese, above note 8, 11–12.

least in international armed conflicts), crimes against humanity and genocide.[11] Antonio Cassese also refers to the principle of universal jurisdiction, in cases of grave breaches of the Geneva Conventions[12] and Additional Protocol I,[13] as well as crimes against humanity, as evidence that the exercise of universal jurisdiction is permitted under international law. Cassese appears to extend that principle to war crimes and genocide as well.[14]

If it is accepted that such crimes attract universal jurisdiction, the consequence is that international law permits states to try another state's nationals for such crimes, regardless of the consent of the state of nationality. For example, the Australian domestic law equivalents of the original Rome Statute crimes (war crimes, crimes against humanity and genocide) apply extra-territorially regardless of the nationality of the alleged perpetrator.[15]

During negotiations to establish the Court at the Rome Conference and the previous Preparatory Committee meetings, Germany had proposed granting the Court universal jurisdiction. The ability of states to exercise jurisdiction over such crimes was one reason for Germany's push. As Cassese notes, 'Germany forcefully expressed the view that international customary law at present authorizes universal jurisdiction over major international crimes'.[16]

This proposal also relied on the argument that if international law permitted a state to prosecute another state's nationals for these crimes on

---

[11] Gerhard Werle, *Principles of International Criminal Law* (Asser Press 2005) 60.

[12] Geneva Convention for the Amelioration of the Condition of the Wounded and Sick in Armed Forces in the Field, opened for signature 12 August 1949, 75 UNTS 31 (entered into force 21 October 1950); Geneva Convention for the Amelioration of the Condition of Wounded, Sick and Shipwrecked Members of Armed Forces at Sea, opened for signature 12 August 1949, 75 UNTS 85 (entered into force 21 October 1950); Geneva Convention Relative to the Treatment of Prisoners of War, opened for signature 12 August 1949, 75 UNTS 135 (entered into force 21 October 1950); Geneva Convention Relative to the Protection of Civilian Persons in Time of War, opened for signature 12 August 1949, 75 UNTS 287 (entered into force 21 October 1950).

[13] Protocol Additional to the Geneva Conventions of 12 August 1949, and Relating to the Protection of Victims of International Armed Conflicts, opened for signature 12 December 1977, 1125 UNTS 3 (entered into force 7 December 1979).

[14] Antonio Cassese, *International Criminal Law* (Oxford University Press 2002) 293–8. See also Cassese, above note 8, 338.

[15] Criminal Code Act 1995 (Cth) s 268, 117.

[16] Cassese, above note 14, 289.

the basis of universal jurisdiction, it was also within states' powers to create an international body which could similarly prosecute alleged perpetrators of such crimes.[17] The Court would therefore have jurisdiction regardless of whether the state of nationality of the accused was a State Party. This concept has been described as a principle that 'States may do together what any one of them could have done separately'.[18]

Although some disagreed with this argument,[19] it appears to be generally accepted that it would have been possible to grant the Court universal jurisdiction, at least in respect of the three original crimes.

## III. UNIVERSAL JURISDICTION AND THE CRIME OF AGGRESSION

There appears however to be some doubt as to the existence of universal jurisdiction over the crime of aggression. Gerhard Werle, for example, argues that a state's authority to prosecute individuals for a crime of aggression is unquestioned 'if it involves the participation of a country's own nationals in a war begun by that state', but he appears to fall short of arguing that universal jurisdiction applies when he acknowledges that prosecution by third states is not an ideal solution.[20] Another commentator argues that although it is generally acknowledged that the principle of universal jurisdiction applies to genocide, crimes against humanity and war crimes committed in international armed conflicts, 'some doubts exist where the crime of aggression and war crimes in non-international armed conflict are concerned'.[21] He also suggests that although 'there appears to be sufficient state practice to support the view that civil war crimes are

---

[17] Elizabeth Wilmshurst, 'Jurisdiction of the Court' in Roy S Lee (ed), *The International Criminal Court – The Making of the Rome Statute – Issues Negotiations Results* (Kluwer Law International 1999) 132.

[18] Lelia Nadya Sadat and S Richard Carden, 'The New International Criminal Court: An Uneasy Revolution' (1999–2000) 88 *Georgetown Law Journal* 381, 412–13.

[19] See, eg, the argument that a state's participation in an international criminal court is derived from treaty law rather than custom, implying that the customary international law rule of universal jurisdiction over international crimes is not relevant: David J Scheffer, 'The United States and the International Criminal Court' (1999) 93 *American Journal of International Law* 12, 18.

[20] Werle, above note 11, 61.

[21] Florian Jessberger, 'Universal Jurisdiction' in Antonio Cassese (ed), *The Oxford Companion to International Criminal Justice* (Oxford University Press 2009) 556.

subject to universal jurisdiction, this does not apply as regards the crime of aggression'.[22]

Interestingly, the German universal jurisdiction proposal to the Preparatory Committee referred only to states being able to 'exercise universal criminal jurisdiction concerning acts of genocide, crimes against humanity and war crimes', but did not mention the crime of aggression.[23] It is unclear why this is the case, although it is clear that Germany did intend the universal jurisdiction regime to apply also to the crime of aggression, once enacted.[24]

## IV. THE ROME STATUTE JURISDICTIONAL SYSTEM AND STATE CONSENT

However, the universal jurisdiction proposal did not receive support at the Rome Conference. Clearly there was not the political will from a sufficient majority of states to provide universal jurisdiction to the Court, as the German proposal was not adopted. Instead, the jurisdictional regime which was adopted under Art 12 is based on the acceptance of the Court's jurisdiction by the state of nationality of the accused or the state in whose territory the alleged crime took place.

Article 12 reads as follows:

> A State which becomes a Party to this Statute thereby accepts the jurisdiction of the Court with respect to the crimes referred to in article 5.
>
> 1 In the case of article 13, paragraph (a) or (c), the Court may exercise its jurisdiction if one or more of the following States are Parties to this Statute or have accepted the jurisdiction of the Court in accordance with paragraph 3:

---

22 Ibid.

23 See Hans-Peter Kaul and Claus Kress, 'Jurisdiction and Cooperation in the ICC Statute' (1999) 2 *Yearbook of International Humanitarian Law* 143, 146–50, who convincingly argue that universal jurisdiction over the three existing crimes is granted by customary international law, but specifically exclude the crime of aggression from this analysis, noting that it was not dealt with in the German discussion paper.

24 See the statement of the German position: 'Permanent Mission of Germany to the United Nations' (May 1998) <http://www.coalitionfortheicc.org/documents/GermanPositiononICC1998.pdf> accessed 7 May 2011.

(a) The State on the territory of which the conduct in question occurred or, if the crime was committed on board a vessel or aircraft, the State of registration of that vessel or aircraft;
(b) The State of which the person accused of the crime is a national.

2 If the acceptance of a State which is not a Party to this Statute is required under paragraph 2, that State may, by declaration lodged with the Registrar, accept the exercise of jurisdiction by the Court with respect to the crime in question. The accepting State shall cooperate with the Court without any delay or exception in accordance with Part 9.

State consent can therefore be evidenced either by the state concerned having become a party to the Rome Statute, or by accepting the Court's jurisdiction ad hoc in a particular case under Art 12, para 3. It is important to note that this requirement for state consent applies only to cases coming before the Court in accordance with Art 13, paras (a) and (c), namely referrals by States Parties or investigations initiated by the prosecutor *proprio motu*.[25]

The requirement for state consent in Art 12 does not apply in respect of cases which come before the Court in accordance with Art 13, para (b), namely referral to the Court by the Security Council of a situation in which a crime appears to have been committed. In such a case it is irrelevant whether the state of nationality of the accused or the state on whose territory the crime was committed is a State Party or has otherwise accepted the Court's jurisdiction.

The consent-based regime for the original three categories of crimes under the Court's jurisdiction is therefore that consent of the state of nationality of the accused, or the state on whose territory the crime is committed is required, except in the case of Security Council referred cases.

For crimes other than those contained in the original Rome Statute, a further complication is added by Art 121, para 5 which provides that:

> Any amendment to articles 5, 6, 7 and 8 of this Statute shall enter into force for those States Parties which have accepted the amendment one year after the deposit of their instruments of ratification or acceptance. In respect of a State Party which has not accepted the amendment, the Court shall not exercise its jurisdiction regarding a crime covered by the amendment when committed by that State Party's nationals or on its territory.

---

25 *Proprio motu* is the term used in the Rome Statute to denote investigations initiated on the prosecutor's own initiative (ie without a referral by a State Party or the Security Council), on the basis of information available to the prosecutor.

The implications of Art 121, para 5 for new crimes, in particular the crime of aggression, arose during the negotiations regarding that crime and will be discussed further below.

The achievement of establishing the Court was undoubtedly a significant step for international criminal justice. It is equally clear that agreement was only able to be reached at the Rome Conference around a system that was based on state consent to jurisdiction. The German proposal for universal jurisdiction of the Court did not have sufficient support to be adopted and instead 'the State consent regime was retained as a concession to the sovereignty of States'.[26]

States accepted a Court with a narrow jurisdictional scope based on 'the two traditional pillars of territoriality and active personality'.[27] This was a result of compromise between various views among delegations at the Review Conference. Perhaps it was felt that the more widely recognised bases of jurisdiction under international law, of territoriality and active personality, would put the Court on a surer footing than the use of universal jurisdiction. This result has been criticised as making the Court's jurisdiction too narrow and indeed granting the Court 'less capability ... than domestic courts of any State'.[28] However, it is certainly much wider than the strictly consent-based regime of the initial International Law Commission draft statute for the Court,[29] which formed the starting point for negotiations in the Court's Preparatory Committee.

Additionally, one should not lose sight of the fact that the adoption of the Rome Statute and the establishment of the Court has also been hailed as 'the United Nations' most significant accomplishment since its establishment in 1945'.[30] Although the Court's consent-based jurisdiction is narrower than some would have liked, it seems that this was one of the prices that had to be paid for reaching agreement at the Rome Conference.

---

[26] Sadat and Carden, above note 18, 413.

[27] Claus Kress, 'The International Criminal Court as a Turning Point' in Antonio Cassese (ed), *The Oxford Companion to International Criminal Justice* (Oxford University Press 2009) 144.

[28] Sharon A Williams, 'Article 12 – Preconditions to the Exercise of Jurisdiction' in Otto Triffterer (ed), *Commentary on the Rome Statute of the International Criminal Court* (Nomos Verlagsgesellschaft 1999) 329, 342. See also Kress, above note 27, 143–4.

[29] *Report of the International Law Commission on the Work of its Forty-Sixth Session*, UN GAOR, 49th sess, Supp No10, UN Doc A/49/10 (1994) 29.

[30] M Cherif Bassiouni, 'Preface' in Otto Triffterer above note 28, XIX, XIX.

## V. STATE CONSENT IN THE CRIME OF AGGRESSION NEGOTIATIONS

Discussions on the role of state consent only began in depth at the November 2008 meeting of the Special Working Group on the Crime of Aggression (SWGCA) – the working group of the Court's Assembly of States Parties, established as a forum for negotiations on the crime of aggression from September 2003 to March 2009.

Up until that time, the discussions of the SWGCA relevant to the issue of consent had focused mainly on the debate over the appropriate mechanism for entry into force of the amendments. In earlier meetings, there was considerable debate in the SWGCA as to whether the amendments relating to the crime of aggression should enter into force under Art 121, para 5 (which, as noted above, requires the acceptance of each state in order for amendments to enter into force for that state), or under the more general entry-into-force mechanism of Art 121, para 4 (which provides for amendments, other than those covered by para 5, to enter into force for all States Parties one year after ratification or acceptance of the amendment by seven-eighths of States Parties). The debate over this question spanned virtually the entire life of the SWGCA.[31]

The ability of the SWGCA to continue this discussion for so long seems to have arisen from the fact that the crime of aggression amendments did not appear to fall neatly under either para 4 or para 5. As stated in a report of the June 2005 inter-sessional meeting of the SWGCA, there was no clear guidance on the matter from the literal language of the Rome Statute and the preparatory work 'did not prove useful since article 5, paragraph 2, had emerged in the final phase of the Rome Conference, after work on the Final Clauses had been concluded'.[32] Moreover, it was noted that Art 121 itself

---

[31] See Assembly of States Parties to the Rome Statute of the International Criminal Court, *Informal Inter-Sessional meeting of the Special Working Group on the Crime of Aggression*, 3rd sess, Doc No ICC-ASP/3/SWGCA/INF.1 (13 August 2004); Assembly of States Parties to the Rome Statute of the International Criminal Court, 7th sess, Doc No ICC-ASP/7/20/Add.1 (19–23 January, 9–13 February 2009) annex II ('*Report of the Special Working Group on the Crime of Aggression*'). Both these documents are reproduced in Stefan Barriga, Wolfgang Danspeckgruber and Christian Wenaweser (eds), *The Princeton Process on the Crime of Aggression: Materials of the Special Working Group on the Crime of Aggression, 2003–2009* (Liechtenstein Institute on Self-Determination at Princeton University 2009) 198–210 [13]–[19], 49–69 [6]–[11].

[32] Assembly of States Parties to the Rome Statute of the International Criminal Court, *Informal Inter-Sessional meeting of the Special Working Group on the Crime*

was drafted prior to the inclusion of the crime of aggression within the crimes falling under the jurisdiction of the Court and therefore had not been drafted with the crime of aggression amendments specifically in mind.[33]

Clearly however, the choice of which entry-into-force mechanism was used impacted heavily on the issue of state consent. If para 4 was used, the crime of aggression amendments would apply to all States Parties once the amendments were accepted by the requisite seven-eighths of States Parties. Although this is admittedly a high threshold, once reached the amendment would also enter into force for the remaining one-eighth of States Parties, regardless of their acceptance of the amendments.[34] Conversely, if para 5 was used, the ability of states to consent to the amendments would be conserved. The effect of the second sentence of para 5 would also need to be taken into account. There is no doubt that the continued debate over the appropriate entry-into-force mechanism was conducted against the backdrop of the issue of state consent to the amendments.

By November 2008 the arguments on both sides were well rehearsed and delegations appeared relatively evenly split, with both mechanisms receiving a large amount of support. The main arguments on both sides are summarised in the reports of the SWGCA[35] and need not be rehashed here. The author's view, however, is that the arguments supporting para 5 were more convincing. Para 4 provides a general entry-into-force mechanism, to which amendments covered by para 5 are the exception. Although admittedly not sufficiently drafted so as to apply unambiguously to the crime of aggression amendments, the reference in para 5 to 'any amendment to articles 5, 6, 7 and 8' seems to be intended to encompass amendments the

---

*of Aggression*, reproduced in Barriga, Danspeckgruber and Wenaweser, above note 31, 198–210 [15]. Article 5, para 2 provided for the adoption of the amendments relating to the crime of aggression 'in accordance with articles 121 and 123' and was deleted as part of the amendments passed at the Review Conference in Kampala.

33 Assembly of States Parties to the Rome Statute of the International Criminal Court, *Informal Inter-Sessional Meeting of the Special Working Group on the Crime of Aggression*, Official Records, Doc No ICC-ASP/4/32 (June 2005), reproduced in Barriga, Danspeckgruber and Wenaweser, above note 31, 167–97 [5]. See also Claus Kress and Leonie von Holtzendorff, 'The Kampala Compromise on the Crime of Aggression' (2010) 8 *Journal of International Criminal Justice* 1179, 1198–9; Roger Clark, 'Ambiguities in Articles 5(2), 121 and 123 of the Rome Statute' (2009) 4 *Case Western Reserve Journal of International Law* 413, 413.

34 Unless the state took the drastic step of withdrawing from the Rome Statute entirely, as para 4 permits.

35 See SWGCA documents, above note 31.

substantive effect of which is to amend the crimes under the Court's jurisdiction, or their definitions.

In an attempt to progress discussions further, the Chairman of the SWGCA, in an informal note on the work programme,[36] suggested that the SWGCA deepen the discussion on the procedure for the entry-into-force of amendments on aggression, in particular the consequences of the second sentence of Art 121, para 5. This deepened discussion focused delegations' attention on issues surrounding state consent to the amendments which had previously not been explicitly discussed.

It became apparent during these discussions that the references in Art 12 and the second sentence of Art 121, para 5 to both a State Party's nationals and a State Party's territory, meant that the consent of two states was potentially relevant. In determining whether the Court had jurisdiction in relation to a crime covered by an amendment made under para 5, it was necessary to look at whether the state of nationality of the accused had accepted the amendment, and also whether the state on whose territory the crime was committed had accepted the amendment.

This gave rise to two questions of interpretation of the Rome Statute which were never resolved by the negotiations. The first of these questions was the issue of where the crime of aggression could be said to have taken place and consequently, which states were states on whose territories a crime of aggression could be said to have taken place for the purposes of Art 12 and Art 121, para 5. Although the SWGCA agreed that the 'conduct of a leader responsible for the crime of aggression would typically occur on the territory of the aggressor State',[37] most states contributing to the discussion also believed that the crime could be said to occur on the territory in which the consequences of the crime were felt (which in the case of the crime of aggression was seen to be predominantly the territory of the state which is the victim of the aggression). This led to many states expressing support for a notion of 'concurrent jurisdiction', which although not defined in the reports of the SWGCA, appeared to refer to a view that the Court could

---

36 Assembly of States Parties to the Rome Statute of the International Criminal Court, *Report of the Special Working Group on the Crime of Aggression*, Doc No ICC-ASP/6/SWGCA/1 (November 2008), reproduced in Barriga, Danspeckgruber and Wenaweser, above note 31, 70–83, Appendix 1 ('November 2008 SWGCA Report').

37 November 2008 SWGCA Report, above note 36, [28].

exercise jurisdiction based either on the acceptance of the amendments by the state of nationality (the aggressor) or the territorial state (the victim).[38]

This notion of 'concurrent jurisdiction' highlights the second question of interpretation of the Rome Statute which remained unresolved by the negotiations. This question can be put as follows: assuming that the crime could be said to take place on the territory of the victim state, what was the effect of the consent of the victim state on the Court's jurisdiction under Art 12 and Art 121, para 5? While Art 12 seemed to allow the Court to exercise jurisdiction on the basis of the victim state's consent, the second sentence of Art 121, para 5 also needed to be taken into account. Did Art 121, para 5 require acceptance of the crime of aggression amendments by *either* the aggressor state or the victim state, or *both* the aggressor state and the victim state? This issue was explored further at the subsequent meeting of the SWGCA in February 2009, where the discussions revealed the complexity of these issues and also that states had divergent views on the answers to this question, despite the support which had earlier been expressed for 'concurrent jurisdiction'.[39] While delegations did not object to the proposition that the Court would have jurisdiction when the aggressor state had accepted the crime of aggression amendments but the victim state had not, views were divided as to whether the Court should have jurisdiction where the victim state had accepted the crime of aggression amendments but the aggressor state had not.[40]

The question of consent of the aggressor state came into focus even more starkly at the subsequent informal inter-sessional meeting on the crime of aggression in June 2009[41] and the final meeting of the Assembly of States Parties before the Review Conference in March 2010.[42] Although some states spoke strongly in favour of a requirement of consent of the alleged

---

[38] Ibid. For a comprehensive analysis of the SWGCA's treatment of this issue, see Netta Goussac, 'Territoriality and the Crime of Aggression' (2008) 6 *New Zealand Yearbook of International Law* 169, 175–8.

[39] Assembly of States Parties to the Rome Statute of the International Criminal Court, *Report of the Special Working Group on the Crime of Aggression*, Doc No ICC-ASP/7/20/Add.1 (February 2009) annex II, reproduced in Barriga, Danspeckgruber and Wenaweser, above note 31, 49–67, Appendix II [8].

[40] Ibid [8]–[11].

[41] Assembly of States Parties to the Rome Statute of the International Criminal Court, *Informal Inter-Sessional Meeting on the Crime of Aggression*, 8th sess, Doc No ICC-ASP/8/INF.2 (10 July 2009), reproduced in Barriga, Danspeckgruber and Wenaweser, above note 31, 23–48 [32]–[37].

[42] Assembly of States Parties to the Rome Statute of the International Criminal Court, 8th sess, Doc No ICC-ASP/8/20/Add.1 (18–26 November 2009) annex II ('Report of the Working Group on the Review Conference') [4]–[8].

aggressor state, views remained divided. The two differing views were not resolved and were taken to the Review Conference reflected in two alternatives to the Chair's proposed 'understandings' on the crime of aggression amendments set out in the Chair's Conference Room Paper:

> [Alternative 1 – 'positive' understanding: jurisdiction without acceptance by the aggressor State] It is understood that article 121, paragraph 5, second sentence, of the Statute does not prevent the Court from exercising jurisdiction in respect of an act of aggression committed against a State Party that has accepted the amendment.
>
> [Alternative 2 – 'negative' understanding: no jurisdiction without acceptance by aggressor State] It is understood that article 121, paragraph 5, second sentence, of the Statute prevents the Court from exercising jurisdiction in respect of an act of aggression committed by any State that has not accepted the amendment.[43]

The issue had thus effectively been recast as a question of whether the alleged aggressor state was required to consent to the amendments before its nationals could be subject to the Court's jurisdiction.

Ultimately, the Review Conference never agreed on a common understanding of the correct interpretation or effect of the second sentence of Art 121, para 5. Neither alternative was included in the final understandings adopted by the Review Conference. Instead, the final result included a compromise outcome on the issue of state consent.

## VI. STATE CONSENT IN THE OUTCOME OF THE REVIEW CONFERENCE

The outcome of the Kampala Review Conference in respect of the crime of aggression contains several important elements relating to state consent. Each element of the outcome will be examined in turn.

### A. Entry into Force under Article 121, Paragraph 5

Firstly, Art 121, para 5 was invoked as the appropriate mechanism for entry into force. Operative Paragraph 1 of the Crime of Aggression Resolution states that the amendments are adopted in accordance with Art 5, para 2, but are 'subject to ratification or acceptance and shall enter into force in

---

43 International Criminal Court, *Review Conference of the Rome Statute of the International Criminal Court – Conference Room Paper on the Crime of Aggression*, Doc No RC/WGCA/1/ (25 May 2010) 7.

accordance with article 121, paragraph 5'.[44] However, the amendments also provide that the Court's jurisdiction over the crime of aggression in *proprio motu* cases or state-referred cases is exercised 'in accordance with article 12'.[45]

## B. No Consent Requirement for Security Council Referrals

The second aspect of the Kampala compromise was that the consent of a state is not required where the alleged crime results from a situation referred to the Court by the Security Council. This is expressed in para 2 of the 'understandings' which were adopted as Annex III to the Crime of Aggression Resolution, which states that '[i]t is understood that the Court shall exercise jurisdiction over the crime of aggression on the basis of a Security Council referral ... irrespective of whether the State concerned has accepted the Court's jurisdiction in this regard'.

## C. Opt-out Mechanism

The third, and perhaps most crucial, aspect of the Kampala compromise relating to state consent was the ability of a state to opt out of the Court's jurisdiction in respect of state referrals or *proprio motu* investigations.

For these cases, Art 15 *bis*, para 4 provides that the Court may 'exercise jurisdiction over a crime of aggression, arising from an act of aggression committed by a State Party, unless that State Party has previously declared that it does not accept such jurisdiction by lodging a declaration with the Registrar'.

Thus, the lodging of an opt-out declaration will have the effect that the Court's jurisdiction over acts of aggression committed by that state is excluded. This effectively introduces a requirement of aggressor state consent, as, regardless of the correct interpretation of Art 12 and Art 121, para 5, or the question of whether aggressor state ratification or acceptance is required, a state which does not wish to grant the Court jurisdiction over crimes of aggression arising from acts of aggression committed by it can achieve this by lodging a declaration. Of course, taking a positive step to opt out of a declaration may subject a state to international criticism.

Article 15 *bis*, para 4 also provides that '[t]he withdrawal of such a declaration may be effected at any time and shall be considered by the State Party within three years'. This allows the flexibility of the Court's jurisdiction over crime of aggression cases to gradually expand as states become

---

44 Crime of Aggression Resolution, operative para 1.
45 Crime of Aggression Resolution, Art 15 *bis,* para 4.

more comfortable with this notion. It also imposes an additional obligation on a State Party which does opt out to at least consider the withdrawal, although it does not oblige the State Party actually to do anything further.

### D. Non-States Parties

The last element of the consent-based result is the exclusion of the Court's jurisdiction over non-States Parties.

Article 15 *bis*, para 5 provides an exclusion for states which are not a State Party to the Rome Statute. It reads: 'In respect of a State that is not a party to this Statute, the Court shall not exercise its jurisdiction over the crime of aggression when committed by that State's nationals or on its territory.'

It is however important to note that the exclusion of the Court's jurisdiction over non-States Parties in Art 15 *bis*, para 5, despite its apparently broad wording, does not totally exclude the Court's jurisdiction over non-States Parties. Art 15 *bis*, para 1 makes clear that Art 15 *bis* contains provisions on the Court's exercise of jurisdiction over crime of aggression cases in accordance with Art 13, paras (a) and (c), namely state referrals and *proprio motu* investigations. The exclusion of non-States Parties in para 5 therefore only applies to such cases. There is no corresponding provision in Art 15 *ter*, which deals with Security Council referred situations. Moreover, as discussed above, para 2 of the understandings in Annex III to the Crime of Aggression Resolution clearly states that the Court has jurisdiction in Security Council referred cases irrespective of state consent. Non-States Parties will therefore potentially be subject to the Court's jurisdiction in cases arising from situations referred by the Security Council, but not in cases arising out of a state referral or *proprio motu* investigation.

## VII. ANALYSIS OF THE KAMPALA OUTCOME ON STATE CONSENT

Ultimately, although the amendments did make clear that Art 121, para 5 was used as the mechanism to bring the amendments into force, the lengthy discussions in the negotiations as to the effect of its second sentence were never resolved, and the Crime of Aggression Resolution is silent on this issue. The reference to Art 12 in the Crime of Aggression Resolution also fails to adequately address the interplay between Art 12 and Art 121, para 5. The issue of state consent to the amendments was therefore not fully resolved. However, the practical significance of this is diminished by the inclusion of the opt-out mechanism, which effectively introduces an alternative way for a state to 'withhold' its consent to the Court's jurisdiction, except in the case of Security Council referrals.

The Kampala outcome has been described as a 'softly consent-based' entry-into-force mechanism, which lies somewhere between the two alternatives of a 'positive understanding' and 'negative understanding' originally proposed by the Chair.[46] According to this argument, the consent of the alleged aggressor state in the form of ratification or acceptance of the amendments is not required for the Court to exercise jurisdiction, but instead the alleged aggressor state can avoid the Court's jurisdiction if it has previously lodged an opt-out declaration. If this interpretation is accepted, nationals of a State Party which had not ratified or accepted the amendments or lodged an opt-out declaration, would be subject to the Court's jurisdiction for involvement in acts of aggression committed by that state.

This argument is supported by the fact that Art 15 *bis*, para 4 was developed as a compromise solution to bridge the gap between those in favour of applying Art 121, para 4 as the appropriate entry-into-force mechanism and those favouring a strictly consent-based regime. The preferred interpretation should therefore be one that is situated somewhere between the two poles. To require ratification or acceptance by the aggressor state would defeat the compromise building nature of Art 15 *bis*, para 4 and is therefore not the preferred interpretation.[47]

It is true that the combination of the use of Art 121, para 5, the reference to Art 12 and the use of an opt-out mechanism was a compromise outcome. The Chair of the SWGCA has explained that the final package, including the opt-out mechanism in Art 15 *bis*, para 4, was presented to the plenary 'as a *sui generis* solution on the basis of the acceptance already given by States Parties under Article 12 of the Rome Statute, which was possible due only to the specific placement of the crime of aggression in the Statute'.[48] While this does seem to indicate the Chair's intention that the entry-into-force mechanism used in the Crime of Aggression Resolution was to be a *sui generis* mechanism falling somewhere between Art 121, paras 4 and 5, the terms of the Crime of Aggression Resolution do not provide much guidance as to what this mechanism might be, or indeed what the legal foundation for amending the Rome Statute other than in accordance with the terms of paras 4 or 5 might be.

---

46 Kress and von Holtzendorff, above note 33, 1212–16.

47 Ibid.

48 Christian Wenaweser, 'Reaching the Kampala Compromise on Aggression: The Chair's Perspective' (2010) 23 *Leiden Journal of International Law* 883, 885–6.

It is also true that the debate surrounding the role of state consent and the correct interpretation of Art 12 and 121 of the Rome Statute was never resolved by the negotiations. The reports of the SWGCA discussed above make clear that a large number of States Parties interpreted the Rome Statute provisions as requiring ratification or acceptance of the crime of aggression amendments by the alleged aggressor state as a pre-requisite to the Court's jurisdiction. Other commentators have continued to support this interpretation, such as Manson, who argues that as a matter of statutory interpretation, the plain meaning of Art 121, Art 15 *bis*, para 4 and operative para 1 of the Crime of Aggression Resolution still require state consent in the form of ratification or acceptance of the amendments.[49]

In the author's view, the Kampala compromise was indeed a creative and inspired one which successfully brought together two seemingly intractable positions in the negotiations. However, the compromise-building quality of the outcome was not that it created a unique entry-into-force mechanism, but that it deliberately left the correct interpretation of the entry-into-force provisions of the Rome Statute unresolved, while at the same time reducing the practical significance of these provisions by introducing a requirement of state consent through the opt-out mechanism.

However, acceptance of a compromise outcome which deliberately left this question unresolved should not imply that the states which argued for a consent-based entry-into-force regime during the negotiations abandoned the interpretation of the Rome Statute underpinning those positions, and agreed to a regime which does not require ratification or acceptance of the amendments by the alleged aggressor state. It would still be open to an accused, if an appropriate case ever arose, to argue that Art 121, para 5 prevents the Court from exercising jurisdiction if the accused's state of nationality has not accepted the amendments. The matter would then be left to judicial decision.

Finally, something must be said about Security Council referred cases. This aspect of the Kampala outcome was relatively uncontroversial, at least in the context of the state consent issue. Security Council referred cases were largely excluded from the discussion described above on state consent during the negotiations, and were dealt with separately.

When this issue was first discussed at the November 2008 meeting of the SWGCA, most states intervening were of the view that, from a policy perspective, states should be subject to the Court's jurisdiction in Security

---

[49] Robbie Manson, 'Identifying the Rough Edges of the Kampala Compromise' <http://www.bepj.org.uk/wordpress/wp-content/uploads/CLF-2010-Manson-final-ed-by-authorTrack-changes-accepted.pdf> accessed 9 August 2011.

Council referred cases irrespective of state consent. Initially, a small number of states put forward a literal interpretation of the second sentence of Art 121, para 5, which, on the face of it, does not distinguish between different modes of referral under Art 12 and could arguably prevent the Court from exercising jurisdiction even in the case of Security Council referred cases where the state of nationality and/or the territorial state had not accepted the amendments.[50] Adopting such a literal interpretation could have meant that states which did not ratify the crime of aggression amendments would not be subject to the Court's jurisdiction, even in the case of Security Council referrals.

The alternative view, favoured by more states, was that the second sentence needed to be read in light of the context and the object and purpose of the Rome Statute, and in relation to Art 12. As discussed above, Art 12 sets out additional preconditions to the exercise of the Court's jurisdiction in *proprio motu* and state referred cases, based on a jurisdictional nexus of territory or nationality.

According to this view, the references in the second sentence of Art 121, para 5 to 'nationals' and 'territory', related to the preconditions in Art 12, which 'established the bases for jurisdiction for state referrals and *proprio motu* investigations, but not for Security Council referrals'.[51] Therefore, the argument ran, Art 121, para 5 could only preclude the Court's jurisdiction in respect of States Parties that had not accepted the amendment on aggression in state referrals or *proprio motu* investigations, but not in Security Council referred cases.

In the author's view it is difficult to follow this argument. Art 12 places preconditions on the Court's jurisdiction in respect of two of the three permissible modes of referral set out in Art 13, which is permissive in the sense that it allows the Court to exercise jurisdiction ('the Court *may* exercise') if the preconditions in Art 12, para 2 are met; that is, if either the state of territoriality or the state of nationality is a party to the Rome Statute. In respect of crimes which are added by an amendment to the Rome Statute, the provisions of Art 121, para 5 also need to be considered. The second sentence acts as a bar on the Court's jurisdiction ('the Court *shall not* exercise its jurisdiction') if the relevant State Party has not accepted the amendment. It seems clear that the bar on the Court's jurisdiction for new crimes under Art 121, para 5 would prevail over the permissive nature of Art 12. The language of the second sentence of Art 121, para 5 is quite clear that if a State Party has not accepted an amendment, the Court does not have

---

50 November 2008 SWGCA Report, above note 36, [9].

51 Ibid [8].

jurisdiction in respect of a crime covered by the amendment when committed by that State Party's nationals or on its territory.

However, despite what seems to be the literal meaning of the second sentence of Art 121, para 5, states generally agreed that from a policy perspective, the provisions on aggression should not restrict Security Council referrals. States were divided however on whether this required an amendment to the Rome Statute or could be achieved by other means.[52] Ultimately the concern as to potential inconsistency with the Rome Statute was not pursued further and states were willing to accept an interpretation of the provisions which granted the Court jurisdiction in Security Council referred cases, regardless of acceptance of the amendments by either the state of nationality or territoriality.

As discussed above, this interpretation ultimately found its way into para 2 of the understandings passed as part of the Crime of Aggression Resolution. The precise legal status of the understandings, and whether an understanding would prevail in the case of any inconsistency with the Rome Statute is, however, not certain, and may well remain subject to review by the Court in an appropriate case.

From the point of view of coherency of international criminal justice, it would be a curious result if a Security Council referral could enliven the Court's jurisdiction over war crimes, crimes against humanity and genocide, but not do so in relation to a crime of aggression arising out of the same situation. This is especially true given the Security Council's role under the UN Charter with respect to aggression. A desire to avoid such an anomalous outcome, and the binding nature of Security Council resolutions under the UN Charter, seemed to provide states with sufficient justification to join the consensus and accept this outcome.[53]

## VIII. THE LEGITIMACY OF THE KAMPALA RESULT

At the most fundamental level, the adoption of the crime of aggression at the Review Conference in Kampala represents the fulfilment of efforts by the international community to criminalise aggression which date back at least 65 years. Since the Second World War and the Nuremberg trials, the international community has recognised the need for international law to criminalise aggressive war-making and the corresponding need for a permanent judicial body to judge those alleged to have committed such crimes.

---

52 Ibid [10].

53 Ibid [8].

One of the earliest resolutions of the General Assembly called for the formulation of the Nuremberg Principles and the preparation of a draft code of offences against the peace and security of mankind, including the crime of aggression.[54] This process eventually led to the negotiations at the Rome Conference establishing the Court. The major piece of 'unfinished business' from the Rome Conference was the crime of aggression, which was largely resolved at the Review Conference where agreement was reached on the definition of the crime and the conditions for the Court's exercise of jurisdiction. It is no exaggeration therefore to say that the adoption of the crime of aggression amendments represents the culmination of the international community's efforts to criminalise aggressive war-making since Nuremberg.

The fact that international criminal justice had, for so long, no mechanism to try those responsible for crimes of aggression, was often cited as a failing of international criminal justice. The adoption of the crime of aggression amendments into the Rome Statute in itself, and their potential entry into force in 2017, is a rectification of that failing. A definition of the crime of aggression has now been incorporated into the Rome Statute and, assuming the requisite two-thirds majority is obtained at an Assembly of States Parties of the Court after 2017, the Court's jurisdiction over the crime of aggression will be enlivened. As the Court's Vice President and Judge, Hans-Peter Kaul, said:

> The previously dominating excuses against the criminalisation of aggression – namely the absence of an accepted definition of the crime and the alleged impossibility to regulate the relationship between the Security Council and the International Criminal Court – have been eliminated. For the first time, the world has a text of international criminal law defining clearer limits for the *jus ad bellum*. For the first time in the history of mankind, there is now a concrete perspective, a unique chance, if sustained and fully implemented, to criminalise aggression and illegal war-making.[55]

---

54 *Formulation of the Principles Recognized in the Charter of the Nürnberg Tribunal and in the Judgment of the Tribunal*, GA Res 177 (II), UN GAOR, 2nd sess, 123rd plen mtg, UN Doc A/Res/177 (II) (1947).

55 Judges Hans-Peter Kaul and Liu Daqun, 'Implications of the Criminalisation of Aggression' (Policy Brief Series No 2, Forum for International Criminal and Humanitarian Law, 2011) 2 <http://www.fichl.org/fileadmin/fichl/documents/FICHL_Policy_Brief_Series/FICHL_PB2.pdf> accessed 7 May 2011.

Despite this significant leap forward, criticisms have been levelled at the outcome of the Review Conference. One of these criticisms has been the fact that the crime of aggression will apply unevenly to different states.[56]

The exclusion of non-States Parties has, in particular, been the target of some criticism. For example, International Criminal Tribunal for the former Yugoslavia and International Criminal Tribunal for Rwanda Appeals Chamber Judge Liu Daqun has argued that those states most likely to commit aggression will remain outside the Rome Statute system:

> An obvious and unfortunate consequence of this arrangement is that the ICC will only have the jurisdiction to prosecute nationals in states least likely to commit acts of aggression. Meanwhile, states most likely to commit acts of aggression will doubtless prefer to remain non-party states to the Statute ... Such a system can hardly be described as progressive – particularly as it allows states to protect their belligerent leaders from prosecution, undermining the credibility of international criminal justice.[57]

While there is validity to these concerns, they are also reminiscent of the earlier arguments surrounding the Court's jurisdiction at the Rome Conference in 1998. As has been shown above, the agreement reached at Rome rejected an outcome which granted the Court universal jurisdiction. It also clearly linked the Court's jurisdiction to a regime based on the consent of the state of nationality or territoriality.

The outcome of the Kampala Review Conference on the crime of aggression is likewise clearly founded on the consent-based regime which was agreed upon for the original crimes under the Court's jurisdiction (reflected in Art 12) and the ability of states to consent to new crimes (reflected in Art 121, para 5).

The Court may exercise jurisdiction over crime of aggression cases arising from a situation referred to the Court by the Security Council, regardless of the consent of states involved. In this regard the crime of aggression is treated in the same way as existing crimes under the Rome Statute.

In relation to state referrals or *proprio motu* investigations, the ability of States Parties to consent to the Court's jurisdiction over new crimes is preserved. States can either rely on a 'negative understanding' of Art 121, para 5 (which would prevent the Court from exercising jurisdiction over crime of aggression cases committed by a State Party's nationals if the state

---

[56] See, eg, Astrid Coracini, 'The International Criminal Court's Exercise of Jurisdiction over the Crime of Aggression – At Last... In Reach... Over Some' (2010) 2 *Göttingen Journal of International Law* 745, 788–9.

[57] Judges Kaul and Daqun, above note 55, 4.

has not ratified or accepted the amendments), or lodge an opt-out declaration which would explicitly exclude the Court's jurisdiction over a crime of aggression arising from acts of aggression committed by it.[58] The consent of the victim state, which some members of the SWGCA had at one stage argued should be enough to trigger the Court's jurisdiction, is not sufficient. Given the lack of agreement in the negotiations on this issue, which has been described above, and the differing interpretations of the existing provisions of the Rome Statute on this point, the author considers that it is appropriate that the end result does not allow the Court to exercise jurisdiction based solely on the acceptance by the victim state.

In relation to non-States Parties, the crime of aggression is also treated in the same way as other crimes under the Court's jurisdiction, with one important exception. For existing crimes, non-States Parties may potentially be subject to the Court's jurisdiction on the basis of the consent of the state in which the crime took place. For example, a war crime perpetrated by the national of a non-State Party on the territory of a State Party would be within the jurisdiction of the Court under Art 12. The crime of aggression amendments rule out this possibility and avoid the associated question of where the crime of aggression takes place by focusing on the acceptance of the amendments by the state alleged to have committed the act of aggression.

The outcome of the Kampala Review Conference, as it relates to state consent, was therefore a conservative one which largely aligns with the jurisdictional regime originally established at Rome. It is true that the outcome means that, in the absence of a Security Council referral, the Court will not have jurisdiction over acts of aggression committed by states who choose to not accept, or to opt out of, the amendments. While some may argue that this undermines the credibility of international criminal justice, given the sensitive and delicate nature of the negotiations, it is probably appropriate for the Review Conference to have taken a more conservative approach and reached consensus agreement, rather than have risked failure by pushing for a broader jurisdiction for the Court.

In this regard, the outcome was similar to that of the negotiations over Art 12 in the Rome Conference. It is therefore perhaps instructive to compare, with the benefit of some ten years' hindsight, the initial reaction following the aftermath of the Rome Conference described above with a more recent view which argues that the prediction that conflict-afflicted states would

---

[58] Note that there is potentially some difference between these two alternatives in the case of potential involvement by individuals in acts of aggression of states other than their state of nationality (or dual nationals). This issue complicates the question of state consent and is not discussed further in this chapter.

never join the Court has proven to be too conservative, and suggests that the limited jurisdictional scheme of Art 12 contributed to the rapid rate of ratifications of the Rome Statute.[59]

In the same way, it is to be hoped that the criticisms made relating to the selective application of the Court's jurisdiction over the crime of aggression can be overcome by widespread acceptance of the amendments, in addition to the ongoing goal of achieving universality of the Rome Statute itself. The legitimacy of the crime of aggression, and international criminal justice, will be enhanced if equal application of the Court's jurisdiction over the crime of aggression is achieved through consent of all states, rather than through an outcome which seeks to impose the Court's jurisdiction on states regardless of consent.

---

59 Sharon A Williams and William A Schabas, 'Article 12 – Preconditions to the Exercise of Jurisdiction' in Otto Triffterer (ed), *Commentary on the Rome Statute of the International Criminal Court – Observers' Notes, Article by Article* (2nd edn, Hart Publishing 2008) 547, 560–61.

# 10. Women and international criminal law: steps forward or dancing backwards

**Helen Durham**

## I. INTRODUCTION

The narrative of the grand international criminal law and justice 'project' as it relates to women is not coherent. Complete consistency of application is something that even the most advanced and nuanced legal systems cannot claim absolutely. The law and its range of prosecution mechanisms is a very blunt instrument in the face of the complexity of human suffering, in particular during times of armed conflict or turbulence. However, to judge hundreds of years' effort to 'end the impunity' of those accused of atrocities exclusively on the basis of the concept of coherence, is to ignore the broader social/political implications that many international legal determinations relating to women have achieved. These achievements, such as the jurisprudential developments clarifying sexual violence and rape as serious international crimes, the inclusion of wider 'gender' elements within the Rome Statute of the International Criminal Court ('Rome Statute') (ICC)[1] and other ways in which prosecutions have assisted and supported women in post-conflict societies (such as by answering questions about missing loved ones), possess legitimacy above and beyond questions of the consistency of application and understanding.

International justice is a wider and broader concept than that which encompasses international criminal law. This wider debate is interesting

[1] Rome Statute of the International Criminal Court, opened for signature 17 July 1998, 2187 UNTS 90 (entered into force 1 July 2002).

and important, and much has been written on the need for active participation of women in all types of international justice initiatives.[2] Indeed, writers such as Millar clearly articulate the need for any 'accountability mechanism, whether truth commissions or some other institutional strategy', to be contextually responsive to the needs of women and allow women to have roles in the actual designs of such mechanisms, not just access to the process.[3] This chapter however will focus upon international criminal law in the more narrow sense, as it relates to prosecutions, rather than explore the broader issues involved in the notion of justice. Despite this, it is important to acknowledge that post-conflict societies choose to deal with the commission of atrocities in a range of ways, and it is crucial to reflect on the impact each of these methods have upon women and issues of gender.

In relation to a key and previously under-prosecuted and under-acknowledged crime, over the last decade the question of whether sexual violence, and in particular rape, is of itself an international crime has been clearly answered. Jurisprudence from ad hoc international enforcement mechanisms, as well as the inclusion of a range of sexual violence crimes within the ICC and numerous hybrid tribunals, leave no doubt that there are internationally recognised limits to the way in which women's bodies can be treated during times of conflict and turbulence.

For many commentators these developments are seen as noteworthy steps forward in the international criminal law's grand project of ending impunity.[4] While historically there are limited instances of prosecution of rape as a war crime, at least up until the last decade or so, never before has the subject matter been examined with such detail and precision. Much discussion is now devoted to the technicalities of *how* sexual violence can be prosecuted as a crime, and not *whether* it deserves such attention. Matters such as the international legal definition of rape and issues relating to the rules of evidence and procedure as they relate to sexual violence have taken over from the urgings for 'something to be done' in this area.

---

[2] See, eg, Sara L Zeigler and Gregory Gilbert Gunderson, 'The Gendered Dimensions of Conflict's Aftermath: A Victim-Centered Approach to Compensation' (2006) 20(2) *Ethics & International Affairs* 171.

[3] Hayli Millar, 'Facilitating Women's Voices in Truth Recovery – An Assessment of Women's Participation and the Integration of a Gender Perspective in Truth Commissions' in Helen Durham and Tracey Gurd (eds), *Listening to the Silences: Women and War* (Martinus Nijhoff 2005) 221.

[4] See for example Jennifer Gong-Gershowitz, 'Forced Marriage: A "New" Crime Against Humanity?' (2009) 8(1) *Northwestern Journal of International Human Rights*, 53 at paragraph 4.

However, to others, especially those from a critical legal theory background, claims that there have been advances in the international criminal legal order for women, due to the articulation of sexual crimes and limited jurisprudence, ring hollow. Haskell writes that such developments must be 'understood as incoherent responses by the post-World War II legal order to the widespread rape of women in armed conflict that has occurred and continues to occur with frequency and severity'.[5] For Haskell and others, international criminal law has not liberated women, and any claims that advances are 'unprecedented' should be challenged with questions about the legitimacy of international law's pluralistic and humanitarian vision.[6] From this perspective it appears that if the crimes continue to be perpetrated, the legitimacy of claiming success at the international normative level is merely noise and action designed to distract viewers from the fact that things are going (perhaps dancing) backwards.

Such views do not take into account developments across the broader international legal landscape which are supported and encouraged by the process of prosecutions. For example, Security Council Resolution 1820 of 2008[7] is the strongest Resolution to date. Dealing with matters such as rape, it locates sexual violence within the discourse of threats to international peace and security rather than deeming it an unfortunate personal consequence of armed conflict.[8] At the other end of the continuum, international criminal prosecutions also support those at a state level in attempts to domestically criminalise sexual violence during conflict. For example, by implementing the Rome Statute into Australian law,[9] the listing of rape and sexual violence crimes as war crimes has cut through any debate about whether the grave breaches provisions[10] of previous war crimes legislation included these specific crimes.

Finally, reflection is required on whether the legitimacy and even coherence of the international criminal legal regime, as it relates to women, can be 'fought over' on the exclusive (and rather narrow) territory of the classification of rape as a war crime. The notion that sexual violence is the

---

[5] John D Haskell, 'The Complicity and Limits of International Law in Armed Conflict Rape' (2009) 29(1) *Boston College Third World Law Journal* 35, 39.

[6] Ibid.

[7] SC Res 1820, UN SCOR, 5916th mtg, UN Doc S/RES/1820 (19 June 2008).

[8] Ibid, at paragraph 15 in particular.

[9] International Criminal Court (Consequential Amendments) Act 2002 ss 268.59 to 268.64, which criminalise rape along with sexual slavery, enforced sterilisation, forced pregnancy and other forms of gender violence.

[10] War Crimes Act 1945, s 6; War Crimes Amendment Act 1988, s 5(6)(e); Geneva Conventions Act 1945, Sched 1, Art 147.

only horror experienced by women during times of armed conflict ignores the importance of the creation of jurisprudence relating to a range of areas, including matters which touch on the methods and means of warfare, the use of specific weapons, the identification via the prosecution process of those previously 'missing', and the dignified treatment of detainees. If sexual violence is the only prism through which to examine the impact of international criminal law on women, a wide range of important factors are ignored, including the capacity for women to be themselves prosecuted for crimes, and their potentially strong agency during and after conflict.

## II. HISTORICAL DEVELOPMENT OF SEXUAL VIOLENCE AS AN INTERNATIONAL CRIME

The earliest recorded prosecution of rape as a war crime can be dated back to the 1474 trial of Peter von Hagenbach before an early form of international tribunal on charges relating to his conduct as governor of the city of Breisach (a position granted to him by the Duke of Burgundy). Von Hagenbach sustained a campaign of systematic violence against the citizens of Breisach and surrounding territories, including sexual violence and rape. A coalition comprising troops from France, Austria, Bern and various other independent towns and cities, captured Breisach and placed von Hagenbach on trial on charges including murder, rape and perjury. The court was ad hoc in nature, with 28 judges appointed by the various members of the coalition. Although Greppi notes that, due to some uncertainty about the timing and circumstances of the formal outbreak of hostilities in this case, it may be difficult to include the charges against von Hagenbach under the rubric of war crimes, it is clear that at the very least they can be considered early prototypes of today's crimes against humanity.[11] Von Hagenbach pleaded a defence of superior orders for his conduct, stating that he was subject only to the authority of the Duke of Burgundy. The court rejected this line of argument and he was executed.[12]

There are other instances of rape during war being prohibited before the codification of international humanitarian law as we know it today. The Belli Treatise of 1563[13] held rape to be punishable by death, and in the

---

[11] Edoardo Greppi, 'The Evolution of Individual Criminal Responsibility under International Law' (1999) 81(835) *International Review of the Red Cross*, 531 at paragraph 9.

[12] Kelly Askin, *War Crimes Against Women: Prosecution in International War Crimes Tribunals* (Martinus Nijhoff 1997), 29.

[13] Pierino Belli, *De Re Militari et Bello Tractatus*, 1563.

1600s Hugo Grotius argued that rape should be punished if committed during war as strongly as if committed during peace.[14] Art 23 of the Treaty of Amity and Commerce[15] between the United States and Prussia in 1785 prohibited the molestation of women and children, and the 1863 Lieber Code,[16] while developed for a domestic context, declared in Art 44 that rape was one of the most serious offences, potentially punishable by death. The 1899 and 1907 Hague Conventions[17] were created mainly to regulate the conduct of hostilities; however, while not directly prohibiting sexual violence, Art 46 of the 1907 Convention states that '[f]amily honor and rights ... must be respected' and this has been interpreted as prohibiting rape. The first Geneva Convention of 1864[18] was concerned with the wounded on the battlefield and consequently held no protections for any of the civilian population.

In this legal context the Charter of the International Military Tribunal (IMT) in Nuremberg did not include rape as a crime, and there were no prosecutions under other crimes such as torture, despite significant evidence of sexual violence.[19] The International Military Tribunal for the Far East (IMTFE) did include a number of cases of sexual violence and rape as 'inhumane treatment', 'ill-treatment' and 'failure to respect family honour

---

14 Kelly D Askin, 'Prosecuting Wartime Rape and Other Gender-Related Crimes under International Law: Extraordinary Advances, Enduring Obstacles' (2003) 21 *Berkeley Journal of International Law* 288, 299.

15 A Treaty of Amity and Commerce Between His Majesty the King of Prussia, and the United States of America, signed September 10 1785. See in particular Art 23.

16 General Orders No. 100, Instructions for the Armies of the United States in the Filed, approved 24 April 1863 (Lieber Code).

17 The Hague Convention (II) with respect to the Laws and Customs of War on Land, 32 Stat. 1803, opened for signature 29 July 1899 (entered into force 4 September 1900) (1899 Hague Convention) and its Annex, Regulations Respecting the Laws and Customs of War on Land (1899 Hague Regulations); The Hague Convention (IV) Respecting the Laws and Customs of War on Land, 1910 UKTS 9, opened for signature 18 October 1907 (entered into force 26 January 1910) (1907 Hague Convention), and its Annex, Regulations Respecting the Laws and Customs of War on Land ('1907 Hague Regulations').

18 Geneva Convention for the Amelioration of the Condition of the Wounded and the Sick in Armed Forces in the Field, 12 August 1949, 75 UNTS 31 ('First Geneva Convention').

19 Documents from the Trials of the Major War Criminals Before the International Military Tribunal at Nuremberg, Vol. VI, 407.

and rights'.[20] Senior Japanese military personnel and the Foreign Minister were found guilty of the crime of rape.[21] There is also evidence of domestic war crimes trials, held under Control Council Law No. 10, in which rape was prosecuted as a crime.[22] For example, under the Australian War Crimes Act 1945 (Cth), rape was specifically listed as a crime and two prosecutions were held resulting in the death penalty in each instance.[23] At the same time the horrendous treatment of women called 'Comfort Women' during World War II went without any prosecution and, until relatively recently, any acknowledgement.[24] Though patchy, inconsistent and at times without focus, there is a history of prosecutions against those who abuse women's bodies during conflict.

In 1949, the inclusion of rape and indecent assault in the Geneva Conventions[25] represented a substantial step forward in formalising the position of crimes of a sexual nature in international humanitarian law. As well as provisions prohibiting such conduct as 'violence to life and person … cruel treatment and torture … outrages upon personal dignity etc', Art 27 of the Fourth Geneva Convention[26] explicitly directs that 'women shall be especially protected against any attack on their honour, in particular against rape, enforced prostitution, or any form of indecent assault'. Despite the outdated and potentially thorny term 'honour', the exclusion of non-female victims of rape and sexual violence, and the failure to accord these crimes grave breach status, it is clear that this demonstrates an intention to solidify the position of rape as a prohibited act in international law. The 1977

---

[20] Kelly Askin, 'Prosecuting Wartime Rape and Other Gender-Related Crimes under International Law: Extraordinary Advances, Enduring Obstacles' (2003) 21(288) *Berkeley Journal of International Law* 302.

[21] Mark Ellis, 'Breaking the Silence: Rape as an International Crime' (2007) 38 *Case Western Reserve Journal of International Law* 225, 226.

[22] Helen Durham and Narrelle Morris, 'Women's Bodies and International Criminal Law: From Tokyo to Rabaul' in Yuki Tanaka, Tim McCormack and Gerry Simpson (eds), *Beyond Victor's Justice? The Tokyo War Crimes Trials Revisited* (Brill 2011) 285.

[23] Ibid.

[24] Chih-Chieh Chou, 'An Emerging Transnational Movement in Women's Human Rights: Campaign of Nongovernmental Organizations on "Comfort Women" Issues in East Asia' (2002) 4(2) *Journal of Economic and Social Research* 153–81 at 161.

[25] Geneva Convention Relative to the Protection of Civilian Persons in Time of War, 12 August 1949, 75 UNTS 287, entered into force 21 October 1950 ('Fourth Geneva Convention') at Art 27.

[26] Ibid.

Additional Protocols[27] expand upon these notions, requiring in Art 76(1) of Additional Protocol I that women be 'the object of special respect ... protected in particular against rape, forced prostitution and any form of indecent assault'. Any person, male or female, affected by non-international armed conflict would also be protected under Art 4(2)(e) of Additional Protocol II, which requires that they be protected against outrages against personal dignity, including rape. However, the updated list of acts which States Parties had the obligation to prosecute for did not directly include crimes of a sexual nature. Art 85 of Additional Protocol I provides a broader list of 'grave breaches' than that found in the Geneva Conventions, and while covering acts of perfidy, indiscriminate attacks, the protection of cultural property and outrageous attacks upon personal dignity based on racial discrimination, no mention can be found of rape or acts of sexual violence.

## III. RECENT JURISPRUDENCE

In the early years of the ad hoc tribunals, solid improvements were made to the legacy of the Nuremberg and Tokyo tribunals. At a structural level, the statutes of both tribunals referred specifically to rape as a crime against humanity,[28] while the statute of the International Criminal Tribunal for Rwanda (ICTR) included rape, enforced prostitution and indecent assault as a violation of Art 3 common to the Geneva Conventions.[29] Both tribunals would go on to take colossal steps forward in developing jurisprudence around rape and sexual violence. Today there is clarity that rape and a range of acts of sexual violence constitute war crimes, crimes against humanity, and in certain circumstances can reach the threshold of genocide.[30] These

---

27 Protocol Additional to the Geneva conventions of 12 August 1949, and relating to the Protection of Victims of International Armed Conflicts, 7 December 1978, 1125 UNTS 3 (hereafter 'Additional Protocol I') and Protocol Additional to the Geneva Conventions of 12 August 1949, and relating to the Protection of Victims of Non-International Armed Conflicts, 7 December 1978, 1125 UNTS 609 (hereafter 'Additional Protocol II'). Both entered into force 7 December 1978.

28 Statute of the ICTY, S.C. Res. 827, U.N. Doc. S/Res/827 (1993) at Art 5; Statute of the ICTR, S.C. Res. 955, U.N. Doc. S/Res/955 (1994) at Art 3.

29 Statute of the ICTR, S.C. Res. 955, U.N. Doc. S/Res/955 (1994) at Art 4.

30 Kelly D Askin, 'The Jurisprudence of International War Crimes Tribunals: Securing Gender Justice for Some Survivors' in Helen Durham and Tracey Gurd (eds), *Listening to the Silences: Women and War* (Martinus Nijhoff Publishers 2005) 132.

developments have not always been easy or linear in progress, and difficulties have been experienced every step along the way. Finding an internationally-agreed upon definition of rape, dealing with issues of confidentiality regarding the provision of evidence, as well as discussions relating to the role of 'consent' in defences, have all been bitterly contested and in many cases are 'works in progress'.

Another legacy of the ad hoc tribunals is the recognition of the need for substantive involvement of women in the investigative and trial process. Former Chief Prosecutor Richard Goldstone has publically addressed the need for women to be involved at all stages of investigations, stating that in the earlier stages of the tribunals he feared that gender-based crimes may have been marginalised due to a lack of understanding of gender issues by the investigative staff and a possible culture of 'gender bias'.[31] The legacy of this understanding of the need for a more competent approach to gender issues can be seen in the mainstreaming of gender issues in later tribunals, including the establishment of the ICC's Gender and Children Unit and the appointment of Catherine MacKinnon as Special Gender Adviser to the Prosecutor.

At the Special Court for Sierra Leone, 10 of 13 defendants were charged with the crimes against humanity of sexual slavery and rape, with an additional six charged with forced marriage.[32] Evidence was presented in *Prosecutor v Brima, Kamara and Kanu* to suggest that women and young girls had been abducted and forced into conjugal relationships.[33] The majority of the Trial Chamber in this case held that these facts were sufficient only for a charge of sexual slavery, finding that the sexual elements of forced marriage should be considered separately from any other conduct associated with forced marriages. The Chamber stated that

> the Prosecution evidence … does not point to even one instance of a woman or girl having had a bogus marriage forced upon her in circumstances which did not amount to sexual slavery. Not one of the victims of sexual slavery gave evidence

---

[31] Dianne Lupig, 'Investigation and Prosecution of Sexual and Gender-Based Crimes before the International Criminal Court' (2009) 17(2) *American Journal of Gender, Social Policy & the Law* 431, 14.

[32] Valerie Oosterveld, 'Lessons from the Special Court for Sierra Leone on the Prosecution of Gender-Based Crimes' (2007) 17(2) *Journal of Gender, Social Policy and the Law* 2.

[33] *Prosecutor. Brima, Kamara and Kanu*, Case No. SCSL-2004–16-T, Trial Chamber Judgment (June 20, 2007) paragraphs 711–12.

that the mere fact that a rebel had declared her to be his wife had caused her any particular trauma.[34]

Doherty J, in dissent, gave lengthy consideration to the non-sexual elements of the crime of forced marriage, such as victims' mental trauma as a result of forced association with their 'husbands', social stigma and isolation from family and community as well as the forced performance of domestic duties, holding that forced marriage did constitute a crime against humanity.[35] Doherty J's approach was upheld on appeal. Oosterveld also notes the potential similarity between cases of forced marriage in the Sierra Leone conflict and evidence in the case of *Prosecutor v Katanga and Ngudjolo Chui*, a current matter before the ICC.[36]

The Rome Statute has reached a new peak in codifying sexual and gender-based offences, building on the work of the International Criminal Tribunal for the former Yugoslavia (ICTY) and the ICTR. In addition to its ground-breaking definitions of crimes of sexual violence, the ICC's rules of evidence provide an unprecedented level of consideration for the needs of witnesses in cases of sexual violence, and the ICC also has the capacity to offer reparations and opportunities for victim participation.[37] In its first years of operation however, the ICC received some criticism for perceived passivity in the face of sexual crimes, causing widespread disappointment, in particular at the failure to incorporate charges of sexual violence into the indictment against Thomas Lubanga Dyilo, despite evidence of possible rape and sexual slavery committed by his troops. SáCouto and Cleary also note disappointment on the part of some commentators at the perceived failure of the court to acknowledge, in particular, the situation of girl soldiers in the context of the conflict in the Democratic Republic of Congo.[38] Setbacks in providing adequate security for witnesses resulted in charges being dropped in the case against Germain Katanga and Mathieu

---

[34] *Prosecutor v Brima, Kamara and Kanu*, Case No. SCSL-04–16-T, Trial Chamber Judgment, paragraph 710.

[35] Ibid, Doherty J. dissenting in part, at paragraphs 14–71.

[36] Oosterveld, above note 32, 11.

[37] See Rome Statute of the International Criminal Court, opened for signature 9 October 1998, UN Doc. A/CONF.183/9 (1998)37 ILM 999 (1998) (entered into force 1 July 2002), at Art 7; also ICC Rules of Procedure and Evidence rules 89–91 & 12 1(10), ICC-ASP/I/3 (September 10, 2002); also Mirjan Damaska, 'The International Criminal Court Between Aspiration and Achievement', 14 *UCLA Journal of International and Foreign Affairs*, 19 (2009) 27.

[38] Susana SáCouto and Katherine Cleary, 'Importance of Effective Investigation of Sexual Violence and Gender-Based Crimes at the International Criminal Court' (2009) 17(2) *American Journal of Gender, Social Policy & the Law* 339, 5.

Ngudjolo (although existing and additional charges were later brought after security issues had been resolved).[39]

Despite these acknowledged imperfections, it does not follow that existing legal mechanisms reflect a cavalier or indifferent approach to the prosecution of sexual and gender-based crimes, nor that the failure to achieve absolute coherence in prosecuting such crimes negates the undertaking as a whole. Rather, the developments in this area can be located firmly along a continuum of marked improvements in access to justice for victims of gender-based crime, flowing consistently from the IMT and IMTFE to the present day. The next step along this continuum is likely to be the continuing effort to improve the circumstances under which victims are able to participate in international justice mechanisms, whether through the improvement of conditions under which victims may testify, or through the establishment of alternative justice mechanisms designed to serve a testimonial rather than an enforcement function. Henry notes the shortfall in the capacity of international criminal tribunals to serve as effective truth-telling forums, citing examples of testimony in which victims were required to describe their experiences in purely factual terms, without reference to their emotional state or to their own perceptions of the significant aspects of the violations they experienced.[40] Henry elsewhere notes the specific problem of cross-examination as a factor increasing the trauma associated with rape and sexual violence.[41] The next steps would therefore seem to be the development of mechanisms whereby victims of sexual violence could give evidence in environments less likely to exacerbate trauma, and the development of alternative truth-telling environments such as parallel public truth and reconciliation proceedings (which may serve victims unable to participate in formal judicial hearings). The possibilities for the development of these alternative mechanisms are endless – from re-workings of the familiar Truth and Reconciliation model, to Terrell's proposal of a reworking of the quasi-judicial 'People's Tribunals'.[42] Given the growing international focus on these issues and the significant potential for development, it is problematic to assume that in the short time that sexual violence has been robustly actionable under international law, a failure to establish a flawless model for testimony is an indictment upon the project as a whole. Indeed, any attempt

---

39 Ibid 6.

40 Nicola Henry, 'The Impossibility of Bearing Witness – Wartime Rape and the Promise of Justice' (2010) 16 *Violence Against Women* 1098, 1113 in particular.

41 Ibid 1105.

42 Fleming Terrell, 'Unofficial Accountability: A Proposal for the Permanent Women's Tribunal on Sexual Violence in Armed Conflict' (2005) 15 *Texas Journal of Women and the Law*, 107.

to do more than cautiously identify the next steps to be taken must be considered to be premature at best.

## IV. BROADER INTERNATIONAL LEGAL DEVELOPMENTS FOR WOMEN

There can be little doubt that the development of international legal jurisprudence on the illegality of rape and sexual violence has resulted in broader policy and legal developments relating to the protection of women during times of conflict and internal tension. Letitia Anderson writes that there is a growing understanding that like war, rape is often politics by other means, and that recent Resolutions by the Security Council on the topic of women and armed conflict demonstrate that sexual violence against women can now be deemed a threat to international peace and security rather than a personal plight.[43] The elevation of this crime to a level where there can be instances of a triggering of corrective action is controversial, but is reflected in the narrative of Security Council Resolutions on this topic, starting with Resolution 1325 and concluding with the 2008 Resolution 1820 which recognised sexual violence as a tactic of war and an impediment to peace.[44] It appears that the most progress on this topic in the last few years can be located in the development of jurisprudence, the creation of UN Resolutions as well as the articulations found in the Rome Statute.

However, the topic of sexual violence against women is still rife with tensions and disagreements about the best way to conceptualise the 'problem'. Anderson states:

> For some, there is no distinction between the aggressive manifestation of sexuality and the sexual manifestation of aggression. Thus conflict-related rape is classified alongside domestic violence and female genital mutilation, as a manifestation of poverty, discrimination or culture. Many consider rape an inevitable by product of war, impervious to prevention. Others place it on par with any classical method of warfare that can be commended, condoned or condemned.[45]

---

[43] Letitia Anderson, 'Politics by Other Means: When Does Sexual Violence Threaten International Peace and Security' (2010) 17(2) *International Peacekeeping* 244, 257.

[44] Amy Barrow, 'UN Security Council Resolutions 1325 and 1820: Constructing Gender in Armed Conflict and International Humanitarian Law' (2010) 92(877) 221, 232.

[45] Anderson, above note 42, 244.

The spectrum of such views flavours the understandings and discourse surrounding the debate about how international criminal law does and should deal with matters of sexual violence against women. For those considering rape in war as an extension of rape in peace, any arguments about the need to include the large number of men sexually abused during conflict into the debate about prosecution may seem both offensive and unnecessary. On the other hand, those that see rape as one of the myriad ways in which battles are fought (from humiliating prisoners of war to a tactic for displacement of the civilian population as communities flee or are torn apart by the humiliation and fear of sexual violence) call loudly for a very inclusive approach to defining and prosecuting rape to be articulated by international courts and tribunals, taking into account the needs of male as well as female victims of sexual violence.[46] This debate has a long way to go, and considering the difficulty faced by domestic courts in prosecuting the range of gendered crimes, it is fitting that the international legal landscape struggles with the concept of how best to criminalise the most personal of all crimes.

## V. 'OTHER' VIEWS OF WOMEN IN INTERNATIONAL CRIMINAL LAW

As noted, exclusively focusing the examination of international criminal law's impact upon only women within the paradigm of sexual crimes, underestimates both women's agency during times of trauma and their capacity to be defendants as well as witnesses, victims or survivors. Nicole Hogg has written about the fate of women in Rwanda prosecuted for crimes such as genocide and has noted that such defendants were seen as '"evil" or "non-women"', almost inhuman as they not only committed crimes against the spirit of humanity but also went against accepted understandings of 'gender'.[47] Much has been written about Pauline Nyiramasuhuko, a trained social worker and former Minister of Family Affairs and Women's Development in Rwanda, the first woman to be found guilty of genocide (for conduct including directly ordering the rape and murder of Tutsi civilians and generalised incitement to genocide through the medium of public radio). Hogg also notes the extent to which Nyiramasuhuko's defence

---

46 Helen Durham and Katie O'Byrne, 'The dialogue of difference: gender perspectives on international humanitarian law' (2010) 92(877) *International Review of the Red Cross* 49.

47 Nicole Hogg, 'Women's Participation in the Rwandan Genocide: Mothers or Monsters?' (2010) 92(877) *International Review of the Red Cross* 69, 70.

employed gender stereotyping in their arguments, citing descriptions of Nyiramasuhuko by defence witnesses as 'very nice, a mother hen', as well as statements made by Nyiramasuhuko herself, referencing her status as a mother as cause to invalidate the charges against her.[48] Nyiramasuhuko's case can also be compared to that of Benedictine nuns Consolata Mukangango and Julienne Mukabutera, who were found guilty of various crimes against the civilian population.[49] Both cases are notable for the extent to which the accused served through their chosen professions as almost perfect avatars of the stereotype of the woman as caregiver – Nyiramasuhuko as a social worker and Mukangango and Mukabutera as nuns – as well as for the brutality of their crimes. It is clear from an examination of the issues raised by Hogg that the added dimension of women engaging in acts of horror repels and fascinates in equal measure. Just as those practicing in the field have identified the extra difficulties in the rehabilitation of female child soldiers compared to their male counterparts, the international prosecution of women accused of heinous crimes also raises a raft of complexities needing further examination to ensure that justice is done in a consistent and impartial manner.[50]

Furthermore, times of turbulence and conflict impact upon women in a vast number of ways, and often sexual violence is not their only or even primary concern when it comes to seeking justice post-conflict. The fate of 'the missing' – the unknown whereabouts of many male relatives – was identified in studies by the International Committee of the Red Cross as one of the primary concerns of women during and after the cessation of hostilities.[51] Any legal developments which result in the need for identification of corpses and remains are thus an extremely significant contribution by international criminal law. Similarly, in most instances it is women who make up the majority of the civilian population during times of fighting and tension, thus any jurisprudence relating to the methods and means of

---

48 Ibid 93.

49 Ibid 98.

50 See, for example, the requirement under Art 88 of the Third Geneva Convention that female prisoners of war not be sentenced to 'a punishment more severe, or treated while undergoing punishment more severely than a male member of the Armed Forces of the detaining power dealt with for a similar offence'. Similarly, general reiteration of the requirement of formal equality is found throughout the Geneva Conventions and their Additional Protocols, generally couched as a need to apply provisions 'without any adverse distinction on the basis of sex'. See First Geneva Convention Art 12; Second Geneva Convention Art 12; Third Geneva Convention Art 16; Fourth Geneva Convention Art 27; Additional Protocol I Art 75; Additional Protocol II Art 4.

51 Charlotte Lindsey, *Women Facing War* (ICRC 2001) 31.

warfare, such as prosecutions dealing with the destruction of civilian infrastructure necessary for the survival of a population, is a step in the right direction for encouraging the protection of women via international criminal law. As the author notes elsewhere, the status of women as a significant proportion of the civilian population gives rise to the need to include generalised protections for civilians under the umbrella of laws protecting women in armed conflict. Similarly, laws regulating the use of weapons which affect women in the conduct of gender-specific tasks (such as the impact of unexploded ordnance upon the ability to collect firewood) are, although not explicitly gender-based, not irrelevant to the question of how international law protects women in armed conflict.[52] Likewise, although violence against healthcare providers in armed conflict may not necessarily be instigated with the intention of targeting women, the particular healthcare needs of women have the potential to place them at risk of additional vulnerability in the context of armed violence.[53] Therefore, any general study of issues causing interruptions to healthcare delivery can and should be seen as an avenue to improving specific protections against gender-based violence, as well as in a more general context.

In the context of the many ways women experience disruption to social order, be it due to conflict or internal tensions, international prosecutions for a range of crimes are one method to strive for increased chances of survival and dignity.

## VI. CONCLUSION

Like its domestic counterparts, international criminal law has been slow and clumsy in its attempts to deal with crimes against women, in particular the most personal and complex of all crimes – those relating to sexual violence. However, in recent years genuine attempts to grapple with the horrors that women face during war have resulted in increased clarity in the codification of sexual violence as a range of international crimes, as well as numerous prosecutions. Indeed the presence of the issue of sexual violence on the agendas of international criminal law must be robustly maintained, but a wider debate about women and war crimes prosecutions should also be encouraged. Much still needs to be done in this area, but to claim that these

---

52 Helen Durham, 'International Humanitarian Law and the Protection of Women' in Helen Durham and Tracey Gurd (eds), *Listening to the Silences: Women and War* (Martinus Nijhoff 2005) 104.

53 Ibid 99.

advances lack legitimacy due to lack of consistency overlooks the inherent nature of any legal system. Haskell writes:

> [D]o international human rights laws concerning rape in armed conflict have any significant merit or value? Can these definitions and new methods of criminalizing rape be recognized as having substance if they are not enforced in any meaningful way? In short, movement may not necessarily equal progress.[54]

These are valuable and necessary questions which need serious reflection. For example, why did the Western world find the rape of women from the former Yugoslavia so horrific while less attention was given to the treatment of women in Darfur? International law is embedded in politics and thus is a victim to the partiality of all narratives about who are the victims most deserving of attention. However, counter to these issues is the fact that today there is not only a clear statement that sexual crimes against women are unacceptable, but also prosecutions to back this up. This has highlighted the issue to other international institutions, such as the United Nations Security Council, and statements and positioning of the topic are now far advanced from where they were even a decade ago.

Finally, the area which needs even more reflection is the broader way international criminal law has impacted upon women – from the increased capacity for them to play a role in the enforcement of institutions, to the wide range of other crimes that impact heavily upon their survival and dignity during turbulent times. International criminal law in this respect is but one of the methods for advancing the security of women throughout the world – it is certainly not the answer to the huge range of problems and difficulties that are faced by them daily. Rather than noisily and ostentatiously dancing backwards, international criminal law needs to be encouraged to continue to make careful but clear, small steps in the right direction.

---

[54] John D Haskell, 'The Complicity and Limits of International Law in Armed Conflict Rape' (2009) 29(1) *Boston College Third World Law Journal* 35, 60.

# 11. Have recent changes designed to benefit victims of international crimes added to the legitimacy of international criminal justice?

**Sam Garkawe**

## I. INTRODUCTION

Since the 1970s, more attention, support and rights have been accorded to victims of crime in both domestic and international criminal justice.[1] While this chapter will describe and critically analyse these changes for victims of *international* crimes, it is important to point out at this early stage that these changes must be seen in the context of a broad social movement[2] (often referred to as the 'victims' movement') stemming from the late 1960s, that arguably has made considerable progress in enhancing the cause of victims of *domestic* crime. While it is true that there are some unique aspects of

1 There is no single definition of a 'victim of crime'. The definition will often depend upon the context and, in particular, where a victim of crime may claim a benefit or right, on the definition found in the particular legislation or instrument that grants the particular right. Some of the main definitions of 'victims of crime' will be mentioned during the course of this chapter.

2 This has spurred a relatively new academic discipline, victimology. Originally a sub-discipline of criminology, it is now arguably a discipline in its own right. See Sam Garkawe, 'Modern Victimology: Its Importance, Scope and Relationship with Criminology' (2001) 14(2) *South African Journal of Criminology* 90. While the discipline of victimology arguably includes other types of victims than crime victims, such as victims of natural disasters, victims of abuse of power and human rights abuses in general, much of the literature and focus has historically been on victims of crime and this continues to be the most frequent subject of victimology. See Sam Garkawe, 'Revisiting the Scope of Victimology – How Broad a Discipline Should it Be?' (2004) 11 *International Review of Victimology* 275. For the purposes of this chapter, the debate over the scope of victimology is largely irrelevant as victims of international crimes are clearly victims of crime.

international criminal justice that make a number of considerations different for victims of international crimes compared with victims of domestic crimes,[3] the two are very much related, and such differences can be easily overrated. This is shown by the fact that the largest single overall achievement of the victims' movement, namely the unanimous agreement by the United Nations General Assembly to the 1985 Declaration of Basic Principles of Justice for Victims of Crime and Abuse of Power (the 'Declaration'),[4] was conceived at the time of its passage as applying primarily to domestic criminal justice.[5] However, as will be shown below, this instrument has been very influential in later international instruments that have dealt with victims of international crimes, and certainly its terms and principles apply equally to victims of both domestic and international crimes.

The term 'international criminal justice' is, in the author's opinion, a broad term that examines the extent to which some degree of 'justice' can be brought to situations where international crimes[6] have been or are being committed. While it may be difficult to categorise international criminal justice as a 'system' of justice (and in fact this is one of the key criticisms of the concept), one can say that a variety of mechanisms have been established or adopted by the international community, regional organisations

---

3 One obvious difference is that an international crime is likely to have involved numerous victims, whereas domestic crimes generally involve one or perhaps a small number of victims. This clearly has implications if rights or benefits are going to be provided to victims; one may have to be more circumspect to accord rights or benefits where numerous victims are involved.

4 Declaration of Basic Principles of Justice for Victims of Crime and Abuse of Power, GA Res 40/34, UN GAOR, Supp No 53, UN Doc A/40/53 (29 November 1985) 213–15. In Art 1, victims of crime are defined as 'persons who, individually or collectively, have suffered harm … through acts or omissions that are in violation of criminal laws operative within Member States … '.

5 See Leroy Lamborn, 'The United Nations Declaration on Victims: The Scope of Coverage' in Zvonimir Šeparović (ed), *Victimology: International Action and the Study of Victims* (Samobor Publishing 1988) 173.

6 In the author's view, an international crime is generally a mass breach of the human rights of people that reaches such a level or scale that the international community regards it as a threat to international society and as such amounts to an international crime. The perpetrators of international crimes will then attract international *individual* criminal liability under international law. These crimes tend to be the most serious crimes known to humankind, the most well-known being genocide, crimes against humanity and war crimes, but others also exist, such as torture, apartheid, slavery, piracy and killing or injuring internationally protected persons.

and individual States to attempt to deal with such situations. These mechanisms have a number of disparate aims that may include provision for offender accountability in some form or another; attempting to document the history of what happened; reconciliation; restoration of peace, stability, the rule of law and social values; and, most importantly from the perspective of this chapter, support and relief for the victims of the international crimes. While the chapter will focus on the issue of victims, we need to bear in mind that these mechanisms generally have a variety of different aims, and any changes made to benefit the cause of victims of international crime must be carried out in what is often a much broader context.

Key among the mechanisms of international criminal justice are the use of criminal trials that have as their primary aim the prosecution of the perpetrators of international crimes. These trials may take place in the domestic criminal courts of the State where the international crime was committed, or in a domestic criminal court in a State other than where the international crime took place (a 'foreign' court); in one of the three 'pure' international courts that were established in the 1990s (see below); or in one of the 'hybrid' or part-internationalised courts created since the turn of this century. The focus in the past was clearly on combating the impunity of alleged offenders of international crimes, and victims were traditionally peripheral to this objective, particularly in those nations and courts that have followed an adversarial system of justice where crime victims are not parties to the criminal trial. The assumption was that bringing offenders to justice would suffice for victims. In these criminal trials it was thus not surprising that victims were rarely offered support and assistance; given little, if any, rights; provided with information they might need; or compensated. Part II of this chapter will examine the key changes to criminal trials in the above types of courts that have been instituted due to the perception that more had to be done to assist and provide support to victims of crime. It will discuss both the positives and negatives of these changes from a victim's perspective, and will also mention the reasons for these changes – some clearly attributable to the victims' movement; others due to the desire of authorities to ensure that victims are prepared to report crime and to cooperate in the prosecution of international crimes; and another more recent factor behind these changes is the growing awareness and advocacy of *restorative* justice principles and practices. It will be shown that a direct consequence of this latter factor has been a more sustained attempt to have victims of international crimes recover restitution or compensation.[7]

---

[7] This is shown by the recent agreement of the UN to the Commission on Human Rights, Basic Principles and Guidelines on the Right to a Remedy and

While in the past and to a large extent even today, the emphasis of international criminal justice among international lawyers and advocates has been on the mechanism of criminal trials, a range of other mechanisms has been established recently by various State and other entities that do not involve the prosecution of offenders. The main non-prosecutorial mechanism prominent from the 1980s onwards has been the investigatory or truth Commission, instituted primarily in parts of Latin America and Africa following the end of oppressive military regimes and/or of governments that systematically violated the human rights of their citizens.[8] These Commissions are established first and foremost to create an accurate and comprehensive historical record of the human rights violations that characterised the period under study, as mandated by the founding document of the particular Commission. Another aim of most Commissions can be to provide help and support to the victims of the human rights violations through various methods, including through the recommendations contained in the Commissions' Reports. The South African Truth and Reconciliation Commission (SATRC) is probably the best known and most discussed of these investigatory Commissions, and certainly in its structure and in many of the recommendations of its Final Report[9] support for the victims of the apartheid regime was emphasised.[10] Part III of this chapter will assess these Commissions from a victim's perspective, describing the main positives and negatives of the measures designed to assist and support the victims of international crimes that these Commissions are mandated to study and report upon. It should be noted that there are other types of non-prosecutorial mechanisms that might be used in, and are part of, the 'system' of international criminal justice. Four of the more prominent mechanisms – immigration measures, lustration, resort to international or regional non-criminal courts and civil suits against perpetrators – will also be briefly mentioned at the end of Part III.

The final part of this chapter will then attempt to draw some overall conclusions concerning the question of whether the changes that have been

---

Reparation for Victims of Gross Violations of International Human Rights Law and Serious Violations of International Humanitarian Law, Res 2005/35, UN Doc E/CN.4/2005/ L.10/Add.11 (19 April 2005) ('Right to a Remedy and Reparation').

[8] For a definitive account, see Patricia Hayner, *Unspeakable Truths: Transitional Justice and the Challenge of Truth Commissions* (2nd edn, Routledge 2010).

[9] Truth and Reconciliation Commission, *Truth and Reconciliation Commission of South Africa Report* (Macmillan Reference Ltd 1998).

[10] See Sam Garkawe, 'The South African Truth and Reconciliation Commission – A Suitable Model to Enhance the Role and Rights of the Victims of Gross Violations of Human Rights?' (2003) 27(2) *Melbourne University Law Review* 334.

instituted on behalf of victims of international crimes detailed throughout Part II (prosecutorial mechanisms) and Part III (non-prosecutorial mechanisms) add to the legitimacy of international criminal justice. A prerequisite to a positive answer to this question is that the changes that have been instituted are beneficial for victims of international crimes. While it is difficult to conclude definitively that all the changes outlined in Parts II and III have in fact been favourable, the author concludes that on balance the changes have been beneficial.

Some comments will then be made as to what have been the main reasons for the questioning of the legitimacy of international criminal justice. Two key criticisms of international criminal justice will be mentioned – first, that it is only a partial and thus not really a 'system' of justice as many situations of international crimes are overlooked; and secondly, that because of the presence of the International Criminal Court (ICC) there is a danger that peace may be jeopardised in situations where leaders refuse to give up power because of the threat of ICC prosecution. It will be argued that an increased focus on aiding victims of international crimes does help to counter these two key criticisms of international criminal justice, and thus it is asserted that the recent attention to the position of victims does, in this respect, add to the legitimacy of international criminal justice. In the author's view, the international criminal justice 'system' has on balance taken an important step forward along the long and difficult path towards legitimacy, by taking the many steps outlined throughout this chapter to address and take seriously victims' situations and perspectives.

## II. AN ANALYSIS OF CHANGES INSTITUTED TO BENEFIT VICTIMS OF INTERNATIONAL CRIMES – PROSECUTORIAL MECHANISMS

As stated in the Introduction, prosecution of international crimes that may involve victims of international crimes can take place in domestic criminal courts, in purely international criminal courts, or in hybrid or part-internationalised criminal courts. Each of these types of criminal courts will be examined in turn, in order to describe and analyse the changes that have been instituted to benefit the victims of international crimes. This analysis will highlight the point made at the very start of this chapter – that there is a close relationship between victim-related initiatives at the domestic level and those at the international level.

## A. The Use of Domestic Criminal Courts to Prosecute International Crimes

Prosecution of international crimes in the domestic courts of the nation where the crimes took place[11] is, at least from most victims' point of view, a better alternative than prosecution that takes place in another State or at an international tribunal. This is because victims will not have to travel far to witness the proceedings and/or testify; they are more likely to understand the court proceedings from a linguistic and cultural point of view; and they will have closer access to support from family and friends. Prior to World War II, such trials in domestic courts were not common as many of the definitions of international crimes had not crystallised sufficiently for domestic legal systems to be able to prosecute.[12] Following World War II, the definitions of international crimes such as genocide and crimes against humanity became more settled, and thus it became more likely for domestic criminal justice systems to adopt these definitions and prosecute these international crimes. In fact, there was little alternative to such domestic prosecutions until the 1990s as no international courts were in existence. Even today, because of the principle that the ICC should be complementary

---

[11] International crimes can be prosecuted in a domestic court provided there are domestic criminal laws in existence that define the international crime as being a crime within the jurisdiction, or the domestic legal system otherwise provides for an international crime to be prosecuted. In such circumstances there will clearly be no problem with jurisdiction as the international criminal jurisdiction principles of universality and territoriality would apply.

[12] The international crime of genocide was never tried domestically or internationally until at least Nuremberg. 'The term genocide received its first formal, legal recognition in the context of the Nuremberg trials': Steven Ratner, Jason Abrams and James Bischoff, *Accountability for Human Rights Atrocities in International Law: Beyond the Nuremberg Legacy* (3rd edn, OUP 2009) 28. With respect to 'crimes against humanity', while an attempt was made to prosecute this as an international crime after World War I, '[t]he Charter of the International Military Tribunal marked the birth of the modern notion of crimes against humanity': at 49. Domestic prosecutions only followed using the first legal definition at Nuremberg as a starting point. The main exception to the lack of domestic prosecution of international crimes prior to World War II was prosecution for war crimes as there was a well-developed body of international humanitarian law that could be traced back into the nineteenth century. However, these trials largely took place in military courts where the focus was on the defendant and whether or not they obeyed the laws of war and not generally on the victims of those crimes.

to domestic criminal jurisdiction,[13] domestic prosecutions of international crime are still of primary consequence.

It is also possible for a foreign court to prosecute international crimes.[14] From a victim's point of view these trials have the disadvantage that they will have to travel to another State to testify or witness proceedings, and it may not take place in their language or in accordance with their understanding of the legal system. However, where the Territorial State refuses or cannot prosecute for some reason, this may be the only alternative available.

The situation of victims in these domestic prosecutions of international crimes is very dependent on the way in which victims are treated generally in the relevant criminal justice system. Two very famous trials where domestic courts have been used to prosecute international crimes provide examples of this. The 1961 *Eichmann*[15] trial in Israel is an example of a foreign court prosecuting international crimes. The Israeli criminal justice system generally is an adversarial one, and many victims of the Holocaust were encouraged to give evidence as witnesses to the trial. History shows that many took this opportunity to 'pour their heart out' in describing what happened to them, possibly going beyond the bounds of what should be strictly allowed under the rules of evidence in an adversarial system, as much of this testimony may have not been sufficiently related to Eichmann's criminal culpability. Yet, for obvious emotional, psychological and political reasons,[16] the Trial Court, consisting of a panel of three judges and no jury (perhaps thus allowing a more liberal interpretation of evidence rules), gave these victim/witnesses much latitude. The important point for present purposes is that they only played the role of witnesses, as it was a trial conducted under an essentially adversarial system that provides victims with no formal role except to give evidence when called by one of the parties (generally the prosecution) to testify. This can be contrasted with the

---

13 See Rome Statute of the International Criminal Court (adopted 17 July 1998, entered into force 1 July 2002) 2187 UNTS 90, preamble [10], Art 1 ('ICC Statute'/ 'Rome Statute').

14 In order for this to occur, not only does the prosecuting State need to have criminalised these international crimes in their domestic legal systems, but it must also have extended the reach of their domestic criminal jurisdiction so that it includes crimes committed anywhere in the world, or at least to the territorial State in which it was actually committed. In such cases there is generally speaking also no problem with jurisdiction as it would be clearly based upon the international criminal jurisdiction principle of universality.

15 *Attorney-General of the Government of Israel v Adolf Eichmann* (1961) 36 ILR 5.

16 See Jonathan Wenig, 'Enforcing the Lessons of History' in Timothy McCormack and Gerry Simpson (eds), *The Law of War Crimes* (Kluwers 1996).

*Klaus Barbie*[17] case in France in the 1980s for crimes against humanity, where about 40 victims of Barbie's human rights violations became civil parties to the trial,[18] and participated in the trial as such, as is allowed under the French criminal justice system.[19]

The contrast in the roles of victims in these two famous domestic criminal trials involving the prosecution of international crimes, reiterates the point made above that the situation of victims in these domestic prosecutions is very dependent on the way in which victims are treated in the relevant criminal justice system. Thus, it is pertinent to examine briefly the recent changes to domestic criminal justice systems, as these generally are translated into changing the position and laws relating to victims in cases where the domestic criminal justice system prosecutes international crime.[20]

It is well accepted that there has been a concerted push throughout much of the developed world to enhance the experiences of victims of crime in domestic justice systems. This has been fuelled by two important concepts (real or imagined). The first was that the victim is the 'forgotten person' of the criminal justice system. This was particularly prominent in adversarial systems of justice, in western nations with 'common law' criminal justice systems where victims of crime were no longer parties to the trial and thus had no decision-making power. Many argued that it was fundamentally unjust in an adversarial criminal trial that the person most affected by the criminal act, namely the victim, seemed to have the least power as they were considered to be mere 'sources of information'.[21] Even in non-adversarial criminal justice systems based on European civil law, where victims can be parties to a criminal trial by becoming a *partie civile* or by an 'adhesion'

---

17 The final appeal decision can be found in *Fédération Nationale des Déportés et Internés Résistants et Patriotes v Barbie* (*Final Appeal Decision*) (1985) 78 ILR 125 (Cour de Cassation [French Court of Cassation]).

18 Known as *partie civile* in French – see below note 22.

19 See Guyora Binder, 'Representing Nazism: Advocacy and Identity at the Trial of Klaus Barbie' (1989) 98 *Yale Law Journal* 1321, 1327–8.

20 Interestingly, in Australia, because international crimes are primarily prosecuted under federal laws (pursuant to the Criminal Code Act 1995 (Cth)) and the Federal Government has not (as at the time of writing) legislated in respect of victim issues, there is doubt as to whether many of the key changes referred to below apply to prosecutions of international crimes. See Sam Garkawe and Michael O'Connell, 'The Need for a Federal, Australia-Wide Approach to Issues Concerning Crime Victims' (2007) 18(3) *Current Issues in Criminal Justice* 488.

21 See War Crimes Research Office, Washington College of Law, *Victim Participation at the Case Stage of Proceedings* (Washington College of Law 2009) 32 ('Victim Participation').

procedure[22] (and thus in theory have many more rights than their counterparts in the common law), the evidence was that these rights were limited[23] and rarely exercised, and even where exercised there was evidence of dissatisfaction with their involvement in the system.[24] The second interrelated concept that struck a strong chord with victim advocates, service providers and policy makers was that victims often suffer from 'secondary' victimisation due to the insensitive treatment by officials and others they deal with in the aftermath of their victimisation. The need to prevent secondary victimisation has clearly become the main driving force behind the victim-related changes to criminal justice, as it is obvious that given the amount of attention paid to victims they are no longer 'forgotten persons'.

Whereas these reasons for the changes regarding victims were certainly prevalent in the first few decades of the modern victims' movement, some commentators now assert that the increased recent attention to victims in domestic crime is due to a greater emphasis and attention on restorative justice theories and practices.[25] In the past the main objective in conducting criminal trials has focused on the need to prosecute the alleged offender (the concept of *retributive* justice), but recently there has been an increasing awareness by national and international criminal justice practitioners and academics that the previous, almost exclusive, fixation with retributive justice does not cater sufficiently for the interests of victims of crime. There

---

22 'The former term has traditionally been used in Belgium, Italy, and France and the latter term in those jurisdictions with a German legal tradition. However, both descriptions reflect the same phenomenon': Matti Joutsen, 'Listening to the Victim: The Victim's Role in European Criminal Justice Systems' (1987) 34(1) *Wayne Law Review* 95, 115.

23 Ibid – 'the victim's role in criminal trials in the Western European countries discussed in this study is generally limited to presenting a civil claim in the criminal process and acting as a witness. It is only in Finland and the Socialist countries that the victim has a more expansive right to present both penal and civil demands.'

24 See Mina Rauschenbach and Damien Scalia, 'Victims and International Criminal Justice: A Vexed Question?' (2008) 90 *International Review of the Red Cross* 441, 446–7. This is referred to in Victim Participation, above note 21, 37.

25 Restorative justice is difficult to define precisely. One possible definition offered by Tony Marshall is that it 'is a process whereby all the parties with a stake in a particular offence come together to resolve collectively how to deal with the aftermath of the offence and its implications for the future'. Tony Marshall, *Restorative Justice: An Overview* (Home Office UK Government 1996) 37. However, authorities such as Professor John Brathwaite argue that it is more commonly defined by what it is not; see John Braithwaite, 'Restorative Justice: How Do We Know It When We See It?', Speech of 22 July 1999 at 'Restoring the Balance between Victims, Offenders & the Community' conference, Brisbane (taken from notes on file with the author).

has been a questioning of past assumptions that bringing such offenders to justice would suffice for victims, and thus there has been a move to looking to *restorative* justice as a means to improve victims' experiences. Ironically, however, it must be said that there is not a unanimous view of the merits of restorative justice among the victims' movement; there are many who are suspicious of restorative justice, particularly for serious crimes, which international crimes are by their very nature. In fact, it is probably fair to say that the move towards restorative justice in recent times has not come, at least initially, from the victims' movement, but more from criminal justice academics and practitioners who were focused on more constructive and compassionate ways to deal with offenders, and with restoring communities and society in general in the case of international crimes.[26] In other words, restorative justice is not just about restoring the victim of the crime; it can also be about restoring the offender back into society, as well as restoring the community. The verdict is clearly still out on the effectiveness and validity of restorative justice in general.[27]

So what have been the key changes to domestic criminal justice systems instituted with the aim of benefiting victims of crime in the modern era? These changes of course will generally apply where domestic courts prosecute international crimes.[28] Among the changes are the following: the provision of State compensation to victims of violent crimes in situations where victims are not able to recover using other means;[29] the establishment of support and advocacy services for victims of crimes, both government and non-government; allowing victims of crime to express their feelings and views of how the crime affected them and their families during sentencing;[30] the institution of 'Victims' Bills of Rights' as either administrative directions to government departments, legislation, or even constitutional provisions in the case of some States in the USA; and the

---

[26] See Sam Garkawe, 'Restorative Justice from the Perspective of Crime Victims' (1999) 15 *Queensland University of Technology Law Journal* 40, 42–4.

[27] For a good overview of the debate, including the issue of the suitability of restorative justice for international crimes, see Chris Cunneen and Carolyn Hoyle, *Debating Restorative Justice* (Hart Publishing 2010).

[28] See, however, above note 3.

[29] See Ian Freckelton, *Criminal Injuries Compensation: Law, Practice and Policy* (Law Book Co 2001).

[30] This is commonly through what are known as 'victim impact statements', but can also take the form of 'victim statements of opinion' (allowed in some States in the USA) or a 'victim personal statement' (United Kingdom). In relation to Australian law, see Michael O'Connell, 'The Law on Victim Impact Statements in Australia' (1999) 2(1) *Journal of the Australasian Society of Victimology* 88. In relation to American law, see Sam Garkawe, 'The Legal Rights of Victims of Crime

enhancement of restorative justice type programmes, such as family conferencing or victim–offender mediation.

Underlining all the above changes is the simple principle at the heart of the Declaration – that 'victims should be treated with compassion and respect for their dignity' (Art 4). Following on from this, it has also been generally recognised that victims should be able to make their own individual choices as to whether they want to be involved in criminal justice proceedings at all,[31] and if they do wish to be involved, the nature of that involvement. What victims might want from the criminal justice system is not an easy question to answer, but a brief discussion on what the research has shown is indicated in the next section of this Part.

While the above list of changes instituted to benefit victims of crime is clearly an impressive one, the above must be balanced against a number of possible negatives. The key overall negative is that the above measures may falsely raise victims' expectations that very often cannot be met and thus can have a detrimental effect on victims from a psychological point of view. This is perhaps the largest danger in granting victims some form of participation or a role in criminal proceedings. Furthermore, when one examines the so-called new 'legal rights' of victims, almost none of them are legal rights in a true sense, as most of the 'Victims' Bills of Rights' make it clear that any breach cannot give rise to a cause of action and cannot impinge on criminal justice decisions that have already been taken.[32] Again, where a 'right' on paper has not been provided, this will add to the problem of expectations that cannot be met.

Another potential problem is that some of the changes have been implemented with a 'law and order' perspective in mind – in other words, they are used to ensure a conviction is obtained or a greater penalty for offenders, rather than to benefit victims. This can reinforce the perceptions of victims and others that they are simply a 'source of information' (see above), and this might again add to their sense of secondary victimisation. A further issue concerns victims who do not fit the stereotype of being totally 'pure' and fully innocent of any wrongdoing – they are often not treated as well as

---

in America' (1992) 1(3) *Journal of the Australasian Society of Victimology* 1. In relation to English law, see *Practice Direction (Criminal Proceedings: Victim Personal Statements)* [2001] 4 All ER 640 (Lord Woolfe CJ).

[31] Subject of course to the requirements of the legal system that may oblige victims to report certain crimes and/or to testify in court proceedings.

[32] See, eg, Victims' Charter Act 2006 (Vic), s 22(1)(a). For an overview and critical analysis of the state of victims' rights in the USA, see Douglas Beloof, 'The Third Wave of Crime Victims' Rights: Standing, Remedy, and Review' (2005) 2 *Brigham Young University Law Review* 255.

the 'perfect' victim.[33] Finally, the additional procedures enabling victims to be involved and/or participate more in the criminal justice system add to costs, delays and possibly to the stress of victims. It is clear that this has been a consequence of many of the above changes. This of course must be balanced against the fact that extra costs and procedures are justified where they are considered to be essential to the 'justice' of the system.

Most of the above positives and negatives concerning the changes in favour of victims apply as equally to domestic prosecutions of international crimes as they do to the prosecution of domestic crimes. However, there may be some differences, including the following:

1) As international crimes may involve numerous victims, support services for victims in the cases concerning international crime may be overwhelmed and governments will probably need to make special provision for extra services.
2) By their very nature, international crimes are likely to involve deeper trauma and this may require domestic support services workers to be especially trained; thus again, more resources need to be made available.
3) International crimes are often committed against minority populations within a society.[34] In such cases, governments will need to ensure that culturally sensitive victim-support services are provided and that criminal courts adopt culturally appropriate procedures and practices.
4) If the international crime occurred on a foreign territory, compensation to victims of these crimes may not be forthcoming as very often a condition of victims recovering from a State compensation fund is that the crime occurred within the territory of the State that administers the funds. Therefore governments may have to make special provisions for these victims. Furthermore, even where the international crime did occur on the Territory of the State that is prosecuting the perpetrator of the crime, that State's compensation scheme

---

[33] This is the case where there is 'shared responsibility for crime' between the offender and the victim, which does occur in certain situations such as pub brawls, violence between friends or workers and where victims of theft may have been negligent in looking after their property. See Andrew Karmen, *Crime Victims – An Introduction to Victimology* (7th edn, Wadsworth Cengage Learning 2010) 106–17.

[34] Exceptionally, it is also possible that international crimes are committed against one section of the population that may even be in the majority, such as the international crimes committed under apartheid, or perhaps the crackdown on dissent in Syria during 2011–2012 .

may be insufficient owing either to the nature of the violations or because the scheme has maximum limits on awards of compensation. In such cases, recovery by victims may have to be supplemented by governments in order to make the compensation meaningful in the context of the particular violations.

To summarise this part of the chapter, many changes to domestic criminal justice systems have taken place that impact on the role and rights of victims. While in the main these have been positive for victims, there are some possible problems, in particular the question of creating false expectations for victims that may leave them worse off psychologically. Victims of international crimes are in a similar position to other victims where cases are prosecuted in a domestic court, although some potential differences were noted above.

## B. The Use of International Criminal Courts to Prosecute International Crimes

There have been five international criminal courts[35] in history – the Nuremberg International Military Tribunal (IMT) and the Tokyo International Military Tribunal for the Far East (IMTFE), both created shortly after World War II; the two ad hoc tribunals, the International Criminal Tribunal for the former Yugoslavia (ICTY) and the International Criminal Tribunal for Rwanda (ICTR), established by the UN Security Council in 1993[36] and 1994[37] respectively; and finally, the permanent International Criminal Court (ICC) agreed to in 1998 pursuant to the Rome Treaty.[38] The changes that have been instituted with respect to victims of international crimes by the later courts indicate a strong trend towards increasing the rights and role of victims in line with the same trends in domestic criminal justice.

---

[35] In the opinion of the author, an international criminal court can be defined as one that is not part of any domestic legal system, is created by the international legal system, and can hold criminal trials and other related proceedings in specially created courts under international law.

[36] See SC Res 827, 3217th mtg, UN Doc S/RES/827 (25 May 1993) <http://www.unhcr.org/refworld/docid/3b00f21b1c.html>. It is significant that the Security Council acted under Part VII of the UN Charter.

[37] SC Res 955, 3453rd mtg, UN Doc S/RES/955 (8 November 1994) <http://www.undemocracy.com/S-RES-955(1994).pdf>.

[38] This contains the Statute of the ICC, which was adopted by the UN Diplomatic Conference of Plenipotentiaries on the Establishment of an International Criminal Court; see above note 13. The Court came into operation from 1 July 2002 pursuant to Art 126 of the Statute.

The first 'international'[39] criminal court in history was the IMT, established to try the remnants of the Nazi leadership. Its founding Statute made no mention of the word 'victim', nor did it mention that victims or witnesses might have rights to protection and support. In fact, the American and British prosecutors did not call any of the victims of the extreme acts of persecution by the Nazi regime to testify.[40] Also established shortly after the end of World War II, the IMTFE had more testimony from witnesses, but like the IMT was dominated by documentary evidence.[41]

Much time passed (due to the Cold War and other factors) until the next step was taken by the international community to establish international criminal courts. The influence of the victims' movement on domestic criminal justice referred to above, as well as the agreement of the UN to the Declaration in 1985, meant that victims' issues would be taken much more into account when it came to the establishment of the ad hoc courts – the ICTY and the ICTR. The Statute of the ICTY introduced a number of innovative and progressive measures to assist and protect victims, which were largely replicated by the Statute of the ICTR following the genocide in Rwanda. It should be noted, however, that one very important additional factor for these victim measures was the international awareness of the widespread allegations of the use of sexual assault as perhaps a systematic policy of warfare during the Bosnian conflict[42] and in the genocide in Rwanda. Due primarily to one very significant part of the victims' movement, namely the feminist movement, there was a strong understanding and acknowledgement of the trauma faced by sexual assault victims when testifying in court, particularly during adversarial trials. This trauma would

39 Although only judges nominated from the four Allied powers (USA, UK, France and the Soviet Union) were able to sit on the IMT, the fact that there was more than one nationality represented among the bench made this court far more 'international' than any previous court. However, compared to modern international courts such as the International Court of Justice (ICJ), the two ad hoc international criminal tribunals and the ICC where judges are elected by the United Nations and come from numerous States, the IMT would hardly qualify as being 'international'.

40 For a detailed account of the role of victims (or lack thereof) at the IMT and the reasons for this, see Sam Garkawe, 'The Role and Rights of Victims at the Nuremberg International Military Tribunal' in Herbert Reginbogin and Christoph Safferling (eds), *The Nuremberg Trials: International Criminal Law Since 1945* (KG Saur Verlag 2006) 86.

41 See BVA Roling and Antonio Cassese, *The Tokyo Trial and Beyond* (Polity Press 1993) 52.

42 See Caroline Kennedy-Pipe and Penny Stanley, 'Rape in War: Lessons of the Balkan Conflicts in the 1990s' (2000) 4 (3/4) *International Journal of Human Rights* 67.

clearly be exacerbated in situations of armed warfare. Given that the ICTY and ICTR were established as fundamentally adversarial courts in nature, it was understood that in order to obtain convictions for these crimes there was an obvious need to support, encourage and protect sexual assault victims in particular so that they would be prepared to provide testimony to the Tribunals.[43] The dependence of the ICTY and ICTR on victim/witness testimony to secure convictions for sexual crimes[44] as part of international crimes was thus a very important reason for the victim measures that were introduced.

What were these measures? First, there was the establishment of Victims and Witness Units[45] to assist and support victims in their dealings with the respective Tribunals.[46] Secondly, the Tribunals were given the power to develop special procedural rules, or measures of protection for victims and witnesses.[47] Thirdly, 'vulnerable' victims, particularly women and children,

---

[43] There was a very different situation confronting victim/witnesses in the Yugoslav context from that which confronted the Allies after World War II. In the Balkans there was a negotiated Peace Treaty (the 1995 Dayton Peace Agreement) whereby the warring parties still retained much power and thus the ability to exact revenge and intimidate victim/witnesses. This required measures to encourage victim/witnesses to come to The Hague to give evidence. This can be starkly contrasted to the situation that followed World War II, where there had been a complete victory over the Nazi regime which no longer posed any threat to victim/witnesses.

[44] Sexual crimes by themselves were not directly prosecuted by the ICTY or ICTR as they are generally not international crimes in their own right. It was important that they were acknowledged as part of an international crime such as a war crime or crimes against humanity, or even genocide. In this manner the aim was to develop international criminal law so that the key international crimes would include, as part of their definition, systematic sexual violence.

[45] The ICTY's Unit has been described as 'the first of its kind in any international context'. See Åsa Rydberg, 'The Protection of the Interests of Witnesses – The ICTY in Comparison to the Future ICC' (1999) 12 *Leiden Journal of International Law* 455, 462.

[46] This includes administrative, financial and practical arrangements to bring a witness from their country to The Hague or Arusha, and basic information to witnesses regarding the work of the Tribunals and trial procedures. The Units also offer emotional support and counselling where appropriate, arrange medical and psychological care where needed, and provide protection to witnesses during their stay at The Hague or Arusha. Another important task of the Units is to make recommendations to the Tribunals regarding special protection measures required for witnesses. See, ibid

[47] See Statute of the International Criminal Tribunal for the former Yugoslavia, Art 22 ('ICTY Statute'); International Criminal Tribunal for the former Yugoslavia, Rules of Procedure and Evidence, Doc No IT/32/Rev.44 (adopted 10 December

were given special consideration in the rules developed by the ICTY and ICTR.[48] The final innovation was that for the first time an international criminal court made an attempt to facilitate victim reparation or compensation.[49]

It is clear that these victim-related measures instituted by the ICTY and ICTR have had some positive results. For example, sexual assault victim/witnesses, after much initial reluctance, started to testify in greater numbers and this did lead to the development of international criminal law in the field of sexual violence issues.[50] The support and help offered by the Victim and Witness Units and the adoption of special rules for vulnerable witnesses such as children were clearly long overdue reforms in the history of international criminal justice. However, this is not to suggest that there were no problems and that there was not dissatisfaction among victim/witnesses. One of the problems was that the formal nature of proceedings only allowed victim/witnesses to testify in the traditional adversarial examination/cross-examination format. Another significant negative was that proceedings in

---

2009) ('ICTY Rules') r 69 (Protection of Victims and Witnesses), r 75 (Measures for the Protection of Victims and Witnesses), r 79 (Provision for Closed Sessions). Such measures of protection have included the following methods, either alone or in combination – facial distortion, the use of pseudonyms, voice distortion, private sessions, closed sessions, use of a remote witness room, video-link testimony and safe conduct. Most controversially, it may also include an order for *total* anonymity of a victim/witness – not only from the press and public, but also from the accused and their lawyers. See *Prosecutor v Tadić* (*Decision on the Prosecutor's Motion Requesting Protective Measures for Victims and Witnesses*) (ICTY, Trial Chamber II, Case No IT-94-I-T, 10 August 1995).

48 For example, ICTY's Rules, r 96 specifies, *inter alia*, that in cases of sexual assault no corroboration of the victim's testimony shall be required, the defence of consent is to be limited and a victim's prior sexual history shall not be admitted in evidence.

49 The ICTY Rules allow there to be a reference to national authorities of a judgment of the ICTY so that victims can enforce this judgment in their domestic courts. However, because of the unlikelihood of victims finding any satisfaction in their own national legal systems, Van Boven has written that the ICTY provisions 'were included in the Rules as a symbolic afterthought rather than being expected to produce concrete results': Theodore van Boven, 'The Position of the Victim in the Statute of the International Criminal Court' in Herman von Hebel, Johan Lammers and Joken Schukking (eds), *Reflections on the International Criminal Court: Essays in Honour of Adriaan Bos* (TMC Asser Press 1999) 77, 80–81. See also Gideon Boas, 'Comparing the ICTY and the ICC: Some Procedural and Substantive Issues' (2000) XLVII *Netherlands International Law Review* 267, 284.

50 See Kelly Askin, *War Crimes against Women: Prosecution in International War Crimes Tribunals* (Martinus Nijhoff 1997).

The Hague and/or Arusha seemed to be too far removed from where most victims lived in the former Yugoslavia or Rwanda. As a result, many victim communities could not relate to or identify with the proceedings, which meant that they lost much of their potential educational and social advantages. While the courts made some attempt to remedy this through outreach and education programmes in victim communities, these were considered by many to be insufficient. Another important criticism was that while the Rwandan and the former Yugoslav criminal justice systems generally provided victims with more of a role in proceedings (potentially at least, given they are based more on civil law European systems), both the ICTR and ICTY were fundamentally adversarial courts where victims have very limited and confined roles.[51] Furthermore, these courts were not focused on reparative measures for victims, and particularly in the case of Rwanda, there was an obvious disparity in the poor living conditions of most victims and the relatively comfortable prison cells of defendants in Arusha.

These considerations were probably borne in mind by those who drafted the Statute of the ICC, which clearly builds upon and further enhances the victim[52] measures utilised by the ICTY and ICTR. While this ICC Statute contains many provisions that deal with the specific concerns and rights of victims,[53] there are two prominent innovations that particularly stand out over and above what is found in the ICTY and ICTR.

The first and most striking is that Art 68(3) of the ICC Statute allows victims, for the first time in international criminal justice, the possibility of having their own legal representation during the trial of 'their' perpetrator. While the ICC will, just like the ad hoc tribunals, still in the main be

[51] 'Critics have also pointed to the fact that neither the ICTY nor the ICTR provide any opportunity for victims to interact with the courts other than as witnesses called to serve the evidentiary needs of a given party in a given case.' War Crimes Research Unit – Washington College of Law, *Victim Participation Before the [ICC]* (Washington College of Law 2007) 2.

[52] ICC, *Rules of Procedure and Evidence*, Doc No ICC-ASP/1/3 (adopted 9 September 2002) r 85 ('ICC Rules') provides the following broad definition of 'victims' for the purposes of the ICC Statute and the ICC Rules:

(a) 'Victims' means natural persons who have suffered harm as a result of the commission of any crime within the jurisdiction of the Court;
(b) Victims may include organizations or institutions that have sustained direct harm to any of their property which is dedicated to religion, education, art or science or charitable purposes, and to their historic monuments, hospitals and other places and objects for humanitarian purposes.

[53] See Van Boven, above note 49; Sam Garkawe, 'The Victim-Related Provisions of the Statute of the International Criminal Court – A Victimological Analysis' (2001) 8(3) *International Review of Victimology* 269.

adversarial in nature, the ICC provisions clearly go beyond the traditional role for victims in adversarial criminal justice systems by granting victims the possibility of their own legal representation. This moves the ICC some way towards adopting more of a civil law approach, and thus the ICC can be seen more as a blend between the two major criminal justice systems of the developed world.

Such a right for a victim to be separately represented and thus able to 'present their views and concerns' is subject to the discretion of the ICC, and will only occur at 'appropriate' stages of proceedings as deemed by the Court. This can only be done where the 'personal interests of victims are affected' and where it is 'not being prejudicial to or inconsistent with the rights of the accused and a fair and impartial trial'. One can see from these phrases found in Art 68 (3) that this is a very discretionary article – what is meant by 'personal interests' of victims, and when are they affected? What exactly are the 'views and concerns' of victims? What are the stages of proceedings where these 'views and concerns' should be presented? How will this ability to have legal representation be 'balanced' against the fair trial rights of defendants, given that the ICC's procedures still consist of significant adversarial elements? Before one can even tackle these issues, there are the preliminary issues of who qualifies as a victim,[54] and at what stage of proceedings can they begin to have representation?[55] Furthermore, it is also obvious that as international crimes by their very nature generally involve numerous victims, and as the ICC Rules give a broad definition of a 'victim',[56] there is a strong need to ensure the efficiency of proceedings that could be overwhelmed by the sheer number of victims wishing to be represented. The ICC Rules of Procedure and Evidence attempt to achieve efficiency in two ways – first, by limiting the number of victims' representatives,[57] and then by placing limitations on the involvement of these representatives.[58] How these provisions will be implemented is up to the discretionary decisions of the ICC Chambers.

The ICC already has an extensive jurisprudence, albeit developing, on many of the above numerous and multifaceted issues that arise in the interpretation of the victim participation scheme found in Art 68(3) of the ICC Statute and in the Rules of Evidence and Procedure that relate to this

---

[54] See Markus Funk, *Victims' Rights and Advocacy at the International Criminal Court* (Oxford University Press 2010) 97–103.

[55] In particular, the role of victims' legal representatives during pre-trial procedures is uncertain – ibid 149–51.

[56] Refer to ICC Rules, above note 52.

[57] Ibid r 90(4).

[58] Ibid rr 89, 91.

scheme. While it is beyond the scope of this chapter to examine these decisions in any detail,[59] some early overall problems have already been identified. One problem is that there is a considerable backload of applications by people seeking to participate as victims in the 'situations' that the ICC is dealing with, and many people have had to wait considerable time before finding out the result of their applications. A second general problem is that those who have been granted 'victim' status must keep applying to an ICC Chamber every time they wish to participate in proceedings in respect of each type of involvement they wish to take, and the ICC has generally ruled that each such application can only be dealt with on a case-by-case basis. This of course has added considerably to delays and ultimately costs, as there is a legal aid scheme for those people who have been declared to be victims. Finally, 'ICC judges implementing the participation scheme have not been consistent in their decisions, meaning that different victims might have different rights depending upon which judges are hearing the case'.[60]

The overall difficulty is that the structure of the scheme only provides the broad outline of how victim representation and participation in the ICC will work in practice, and thus the Court must constantly exercise its individual discretion when making practical decisions on each aspect of the victim participation and representation scheme. One possible solution to this problem is for the ICC to articulate the reason for the existence of the participation scheme, and to thus fashion the exercise of their discretion on this basis. While 'none of the decisions regarding victim participation at the ICC to date include an in-depth exploration of the scheme's purpose',[61] most commentators, and the ICC itself[62] are clear that 'the primary motivation behind the creation of a victim participation scheme within the ICC context was a desire to achieve restorative – as opposed to strictly retributive – justice'.[63]

---

59 For a good summary of the key decisions of the ICC from 2005 (when the first applications by people claiming to be victims were dealt with) up to July 2010, see ICC, The Office of Public Counsel for Victims, *Representing Victims before the International Criminal Court: A Manual for Legal Representatives* (ICC 2010) <http://www.icc-cpi.int/Menus/ICC/Home>.

60 War Crimes Research Unit – Washington College of Law, above note 51, 1.

61 Ibid 2.

62 See Assembly of State Parties, Report of the Court on the Strategy in Relation to Victims, 8th sess, UN Doc ICC-ASP/8/45 (10 November 2009)1: '3. A key feature of the system established in the Rome Statute is the recognition that the ICC has not only a punitive but also a restorative function. It reflects growing international consensus that participation and reparations play an important role in achieving justice for victims.'

63 War Crimes Research Unit – Washington College of Law, above note 51, 2.

However, given the complexities and the uncertainties of what exactly is 'restorative justice' this seemingly simple explanation for the participation scheme does not necessarily show the ICC how to exercise the many discretions it has in the area of victim participation; nor can one exclude other interrelated reasons for the scheme, such as the desire that it would lead to more cooperation between victims and the ICC in general, or that it is intended to implement international instruments such as the Declaration and the Right to a Remedy and Reparation. In respect of the latter reason, the language used in one of the key provisions of the Declaration found in Art 6(b)[64] replicates much of the language found in Art 68(3) of the ICC Statute. The author would also argue that a significant reason for the participation scheme is to ensure victims are able to exercise their rights to procedural fairness.[65]

While the above matters can assist the ICC to exercise its discretion on victims' issues, it is submitted that ultimately the purpose of the participation system should be guided by the extensive research already carried out in criminal justice that explains what victims might desire from the criminal justice system. This research has largely informed many of the changes to domestic criminal justice as outlined in the section above. A number of aspects stand out. First, and probably most importantly, victims want *information* regarding 'their' cases – where is it up to? When will it be heard? What are the steps it will go through? When do I need to be at Court? What options do I have in terms of involvement in the case? Secondly, victims also want clarity about their role in the proceedings – what happens when I stand up in court? Who can I have by my side during the proceedings? Thirdly, victims clearly want respect and to be treated with dignity, the key principle underlying the Declaration (Art 4). They certainly do not expect to suffer from secondary victimisation at the hands of professionals associated with the court proceedings. Fourthly, many victims want compensation in a tangible form for their suffering. The violations could have

---

64 This includes the phrases: 'views and concerns'; 'appropriate stages of proceedings'; where their 'personal interests are affected'. One major difference between this clause and Art 68(3) of the ICC Statute is that the former does not mention the possibility of victims having a legal representative.

65 This is an administrative law concept perhaps restricted to common law jurisdictions. It basically means that when a decision is about to be made that affects the rights and interests of a particular person, that person should at least have the opportunity to present facts and/or their arguments to the decision-maker *before* the decision is taken. This is applicable to crime victims as it is submitted that many discretionary decisions made during stages of the criminal justice process impact on the rights and interests of the victim; it is hoped that something like the ICC participation scheme can lead to procedural fairness for victims.

seriously impacted upon them financially, in terms of their direct medical, dental and psychological bills, and possible property loss, and also in terms of damage to their current and/or future earning capacity. Finally, victims also want to know that they are being heard, but not necessarily in order to participate in proceedings. In fact, the research has shown that many victims do not want the stress and costs (financial and emotional) of participating, and prefer to leave the running of the case to the relevant authorities.

So has the participation scheme been beneficial overall for victims? Of course, given what has been said above and the fact that we are in the early days of seeing how the ICC will actually work (remembering that at the time of writing, no verdicts have been pronounced), it might be premature to come to any conclusion. There are certainly many potential benefits of the participation scheme. In the author's opinion, it does give victims a better chance to achieve their aims (which victims of domestic crimes also desire) – information about the case and their potential role in proceedings, the opportunity to be heard (without being forced to take a role or seek participation), respect that the possibility of having their own representation may give them, dignity because the international community is more in tune with their rights, and the greater chance of reparation owing to the establishment of the Trust Fund. While the participation scheme may not satisfy all the desires of victims, it is a remarkable step in international criminal justice that at least represents a genuine attempt to involve them and deliver their wishes.

The establishment of specific institutions to aid victims and ensure the scheme lives up to expectations is a very important part of the benefits for victims. One such institution is the Office of Public Counsel for Victims as an independent entity within the ICC Registry.[66] While it does not have large resources at its disposal, it has played a positive role in conducting research on victims' issues and in providing briefs on victims' issues to the ICC when requested. It has also been responsible for the training and education of many lawyers who are going to represent victims, and for keeping a list of such lawyers for victims' benefit. Individual lawyers working for the office are permitted to act for victims themselves, particularly where victims or the ICC request this, or victims have no other lawyers to turn to. There are other significant community and NGO organisations that also play a positive role with limited resources in advocating for victims, conducting research and providing support for victims. One prominent organisation is the Victims' Rights Working Group (the VRWG), which:

---

66 Their website can be accessed via the ICC website – see above note 59.

> is a network of over 300 national and international civil society groups and experts created in 1997 under the auspices of the Coalition of the [ICC]. It was created by a number of international NGOs and experts but over the years has evolved to include NGOs from a wide array of countries including those countries most affected by the [ICC]. ... The VRWG's current work seeks to ensure that the [ICC] provisions [regarding victims] are effectively implemented, making justice for victims a possibility for the first time. Particular attention is paid to ensuring that re-victimization is prevented.[67]

On the drawbacks of the participation scheme for victims, it is clear that all the possible procedures described above that include initial applications by potential victims' to seek the status of a 'victim' under the Statute, and then if successful, to participate in proceedings, involve a multitude of discretionary decisions of the ICC that must be heard and litigated every step of the way. This has already added significantly to the costs and delays in finalising cases before the ICC and will continue to do so, even if in the future the ICC is able to articulate more clearly the rules relating to victim involvement as suggested by some commentators.[68] This mirrors arguments often made in domestic criminal justice that greater victim involvement in the criminal trial may be counter-productive as it may add to victims' stress, inconvenience and cost, and could create false expectations that cannot be fulfilled. However, while this criticism clearly has some truth, it needs to be seen in the context that sometimes there is a price for justice, and additional costs should never get in the way of what is essential to ensure basic fairness. The other negative consequences of victim participation, such as the additional delays, are likewise also inevitable but should again be seen as part of ensuring justice.

The creation of false expectations for victims is possibly the most valid criticism of the participation scheme, and those dealing with victims should be aware of this issue and take steps to minimise it. The education of victims and victim communities in how the ICC works and what choices they can exercise in their dealings with the Court, is of course vital to keep expectations realistic. To the ICC's credit, it has tried to learn the lessons of the ICTY and ICTR in respect of the problems caused by a lack of victim consultation and education, and it has placed much more emphasis on outreach programs in affected communities, particularly in those States where it is directly involved. The Office of the Prosecutor, for example, has established offices on the ground in some of the States where 'situations' are

---

67 VRWG, 'Home' (*Victims' Rights Working Group*) <http://www.vrwg.org/> accessed 10 August 2011.

68 For example, see many of the recommendations found in the War Crimes Research Unit – Washington College of Law, above note 51.

being investigated by that office. The Trust Fund for Victims (see below) also is spending money on outreach programmes, and many NGOs are also assisting with outreach programmes. A detailed study by the VRWG of outreach programmes, including an analysis of questionnaires answered by victims mainly from the Democratic Republic of Congo and Uganda, was recently completed. This study indicated that while more resources needed to be devoted to outreach programmes, and there were inherent problems in the remoteness and lack of infrastructure of many victim communities, as well as ongoing security concerns, victims who participated in educational outreach programmes about the ICC were generally appreciative and more informed about the ICC's work.[69] In summary, while there are clearly some negatives concerning the victim participation programme such as extra costs, delays and problems with unmet expectations that may leave victims worse off psychologically, in the author's opinion, they are understandable and do not detract significantly from the overall benefits of the participation scheme.

The second major innovation of the ICC is that also for the first time in international criminal justice there is a genuine attempt to create a reparation scheme for the victims of the crimes under the jurisdiction of an international Court, which has some parallels to State-administered compensation schemes for victims of violent crimes in domestic criminal justice. Article 75(1) of the ICC Statute provides that the 'Court shall establish principles relating to reparations to, or in respect of, victims, including restitution, compensation and rehabilitation'. The Court may order that the award for reparations to victims be made through the Trust Fund established for the benefit of victims and their families under Article 79.[70] This is the primary mandate of the Trust Fund. The creation of this fund is clearly intended to ensure that the ICC will have access to some tangible assets when it makes reparation awards to victims of international crimes. Significant sums of money have been collected, mainly from various voluntary donors (including States and a variety of private individuals), enabling the Trust Fund to hold considerable assets. However, to the author's knowledge little or nothing has been collected from defendants at the time of writing. Given there have been no actual convictions by the ICC it is too early to say to what extent (if any) the reparation function of the Trust Fund will yield tangible results to victims of the international crimes

---

[69] See the Report: Victims' Rights Working Group, *The Impact of the ICC on Victims and Affected Communities* (VRWG 2010).

[70] ICC Rules, r 98 sets out how this works in practice. Note that under r 97, reparations can be assessed on an individualised or collective basis and the Court may appoint experts to aid it in its assessment of reparations.

that the ICC has prosecuted. However, the Trust Fund also has a second mandate – to use its resources for the benefit of victims generally, although this must be subject to the provisions of Art 79 of the Rome Statute. There does not need to have been a conviction for it to allocate funds for this mandate. Currently 'the Trust Fund for Victims is providing a broad range of support for victims under this second mandate – including vocational training, counselling, reconciliation workshops, reconstructive surgery and more – to an estimated 70,000 victims of crimes under the ICC's jurisdiction'.[71] This aspect of the ICC's work must surely be a good thing, although given the nature of international crimes and the sheer number of victims in 'situations' the ICC is currently involved in, such as Darfur, the Congo and Uganda, there will never be enough resources to satisfy all victims, and expectations may again be raised too high.

To summarise this section of the chapter, the three 'pure' international criminal courts established in the 1990s have made changes that clearly attempt to benefit the victims of international crimes. Whereas the changes provided by the two ad hoc tribunals have mirrored to a large extent the changes that have been instituted in domestic criminal justice systems (particularly those with adversarial systems), and were primarily designed to encourage victim/witnesses to cooperate and give evidence, the changes instituted by the ICC have arguably been further reaching. The two key victim changes of the ICC, allowing victims the possibility of their own legal representation and a greater chance of receiving reparation, are driven to some extent by restorative justice philosophies. Clearly, once again there has been a genuine intention for these changes to benefit victims of international crimes, and no doubt some of these changes are sensible and overdue. The main problem is that victim expectations may not be achievable because the success of proceedings and reparations will depend on the discretion exercised by the ICC. Furthermore, many victims who might be equally deserving may not know about the ICC at all, or may be too shy, scared or simply unable to become involved. Clearly, one of the most important areas that will need attention is the outreach and education programme within victim communities. Carried out properly with adequate resources, this can ensure that victims have realistic expectations, and that every victim who wishes to be involved is informed of their rights in this respect.

---

[71] See ICC, 'Welcome/Bienvenue' (*The Trust Fund for Victims*) <http://www.trustfundforvictims.org/> accessed 5 April 2011 – the Reports of the Trust Fund can be downloaded from this website.

### C. The Use of 'Hybrid' or Partly Internationalised Criminal Courts to Prosecute International Crimes

The final type of criminal court that may prosecute international crimes are the hybrid or partly internationalised courts that have come into existence only this century. These institutions are intended to utilise the best aspects of both domestic and international criminal courts, while minimising the disadvantages of each.[72] Such courts are located locally – in the State where the crime took place; they may be existing criminal courts or especially created for the specific purpose of trying international crimes, such as the Extraordinary Chambers in the Courts of Cambodia. These courts become hybrid or part-internationalised because they may have international judges, prosecutors, defence lawyers and/or support personnel to assist and work together with their local equivalents, with the aim of providing greater objectivity in proceedings that may be lacking if it was purely a domestic criminal court. Examples of such courts were or are found in East Timor, Sierra Leone, Cambodia, Kosovo, Bosnia, Lebanon, and perhaps Serbia and Iraq.[73]

Because these courts are located within, and are considered to be part of, the domestic criminal justice system of the State in which they are held, the manner in which victims interact with and are treated by these courts will generally depend upon the position of victims in that system. The comments and considerations discussed in the section on the use of domestic criminal courts to prosecute international crimes are for the most part applicable for these courts. The involvement of international personnel could mean that international standards on the treatment of victims are more likely to be

---

[72] For an overview see Kai Ambos and Mohamed Othman (eds), *New Approaches in International Criminal Justice: Kosovo, East Timor, Sierra Leone and Cambodia* (Max-Planck-Institute 2003); Laura Dickinson, 'The Promise of Hybrid Courts' (2003) 97 *American Journal of International Law* 296.

[73] There is some debate over whether the Iraqi High Tribunal and the Serbian War Crimes Chamber are simply domestic courts or are in fact hybrid courts. Compare the following viewpoint: 'entities such as the Iraqi High Tribunal and the Serbian War Crimes Chamber … are little more than domestic courts assisted by international advisors' (Ratner, Abrams and Bischoff, above note 12, 247), with the view of Laura Dickinson when discussing the Iraqi High Tribunal: 'Yet, in the end Iraq chose to create a hybrid of the two; a court that has some international and some domestic components (although … in its current structure it more closely resembles a domestic court)' (Laura Dickinson, 'IHT Should Consider Appointing Foreign Judges to Enhance the Legitimacy and Capacity of the Court' in Michael P Schart and Gregory S McNeal (eds), *Saddam on Trial: Understanding and Debating the Iraqi High Tribunal* (Carolina Academic Press 2006) 92).

adhered to, and outreach and education programmes for victim communities may be more likely to take place as funding may be more forthcoming given that the involvement of the international community often means more resources are available. On the negative side, there may be resentment in the local population of the resources devoted to the hybrid institution that victim communities, in particular, think might be better spent on reparation to victims or more general welfare measures.[74] Furthermore, the attention and involvement of the international personnel together with greater resources devoted to outreach and education programmes for victim communities may make any victim involvement in the court much more likely, and this may overwhelm the system. In Cambodia for example, this might lead to a closing down or a curtailment of what is in fact a more generous scheme of victim and survivor involvement in the Extraordinary Chambers in the Courts of Cambodia than the ICC's scheme.[75]

## III. AN ANALYSIS OF THE CHANGES THAT HAVE BEEN INSTITUTED TO BENEFIT VICTIMS OF INTERNATIONAL CRIMES IN NON-PROSECUTORIAL MECHANISMS

The primary non-prosecutorial mechanism prominent since the 1980s has been the investigatory Commission, sometime referred to as a 'truth' Commission, and in some cases, the word 'reconciliation' appears in the title of the Commission. As stated in Part I, these Commissions are established first and foremost to create an accurate and comprehensive historical record of the human rights violations that characterised the period under study, as generally mandated by the founding document of the

74 Anecdotal evidence reveals this did seem to be the case, for example in Sierra Leone.

75 'With a groundbreaking scheme for survivor participation – stretching far beyond the [ICC] ... The Court's Internal Rules accord a role to all survivors ... and conceive of certain recognized victims as full parties to the proceedings ... Due to inadequate planning, funding and commitment from key stakeholders, however, this initiative is currently being considered and may be eliminated after use in only one trial.' Sarah Thomas and Terith Chy, 'Including the Survivors in the Tribunal Process' in John Ciorciari and Anne Heindel (eds), *On Trial: The Khmer Rouge Accountability Process* (Documentation Centre of Cambodia 2009) 214. See also ABC Radio, 'Victims Advocate Steps Away from Khmer Rouge Tribunal', *Radio Australia*, 14 November 2011 (Kanaha Sabapathy, Seng Theary, Claire Duffy, Phay Siphan) <http://www.radioaustralia.net.au/international/radio/onairhighlights/victims-advocate-steps-away-from-khmer-rouge-tribunal>.

particular Commission. They normally arise either as part of a negotiated settlement to a conflict or division in a society (as in South Africa), or as a means by which an incoming government decides to deal with its past (as in Argentina and Chile). They have been mainly established by the new government, either directly by the executive, or by means of legislation. It is also possible for international organisations (such as the UN in the case of El Salvador), non-governmental organisations and even political parties (the African National Congress in South Africa created two) to sponsor them. Their mandate will almost always be established in writing at the time of the Commission's formation. Beyond the formal words of the mandate, factors such as the resources available to the Commission, its time limitations, political conditions within the State, and the scale of the abuses will also have a significant effect on the mandate, and importantly, how it is interpreted by the Commission itself.[76]

So what are the benefits of such Commissions from a victim's perspective? Their main aim is to discover the 'truth' about what happened during the period of their mandate. This is of vital interest to many victims; many say it is a necessary first step on the road to recovery. Commissions often have the flexibility, the personal resources (such as trained historians) and the ability to ask broad questions about the nation's past history of oppression. They are not bound only to study one case at a time, do not need to prove every fact beyond a reasonable doubt, and are not restrained by complex and restrictive laws of evidence, as criminal courts may be. Furthermore, where there are incentives for perpetrators to come forward and tell the truth, such as what occurred with the amnesty process of the SATRC, this may uncover truths that would normally not have been revealed. Whereas criminal courts must confine themselves to the question of the criminal liability of the particular defendant they are prosecuting, Commissions can seek deeper into the past. They can hold institutional hearings on the behaviour of different professions and parts of society during the era of repression, on different categories of victims, such as children and victims of sexual violence, and on particular aspects or incidents during the period under study.[77] This is not to say that criminal

---

[76] For the most comprehensive account of the history of these Commissions and an analysis of those created before the turn of the century, see Patricia Hayner, *Unspeakable Truths: Confronting State Terror and Atrocity* (Praeger Publishers 2001). This book has now been updated – see Hayner, above note 8.

[77] For example, the SATRC conducted institutional hearings on the business and labour, legal, prison, health, faith and media sections of South African society during the apartheid era. Special hearings were also carried out on compulsory military service, children and youth, and women.

courts cannot likewise be important discoverers of the truth, particularly when a Head of State is the defendant, and a broad indictment that covers a large amount and scope of criminal wrongdoing becomes the basis for the trial;[78] but is not a common situation, and Commissions overall seem to have broader mandates and abilities to extract the truth.

A second important benefit of Commissions is that victims are generally able to tell their 'story' in the way they wish because many Commissions establish a forum for victim hearings that attempt to create as informal, sympathetic and reassuring an atmosphere as possible, preferably without applying formal rules of evidence. There is clearly therapeutic value for victims of traumatic events in telling their story in a supportive atmosphere, and importantly, as part of a publicly-recognised process.[79] By way of contrast, under a criminal trial approach victims are often limited in their testimony by formal rules of evidence and procedure, and may be subject to rigorous and often traumatic cross-examination by defence lawyers.

Another vital benefit of Commissions for victims is that they are likely to be able to recommend broad reparation measures (normally in their Final Report), including monetary payments. It is usually within most Commissions' mandates to make reparation recommendations, although ultimately only governments can implement most of them. These recommendations can go far beyond merely monetary amounts for victims. For example, the SATRC made very broad recommendations that included various interventions to help individuals in legal or administrative matters,[80] 'community' and national interventions,[81] 'community rehabilitation' measures,[82] and

---

[78] Certainly this was the aim of the Milošević trial at the ICTY. Had Milošević survived and a judgment been rendered, it probably would have been of significant historical importance.

[79] Psychologist Brandon Hamber states: 'Providing space for victims to tell their stories, particularly in public forums, has been of use to many. It is indisputable that many survivors and relatives of victims have found the public hearing process psychologically beneficial.' Brandon Hamber, 'The Burdens of Truth: An Evaluation of the Psychological Support Services and Initiatives Undertaken by the South African Truth and Reconciliation Commission' (1998) 55 *American Imago* 9, 18.

[80] Examples are exhumations, reburials and ceremonies, provision of headstones and tombstones, declarations of death, the issuing of death warrants, expungement of criminal records and the expediting of other outstanding legal matters. See Truth and Reconciliation Commission, above note 9, vol 5, ch 5, [78]–[85], 188–9.

[81] Examples might be the renaming of streets and facilities, erecting memorials and monuments, conducting culturally appropriate ceremonies to commemorate

finally various institutional reforms were recommended that would guarantee non-repetition of the apartheid era abuses. This broad list of different forms of reparations is something that simply cannot be achieved using criminal justice type mechanisms. Criminal courts are generally not geared to do such work, although it is acknowledged that the ICC reparation scheme as discussed above constitutes an attempt to go some way towards these goals. Of course, whether governments take up the recommendations of Commissions is another matter and will often depend upon political, financial and social factors beyond the control of Commissions and victims.

There are of course many possible negatives of Commissions from a victim's perspective. Recommendations that are not implemented by governments are clearly a source of frustration and bring about the false expectations of victims that may leave them psychologically worse off. This is also the case where the 'truth' does not seem to have been uncovered, and partial truths are perhaps even more damaging for victims. If adequate support services have not been made available to victims, then even finding out the truth may be traumatising, at least initially. Most Commissions, unlike the SATRC, have tended to provide perpetrators with an amnesty without any requirements on them to do anything. Some Commissions do not allow perpetrators to be named in the Final Report, and this can be very damaging for victims.[83] Finally, Commissions sometimes have limited definitions of who is a 'victim' to work with, or choose to interpret their mandate restrictively and thus confine narrowly their working definition on who are the victims. People falling outside these official definitions but who may also be victims of international crimes can feel cheated by their lack of access to the Commission, its hearings and any services it provides (such as counselling), and would not be subject to its reparation recommendations.[84]

---

the victims of repression and even the institution of a national day of remembrance. See Truth and Reconciliation Commission, above note 9, vol 5, ch 5, [86]–[93], 189–90.

82 These might include the improvement of health and social services, skills training, the need for specialised trauma counselling services, family-based therapy and help with education and housing provision. See Truth and Reconciliation Commission, above note 9, vol 5, ch 5, [94]–[113], 190–93.

83 See Ratner, Abrams and Bischoff, above note 12, 265.

84 A good example of this was the fact that victims of legal discriminatory policies in South Africa, such as forced removals to 'homelands', were not considered to be 'victims' under the mandate of the SATRC. See Truth and Reconciliation Commission, above note 9, vol 1, ch 4, [42]–[59], 60–65. For a criticism of this see Mahmood Mamdani, 'A Diminished Truth' in Wilmont James and Linda Van de Vijver (eds), *After the TRC: Reflections on Truth and Reconciliation in South Africa* (Ohio University Press 2001) 58.

Other types of non-prosecutorial mechanisms are part of and might be used in the 'system' of international criminal justice. Four such mechanisms feature in the literature. The first mechanism provides immigration measures against the perpetrators of international crimes (used primarily in the USA), which normally take the form of denaturalising and then deporting a perpetrator who has deliberately lied when he or she obtained their citizenship or their right to live in their State of residence.[85] A second non-prosecutorial mechanism is 'lustration', the removal or 'selective purging' of certain categories of people from public office and/or removing their benefits; this is used primarily in Eastern Europe and to a lesser extent in Latin America.[86] A third possible mechanism is taking action in an international or regional court against a State said to have been responsible for international crimes being committed.[87] These bodies are not criminal courts, they do not have jurisdiction over individuals and are more geared towards deciding on State responsibility for violations of international law. However, they can establish an authoritative factual record and adjudicate State responsibility, and thus provide some psychological satisfaction for victims. In fact, each of these three mechanisms has the ability to provide some psychological benefit for victims in situations where the final decision that results from the mechanism is favourable to the victim. The problem however is that in each one of these three mechanisms victims cannot take the initiative, nor can they really achieve material results, only a sense of psychological satisfaction.

The final possible mechanism, the use of civil suits against perpetrators and those who support or cooperate with them, is potentially a much better mechanism for victims. Not only do they allow victims to take the initiative, but they also allow for the possibility for victims to benefit tangibly from the mechanism by being awarded a judgment in their favour.[88] While clearly more should be done by States to allow, encourage and facilitate victims of

---

85 See Matthew Lippman, 'The Denaturalization of Nazi War Criminals in the United States: Is Justice Being Served?' (1985) 7(2) *Houston Journal of International Law* 169.

86 For a detailed account and analysis of lustration see 'Symposium: Law and Lustration: Righting the Wrongs of the Past' (1995) 20(1) *Law & Social Inquiry 1.*

87 The best example was the case brought in the ICJ by Bosnia against the then Federal Republic of Yugoslavia alleging breaches of the Genocide Convention. See *Application of the Convention on the Prevention and Punishment of the Crime of Genocide* (*Bosnia and Herzegovina v Federal Republic of Yugoslavia*) (*Preliminary Objections*) [1996] ICJ Rep 616.

88 Of course, actually collecting on the judgment may prove to be even more difficult. It should be noted that such a mechanism is mainly applicable in

international crimes to take this course of action within their domestic civil legal system,[89] this topic is beyond the scope of this chapter.

## IV. SOME CONCLUSIONS ON WHETHER THE CHANGES DESIGNED TO BENEFIT VICTIMS OF INTERNATIONAL CRIMES HAVE ADDED TO THE LEGITIMACY OF INTERNATIONAL CRIMINAL JUSTICE

This chapter has described and examined many of the key changes brought to the mechanisms of international criminal justice in order to benefit the situation and position of victims of international crimes. It has been shown that at times these changes have not necessarily resulted in the advancement of the situation for victims of international crimes, and in fact some may be counter-productive. We have also seen that many of the changes are long overdue and sensible, having added a sense of justice for victims. It is thus a difficult balancing exercise to come to a definitive answer as to whether the changes have been a good thing overall, and more particularly, whether they have added to the legitimacy of international criminal justice. As stated already in the Introduction to this chapter, the author's conclusion is that on balance the answer is 'yes' to both questions.

Let us take the first question – have the changes outlined in Parts II and III been to the overall benefit of victims of international crimes? One key reason for the conclusion that the changes have on balance been beneficial is that those changes that have not worked out to be to the advantage of victims of international crimes (that is, those on the negative side of the ledger) must be understood in the context that one cannot judge these changes purely from the perspective of victims. The changes must be seen in a broader context, and it is important that they conform to and are restrained by the interests of other key stakeholders in the international criminal justice system. Thus even if they are instituted with the best of intentions to benefit victims, the system must ensure that the key interests of other stakeholders are respected, which often acts to temper the changes.

jurisdictions where there is an adversarial system of criminal justice. In non-adversarial systems of criminal justice, the victim's civil claim may be heard as part of the criminal case brought against the defendant.

89 For example, more States could enact legislation such as that found in the USA, namely the Alien Torts Claim Act 1799 *and the* Torture Victim Protection Act 1992. These enable victims/survivors of some international crimes to sue in tort in USA Federal courts, even though the international crime did not occur in the USA.

The most obvious other stakeholders here are accused persons, and this is why, for example, the ICC has been so careful and tentative in providing guidelines on the rights to victims, as the ICC Statute Art 68(3) participation right must be subject to the rights of accused persons. Another example is that the good intentions of the SATRC in inviting victims to tell their story without any hint of the accused person being present or having a role in the Human Rights Committee hearings, had to be modified because of due process restraints brought about by the judicial intervention of an alleged perpetrator.[90] The other stakeholder is the international community which must largely bear the costs of the international criminal courts. Victim initiatives such as legal representation during cases at the ICC are therefore subject to the valid objective of conducting reasonably expeditious trials, as this will keep costs and delays to reasonable levels. In short, while it is easy to be negative about those victim initiatives that have not worked out as well as their original intentions, they must be seen in the context of how these changes must operate in practice. This is not to deny or minimalise the negative side of the ledger for victims of these changes, but to perhaps emphasise the need for continued vigilance to ensure that these negatives are minimised, and that any solutions to them must be found within the broader context under which they must operate.

So do the changes made purportedly to benefit victims add to the legitimacy of international criminal justice? In order to attempt to answer this question, one must first ask why the validity of the system of international criminal justice has been questioned. The key criticism already alluded to is that the use of the word 'system' to describe international criminal justice is a dubious one. Is there really a 'system' of international criminal justice? Is wrongdoing amounting to international crimes addressed with a reasonable degree of coherency and consistency, and without politics intruding? We have seen that various mechanisms have been expanded or instituted to tackle situations of international crime, but it is clearly far from comprehensive as they only apply in certain situations or under certain circumstances. The key criticism has been that there have been significant gaps in the prosecution of those who commit massive violations of human rights; for example, over recent decades when international criminal courts have come into being, the emphasis seems to be particularly on Africa and not on other continents. More importantly, there have been so many examples of impunity: of brutal dictators not being prosecuted or having to experience some form of accountability, and being

---

90 See *Du Preez v Truth and Reconciliation Commission* (1997) 4 BCLR 531.

able to live out their lives in comfortable exile. Furthermore, where individuals from one of the big five powers in the Security Council are possibly involved in international crimes, experience has shown that international criminal justice is non-existent or ineffective. Of course this impacts on all the victims of these alleged perpetrators of international crimes, who are deprived of the psychological satisfaction of seeing 'their' offender being made accountable for their actions, or in many situations, of even the 'truth' about what happened being recognised.

This last criticism clearly has considerable merit. But looking at the perspective of victims of international crimes, one can see that by strengthening their position, the legitimacy of international criminal justice can be enhanced. The above criticism takes a very retributive perspective of international criminal justice and thus may not represent the full picture from a victim's point of view. It ignores the benefits and value to victims of the non-prosecutorial mechanisms discussed in Part III, many of which may benefit victims of international crimes even without a hint of prosecution or other forms of accountability. In particular, where an investigatory commission is established with the interests of victims in mind, this may benefit victims in a number of ways – by the process of being able to tell their story in a friendly, non-adversarial environment; the possibility of receiving tangible benefits such as medical and psychological help and in sorting out various legal matters relating to the international crimes; perhaps a sum of money from the incoming government, and the erection of memorials to their loved ones. This surely must add to the legitimacy of the international criminal justice system even where there is no prosecution or other form of accountability for perpetrators. This of course does not entirely meet the criticism of lack of systematic coverage in situations, because in places such as Mozambique no mechanisms (prosecutorial or non-prosecutorial) were established at all. But these situations are becoming the minority – most transitional governments are providing something for victims even where it is too dangerous and too difficult and/or impractical to prosecute or force perpetrators to undergo other forms of accountability.

Another key criticism of international criminal justice, and the ICC in particular, is that there are situations where the inflexibility of or insistence upon prosecution of perpetrators of international crimes may jeopardise a possible peaceful outcome to a conflict, and this may end up being counter-productive.[91] For example, if the ICC had been fully functional at the time of the creation of the SATRC, would it have determined that the

[91] See Michael Scharf, 'Trading Justice for Peace: The Contemporary Law and Policy Debate' in Edel Hughes, William Schabas and Ramesh Thakur (eds),

'amnesty for truth' arrangement contemplated by the SATRC made South Africa 'unable or unwilling'[92] to prosecute international crimes under apartheid, and thereby insisted that the perpetrators of international crimes under apartheid be indicted by the ICC prosecutor?[93] While this is now a theoretical question, the situation in Uganda is probably the best example of how this issue might undermine the credibility of international criminal justice. The indictments against the leaders of the Lord's Resistance Army (LRA) by the ICC prosecutor, initially fully supported by the government of Uganda, have proven to be a stumbling block to a possible peace agreement, as the leaders of the LRA are not prepared to sign an accord unless the indictments against them are dropped. Despite the Ugandan government now being agreeable to this, the ICC prosecutor made it clear that he would not do this and would not be swayed by political considerations. Looking at this dilemma from a victim perspective, it seems that an insistence on justice may be for the benefit of past victims, but the sacrifice of a possible peaceful outcome could mean many new victims of any resultant outbreak of further hostilities would be created. A victim perspective thus may not provide a clear answer to this dilemma. Some may argue that whatever advantages there are of prosecution to former victims, this is outweighed by the prevention of further victimisation. Past victims need not be left out altogether if the non-prosecutorial options discussed in Part III are implemented, with a view to providing victims with tangible benefits such as reparation, memorials, and access to health interventions. Thus in Uganda if the ICC prosecution were to be dropped and a peace treaty entered into, part of the peace treaty should include these kinds of benefits for the previous victims of the LRA. This would, so the argument goes, provide a form of justice that, while imperfect, may be better than allowing peace to be jeopardised and thereby creating a whole new group of victims. Wherever one stands on this difficult dilemma between peace and justice, attention to the position and support for victims can help to minimise the inevitable criticism that will come, whichever path is taken.

For both of the above major criticisms of international criminal justice discussed above, it is the author's view that the increased attention to victims of international crimes in both prosecution and non-prosecutorial mechanisms has added to the legitimacy of international criminal justice. If

---

*Atrocities and International Accountability: Beyond Transitional Justice* (United Nations University Press 2007) 246.

92 This is the language used in the ICC Statute, Art 17.

93 See William Schabas and Ramesh Thakur, 'Concluding Remarks: The Questions That Still Remain' in *Atrocities and International Accountability*, above note 91, 275, 279–80.

international criminal justice is not designed to benefit its victims, one may well ask, then what is it for?

# 12. International criminal justice and military perspectives

**Geoffrey Skillen***

## I. INTRODUCTION

Historically, there is little evidence of military commanders being among the most fervent champions of international humanitarian law (IHL), or the law of war. Sir Arthur 'Bomber' Harris, the commander of the Royal Air Force's Bomber Command during World War II, famously said: 'International law can always be argued pro and con, but in this matter of the use of aircraft in war there is, it so happens, no international law at all.'[1]

It is unlikely that this view would allow for enthusiasm for any notion of international criminal justice. How should the contemporary institutionalisation of the idea of international criminal justice, embodied in the establishment of a number of international courts and tribunals since 1993, be viewed by military forces? Should they be wary of it, or should they welcome it?

This chapter argues that a well-trained and disciplined military force that exhibits a commitment to the observance of IHL, has nothing to fear from international criminal justice and should adopt a 'business-as-usual' approach. In some respects, such a commitment can be seen as positive.

In early 1995 the author was the Director-General of Legal Services of the Australian Defence Force (ADF) and in that capacity, joined in the work towards the development of the Australian Government's position on the proposal to establish an international criminal court. As with all treaty negotiations, there is an irresistible and natural inclination to approach the task with a view to achieving what a state regards as the optimum outcome for it, which, in the case of a multilateral treaty, may or may not coincide

* The views expressed in this chapter are personal and do not necessarily represent those of the Australian Government or of the Australian Red Cross.

[1] Quoted in W Hays Parks, 'Air War and the Law of War' (1990) 32 *Air Force Law Review* 1.

with the greater good. Viewed in this light, the interests of the Defence Force were pretty clear at the outset – no military force would want to see its soldiers tried for war crimes by a foreign or international tribunal. It was hard to avoid the conclusion that no good could come of this for the ADF, and that the best strategy would be to limit the scope of the new institution so as to minimise its impact on the military. This attitude was evident among many of the military delegates at the Preparatory Committee meetings in New York held before the Rome Conference.[2] The agenda was that if a court was to be established, it should in no circumstances ever be in a position to try one's own soldiers.

Some military thinkers, particularly from the United States, have expressed misgivings about the prospect of the trial of soldiers before the International Criminal Court (ICC).[3] Probably the most extreme reaction to the perceived threat posed by the ICC to military forces came in the form of the United States' American Servicemembers' Protection Act.[4] Speaking in support of the Act, the Chairman of the Senate Committee on Foreign Relations said: 'If other nations are going to insist on placing Americans under the ICC's jurisdiction against their will, then Congress has a right and responsibility to place a cost on their obstinacy, and to ensure our men and women in uniform are protected.'[5] The Act contained a range of measures designed to protect members of the US military from the reach of the ICC, including the now infamous authority to free American military personnel held captive by the ICC.

So how can it be argued that military forces should be supportive of the notion of international criminal justice, rather than instinctively oppose it or seek to limit its reach?

---

2 The Preparatory Committee for the Establishment of an International Criminal Court was mandated by the United Nations General Assembly in Resolution 50/46 of 11 December 1995. The Committee met six times between March 1996 and April 1998.

3 See, eg, Joel F England, 'The Response of the United States to the International Criminal Court: Rejection, Ratification or Something Else?' (2001) 18(3) *Arizona Journal of International and Comparative Law* 941, 976.

4 American Servicemembers' Protection Act, S. 2726, 106th Cong. (2000).

5 United States Congress, Senate Committee on Foreign Relations, *The International Criminal Court: Protecting American Servicemen and Officials from the Threat of International Prosecution – Hearing Before the Senate Committee on Foreign Relations: One Hundred Sixth Congress: Second Session: June 14, 2000* (US Government Printing Office 2000).

## II. MILITARY FORCES ARE INSTRUMENTS OF STATES

The interest of states in the concept of international criminal justice is affirmed in these preambular paragraphs from the Rome Statute of the International Criminal Court ('ICC Statute'):

> Affirming that the most serious crimes of concern to the international community as a whole must not go unpunished and that their effective prosecution must be ensured by taking measures at the national level and by enhancing international cooperation ...
>
> Determined to put an end to impunity for the perpetrators of these crimes and thus to contribute to the prevention of such crimes ...
>
> Determined to these ends and for the sake of present and future generations, to establish an independent permanent International Criminal Court in relationship with the United Nations system, with jurisdiction over the most serious crimes of concern to the international community as a whole ...[6]

Clausewitz asserted that war is the continuation of politics by other means.[7] Military forces cannot and should not be seen as entities totally divorced from the states they represent. Military forces are in fact instruments of states, whose role within the state is underpinned by the liberal concept of the subservience of the military to civilian authority. Just as states have an interest in a functioning regime of international criminal justice, so too do their military forces. Indeed, as argued below, in some respects military forces have a particular interest in this.

## III. ACCOUNTABILITY OF THE ENEMY

The prospect of one's own soldiers being tried for war crimes before an international tribunal is one thing, but what about the accountability of the enemy? Is there not an argument that the establishment of international tribunals might improve the likelihood of accountability for the perpetrators of crimes of which a state's own soldiers are the victims?

The interest of states in accountability for war crimes committed against its own citizens is evident in Australia's War Crimes Act 1945 ('War Crimes

---

[6] Rome Statute of the International Criminal Court, opened for signature 17 July 1998, 2187 UNTS 90 (entered into force 1 July 2002).

[7] Carl von Clausewitz, *On War: Vom Kriege* (Forgotten Books 1832).

Act'), which empowered Australian military courts to try war crimes committed against Australian residents during World War II.[8] In the majority of the 922 trials that were conducted under this legislation between 1945 and 1951, the victims were Australian military personnel, mainly prisoners of war.[9]

The jurisdiction provided for in the War Crimes Act relies on the passive personality principle, under which states claim jurisdiction to try foreign nationals for offences committed abroad that affect their own citizens.[10] Recognition of the significance of the victims of international crimes is found in more contemporary authorities, including the establishment of the ICC's Office of Public Counsel for Victims.[11]

Looking at Art 8 of the ICC Statute, 33 war crimes can be identified for which the victims could be members of military forces, of which five are crimes in which the victims are prisoners of war or combatants.[12] Given that the establishment of the ICC recognises that states have often failed in their duty to bring to justice the perpetrators of crimes within their jurisdiction,[13] military forces should welcome the increased prospect of accountability for crimes committed against their personnel.

---

[8] War Crimes Act 1945 (Cth) s 7 provides: 'A military court shall have power to try persons charged with war crimes committed, at any place whatsoever, whether within or beyond Australia, against any person who was at any time resident in Australia, and for that purpose, subject to any direction by the Governor-General, to sit at any place whatsoever, whether within or beyond Australia.'

[9] See 'Stolen Years: Australian Prisoners of War' (*Australian War Memorial*) <http://www.awm.gov.au/exhibitions/stolenyears/ww2/japan/warcrimes/> accessed August 2011.

[10] The passive personality principle is sometimes asserted by states to claim jurisdiction to try a foreign national for offences committed abroad that affect its own citizens. It is recognised in a number of Conventions, for example in the Convention against Torture and Other Cruel, Inhuman or Degrading Treatment or Punishment, Art 5(1) (c) of which provides: 'Each State Party shall take such measures as may be necessary to establish its jurisdiction over the offences referred to in article 4 in the following cases: … [w]hen the victim is a national of that State if that State considers it appropriate.'

[11] ICC, *Regulations of the Court*, Doc No ICC-BD/01–01–04 (adopted 26 May 2004) Art 81 ('ICC Regulations').

[12] ICC Statute, Arts 8(a)(v), (vi), (b)(vi), (xi), (c)(ix).

[13] ICC Statute, Preamble para 5 states: 'Determined to put an end to impunity for the perpetrators of these crimes and thus to contribute to the prevention of such crimes.'

## IV. INTERNATIONAL CRIMINAL JUSTICE AND MILITARY DISCIPLINE

What influence does international criminal justice exert on military disciplinary authority? Does the prospect of accountability before an international tribunal encourage or discourage the exercise of authority under domestic military law? Recall that the preamble to the ICC Statute states 'that it is the duty of every State to exercise its criminal jurisdiction over those responsible for international crimes'. The state's criminal jurisdiction over its soldiers for war crimes can be exercised through its normal criminal laws,[14] or its laws regulating the discipline of its military forces.[15]

In Australia, three members of the Defence Force were charged under the Defence Force Discipline Act 1982 for offences arising from an incident in Afghanistan on 12 February 2009 that resulted in the death of six civilians and injury to four others.[16] Much controversy surrounded the decision to lay the charges. The decision was attacked by media commentators[17] and criticised by the leader of the Australian Opposition.[18] Significantly, some media attention focused on possible interest in the case by the Prosecutor of the ICC. One report made the improbable claim that:

> The charging of Australian commandos over the deaths of six Afghan civilians headed off an international investigation into the killings. A spokeswoman for the International Criminal Court told the *Herald* yesterday that investigators from the court had begun inquiries into the killings, which happened when the commandos threw grenades into a room containing five children and an armed man.[19]

---

[14] Criminal Code Act 1995 (Cth) div 268.

[15] Defence Force Discipline Act 1982 (Cth).

[16] Director of Military Prosecutions, 'Civilian Casualty Incident in Afghanistan' (Media Release, 12 February 2009) ('Civilian Casualty Incident').

[17] Radio announcer Alan Jones referred to the Director of Military Prosecutions, Brigadier Lyn McDade as 'a Brigadier without a brigade, a woman who's never seen the signs let alone heard the sounds of battle', see: Sydney Talkback Radio 2GB, *The Alan Jones Breakfast Show*, 13 October 2010 (Alan Jones).

[18] Australian Opposition Leader Tony Abbott said that the soldiers 'are being thrown to the wolves by the Government', see: Philip Coorey, 'Soldiers Thrown to the Wolves Says Abbott' *Sydney Morning Herald* (online, 13 October 2010).

[19] Dan Oakes, 'Afghan Charges Stalled Hague War Crimes Case' *Sydney Morning Herald* (online, 30 September 2010).

The report went on to assert that there was uncertainty about how much the prospect of the ICC prosecuting the soldiers influenced the decision to charge them under Australian military law.

The possibility of interest in this case by the Prosecutor of the ICC is so remote that it can be dismissed out of hand. The ICC Statute makes clear in Art 1 that it has jurisdiction over 'the most serious crimes of international concern'. In addition, Art 8 provides that: 'The Court shall have jurisdiction in respect of war crimes in particular when committed as part of a plan or policy or as part of a large-scale commission of such crimes.'

As tragic as the incident in Afghanistan undoubtedly was, there can be no interpretation of it that would satisfy these tests. Any doubt about the determination of the then Prosecutor of the ICC to restrict himself to the mandate so clearly expressed in the ICC Statute was surely dispelled when he issued a statement in 2006 setting out reasons why he declined to investigate allegations that war crimes had been committed in Iraq by the military forces of States Parties to the ICC Statute.[20] The Prosecutor specifically found that: 'The information available at this time supports a reasonable basis for an estimated 4 to 12 victims of wilful killing and a limited number of victims of inhuman treatment, totaling in all less than 20 persons.'

However, the Prosecutor had little difficulty in concluding that the gravity requirements of the ICC Statute had not been met, stating that: 'According to the available information, it did not appear that any of the criteria of Article 8(1) were satisfied.' Accordingly, the Prosecutor found that he had no need to reach a conclusion about complementarity.

A number of conclusions can be drawn from this. First, Moreno Ocampo had a commendable determination to act in accordance with the mandate in the ICC Statute. More to the point, military forces have no reason to fear that the existence of an institutionalised regime of international criminal justice, in the form of the ICC, will supplant the proper exercise of military disciplinary authority.

Hence, Australian media speculation about the interest of the ICC in the Afghanistan case is fanciful in the extreme and completely unwarranted. The Prosecutor reported that as at 31 July 2010, he had received a total of 8,792 communications about matters that he might investigate.[21] Most likely, information about the Australian case is included in this statistic. The fact that the Prosecutor had acted in relation to only one situation referred to

---

20 Letter of Prosecutor of the International Criminal Court regarding the situation in Iraq, of 9 February 2006.

21 ICC, *Report of the International Criminal Court*, 65th sess, Agenda Item 74, UN Doc A/65/313 ( 19 August 2010) paragraph 65 ('ICC Report').

him,[22] was further evidence that the ICC is unlikely to take an interest in crimes allegedly committed by individual soldiers.

Moreover, the complementarity provisions in the ICC Statute would act as a complete bar to an investigation and prosecution before the ICC in any case in which a state demonstrates willingness and ability to deal with it itself. Article 17(1)(b) of the ICC Statute provides that the Court shall determine that a case is inadmissible where: 'The case has been investigated by a State which has jurisdiction over it and the State has decided not to prosecute the person concerned, unless the decision resulted from the unwillingness or inability of the State genuinely to prosecute.'

To return to the example of the Australian case, it was the subject of a comprehensive investigation by the ADF Investigative Service, followed by a detailed consideration of the evidence by the Director of Military Prosecutions.[23] There can be no doubt that Art 17 would require that this case be ruled inadmissible, were it to be brought before the ICC. Suggestions in the Australian media that the decision to charge the soldiers under Australian military law was influenced by the prospect of interest on the part of the ICC are completely unfounded. Even a decision not to lay charges would not alter this conclusion, on a proper reading of Art 17(1)(b), given the comprehensive investigation and consideration by the prosecuting authority.

In more general terms, the carefully crafted concept of complementarity, which can be regarded as the cornerstone of the ICC Statute, ensures that a military force with a tradition of holding soldiers accountable for their actions in time of armed conflict can have no legitimate fear of the prospect of a trial before the ICC. Ensuring that soldiers would remain subject primarily to domestic jurisdiction was one of the principal demands of many drafters of the ICC Statute.

It is doubtful that the ICC Statute would have been as widely accepted as it has been,[24] had states not been confident about the unrestricted operation of their domestic jurisdiction over members of their military forces. In Australia's case, this is made abundantly clear in the legislation that criminalises the offences within the ICC's jurisdiction, which provides:

---

22 For information on the situation in Kenya, see: International Criminal Court, 'Kenya – Situation in the Republic of Kenya' (International Criminal Court) <http://www.icc-cpi.int/Menus/ICC/Situations+and+Cases/Situations/Situation+ICC+0109/> accessed August 2011.

23 See Civilian Casualty Incident, above note 15.

24 As at August 2011, there were 115 States Parties to the ICC Statute: <http://www.icc-cpi.int/menus/icc/about%20the%20court/icc%20at%20a%20glance/icc%20at%20a%20glance?lan=en-GB> accessed August 2011.

> It is the Parliament's intention that the jurisdiction of the International Criminal Court is to be complementary to the jurisdiction of Australia with respect to offences in this Division that are also crimes within the jurisdiction of that Court. Accordingly, the International Criminal Court Act 2002 does not affect the primacy of Australia's right to exercise its jurisdiction with respect to offences created by this Division that are also crimes within the jurisdiction of the International Criminal Court.[25]

There is no doubt that offences that may be committed by members of the ADF were uppermost in the minds of the drafters of this legislation.

## V. THE INFLUENCE OF INTERNATIONAL CRIMINAL JUSTICE ON THE CONDUCT OF MILITARY OPERATIONS

Should international criminal justice influence the way in which military operations are conducted? Should soldiers be reluctant to act in ways that are dictated by military utility for fear of being held criminally liable for their actions?

One commentator has noted that differences between American and European conceptions of a rule-governed international order can be observed via an examination of the legal regimes governing the conduct of American and British troops in Iraq. British troops were obliged to act in accordance with a much more restrictive legal regime than their American counterparts, 'based on changes introduced subsequent to Britain's membership of the International Criminal Court'.[26]

There may have been changes to British rules of engagement or other military instructions introduced at some point after the United Kingdom became party to the ICC Statute in October 2001, but it would be surprising if adherence to the ICC Statute was the catalyst for any such changes.

The simple fact is that the ICC Statute is not intended to create new legal norms. The UN Office of Legal Affairs draws a distinction between its work on codification and progressive development of international law.[27] The

---

25 Criminal Code Act 1995 (Cth) s 268.1.

26 Chris Brown, 'Conceptions of a Rule-Governed International Order: Europe vs. America?' (2006) 20(3) *International Relations* 309.

27 See United Nations Office of Legal Affairs, 'Codification Division' (United Nations Office of Legal Affairs, 2010) <http://untreaty.un.org/ola/div_cod.aspx?section=cod> accessed August 2011.

adoption of the crimes within the jurisdiction of the ICC was always understood to be an exercise in codification rather than progressive development.[28]

Article 8 of the ICC Statute represents what the participants in the Rome Conference of 1998 were prepared to regard as the war crimes recognised under IHL at that time. In some respects, Art 8 can be criticised as a 'lowest common denominator' of the catalogue of recognised war crimes. Many participants would have been prepared to include others,[29] particularly crimes in non-international armed conflict.[30] However, some participants in Rome argued that the ICC Statute should recognise no war crimes in non-international armed conflict at all.[31]

Given that the ICC Statute creates no new legal norms, it is difficult to mount a cogent argument that the military forces of a State Party ought to, or are bound to observe different or more restrictive rules. The norms reflected in Art 8 are drawn from a number of sources, many of which pre-date the ICC Statute by decades.[32] States were already bound by these norms, either because they are contained in treaties to which the state is a party, or because they have long been recognised as part of customary international law.

Similarly, the possibility of trial before the ICC cannot be cogently argued to restrict actions taken in conflict that might be justified by military utility. Violations of IHL ought to be investigated and prosecuted by national authorities. This was the rule before adoption of the ICC Statute and remains the rule today. States that adhere to this rule need not consider

---

[28] The report of the International Law Commission which included the Commission's draft statute for an international criminal court (Document A/49/10, Report of the International Law Commission on the work of its forty-sixth session, 2 May to 22 July 1994) stated, at 38: 'the statute is primarily an adjectival and procedural instrument. It is not its function to define new crimes.'

[29] See, eg, Knut Dörmann, 'War Crimes Under the Rome Statute of the International Criminal Court, with a Special Focus on the Negotiations on the Elements of Crimes' (2003) 7 *Max Planck Yearbook of United Nations Law* 341, 345–7.

[30] Ibid 347–8.

[31] Ibid 347.

[32] ICC Statute, Art 8(b)(v), which states: 'Attacking or bombarding, by whatever means, towns, villages, dwellings or buildings which are undefended and which are not military objectives', is drawn from International Conferences (The Hague), *Hague Convention (IV) Respecting the Laws and Customs of War on Land and Its Annex: Regulations Concerning the Laws and Customs of War on Land*, 18 October 1907, annex art 25 <http://www.unhcr.org/refworld/docid/4374cae64.html> accessed 22 August 2011.

the additional possibility of trial before an international tribunal as a limiting factor on their ability to prosecute military action.

## VI. INTERNATIONAL CRIMINAL JUSTICE AND TRAINING IN IHL

A subtly different question is whether international criminal justice influences, or ought to influence, the training of soldiers in IHL. Bruce Oswald has argued that 'when planning for, managing and conducting contemporary military operations, states that are signatories to the Rome Statute of the International Criminal Court … must establish firm boundaries within which their troops must operate'.[33]

It can equally be argued that the training of soldiers in IHL ought to include instruction in all the norms of IHL that bind the State and that, in theory at least, international criminal justice ought to have no influence on the norms taught as part of the curriculum.

This is the approach adopted in the Royal Australian Air Force's *Operations Law for RAAF Commanders*.[34] This publication is described in its Foreword as 'a useful starting point for commanders to enable them to have the basic legal knowledge vital to their ability to conduct, or be prepared to conduct, operations'. It describes the basic principles of the law of armed conflict, or IHL, that apply to Air Force commanders, such as military necessity, humanity, proportionality and distinction.[35] It states that the sources of IHL are customary international law and the principal treaties that are traditionally cited, including all those that establish so-called Hague law and Geneva law.[36]

It refers to the establishment of the ICC (which occurred after publication of the first edition in 1994), describing the ICC and its jurisdiction, examining the concept of complementarity and noting that Australia is a party to the ICC Statute and has enacted legislation to implement it in Australian law. However, it does not rely on the ICC Statute as a source for the norms derived from the law applicable to Air Force commanders.

---

33 Bruce Oswald, 'Detention of Civilians on Military Operations: Reasons for and Challenges to Developing a Special Law of Detention' (2008) 32 *Melbourne University Law Review* 524.

34 RAAF, *AAP1003 – Operations Law for RAAF Commanders* (2nd edn, Air Power Development Centre 2004).

35 Ibid 49–53.

36 Ibid 47–9.

This is not to say that international criminal justice is irrelevant to training military forces in IHL. Quite the contrary: the jurisprudence of bodies such as the International Criminal Tribunal for the former Yugoslavia (ICTY) and the International Criminal Tribunal for Rwanda (ICTR), has contributed significantly to the understanding of key concepts in war crimes, crimes against humanity and genocide. This has been well documented by numerous commentators.[37] This rich body of learning should not be ignored in training military forces in IHL. It is referred to extensively in the International Committee of the Red Cross's *Study on Customary International Humanitarian Law*.[38]

## VII. THE EXECUTION OF INTERNATIONAL ARREST WARRANTS BY MILITARY FORCES

International courts and tribunals do not have police forces as part of their organic structure. Might military forces be required to search for, arrest and detain persons who are wanted to face trial before international courts and tribunals?

This has already occurred in the former Yugoslavia.[39] The ICTY has required NATO forces to arrest persons who have been indicted by the ICTY and to deliver them to the custody of the Tribunal. The Tribunal has made Rule 59 *bis* in its Rules of Procedure and Evidence,[40] which provides that:

> on the order of a permanent Judge, the Registrar shall transmit to an appropriate authority or international body or the Prosecutor a copy of a warrant for the

---

[37] See, eg, Gideon Boas and William Schabas, *International Criminal Law Developments in the Case Law of the ICTY* (Martinus Nijhoff 2003); Human Rights Watch, *Genocide, War Crimes and Crimes Against Humanity – A Digest of the Case Law of the International Criminal Tribunal for Rwanda* (Human Rights Watch 2010).

[38] Jean-Marie Henckaerts and Louise Doswald-Beck, ICRC, *Study on Customary International Law* (Cambridge University Press 2005).

[39] See generally Han-Ru Zhou, 'The Enforcement of Arrest Warrants by International Forces From the ICTY to the ICC' (2006) 4(2) *Journal of International Criminal Justice* 202.

[40] See International Tribunal for the Prosecution of Persons Responsible for Serious Violations of International Humanitarian Law Committed in the Territory of the Former Yugoslavia since 1991, Rules of Procedure and Evidence, Doc No IT/32/Rev. 44 (adopted 11 February 1994).

> arrest of an accused, on such terms as the Judge may determine, together with an order for the prompt transfer of the accused to the Tribunal in the event that the accused be taken into custody by that authority or international body or the Prosecutor.

Orders made under this rule have been transmitted to and executed by NATO forces. This has been controversial, and the validity of the practice has been debated before the Tribunal in a number of cases.[41] It is likely that orders given by the ICTY to military forces to execute arrest warrants issued by it, would be binding on states, given that the Statute of the International Criminal Tribunal for the former Yugoslavia was adopted by the UN Security Council acting under Chapter VII of the United Nations Charter ('UN Charter').

The ICC Statute requires states to comply with requests for arrest and surrender made by the Court.[42] But there is nothing in the ICC Statute or the Court's Rules of Procedure and Evidence[43] that is comparable to Rule 59 *bis* in the ICTY Rules of Procedure and Evidence that would empower the Court to order an international body such as NATO to arrest and surrender an accused. Article 87(6) of the ICC Statute provides that '[t]he Court may ask any intergovernmental organization to provide information or documents. The Court may also ask for other forms of cooperation and assistance which may be agreed upon with such an organization and which are in accordance with its competence or mandate.'

By using the term 'ask', this provision has the effect that intergovernmental organisations are not under an obligation to cooperate with the Court or the Prosecutor. Therefore, assuming such an intergovernmental

---

[41] The arrest of suspects by NATO forces has been upheld in *Prosecutor v Nikolić* (*Decision on Defence Motion Challenging the Exercise of Jurisdiction by the Tribunal*) (ICTY, Trial Chamber II, Case No IT-94–2-PT, 9 October 2002); *Prosecutor v Mrkšić (Decision on Defence Interlocutory Appeal on Communication with Potential Witnesses of the Opposite Party)* (ICTY, Appeals Chamber, Case No IT-95–13/1-AR73, 30 July 2003); *Prosecutor v Simić* (*Decision on Miroslav Tadić's Application for Provisional Release*) (ICTY, Trial Chamber, Case No IT-95–9-PT, 4 April 2010).

[42] ICC Statute, Art 89(1) provides that: 'The Court may transmit a request for the arrest and surrender of a person … to any State on the territory of which that person may be found and shall request the cooperation of that State in the arrest and surrender of such a person. States Parties shall, in accordance with the provisions of this Part and the procedure under their national law, comply with requests for arrest and surrender.'

[43] ICC, Rules of Procedure and Evidence, Doc No ICC-ASP/1/3 (adopted 9 September 2002).

organisation is unwilling to risk its troops in enforcing an arrest warrant, it may simply refuse the request.

Prosecutor Moreno Ocampo reported on failures to cooperate in the execution of arrest warrants issued by his office. As at 31 July 2010, nine arrest warrants had not been executed.[44] Four of these warrants were issued pursuant to the referral to the Court of the situation in Darfur, Sudan, by the UN Security Council in 2005,[45] indicating that the obligation in the UN Charter to cooperate with decisions by the Security Council has not been effective in obtaining cooperation by unwilling states.

Accordingly, military forces can expect to be called on to provide greater assistance in securing the cooperation of states in enforcing warrants issued by international courts and tribunals. In some cases, it may be that a state or multinational military force deployed on the ground is the only body with the capabilities to execute an arrest warrant. The experience of the ICTY and NATO in this regard can be viewed as a precedent. The ICC reports that it has entered into negotiations to conclude cooperation agreements with the African Union, the Organization of American States, the League of Arab States and the Commonwealth Secretariat.[46]

Military forces who witness the commission of international crimes may also be expected to give evidence before international courts and tribunals.

The effect on the conduct of the primary mission of a military force that has been deployed to a theatre of conflict which may result from the execution of arrest warrants and the giving of evidence before tribunals, is a legitimate concern for military forces and the governments they represent. However, given the interests of states, the role that their military forces might need to play should be seen as a necessary contribution to the establishment and maintenance of a functioning regime of international criminal justice.

## VIII. CONCLUSION

Looked at from the perspective of the ADF, the institutionalisation of international criminal justice is a welcome development. A military force with a tradition of holding soldiers accountable for their actions in times of armed conflict can have no legitimate fear of the prospect of a trial before an international court. The concept of complementarity ensures that this is so.

---

44 ICC Report, above note 20, 13.

45 SC Res 1593, UN SCOR, 60th sess, 5158th mtg, UN Doc S/RES/1593 (31 March 2005).

46 ICC Report, above note 20, 21.

The conduct of the inaugural Prosecutor disclosed no inclination to pursue unwarranted accusations against the members of military forces committed to proper, accountable and transparent self-regulation.

The significance of the creation of the ICC and its attendant publicity has promoted a welcome focus on the duty of military forces to train in and demonstrate awareness of IHL. The ADF has a well-deserved reputation for commitment to IHL, and, from its perspective, the institutionalisation of international criminal justice can only be viewed as a positive change.

# Index


accountability 229, 230, 255, 271, 300, 301, 306, 307, 308
accused *see* defendant
adversarial 55, 56, 62, 68, 70, 73, 82, 92, 101–3, 271, 275, 276, 286
aggressor 139, 232, 241–4, 246, 247
al-Bashir 178, 180
amnesty 15, 297, 302
anti-terrorism *see* counter-terrorism
armed conflict 44, 48, 105, 110, 111, 112, 120, 158, 159, 188, 193, 204, 205, 214, 235, 256, 264, 267, 316
atrocities 1, 2, 10, 12, 16, 22, 131, 255

Barayagwiza 103, 167
Barbie 138, 276
Bemba 72, 74, 78, 91, 95
Bizimungu 69, 94, 96
Blaškić 74, 78, 81, 91, 97
Bosnia 4, 65, 80, 126, 144, 282, 293

Charter of the United Nations 3, 5, 6, 207, 209–12, 249, 316
coherency 3, 10–12, 125–7, 177, 190–230, 249, 254, 256, 300
collective will 123, 129
collective responsibility 131, 134
commission of inquiry 109, 112–14
compensation *see* reparations
Congo 180, 262, 291
cost 12, 90, 120, 131, 140, 141, 153, 165, 167, 170–74, 191, 197, 202, 280, 287, 289, 290, 291, 297
counter-terrorism 190, 192, 201, 202, 218, 226, 230
crime of aggression 124, 138, 164, 231, 232, 235, 236, 238–53
crimes against humanity 108, 119, 131, 257, 260, 261, 274, 314
*see also* genocide; rape; torture
cross-examination 32, 35, 57, 58, 60, 61, 62, 66, 263

Darfur 112, 113, 114, 169, 173, 233, 268, 292, 316
defence 12, 26, 27, 31, 36, 37, 39–42, 53, 56–8, 60–62, 66, 68–104, 134, 147, 148, 154, 175, 181, 183, 227, 257
defence counsel *see* defence
defendant 7, 10, 11, 18, 25–43, 52, 53, 55, 58, 61, 68–76, 79, 83, 84, 88, 93, 96–8, 101–3, 128, 161, 181, 182, 247, 286, 300
delay *see* timeliness
detention 102, 204
determinacy 215, 218, 219
disclosure 52, 53, 56, 69, 71, 72, 74, 76, 82–9, 92–8, 101
distinction, the principle of 110, 111, 118
due process 81, 208, 209
Dujail 34, 35, 40

Eichmann 24, 128, 134, 135, 275
Erdemović 71, 147, 149, 188
European Court of Human Rights (ECHR) 70, 78, 79, 209, 210–12
European Court of Justice (ECJ) 206–8
evidence
  springboard 87, 89
  exculpatory 84, 88, 89
  inculpatory 84, 86
exculpatory 53, 72, 84, 88, 91–3, 111
expediency *see* timeliness

fair trial 4, 42, 44, 68–70, 76, 79, 84, 97, 181, 182, 184, 200 fragmentation 125–7, 203, 208

Gaddafi 23, 107, 116, 117, 212
Galić 74, 81, 118–20
genocide 2, 16, 20, 21, 23, 126, 130, 132, 137, 138, 141, 144, 234–6, 249, 260, 265, 274
*see also* crimes against humanity
Germany 5, 15, 136, 137, 139, 179, 181, 234, 236

Halilović 77, 80, 82, 86, 100, 101
Hague, The 9, 25, 31, 141
history 13, 22, 64, 65, 68, 102, 123–44, 145–89, 218, 230, 255, 257–60, 272, 281, 282, 294, 295
Holocaust 21, 127, 128, 137, 138, 275
human rights 6, 12, 15, 68, 101, 143, 181, 184, 186, 201, 206, 209, 210, 213, 226–9, 272, 276, 294, 300
Hussein 25, 28, 29, 34, 35, 39, 40, 42, 168, 169, 177

illegitimacy 192, 208, 212, 216, 229, 230
impunity 6, 19, 48, 65, 179, 254, 271, 300
incoherence 11, 191, 202, 203, 205, 212
inculpatory 84, 86, 87, 88
indeterminacy 192, 215, 216, 218, 226, 230
indictment 51, 52, 62, 71, 72, 74–6, 80, 98–100, 137, 178, 296, 302
individual agency 134, 140, 141
individual liability *see* individual agency
International Court of Justice (ICJ) 9, 126
International Covenant on Civil and Political Rights (ICCPR) 70, 97, 183, 223
International Criminal Court (ICC) 6, 7, 9, 19, 23, 46, 48, 61, 65, 69, 70, 72, 78, 84, 85, 88, 89, 91–3, 97, 99, 105, 106, 120, 122, 143, 144, 164, 165, 168, 169, 172, 173, 177, 179, 180, 183, 184, 186, 216, 231, 251, 262, 273, 274, 284–92, 300–302, 305, 307, 309–13, 315, 316
International Criminal Law 8, 9, 17, 47, 48, 50, 93, 123, 127, 130, 133, 136, 140, 145, 146, 150, 153, 170, 174, 188, 189, 192, 216, 233, 254–6, 265–8, 284
International Criminal Tribunal for the former Yugoslavia (ICTY) 4, 5, 30, 37, 39, 45–60, 63, 65, 66, 70, 71, 73, 75, 81, 84, 86, 93, 99–101, 105, 108, 113, 120, 126, 130, 131, 139, 144, 146, 147, 157–9, 167, 171, 172, 180, 182, 186, 187, 251, 282–5, 314, 315
International Criminal Tribunal for Rwanda (ICTR) 16, 47, 48, 65, 69, 81, 92, 158, 167, 171, 180, 182, 186, 251, 260, 262, 281–5, 290, 314
International Criminal Tribunal for Sierra Leone (ICTSL) 13, 41, 65, 160, 168, 171, 261
International Human Rights Law 200, 205, 223
International Humanitarian Law (IHL) 110, 186, 197, 198, 203–5, 213, 214, 257, 259, 312–14, 317
International Law Commission (ILC) 6, 238
International Military Tribunal (IMT) 142, 146, 150, 154, 155, 179, 181, 184, 188, 258, 281, 282
International Military Tribunal for the Far East (IMTFE) 142, 258, 263, 282
Iraq 11, 22, 144, 169, 177, 209, 212, 293, 309, 311

judges 7, 25, 26, 29, 30, 32, 37, 39–42, 49–51, 58–60, 62, 128, 142, 154–65, 184, 186, 227, 287
judicial
control 59, 60
case management 56–61
discretion 162, 164, 165

process 26, 27, 30, 38, 40, 50, 64, 65, 69, 208
jurisdiction 7, 9–11, 48, 52, 65, 66, 70, 85, 120, 138, 155, 157, 164, 165, 167, 171, 206, 210, 218, 219, 232–8, 240–49, 251, 252, 291, 298, 307, 309–11
universal 232–6, 251

Karadzić 33, 34, 46, 52, 53, 55, 180
Kosovo 23, 110, 112, 172, 187, 293
Krstić 86, 88, 91
Kupreskić 71, 75, 159, 160

law of armed conflict 157, 163, 188, 193, 313
law on the use of force 199
laws of war 214, 215
Lebanon 192, 218, 227
legitimacy 3, 5, 8, 10–12, 18, 19, 93, 125, 173, 190–230, 232, 249–53, 256, 268, 269–303
Libya 2, 7, 18, 23, 64, 105–7, 109–11, 114, 117, 118, 120, 143, 173, 174, 177, 178, 189, 212, 233
Lubanga 74, 77, 79, 83, 86–90, 94–6, 184, 262

Manson 30, 31
Milosević 28, 29, 31, 32, 42, 54, 55, 98, 100, 103, 106, 118, 126, 130, 132, 139, 172
Milutinović 53, 100
Mladić 60, 130, 180
Moussaoui 28, 31

natural 11, 154–7, 159, 160, 161, 164, 165, 227
naturalism *see* natural
non-adversarial 272, 273, 276, 294, 298, 301, 302
non-prosecutorial *see* non-adversarial
norm 6, 7, 18, 110, 125, 142, 163, 186, 190, 191, 193–7, 199, 201–5, 212, 213, 216, 218, 219, 224, 229, 311–13
normative 18, 127, 187, 191, 194, 195, 200–203, 256
North Atlantic Treaty Organisation (NATO) 23, 46, 109, 143, 167, 172, 187, 314–16
*nullum crimen sine lege* 155, 156, 161, 162
Nuremberg 3, 4, 6, 11, 26, 47, 131, 134, 137, 143, 147–51, 154–7, 164, 166, 170, 181, 184, 188, 231, 249, 250, 258, 260

Office of the Prosecutor (OTP) 106, 110, 112, 122, 172, 290

politics 5, 8, 12, 14, 17–19, 23, 46, 47, 55, 99, 101, 108, 125, 128, 131–3, 140, 142, 154, 167, 191, 203, 205, 206, 208, 209, 212, 213, 216, 218, 221, 224–6, 228, 236, 264, 268, 274, 297, 300, 306
positive 7, 154, 155, 156, 157, 162, 164, 165, 227
positivism *see* positive
proportionality, the principle of 39, 110, 111, 118, 187
prosecution 51, 53, 55, 56, 59, 60–63, 68–104, 110, 111, 142, 170, 173, 174, 205, 219, 235, 254–6, 263, 271, 273–6, 280, 314

rape 254–65, 268
*see also* crimes against humanity; sexual assault; sexual crimes; sexual violence
reconciliation 6, 7, 12–14, 16–19, 22, 64, 65, 263, 272, 292, 294
reparations 19, 271, 278, 280, 281, 284, 288, 291, 292, 297
reporting 14, 150, 151, 154
restitution *see* reparations
restorative justice 12, 15, 271, 277–9, 288, 292
retributive justice 5, 7, 12, 36, 277
Rome Statute 9, 23, 49, 50, 70, 74, 84, 85, 87, 97, 106, 119, 120, 130, 158, 161, 162, 164, 165, 173, 178,

183, 184, 231–3, 236, 237, 239, 241, 242, 245–54, 256, 262, 306
Rome Treaty *see* Rome Statute
rule of law 10, 141, 142, 155, 207, 271
Rwanda 2, 5, 16, 18, 167, 177, 180, 265, 282, 285

Sarajevo 106, 118, 119, 121, 122
Second World War 48, 65, 153, 177, 179, 249, 274
Security Council 2, 5, 11, 18, 23, 64, 106, 112, 139, 143, 144, 167, 169, 171, 173, 177, 178, 180, 194, 196, 197, 203, 206–12, 215–17, 219, 222, 225, 227, 237, 244, 245, 248, 249, 256, 264, 301, 316
self-representation 25, 31–4, 37, 38, 42, 53–5
September 11 (9/11) 12, 190, 195, 199, 200, 204, 213, 215, 225
Serbia 23, 32, 126, 130, 140, 293
Šešelj 32, 33, 37, 42, 54, 103
sexual
  assault 282–4
  crimes 256, 262, 265, 268, 283
  violence 254–67, 284, 295
  *see also* rape
Sierra Leone 2, 13, 18, 168, 262
soft law 190, 197, 225, 229
South Africa 15, 170, 295, 302
Special Court for Sierra Leone (SCSL) *see* International Criminal Tribunal for Sierra Leone
stay 69, 90, 93, 96
Sudan 2, 23, 169, 180, 233, 316

Tadić 87, 126, 130, 131, 158, 159, 182
terrorism 10, 31, 45, 190–230, 233
timeliness 36, 37, 39, 46, 72, 77, 81, 82, 85, 88, 97, 104, 237, 280, 290, 291
torture 10, 200, 201
  *see also* crimes against humanity
transparency 229, 230
tribunals
  adhoc 6, 74, 85, 106, 110, 122, 162, 164, 172, 180, 184, 260, 261, 285, 292
  hybrid 6, 168, 255
  military 12, 142, 184, 186, 258
truth and reconciliation 14, 19, 263
  commissions 2, 13–15, 17, 18, 22, 272

Uganda 2, 15, 133, 180, 291, 292, 302
United Nations 25, 45, 48, 105, 173, 194, 211, 233, 238, 270, 306, 315
United Nations Human Rights Council (UNHRC) 106, 109, 115
United Nations War Crimes Commission (UNWCC) 151, 153
Universal Declaration of Human Rights (UDHR) 158, 182

Versailles 123, 124, 132, 133, 143
victim
  movement 269, 270, 277, 278, 282
  organisations 78
  participation 18, 95, 262, 286–8, 290, 291
  rights 18, 19
victor's justice 3, 5, 11, 166–9, 179

war crimes 2–14, 48, 65, 106, 120, 141, 148, 157, 161, 162, 215, 233–6, 249, 252, 255–7, 259, 260, 307, 309, 312
  *see also* crimes against humanity
war criminal 3, 8, 9, 175
witness 18, 27, 37, 51, 56–60, 66, 85–8, 112, 114, 121, 182, 183, 262, 275, 282, 284, 292
women 254–68

Yugoslavia, the former 14, 18, 45, 46, 48, 52, 55, 59, 65, 131, 157, 172, 180, 268, 285